Marxism and America

Manchester University Press

Marxism and America

New appraisals

Edited by

Christopher Phelps
and Robin Vandome

MANCHESTER UNIVERSITY PRESS

Copyright © Manchester University Press 2021
While copyright in the volume as a whole is vested in Manchester University Press, copyright in individual chapters belongs to their respective authors, and no chapter may be reproduced wholly or in part without the express permission in writing of both author and publisher.

Published by Manchester University Press
Oxford Road, Manchester M13 9PL

www.manchesteruniversitypress.co.uk

British Library Cataloguing-in-Publication Data
A catalogue record for this book is available from the British Library

ISBN 978 1 5261 4976 3 hardback
ISBN 978 1 5261 7192 4 paperback

First published 2021
Paperback published 2023

The publisher has no responsibility for the persistence or accuracy of URLs for any external or third-party internet websites referred to in this book, and does not guarantee that any content on such websites is, or will remain, accurate or appropriate. Unless otherwise stated, all URL references mentioned were last accessed on January 1, 2021.

Typeset
by Deanta Global Publishing Services

Contents

Figures	*page* vii
Notes on contributors	viii
Preface – Nelson Lichtenstein	xii
Acknowledgments	xiv

	Introduction: the Marx–America dialectic *Christopher Phelps and Robin Vandome*	1
1	The blue and the gray and the red: Marxism and Civil War memory *Matthew E. Stanley*	17
2	"What *is* the correct revolutionary proletarian attitude toward sex?": red love and the Americanization of Marx in the interwar years *Jesse F. Battan*	43
3	Marxism and Americanism: A. J. Muste, Louis Budenz, and an "American approach" before the Popular Front *Leilah Danielson*	71
4	Women, the family, and sexuality in U.S. Communist Party publications: refashioning Marxism for the Popular Front era *Jodie Collins*	95
5	Rethinking Karl Marx: American liberalism from the New Deal to the Cold War *Andrew Hartman*	119

6	Black Marxism off the color line: W. E. B. Du Bois and Oliver Cromwell Cox as democratic theorists *Paul M. Heideman*	144
7	"Not picketing in front of bra factories": Marxism, feminism, and the Weather Underground *Sinead McEneaney*	170
8	A people's history of Howard Zinn: radical popular history and its readers *Nick Witham*	195
9	Class, commodity, consumption: theorizing sexual violence during the feminist sex wars of the 1980s *Mara Keire*	217
10	Will the revolution be podcast? Marxism and the culture of "millennial socialism" in the United States *Tim Jelfs*	241
11	Does the American experience refute Marxism? *Kim Moody*	264

Index   291

Figures

0.1	Eugene V. Debs (Getty Images)	*page 5*
1.1	Joseph Weydemeyer (International Institute for Social History)	23
3.1	Electric Auto-Lite strike (George Blount / Toledo Lucas County Public Library)	72
4.1	Earl Browder (Social Movements Collection, University of Hawaii)	97
4.2	*Working Woman* (Marxist Internet Archive)	101
4.3	*Woman Today* (Marxist Internet Archive)	110
5.1	"Communism is Americanism of the 20th Century" (Communist Party USA)	125
7.1	Cathy Wilkerson (Federal Bureau of Investigation)	171
8.1	Howard Zinn (Jeff Albertson / University of Massachusetts Amherst Libraries)	197
9.1	The pornographic commodity (Andreas Feininger, Museum of the City of New York)	225
10.1	*Chapo Trap House* (Wikipedia Commons)	242
11.1	Average rate of profit of the G7 nations (Michael Roberts)	268
11.2	U.S. productivity and typical worker's compensation (Economic Policy Institute)	272
11.3	Growth in average wages and labor productivity (International Labour Organization)	276

Notes on contributors

Jesse F. Battan is professor of American Studies at California State University, Fullerton. He has written numerous articles on sexual radicalism in the nineteenth and twentieth centuries for *The Journal of the History of Sexuality, The Journal of Social History*, and other journals, co-edited *Meetings & Alcôves: Gauches et Sexualités en Europe et aux Etats-Unis depuis 1850* (Editions Universitaires de Dijon, 2004), and is currently at work on a book to be titled *Incompatible Bedfellows: Love and Freedom in Early-Twentieth Century America*.

Jodie Collins is a collaborative doctoral student at the University of Sussex and the British Library. Her project, funded by the Arts and Humanities Research Council (AHRC), examines the pamphlets produced by radical groups such as the Communist Party USA during the interwar period. Collins works with the British Library's American collections to collate, promote, and make accessible the hundreds of political pamphlets available at the Library.

Leilah Danielson is professor of history at Northern Arizona University where she teaches a range of classes on U.S. politics and culture and foreign relations. She is the author of *American Gandhi: A. J. Muste and the History of American Radicalism in the Twentieth Century* (University of Pennsylvania Press, 2014) and co-editor of *The Religious Left in Modern America: Doorkeepers of a Radical Faith* (Palgrave Macmillan, 2018), as well as the author of a number of articles exploring the intersection between religion, race, and American social movements.

Andrew Hartman is professor of history at Illinois State University and the author of two books, *Education and the Cold War: The*

Battle for the American School (Palgrave Macmillan, 2008) and *A War for the Soul of America: A History of the Culture Wars* (University of Chicago Press, 2015). He is co-editor of *American Labyrinth: Intellectual History for Complicated Times* (Cornell University Press, 2018) and the recipient of two Fulbright Awards. Hartman is currently at work on his third book, *Karl Marx in America*, to be published by the University of Chicago Press.

Paul M. Heideman is the editor of *Class Struggle and the Color Line: American Socialism and the Race Question, 1900–1930* (Haymarket Books, 2018). He received his Ph.D. in American Studies from Rutgers University-Newark, and is currently a Ph.D. candidate in Sociology at New York University. His work has appeared in *Jacobin*, *Historical Materialism*, and *In These Times*.

Tim Jelfs, assistant professor in American studies at the University of Groningen in the Netherlands, is the author of *The Argument About Things in the 1980s: Goods and Garbage in an Age of Neoliberalism* (West Virginia University Press, 2018), which won the British Association of American Studies Arthur Miller Institute Prize.

Mara Keire is a Senior Research Fellow at the Rothermere American Institute, University of Oxford. She is the author of *For Business and Pleasure: Red-Light Districts and the Regulation of Vice in the United States, 1890–1933* (Johns Hopkins University Press, 2010) and is currently writing a book on feminism and sexual violence from the second wave to #MeToo.

Nelson Lichtenstein is distinguished professor of history and director of the Center for the Study of Work, Labor, and Democracy at the University of California, Santa Barbara. The recipient of numerous awards, he is the editor of twelve edited collections and the author of the books *Labor's War at Home: The CIO in World War II* (Cambridge University Press, 1982), *Walter Reuther: The Most Dangerous Man in Detroit* (University of Illinois Press, 1997), *State of the Union: A Century of American Labor* (Princeton University Press, 2003), and *The Retail Revolution: How Wal-Mart Created a Brave New World of Business* (Henry Holt, 2009).

Sinead McEneaney is based in the history department at the Open University. Her research primarily focuses on gender and race in the 1960s. Most recently, she has published on sex and sexuality in the underground press in the United States and on housing activism in Ireland.

Kim Moody is a visiting scholar at the University of Westminster and author of numerous books on labor politics and history including, most recently, *In Solidarity: Essays on Working-Class Organization and Politics in the United States* (Haymarket Books, 2014), *On New Terrain: How Capital is Reshaping the Battleground of Class War* (Haymarket Books, 2017), and *Tramps and Trade Union Travelers: Internal Migration and Organized Labor in Gilded Age America, 1870–1900* (Haymarket Books, 2019).

Christopher Phelps is associate professor of American history at the University of Nottingham. He is the author of *Young Sidney Hook: Marxist and Pragmatist* (Cornell University Press, 1997; 2nd ed., University of Michigan Press, 2005) and co-author, with Howard Brick, of *Radicals in America: The U.S. Left since the Second World War* (Cambridge University Press, 2015). His scholarship has received awards from the Historians of the Twentieth-Century United States and the Labor and Working-Class History Association.

Matthew E. Stanley is assistant professor of history at Albany State University. He is the author of *The Loyal West: Civil War and Reunion in Middle America* (University of Illinois Press, 2017) and the forthcoming *Grand Army of Labor: Workers, Veterans, and the Meaning of the Civil War* (University of Illinois Press, 2021). Stanley has also written on history and politics for, among other publications, *Counterpunch*, *Process History*, *The Huffington Post*, *International Socialist Review*, *Socialist Worker*, and *Jacobin*.

Robin Vandome is assistant professor in American intellectual and cultural history at the University of Nottingham. He obtained his Ph.D. from Cambridge University and is the author of articles published in the *Journal of American Studies*, *American Periodicals*, and other journals. He is researching a biography of the early twentieth-century radical writer Joseph Freeman.

Nick Witham is associate professor of United States History at University College London and co-editor of the *Journal of American Studies*. He is the author of *The Cultural Left and the Reagan Era: U.S. Protest and Central American Revolution* (I.B. Tauris, 2015), and co-editor of *Reframing 1968: American Politics, Protest and Identity* (Edinburgh University Press, 2018). He is currently writing *The Popular Historians: American Historical Writing and the Search for an Audience, 1945–present*, to be published by the University of Chicago Press.

Preface

In the very last scene of Raoul Peck's film *The Young Karl Marx*, Fred, Jenny, and Karl are at a candlelit table hurriedly editing the *Communist Manifesto*. Karl writes, "A bogeyman is haunting Europe." Jenny injects, "No, no, wrong word." Karl replaces it with *spectre*. Then a paragraph is gone missing, papers are hurriedly shuffled, and they insert the fugitive lines.

That sense of collaborative creation, of the human impress that shaped a world-historic doctrine, is central to the study of the Marxist idea as it flows through history and onto the variegated national landscapes upon which it has flourished and floundered. This liquidity and engagement are found in abundance among these eleven essays edited by Christopher Phelps and Robin Vandome. This is not to say that Marxism, in America or elsewhere, can mean *anything*. Rather, as E. P. Thompson famously put it, the working-class struggle "arises at the intersection of determination and self-activity," thereby opening our understanding of both consciousness and conflict to a high degree of contingency.

For a collection of essays on Marxism in America, it is refreshing to find that the stale controversy over the extent to which capitalism and the working-class movement in the United States are "exceptional" is for the most part missing from these pages. That is partly because both scholarship and economic reality have converged to make the case that American capitalism is no longer a "variety" whose trajectory is all that different from the political economies of Europe and East Asia, the other two great loci of economic power.

More importantly, perhaps, the old argument that the American working class has been exceptionally fractured and ideologically complicit in its own impotency no longer holds much explanatory power. It is not simply that a global neoliberalism has degraded social democracy and dampened working-class struggle where it once seemed so well entrenched. Rather, contributors to this essay collection demonstrate that Marxist categories of analysis are properly subject to much reconfiguration. This includes such seemingly bedrock concepts as class, production, exploitation, and the struggles that arise from labor's conflict with capital. In the United States that fight goes on, but these scholars show how it manifests itself in a remarkably effervescent fashion, with several essays putting issues of race, sexuality, and identity at the center of Marxist discourse. Rather than marginalizing class consciousness, however, this cultural turn demonstrates that in the United States, perhaps even more than other countries, class struggle proceeds through a lens that foregrounds racial, religious, and gender inequalities and the movements that seek to rectify them.

In the nineteenth century, European Marxists thought American capitalism immature. By the middle decades of the twentieth century, Marxists the world over saw American capitalism as in the vanguard. In more recent decades, however, a stagnation of living standards and the difficulties that the nation has faced in coming to terms with both the financial crisis of 2007–2008 as well as the coronavirus disaster twelve years later have made it clear that a dysfunctional American state, and the misshapen political economy that sustains it, has actually undergone a process of underdevelopment.

A century ago, Rosa Luxemburg put the issue before us in the starkest terms: "Either transition to socialism or regression to barbarism." Written in the most expansive Marxist tradition, these essays help illuminate that choice.

Nelson Lichtenstein

Acknowledgments

We wish to thank all of the many participants in the conference "Marx and Marxism in the United States: A One-Day Symposium," held at the University of Nottingham, May 11, 2019. The conference was sponsored by the British Association for American Studies (BAAS) as well as the Faculty of Arts and School of Cultures, Languages, and Area Studies at the University of Nottingham. That day's lively discussion sharpened the work that follows. A majority of the essays that follow were developed from talks delivered on that occasion, and we thank those participants as well as the several authors not present at the original conference who agreed to contribute additional essays to round out the volume. At Manchester University Press, Emma Brennan has been brilliant in support of the book, and the remainder of the staff has our gratitude for their work in all phases of its production.

Introduction: the Marx–America dialectic

Christopher Phelps and Robin Vandome

Since the financial crisis of 2008 and the Great Recession that followed, American politics has seen a striking socialist revival. Perceptions of capitalism among young adults in the United States have deteriorated steadily, while socialism's favorability has risen such that even *Teen Vogue* may now be found running favorable articles on Karl Marx.[1] The youthful interest in socialism began with the Occupy Wall Street movement of 2011, which succeeded in dramatizing economic inequality and the rapaciousness of the financial system but dispersed so rapidly that many inspired by it came to desire more effective, coherent modes of left-wing political action. That impulse coincided with the presidential campaigns of Senator Bernie Sanders, who attracted a surprising extent of popular support in 2016 and 2020 without sacrificing his identification as a democratic socialist. Together with the electrifying upset victory of Alexandria Ocasio-Cortez in her Bronx race for the House of Representatives in 2018, followed by successive elections of other left-wing candidates, the Sanders campaigns succeeded in making a socialist agenda "hip" for the first time in decades, along with a vision of comprehensive and universal health care, free university education, and a redistribution of wealth away from the topmost one percent of the population. As a result, the Democratic Socialists of America have surged to more than 40,000 members, most of them below the age of thirty.[2]

This new interest in socialism is not, to be sure, wholly Marxist in character. Broadly, it is animated by a classic social–democratic politics: a strategy of electoral campaigning more than mass action, and policies that correct for capitalism's worst inequalities rather than seek the abolition of private property. Marxism, by contrast, has at its center of vision the replacement of capitalism with common ownership of the means of production. Nevertheless, the renewal of socialist politics—coinciding with Black Lives Matter, immigrant rights organizing, increasing strike activity, climate justice campaigning, the feminist #MeToo movement, and myriad other forms of ferment from below—has been accompanied by a renaissance of interest in Marxist analysis. The socialist commentary supplied by such periodicals as *Jacobin* (founded in 2010) has, for example, drawn upon Marxist frameworks for understanding class society and political economy, casting capitalism as innately unequal and crisis-prone, while propounding a strategic view of social democracy as a transitional form pointing toward a more thoroughgoing socialism.[3] In this manner, the hue of the new politics does not preclude Marxist theory, much as was the case in the twentieth-century heyday of American socialism. Even if relatively few of the study groups reading Marx's magnum opus *Capital* in the years following the 2008 financial crisis made it all the way through the book, stopped short by its notoriously turgid opening chapters, a new generation on the left has grown comfortable with Marx and Marxism.

American interest in Marxism reciprocates the intense interest in the United States evinced by Karl Marx and Friedrich Engels. Despite residing for their whole lives in Germany, France, and England, Marx and Engels wrote for the *New York Tribune*, exchanged letters with Americans, and provided analyses of American events for European audiences, particularly in interpreting the U.S. Civil War.[4] As a young man, Engels cited the numerous early American experiments in communal property as evidence of socialism's viability. "Communism, social existence and activity based on community of goods, is not only possible but has already been realized in many communities in America," he wrote.[5] Before long, he and Marx would eschew such small-scale efforts or intentional communities, declaring them "utopian." Small-scale co-operative endeavors in agrarian and craft production were incapable of competing against an expanding industrial capitalism. Rather than such trial demonstrations of the virtues of collective property in local experiments, the transformation of the whole of society through the working-class movement was to Marx and Engels the most effective method of social transformation.

Nevertheless, Marx and Engels continued to observe other developments in the United States with great interest, seeing both limits and promise in its place in world history. In 1852, Marx wrote that America was "as yet by no means mature enough to provide a clear and comprehensible picture of the class struggle."[6] Yet during the time of the International Workingmen's Association, an attempted alliance of working-class organizations in multiple countries later known as the First International (1864–1876), Marx corresponded with associates in America. When he came to write *Capital* (1867), he viewed the recently concluded American Civil War, with its vast expropriation of slave property, as world-historical in its revolutionary import. Emancipation from slavery, Marx observed, was essential, for "every independent movement of the workers was paralyzed so long as slavery disfigured a part of the Republic. Labor cannot emancipate itself in the white skin where in the black it is branded." In the American abolition of slavery, he thought, Europe could find inspiration for the abolition of capital: "As in the eighteenth century the American war of independence sounded the tocsin for the European middle class, so in the nineteenth century the American Civil War sounded it for the European working class."[7]

Despite the affinity that Marx and Engels felt for its revolutionary potentiality, the United States has experienced repeated bouts of political hysteria—most conspicuously after the Haymarket affair of 1886, in the 1919 Red Scare, and during the McCarthy era of the 1950s—in which the society's most powerful forces persecuted socialism and communism with a degree of fervor and venom wildly disproportionate to their actual influence in American life. Many theorists and journalistic commentators have asserted that America's political essence is a liberal democracy impervious to Marxism, often pointing to the country's unique national formation without feudal antecedents.[8] Engels himself, in the years after Marx's death and toward the end of his own life, called Americans "extremely conservative, precisely because America is so purely bourgeois, without any feudal past." His thoughts were occasioned by his visit to the United States in a brief trip in 1888, the only time either he or Marx set foot in the country. America, he complained, was "still in swaddling clothes in theory" because it was "a nation—a *young* nation—so conceited about its 'practice' and at the same time so frightfully dense theoretically." Unlike those who would posit an intrinsically capitalist America, however, Engels did not consider these traits its destiny. He contended that the exploitative social conditions and vast inequalities of the Gilded Age meant that "the last Bourgeois Paradise on earth is fast changing into a Purgatorio." Denying that either the pragmatic streak in American thought or the country's bourgeois formation would inhibit socialism, he held that "things over there will nevertheless move faster than anywhere else" for "unless I am greatly mistaken the Americans will astonish us all by the magnitude of their movement."[9]

That America and Europe moved by different tempos did not, then, mean that America was "exceptional"—exempt from capitalist crises, great class contestations, or socialist promise. By the early twentieth century, after the deaths of Marx and Engels, the United States would indeed generate a massive socialist movement in the era of the Socialist Party's standard-bearer Eugene V. Debs (Figure 0.1), a former railroad worker union leader who advocated "the revolutionary action of the workers," garnering impressive vote tallies for the presidency in 1912.[10] At a time when Germany's Social Democratic Party was at its apex as the parliamentary crown jewel of the Second International (1889–1916), these American developments were correlative, not exceptional. The United States did not, however, come close to experiencing a socialist revolution or even building an enduring labor or social–democratic party rooted in the unions, as would become commonplace in Europe. Marxist analyses may be astutely applied to any number of features of American life, and socialist politics have earned the approval of millions of American voters in certain circumstances, but any realistic appraisal must concede that the influence of Marxism in the United States has, in political terms, been distinctly limited.

When the United States came under the gaze of twentieth-century European Marxists, therefore, distinctions were often uppermost in mind as they viewed it as an alien land and culture, one whose relatively weak socialist presence demanded an explanation. The year 1917 saw two Russian revolutions—in February against the czar, in October of the Soviets—but at its beginning Nikolai Bukharin, Alexandra Kollontai, and Leon Trotsky, who would play crucial roles in the Russian events, were all residing in New York. Trotsky was enraptured by his Bronx apartment with its "electric lights, gas cooking-range, bath, telephone, automatic service-elevator, and

Introduction

Figure 0.1 "I would rather a thousand times be a free soul in jail than to be a sycophant and coward in the streets," said Eugene V. Debs, leader of the Socialist Party, in the speech against the First World War that would result in his incarceration. His speech to the jury opposed "Kaiserism" while positing an American revolutionary tradition and constitutional right to freedom of speech. Canton, Ohio, June 16, 1918. *Courtesy Getty Images.*

even a chute for the garbage," but while appreciating these consumer comforts of American capitalism he looked down with disdain upon a "bourgeoisified" Debsian Socialist Party made up of "doctors, lawyers, dentists, engineers, and the like."[11] He had somehow missed the support for the Socialists among the impoverished women garment workers of the Lower East Side who had waged mass strikes, or among the hardscrabble sharecroppers and tenant farmers of Oklahoma, where the party had its strongest state presence.[12]

At the same time, European observers could catch glimpses of a universal future arising from American economic and cultural dynamism. Writing in his notebooks in a fascist prison in Italy, Antonio Gramsci speculated in 1929 about the production techniques of Henry Ford and Frederick Winslow Taylor, together with "Americanism," the patterns of cultural life that he defined as "an ideology of the kind represented by Rotary Clubs." These were both an extension of certain aspects of European civilization, he thought, namely its capitalist development, and "an advance criticism of old strata which will in fact be crushed by any eventual new order."[13] The American ideology of the Rotary Clubs was, then, capitalism's apotheosis.

The 1940s, similarly, saw Theodor Adorno and Max Horkheimer of the Frankfurt School in exile in New York and Los Angeles, where Horkheimer recoiled from American pragmatist philosophy as the abnegation of social theory and liquidation of truth. That view was diametrically opposed to that of the young Sidney Hook, John Dewey's student, widely perceived as the best American Marxist philosopher of the 1930s, who detected synergies between historical materialism and the democratic–experimental method of pragmatism, although his accommodation with moderate anti-communist liberalism may only have affirmed for Horkheimer the perils of pragmatism.[14] Jazz, meanwhile, was loathed by Adorno, who saw in it not improvisation but a "factory-made," proto-totalitarian output of the "culture industry," rife with "castration symbolism."[15] Indelibly imprinted with the trauma of Nazism, wary of mass culture, Adorno and Horkheimer were exceptionally pessimistic but taken together with Trotsky's experience in the Bronx and Gramsci's lamentation of the culture of the Rotary Club, they illustrate the tendency of European observers steeped in Marxism to recoil from American life even as they denied that it possessed any exceptional qualities—and even as they viewed it, indeed, as the very epitome of late capitalism.

The Marx–America dialectic, as these encounters suggest, is further complicated given the porousness and instability of what it has meant to be "American," the meaning of which has been disputed by its own citizenry, reshaped by millions of immigrants and temporary visitors, challenged by millions on the American continents who contest any single nation's claim to possess the word, and influenced by global interlocutors and circuits. No less fraught is the challenge of fixing a meaning to Marxism, which is less a set body of thought than a constellation of insights and methods, an international, varied, and often contradictory tradition to which no simple, uniform definition may be ascribed. Perhaps Marxism may at a minimum be said to hold to a materialist view of history, perceiving history not in terms of spiritual design but as a process determined by such factors as the organization of production, social classes in irreconcilable conflict, technological innovation, economic booms and contractions, and other social forces. Politically, Marxism champions the vast majority, the wage earners who do not own the means of production and must work for others in order to survive, believing no left-wing strategy sound that is not centered upon their participation. Finally, Marxism aspires to socialism, the creation of a classless society of shared ownership and abundance.

From its inception, Marxism attracted adherents in the United States. In the nineteenth century, they were limited largely to German–American immigrants who shared the language of Marx and Engels, most of whose work was not yet translated into English. A far more general dissemination of Marxism came in the first half of the twentieth century, first under the Socialist Party and then in the interwar moment when the Communist Party of the United States of America (CPUSA) was dominant while numerous smaller groups, publications, and individual thinkers besides the Communists laid competing claim to the Marxist tradition. That was a time when American labor movements were militant and dynamic, when organizations of the left attracted tens of thousands of members, and when American intellectuals fostered a vibrant Marxist culture. It was also, however, a time when cords of loyalty bound American Communist leaders with increasing tightness to the Soviet Union, which was becoming despotic as Joseph Stalin amassed state power. The very phrase "American exceptionalism," indeed, originated as the taunt by which Stalin deposed CPUSA head Jay Lovestone, compelling the Party's absolute loyalty. The Cold War saw the declension of the Communist Party, and the New Left of the 1960s sought to transcend what it considered a moribund Old Left, but various American thinkers remained animated by Marxism, from Herbert Marcuse to Angela Davis. Many student radicals by the end of the 1960s, having understood the limitations of campus uprisings without a broader social base, were drawn to Marxism only to encounter conservative headwinds in the 1970s. Set back once again by the New Right's surge in the 1980s and the "end of socialism" after 1989, American Marxism entered a doldrums, broken only by its recent renaissance.

This collection of essays brings together eleven scholars of U.S. history and culture—some new voices, others seasoned leaders in their fields—to provide a set of original appraisals of the relationship of Marxism and America. Most, but not all, of the chapters were first delivered as papers at a conference on "Marx and Marxism in the United States."[16] The contributions have been selected for quality and freshness of perspective, not ideology or particular stance. They are arranged by chronological order of subject matter so that if read in order they provide a kaleidoscopic intellectual and political history proceeding from the Civil War to the present. Michael Denning once suggested that the genesis of American Studies lay in the Cold War aspiration to erase Marxism; in this volume, as in his work, may be found contributions to the capacity of American Studies to elucidate Marxism.[17]

The crucial questions taken up include the following: How has Marxism—a varied, international, and above all internationalist tradition—engaged with the United States of America, itself a contested polity and culture? Is the United States innately insusceptible to Marxism? If so, what accounts for Marxism's recurrent appeal to at least some Americans? If not, what accounts for Marxism's historic weakness in the United States relative to that in numerous other countries? What notable contributions has Marxism made to American society and culture despite resistance to its influence? What toll has been exacted by the systematic marginalization of Marxism in American thought and political culture? How has Marxism, a body of thought focused upon class and production, engaged with gender, race, sexuality, empire, and other structural aspects of American life? How is the history of American Marxism in need of reconsideration or clarification?

While no singular way exists to answer any of these questions, let alone all of them at once, the thematic character of the problems they pose indicates an alternative way to contemplate the contributions that follow. In addition to their chronological ordering, the essays might also be read in comparison and contrast to one another, insofar as they speak to Marxism's antinomies—its inescapable tensions, oppositions, enigmas, and paradoxes. These antinomies help explain why thinkers who adhere to Marxism have evinced such radically different approaches and understandings of it. Here we suggest four such antinomies, the first three intrinsic to Marxism, the last extrinsic:

1. *Orthodoxy and heterodoxy*: The inclination to imbue Marxism with the trappings of religious infallibility is nothing new. Engels faulted Marx's first American followers, the German immigrants of the '48er generation, not only for failing to learn English and engage with native-born workers but as "people who claim to be orthodox Marxists, who have transformed our concept of movement into a rigid dogma to be learned by heart," making them "merely a sect."[18] The "orthodox" claim to fidelity to the letter of Marx was problematic, then, in the First International, just as it would be in the Second and Third. The danger of ossification—theory's hardening until it becomes a brittle dogma in the hands of self-construed pious Marxists—is a danger that Marx himself eschewed, writing, famously, "Je ne suis pas un Marxiste." Orthodoxy is not the sole danger, however, for heterodoxy presents risks as well in the prospect of straying so far from the path as to be unrecognizable or stretching core ideas so far as to leave Marxism bereft of any integral meaning. This creates interesting questions. What if, for example, those inspired by "Marxism" harbor doubts as to whether an outlook that seeks to transform the world through social movements should be named after one figure and beholden to his texts more than two centuries after his birth? Wouldn't Marx himself prefer to find another name, so as to end the religiosity intrinsic in such ritual?

American radicalism has seen tendencies toward both orthodoxy and heterodoxy. From the 1920s to the 1950s, the CPUSA positioned itself as a prominent custodian of doctrinal authority, but Jodie Collins (Chapter 4) suggests that at the very height of its influence during the Popular Front of the late 1930s, American Communism's attitudes toward family, gender, and sexuality showed a marked abnegation of Marx and Engels's views on those topics. Jesse Battan (Chapter 2) suggests, conversely, that it was V. F. Calverton and Samuel D. Schmalhausen, independent radicals derided as "sex boys" by more orthodox polemicists, who better shaped a revolutionary outlook on the sex question in the 1920s by amalgamating Marx and Freud, even as they departed freely from numerous aspects of the doctrines of Marx and Engels. "Orthodoxy" in the Stalin era, then, was stultifying, rigid, and adapted to the cultural conventions of bourgeois society, while the "heterodox" initiatives showed, in their very creativity, more fidelity to the spirit and method of Marx, even if contravening his utterances.

2. *Class and identity*: The proletariat, or wage-earning working class, was for classical Marxism, if not all its subsequent variants, the center of gravity. Marx assigned the proletariat a decisive mission since to him history was a tale of class struggles. As a social system premised upon the imperative of private profit, he wrote, capitalism pits property owners against workers compelled to generate more value through their productivity than the capitalists return in the form of wages. Every contest within society over the resultant surplus value, as one homespun American interpretation put it, either "advances the interests of the *takers*, or it advances the interests of the *makers*."[19] When strikes and other clashes erupt, for Marx they are not futile; in an exploitative order, they are inescapable, and they point toward and will ultimately be resolved by the achievement of communism, a society of shared wealth and abundance that will eliminate classes. What, then, would such an outlook make of an astonishingly heterogeneous society like the United States, where race, gender, sexuality, nationality, ethnicity, religion, and other forms of identity besides class take on great significance? How can Marxism, which sees class as a condition determined by relationship to the means of production, account for such variables? Is Marxism inescapably, as many critics have alleged, a form of class reductionism?

If so, it would be hard to explain the preoccupation of Marx and Engels with, say, the family, gender, and sexuality, signal themes in this volume. In *The German Ideology* (1845–1846), Marx and Engels described the family, with its imperative to propagate, as "the only social relationship" in human society at its origins. In the primordial anthropological past, they explained, class society emerged through property, an institution arising from the slavery of women and children to men within the family. Male domination, in short, led to class.[20] This should make it unsurprising that class is far from the only form of identity addressed by Marxism in the array of essays here. Paul Heideman (Chapter 6) examines two African-American thinkers, W. E. B. Du Bois and Oliver Cromwell Cox, who found in Marxism not only an explanation for how capitalism generated racial oppression and a means to end it, but also a prism for contemplating democracy. Matthew Stanley (Chapter 1), in his sketch of the Civil War in socialist memory, shows both how some Marxists flattened the American past in their quest for an American socialism, insufficiently attentive to racial oppression, while others extracted from the war's legacy deeper revolutionary meanings. Taking up the "sex wars" of the 1980s, Mara Keire (Chapter 9), offers a new interpretation of the radical feminists Andrea Dworkin and Catharine MacKinnon—usually perceived as searing critics of the left—that maintains they drew upon Marxism in their critique of pornography as a commodity form, reconstruing gender *as* class. The generational cohort as a phenomenon is attended to by Tim Jelfs (Chapter 10) in his examination of the new heterogenous socialism emergent among millennials and their enthusiasm for the podcast, which augments, if not supplants, the print culture that sustained traditional Marxism. These contributions suggest an oscillation between solidarity and self-determination. They also suggest a need for analytical nuance, because depending upon its framing, Marxism has variously enabled or obstructed comprehension of such identities as race, gender, sexuality, nationality, and age. As a theory centered on social class, Marxism has, when applied to the various identities of American capitalist society, generated both contradictions *and* insights, in a process of continuous intellectual struggle.

3. *Revolution and reform*: Marxism, born in the crucible of 1848, that year of European revolutions, of the "springtime of peoples" and the *Communist Manifesto*, has always had at its core the aspiration of the revolutionary reconstitution of society. It is, however, not at all interested in standing apart indifferently from conditions in the present, accepting them fatalistically, which led even the *Manifesto* to propose such immediate reforms as a graduated income tax. This reform–revolution antinomy plays out in the history of the American left as a dialectic. The Scylla of "the progressive," capable of modifying but not superseding the strictures of existing society, is countered by the Charybdis of the would-be "insurrectionary" who accomplishes nothing but the isolation of the would-be vanguard in a sectarian fantasy. The first danger is exemplified by the siren song of liberalism in the New Deal era. Andrew Hartman (Chapter 5) suggests that the CPUSA's Popular Front absorption within the New Deal constitutes a good part of the answer to the mystery of why Marxism did not flourish in the 1930s during capitalism's massive crisis of the Great Depression. The second danger is epitomized by the adventurist delusions of Weatherman, a tiny offshoot

of the sixties New Left that imagined that a few hundred radicals could by acts of individual violence spark an American revolution. Sinead McEneaney (Chapter 7) examines how the Weatherwomen, who disdained feminism as "picketing in front of bra factories" and elevated race and empire above gender, short-circuited a historic opportunity for radicalism and feminism to inform one another in the era of the women's liberation movement.

More subtle dilemmas of tactics and strategy, of reform and revolution, arise in perpetuity in the history of Marxian thought. Few have managed to resolve them more cogently than Rosa Luxemburg, the Polish-German Jewish revolutionary. Spurning reformism, a gradualism that blunts militancy and casts itself as practical but accepts the horizon of the existing society, she posited as a better means to secure desired reforms a militant, uncompromising politics focused primarily upon building working-class power so as to provide the foundation for eventual social transformation from below.[21] Americans have made notable contributions to the theory and practice of such a method, from the left wing of the early Socialist Party through the dissenting strands of 1930s and 1960s radicalism, as well as in the thought of individual thinkers such as the Trinidadian émigré C. L. R. James, who spent a decade in the United States working out a theory of revolutionary politics and trying to draw up an analysis of American capitalism.[22] In America as in Europe, however, such a libertarian and democratic revolutionary socialism remained a minoritarian perspective, helping to explain the contemporary weakness of socialism on both continents.

4. *Marxism and America*: Far beyond the initial musings of Marx and Engels, the United States of America has presented a series of interpretative problems for Marxist analysis and socialist politics. That the country with the most advanced capitalist economy in the world would be markedly weak in the intellectual caliber of its contributions to Marxism and in the capacity of Marxism to attract adherents has long reverberated as a puzzle in need of investigation. Some suggest that the answer lies in the liberal roots of the American polity. Others point to a popular culture defined by practicality, with a superficial preference for "getting things done," the inclination toward practice rather than theory resulting in proneness toward opportunism. That conjecture might find substantiation in stories

such as one that the first hedge fund—that quintessential institution of Wall Street's global financialized capitalism—was founded in 1949 by an American who in the Great Depression attended the Marxist Workers School in Berlin, ran secret anti-fascist missions for the Leninist Organization, and toured the Spanish Civil War.[23] Surely this is not the only case of grounding in *Capital* producing investment acumen, since in bear markets even the business press has a propensity for turning out admiring portraits of Marx.

"America will never become a socialist country," said the President of the United States in the 2019 State of the Union address, drawing upon old Cold War tropes.[24] Yet claims of an essentially capitalist America implacable to any Marxist influence and inured to all theory are overdone. Leilah Danielson's evocation of A. J. Muste's band of thinkers (Chapter 3) reveals the way a "foreign" doctrine such as Marxism can inform a self-declared "American approach" steeped in indigenous revolutionary traditions and rooted in the activity of the contemporary labor movement. Nick Witham (Chapter 8), in his essay on Howard Zinn's bestselling work *A People's History of the United States*, shows how an idiosyncratic, existentialist, Marxist-hued radical history helped shape American popular historical understanding, even during the conservative reign of Ronald Reagan. This is not to deny that particularities of American culture present difficulties for Marxism, including a national chauvinist "Americanism" construing the United States to be in direct contrast to Marxism and all things European, or an insistence on the vernacular that veers toward rhetorical populism rather than the class categories preferred by the Marxist idiom. Yet the labor studies scholar Kim Moody (Chapter 11) presents a vigorous challenge to the perennial charge of American exceptionalism in his examination of capitalism and working-class politics today. None of these essays feigns a comprehensive answer to Werner Sombart's old question, "Why is there no socialism in the United States?" They do, however, suggest Marxism's enduring vitality and relevance in an America so often resistant to its teachings.

In recent years, given rising anxieties about economic inequality, even many liberals have mellowed toward Marx. Louis Menand writes that Marx was a humanist "whose thought was dedicated to human freedom," that "for better or worse, it just is not the case that his thought is obsolete," and that even if a revolutionary overthrow of the capitalist order has thus far not materialized "he is not wrong yet."[25] However, such generosity vies in the liberal mind with a tradition of skepticism typified by Daniel Bell's landmark work *Marxian Socialism in the United States* (1952), which dismissed American socialism as "in the world, but not of it." Socialists were, Bell held, melioristic and therefore proposed reforms, but refused "to accept responsibility for the actions of the government itself," a trait Bell thought made them otherworldly. Why American socialists should have taken on the burden of responsibility for a state they never controlled is a mystery, but toward the end of his book even Bell was prepared to concede that many policies adopted in the twentieth century were first advocated by socialists, including old-age pensions, unemployment insurance, a limited workday, and the right of workers to organize unions. He admitted that among union leaders, in intellectual life, and in numerous other ways, "socialism has, as a pale tint, suffused into the texture of American life and subtly changed its shadings."[26] For a doctrine not "of the world," then, socialism had somehow colored the world.

Today a new generation has turned to socialism, adapting Marxism to praxis in new ways. Is it impermissible to imagine these youth infusing their own colorations into American life—or even to hope that they might wrest much more from bourgeois society than a "pale tint" of influence? As late capitalism creates multi-million-dollar penthouses while half a million people sleep nightly on American streets, lavishes more energy on creative accounting than research and development, pumps carbon into the atmosphere heedless of melting ice caps and species extinctions, tends toward the erosion of democratic norms if not outright authoritarian rule in both state and workplace, and fosters one inane bigotry after another as scapegoats for the insecurities it has generated in everyday life, it would seem that very little is left to lose—while a world awaits to be won—in reclaiming the best of a long tradition of revolutionary imagination.

Notes

1 "Socialism as Popular as Capitalism among Young Adults in U.S.," Gallup, November 25, 2019 https://news.gallup.com/poll/268766

/socialism-popular-capitalism-among-young-adults.aspx; "Who is Karl Marx?" *Teen Vogue*, May 10, 2018 www.teenvogue.com/story/who-is-karl-marx?

2 Morgan Gstalter, "Democratic Socialists of America see membership spike after Ocasio-Cortez win," *The Hill*, June 28, 2018 https://thehill.com/blogs/blog-briefing-room/news/394679-democratic-socialists-of-america-see-membership-spike-after; "America's New Left," *New Left Review* 116/117 (Mar/June 2019): 118–35.

3 Sarah Leonard and Bhaskar Sunkara, *The Future We Want: Radical Ideas for the New Century* (New York: Metropolitan, 2016); Bhaskar Sunkara, *The Socialist Manifesto* (London: Verso, 2019).

4 Karl Marx and Friedrich Engels, *The Civil War in the United States*, ed. Andrew Zimmerman (New York: International Publishers, 2016); Karl Marx and Friedrich Engels, *Letters to Americans, 1848–1895* (New York: International Publishers, 1953).

5 Engels, "Description of Recently Founded Communist Colonies Still in Existence" (1844), in *Marx and Engels on the United States* (Moscow: Progress, 1979): 33.

6 Marx to Joseph Weydemeyer, March 5, 1852, in *Marx and Engels on the United States*, 71.

7 Marx, *Capital*, in *Marx and Engels on the United States*, 212–13.

8 The quintessential expression is Louis Hartz, *The Liberal Tradition in America* (New York: Harcourt, Brace and World, 1955).

9 Engels to Florence Kelley-Wischnewetzky, June 3, 1886, and Engels to Friedrich Adolph Sorge, August 8, 1887, February 8, 1890, and March 18, 1893, in *Marx and Engels on the United States*, 307, 319, 331.

10 *Eugene V. Debs Speaks* (New York: Pathfinder, 1972), 204.

11 Leon Trotsky, *My Life* (New York: Charles Scribner's Sons, 1930), 274.

12 Meredith Tax, *The Rising of the Women: Feminist Solidarity and Class Conflict, 1880–1917* (New York: Monthly Review, 1980); James R. Green, *Grass-Roots Socialism: Radical Movements in the Southwest, 1895–1943* (Baton Rouge and London: Louisiana State University Press, 1978).

13 Antonio Gramsci, *Selections from the Prison Notebooks* (New York: International Publishers, 1971), 317.

14 Max Horkheimer, *Eclipse of Reason* (New York: Oxford University Press, 1947); Sidney Hook, *Towards the Understanding of Karl Marx* (New York: John Day, 1933).

15 Theodore W. Adorno, "Perennial Fashion—Jazz" (1953), in *Prisms* (Cambridge: MIT, 1986), 119–32.

16 "Marx and Marxism in the United States: A One-Day Symposium" was held at the University of Nottingham, May 11, 2019. Andrew Hartman's

paper, included here, was the keynote address. The plenary, with contributions from Christopher Phelps, Jennifer Luff, Alex Goodall, Jonathan Bell, and Molly Geidel, is published as "Roundtable: Antecedents of 2019," *Journal of American Studies* 53 (November 2019), 855–92.

17 Michael Denning, "'The Special Conditions': Marxism and American Studies," *American Quarterly* 38 (1986), 356–80. For another example of this reversal, see "Marx and the United States," a special issue of *Amerikastudien/American Studies* 62 (2017), edited by Dennis Büscher-Ulbrich and Marlon Lieber, which includes a creative essay by Denning on how to read *Capital*.

18 Engels to Friedrich Adolph Sorge, June 10, 1891, in *Marx and Engels on the United States*, 325.

19 Mary Marcy, "The Class Struggle," *International Socialist Review*, XVI (October 1915): 208.

20 Karl Marx and Friedrich Engels, *The German Ideology* (London: Lawrence & Wishart, 1968), 40, 44.

21 Rosa Luxemburg, *Reform or Revolution* (New York: Pathfinder, 1970).

22 Christopher Phelps, "C. L. R. James and the Theory of State Capitalism," in *American Capitalism: Social Thought and Political Economy in the Twentieth Century*, ed. Nelson Lichtenstein (Philadelphia: University of Pennsylvania Press, 2006), 156–74.

23 Sebastian Mallaby, *More Money Than God: Hedge Funds and the Making of a New Elite* (London: Bloomsbury, 2010), 1.

24 "Painting Socialists as Villains, Trump Refreshes a Blueprint," *New York Times*, February 6, 2019 www.nytimes.com/2019/02/06/us/politics/socialism-donald-trump.html?searchResultPosition=1.

25 Louis Menand, "Karl Marx, Yesterday and Today," *New Yorker*, October 3, 2016 www.newyorker.com/magazine/2016/10/10/karl-marx-yesterday-and-today.

26 Daniel Bell, *Marxian Socialism in the United States* (New York: Princeton University Press, 1967), x, 191–92.

1

The blue and the gray and the red: Marxism and Civil War memory

Matthew E. Stanley

The template for the Marxist memory of the U.S. Civil War began while the conflict was still underway. Covering the war era for the *New York Tribune* and Vienna's *Die Presse*, Karl Marx imagined the struggle as being between two social systems, one of which, the Confederate, was part of a "crusade of property against labor."[1] He also predicted the losing prospects of such a cause. The Confederacy, far from constituting a "solid" bloc, Marx insisted, was an oligarchical faction attempting an improbable coup d'état. Anticipating the guerilla conflicts, food riots, anti-conscription upheaval, mass soldier desertions, and, most especially, the "general strike" of enslaved peoples that came to characterize rebel defeat, Marx underscored the Confederate project's fundamental regressiveness and internal contradictions—its class conflict and popular discontent. Scholars since have scrutinized what they view as Marx's overly sympathetic view toward Lincoln, his inflation of antislavery sentiment among Northern workers, the way his taxonomy of workers perhaps prioritized (mostly white) wage earners, and his overlooking of the imperial nature of the Union war effort, especially in the West.[2] Nevertheless, Marx reckoned correctly that the South's cabal of "slaveocrats" would only yield to a revolutionary waging of war that might unleash the socially disruptive potential of those disaffected classes—chiefly through the destruction of chattel bondage.[3]

Marx also recognized the agency of common people and grew increasingly influenced by what Herbert Marcuse described as "living workers changing living reality by their action."[4] Penning his masterwork as he analyzed the political situation in North America, the War of the Rebellion came to have a considerable impact on the nature and structure of *Capital*. As Raya Dunayevskaya explained, "It was under the impact of the Civil War and the response on European workers ... that the International Working Men's Association, known as the First International, was born."[5] The book's "American roots" are perhaps best characterized by the author's maxim that "labor cannot emancipate itself in the white skin when in the black it is branded," and his observation that slavery's death created new possibilities for interracial class-based solidarity, particularly in the form of the eight-hour workday. This held international significance. For Marx, the Civil War was nothing less than "world-transforming," and the destruction of chattel slavery alongside agitation against serfdom in Russia constituted "the most momentous thing happening in the world."[6]

While Marx and his collaborator Friedrich Engels did not view the Union cause as synonymous with proletarian revolution, they *did* understand the triumph of political democracy and bourgeois capitalism as stepping stones toward working-class liberation. The war provided an organizational impetus for the international workers' cause.[7] In the International's 1864 address to Abraham Lincoln, Marx predicted that chattel slavery's dismantling would inaugurate a "new era of emancipation of labor," fostering liberal capitalism and, eventually, the requisite class consciousness needed to overthrow the economic system.[8] Praising Ohio Senator Benjamin F. Wade's call for a "more equal distribution of wealth" in his preface to the first edition of *Capital*, Marx avowed that the war had "sounded the alarm bell" for the European working class and that the "eyes of Europe and the world" were "fixed upon" the events of Reconstruction.[9] In his letter to the National Labor Union in May 1869, just as the world's first experiments in large-scale interracial democracy were playing out in the South, Marx explained that Union victory had "opened up a new epoch in the annals of the working class ... now at last the working classes are bestriding the scene of history."[10]

Having witnessed the contact between German-speaking Union soldiers and African Americans in what was perhaps "the earliest collaboration between socialists with a self-emancipating proletariat," Marx foresaw the prospect of a multi-ethnic movement among the world's most diverse working class arising from slavery's collapse.[11] He deemed the postwar era a "revolutionary phase" and hoped it might bring about "the rescue of an enchained race and the reconstruction of a social world."[12] Marx's radical counterparts across the Atlantic agreed that emancipation meant little without economic as well as political democracy, including access to land, safer working conditions, and greater control over their own labor and its profits. But even Marx's disappointment with the abandonment of Reconstruction and the failure of the U.S. political system to produce a viable labor party could not conceal his appreciation for the wartime gains made by workers, including freedpeople.[13] As Robin Blackburn explains, for Marx and Engels, "every revolutionary effort, when analyzed properly, laid the groundwork for ever more successful revolution."[14]

Marx was hardly alone in forging historical consciousness with a view toward the future. Nor was he distinctive in his urge to dispense with unavailing remnants of the past, famously asserting in *The Eighteenth Brumaire* that "the tradition of all dead generations weighs like a nightmare on the brains of the living."[15] Likewise, Marxist historiography is not exceptional in its drift toward teleology. Yet Marxist Civil War memory *is* unique in its emphasis on modes of production (denaturalizing capitalism) and the war as an ongoing project of transformation from below, or what Enzo Traverso labels a "strategic memory of past emancipation struggles, a future-oriented memory."[16] Indeed, although Reconstruction's downfall precluded the larger transformation of capitalist relations and landed property, what Marx termed the "American Anti-Slavery War" galvanized nineteenth-century workers' movements much as the American Revolution had inspired the bourgeois revolutions of previous generations. American Marxists since Marx have shared the great thinker's interest in the Civil War owing to its continuous contemporary relevance related to class injustice, inequality, and, above all, the unfinished matter of black civil rights.[17] A synthesis and reinterpretation of Marxist Civil War memory and leftist historiography reveals a variety of radical remembrances and their residual impact on scholarly paradigms, with implications for the significance of class in the study of memory.

Beyond an expressed adherence to Marxism, socialism, or revolutionary politics, the red memory of the war possessed certain hallmarks, emphasized by its progenitors in various proportions: materiality, workers, internationalism, and futurism. Above all, Marxians spotlighted proletarian agency. In their view, the war may have begun over wider issues, especially the clash between free and slave labor systems, but it was fought by masses of working people. More critically, its liberationist elements could be made to serve the interests of workers through a self-emancipation movement *led by workers*. Because regional and national identities hindered class consciousness, Marxists at the time tended to view the war's pivotal intellectual and historical linkages as international, rather than sectional or national, and later socialists worked to situate the contest into a transnational schema. This emphasis on internationalism contained elements both empirical and aspirational. In other words, not only had the war been part of a world-historical process that broke the power of landed aristocracy even as it ushered in new forms of capital aggregation and economic dominion, its emancipatory program was the precursor to a broader deliverance from "wage slavery" and therefore heralded a left future.

The Civil War has always provided socialists a means of understanding historical process *and* Americanizing their cause. While Marx and Engels were perhaps correct to identify political liberalization (emancipation and Radical Reconstruction) in the world's fastest-growing industrial economy with the potential for accelerated class struggle, they failed to grasp the extent to which racial and ethnic animosities, entrenched ideas regarding merit and mobility, a dynamic bourgeoisie, and the success with which elites were able to paint socialism as a violent immigrant conspiracy would become roadblocks to the consciousness and institutional and political coherence of a self-defined working class. Yet the appropriation of popular historical memory proved a way to facilitate the class solution by bridging the tenets of European socialism and the traditions of American reform. As Paul Buhle notes, "textualist" Marxists, whose immigrant backgrounds, theoretical inclinations, and somewhat provincial ethnic institutions limited their exposure to wider U.S. culture, needed a way to meld their revolutionary movement with indigenous radicalism. Through the efforts of "Americanizing" socialists, the Civil War's lessons became a way for early Marxists to appeal to white veterans, African Americans, women's rights advocates, and homegrown reformers of various stripes with backgrounds in abolitionism, transcendentalism, spiritualism, or anti-monopolism.[18]

Indeed, the postwar labor movement was, to some extent, "abolitionized"—refracted through the semantics, ideas, and personalities of the sectional conflict. Marxists in particular invoked the language and imagery of emancipation; elicited the sectional impulse and entreated the veteran; and looked to abolitionism and Radical Republicanism as symbolic and organizational templates, often viewing the liberation of black slaves as not a threat, but a *model* of broader worker liberation.[19] Although many understood black liberation as unrelated or even a hindrance to the fuller "emancipation of [white] labor," myriad white workers also saw the destruction of slavery—what Marx termed the "movement of slaves" into the greatest slave rebellion in world history—as a blueprint for their own emancipation.[20] Rejecting the notion of "free labor" as the mere absence of legal enslavement, countless industrial laborers used collective memory to challenge property rights *beyond* property in man. Rather than recalling the abolitionist movement, as many antebellum workers had, as altogether bourgeois, or viewing slavery's opponents as mere pragmatic allies whose aim of free labor converged with their own, organized workers—and revolutionary socialists in particular—saw themselves as postscripts to the abolitionist cause. In appropriating the antislavery spirit, they forged their own internationalist and revolutionary vein of Civil War memory, constructing "red Abe Lincolns" and "red John Browns" as symbolic threats to exclusive property rights and harbingers of a greater social upheaval.

This discourse emanated not only from the top down, from labor leadership to the shop floor, but also from the bottom up, as workingmen converted rural mills, urban docks, factory yards, campaign stumps, convention halls, and printing houses into critical sites of memory production, framing their struggle as a "second civil war" or a "third American revolution." Wielding war memories, labor organizations, and political movements used class (rather than race or section) as a means of reconciling workers across North–South lines. They did so in numerous ways and through assorted means, both inside and outside formal politics, and with various levels of sincerity, pragmatism, and long-term strategy. Yet these sustained attempts at class-based rapprochement were repeatedly torpedoed by social and political forces that proved inherently antithetical to class unity: nationalism, militarism, regionalism, religion, and partisanship, as well as exploited divisions of ethnicity, gender, and, most especially, race. Despite tension within the labor movement between a mode of Civil War commemoration rooted in nationalism and reform and a Marxian memory centered on internationalism and revolutionary redemption, radical worker movements all shared the common feature of having employed collective memory to attempt to bridge wartime "division" not primarily through shared whiteness or sectional loyalty, but through class and trade solidarity.

The groundwork for an interpretation of the Civil War as the opening phase of a greater struggle from below dates to wartime revolutionaries: Forty-Eighters, socialist émigrés, radical trade unionists, German-American Turners, labor-oriented abolitionists, and "red republicans" for whom free labor ideology existed within a class prism. Socialists in particular infused the meaning of the war with economic radicalism and internationalism, an alternative to the dominant liberal nationalism of the era.[21] Such revolutionaries—a number of whom, including Marx's associate Joseph Weydemeyer (Figure 1.1), served in the Union Army—represented the leftmost edge of what Matt Karp calls "antislavery as class struggle." Indeed, while the vast majority of white Northerners, including bourgeois Republicans, had little interest in black equality, detested abolitionism, and, in the words of W. E. B. Du Bois, "went to war without the slightest idea of freeing the slave," the nascent Republican Party utilized class and material (though not socialist) arguments to oppose the slave system.[22] Radical workers especially came to denounce what Labor Reform Association founder and eight-hour workday advocate Ira Steward referred to as the "rebel aristocracy."[23] Yet they also emphasized "slavery" as an economic condition that was transferable to workers in a factory setting. In other words, the labor left broke with antislavery liberal orthodoxy by both casting disloyal owners (slaveholders) and their unfree labor (slaves) against the patriotism of *worker* organization (and often worker internationalism) and by portraying chattel bondage as a dimension of *working*-class conflict.

Meanwhile, "walkouts" of enslaved people and slave seizures by Union soldiers set the pace for emancipation, their definitions of freedom galvanizing a social revolution.[24] But using the war as a revolutionary symbol meant balancing aspirations with real-time

Figure 1.1 Joseph Weydemeyer, shown here in his Union uniform, was an early follower of Karl Marx and Friedrich Engels and a participant in the revolutions of 1848 in Germany who emigrated to the United States and helped found its first Marxist organization, the Proletarierbund, in 1852. He then helped establish the American Workers League before joining the Union Army during the Civil War, rising to the rank of Colonel, and corresponding all the while with Marx and Engels in support of the creation of the International Workingmen's Association, or First International. *Courtesy International Institute for Social History, Amsterdam.*

limitations. The First International initially believed, and workers continued to hope, that the Civil War would summon a new dawn for the power and possibilities of working people. However, the realities of the Gilded Age—widening inequality, political corruption, reactionary bureaucratization, and the abandonment of workers by both parties—tempered any unwarranted optimism.[25] Emancipation provided a model for radical democracy, but the war itself had expedited many of the harshest features of industrial capitalism. This duality combined with the tendency of white radicals to overemphasize the role of *white* workers. The result was a devaluing of the agency of enslaved people during the war—and the prerogatives of non-white workers in the present—that would become typical of the labor left's memory of the Civil War well into the twentieth century.

Beginning with the National Labor Union's eight-hour movement, postwar tradesmen and farmer-labor insurgencies consistently painted battles against "wage slavery" as continuations of the antislavery fight. This entailed either a broadening "emancipation" northward (sometimes racialized to benefit "white slaves") or making good on the war's ostensible promises of an expanded democracy. Speaking in Chicago in January 1865, William H. Sylvis insisted that although the ongoing "political revolution" was coming to a close, a "social revolution"—a "collision between classes"—was still taking place across Northern cities, where wage labor had become tantamount to bondage.[26] The conclusion of the slaveholder's rebellion and the end of the abolitionist movement had opened up new imaginative outlets for a republicanism centered on combating the inequalities of industrial capitalism through expanded definitions of "free labor."[27] Such sentiment materialized not only in craft unions, but through agrarian radicalism in Virginia, where Readjusters employed antislavery vernacular to propel their interracial insurgency, foretelling both the achievements and dilemmas of later populist struggles.

The collapse of Reconstruction, the Great Railroad Strike of 1877, and the overall decline of the Republican free labor ideal led to calls for a more democratic economy by disparate yet often reinforcing political movements—anti-monopolism, greenbackism, trade unionism, and socialism—and their corresponding political parties. Members of the Greenback–Labor Party conceived their organization as a fulfillment of the promises of free labor—the idea that independence lay with land ownership and that no man had a right to exploit more land than he could cultivate.[28] Through the GLP, whose political pedigree would also link antislavery to the Knights of Labor and the People's Party, veterans used specific interpretations of the war as a bridge out of major party politics and toward populism, socialism, anarchism, and labor radicalism.[29] At the same time, conditions in industry's "human jungle" led to increased battles between capital and labor and new imaginings of "slavery," often qualified with specific conceptions of whiteness ("white slavery").[30] Labor unions, unprecedented in size, influence, and trade inclusivity, constituted the most salient challenge to the developing industrial order. The Knights of Labor, for one, borrowed directly from antislavery traditions, as industrial "slavery" and worker "emancipation" proved critical to how the Knights imagined, dialogued, and strategized about the conditions of production.

The Socialist Labor Party (SLP) and emerging anarchist networks, many of which were influenced by Marxist conceptions of class struggle and historical materialism, furthered more explicit war memories. In pursuit of what they termed a "second emancipation," this one of the entire working class, socialists co-opted a variety of antislavery language, songs, and symbols as they sought the abolition of "industrial slavery." Both Daniel De Leon's industrial unionists and the revolutionary anarchists of Chicago viewed their cause as a "New Abolitionism" that inherited and transcended free labor precepts. Their imaginings of "communist John Browns," property-seizing Abe Lincolns, and industrial "slave pens" "reddened" the memory of slavery and emancipation and married their politics to "a native Garrisonian and John Brown-derived tradition of political terrorism and moral action."[31] This protraction of abolitionism saw the conflict between labor and capital as an extension of the "property question" that had existed prior to the Civil War.[32] Even as capitalists, like the Slave Power before them, painted working-class mobilization as an "American Commune," especially in the aftermath of the Haymarket bombing, socialists and anarchists built on the redistributionist claims of abolitionists and freedpeople—and exceeded those of trade unionists—by openly challenging not only the legitimacy of slave property or plantations, but also of the mechanisms of production and property rights altogether. Yet both groups generally dismissed racial distinction, as most saw the only difference between chattel slavery and "white slavery" as the difference between slaves sold *at* the market and slaves sold *in* the market. Nevertheless, the SLP's vision of a "socialist army" in "a war for social emancipation" prefigured that of later socialists.

In the early twentieth century, the Socialist Party of America and Industrial Workers of the World expressed their politics in antislavery vernacular, grafting war memories onto a variety of labor personalities and campaigns. Socialist editors promoted incremental reform and Christian socialism; politicians quoted Lincoln and John Brown alongside Marx and Eugene Debs to validate calls for industrial liberation.[33] This left nationalism encouraged workers to renew the war's insurgent militancy in the name of a supplementary "emancipation." The most prominent Socialist newspaper, the *Appeal to Reason*, consistently presented the war as a momentous—albeit incomplete—occasion of human freedom. While memory creation tended to reflect either the SP's racially conservative or egalitarian wings, Socialists argued that the Emancipation Proclamation, as well as Radical Republican activist economic planks and bids for land redistribution, had also provided an analogue for the seizure and decommodification of private property. Former calls to "confiscate the slaves!" were now followed by those to "confiscate the industries!" However, the mandated patriotism and government anti-radicalism and labor repression during the First World War and the Red Scare—censorship, deportations, mass arrests, beatings, brandings, murders, and lynching—marginalized demands for international working-class revolution and drained left nationalism of its insurgent edge, weakening the class war interpretation. Diminution of radicalism reinforced the conservative nationalism of popular Civil War memory, channeled largely through the American Federation of Labor (AFL).

Early twentieth-century Marxist cultural politics also embodied one of the consistent pitfalls of the American radical memory: the neglect of racial analysis. The general failure of white radicals to account for black memory and black history—which ranged from professed colorblindness to outright white supremacy—was part and parcel of their shortcomings in mobilizing black workers. Many white socialists, including Debs, *did* vigorously attack the color line, helping cultivate an influential cadre of black socialists who predated the black Marxism of Cyril V. Briggs and Hubert Harrison, as well as the better-known antiracist work of the Communist Party. However, white consciousness or racial supremacy led the vast majority of white socialists to snub the extent to which Marxist theory applied especially to the most disproportionately working-class and most organizationally isolated population. Although the SLP, left anarchists, and the SP officially backed universal political rights regardless of race, sex, and color, they did not meaningfully address race-specific grievances such as lynching, convict leasing, racial banishment, or the mass deprivation of civil liberties, or propose measures to advance African Americans specifically.[34] Most insisted that the capitalist "slave factory" was "more intense in its horrors than the famous slave pen," and that the "race question" would be resolved naturally through the destruction of capitalism.[35]

Such deficiencies exacerbated the labor left's gargantuan task of seizing the popular narrative of a "continued Civil War." More powerful memory makers, including the middle-class dominated veterans' organizations, espoused reactionary ideas regarding economic competition, fetishized individualism, social hierarchy, and national empire, censuring all labor organization as "communistic." Leftist class reconciliation, or the attempt to achieve class-based interracial reconciliation across North and South, was further complicated by the fact that conservative politicians, publishers, businessmen, and civic groups and militias also embraced white (and not class-based) Blue-Gray reunion within the added dimension of enforcing order and suppressing labor organization and third-party insurgency. Industrialists, meanwhile, sat popular generals on corporate boards and disproportionately employed Union veterans as private guards, detectives, and police forces—the hit force of capital.

The revolutionary interpretations of the Civil War that sprung from and disseminated well beyond the First and Second Internationals largely failed to integrate the racialization of capitalism into their politics of collective memory.[36] The Third International and the Communist Party of the United States of America (CPUSA), however, *did* develop coherent, historical theories about how racism interacts with capitalism, sometimes to the benefit of white workers, but more critically, how it adds layers of exploitation onto non-white people. Party leaders including William Z. Foster and Earl Browder consistently invoked antislavery themes to link the "common man" Lincoln to struggling Depression-era workers, appeal to African Americans on behalf of "Self-Determination for the Black Belt," or buttress the party strategy of "Communism is Twentieth Century Americanism." Party conventions and the pages of the *New Masses* (1926–1948) featured assorted Civil War themes within socialist–realist imagery, including placards of John Brown and Frederick Douglass in 1936 and a colossal likeness of Lincoln in Chicago in 1939. Each February, Communists commemorated the sixteenth president's birthday with Lincoln-Lenin rallies. They named community clubs after antislavery luminaries: John Brown, Harriet Tubman, Frederick Douglass, Sojourner Truth, and Elizabeth Cady Stanton, among others. The party, which leader Earl Browder called "the most consistent fighter … for the defense of our flag," used such cultural representation to "carry on the work" of Lincoln and the antislavery generation.[37] In fact, according to Nina Silber, U.S. Communists were the inheritors of "an intellectual legacy that saw in the Civil War period the roots on an indigenously American radical tradition."[38] Black Communists including Hosea Hudson and Angelo Herndon likened their organizing efforts to a restored abolitionism that might "finish the job of freeing the Negroes" or even "complete the unfinished tasks of revolutionary Reconstruction."[39] "The first Civil War didn't free [black tenant farmers]," one comrade maintained. "But this one will."[40]

Yet by the time the historical dynamics of interracial class struggle became commonplace among white radicals in and beyond the 1930s, including tying antiracism to anti-capitalism and avowing that the liberation of *all* depended on the capacity of white workers to overcome race prejudice, the possibilities of revolutionary industrial unionism had been largely suppressed—folded into the Democratic Party, negotiated into the reformist AFL, or simply stomped out of existence. Numerous academic Marxists and social historians nevertheless incorporated aspects of this "red memory," including how the destruction of slave property kindled aspirational "emancipations" in which laborers sought to transcend civic equality through land redistribution or the transformation of productive relations. Marxian historians since 1917 have applied Marx's and Engels's early concept of "bourgeois revolution" to describe the Civil War's essence. Yet the idea of the sectional contest as a "revolution" sprung from freedpeople and radical workers, alongside antislavery editors and labor-minded abolitionists such as Wendell Phillips, Radical Republicans like Thaddeus Stevens, and Union officers including James A. Garfield situated the struggle within the broader nineteenth-century Atlantic context of liberal nationalist conflicts and wars of unification.[41] Other observers attached materialist or class-based explanations to the revolutionary model. It was Vermont Senator Justin Smith Morrill who in 1862 described the war as "the old struggle of a class for power and privilege and which has so often convulsed the world repeating itself in our history."[42]

By the 1920s, leftists had accepted and integrated the basics tenets of Charles and Mary Beard's concept of a "Second American Revolution." Popularized in their classic *The Rise of American Civilization* (1927), the Beards' thesis held that the war was one between two antagonistic economic systems in which "the capitalists, laborers, and farmers of the North and West drove from power in the national government the planting aristocracy of the South."[43] Slavery was almost incidental. Although Herbert Morais, the first editor of Marx and Engels's Civil War writings, chided the Beards' neglect of slavery and African Americans, there were often minimal interpretative differences between Progressive school "economic" historians and Marxists writing during High Stalinism. Both viewed the Civil War as predicated on capitalist expansion by manufacturers and commercial farmers against an also expansionistic slaveholding class characterized variously as illiberal capitalist, pre-capitalist, late-stage feudalist, or merchant capitalist, or even vaguely as "agrarian." Influenced by Beardianism and contemporary European Marxist scholars including Georges Lefebvre and Christopher Hill, who respectively charted the French Revolution and the English Civil War as class conflicts that freed the capitalist impulses of the urban middle classes from their feudal restraints, Marxist historians came to emphasize the bourgeois nature of the Union project. They also highlighted Marx's notion that the North's industrial bourgeoisie had to be rescued in some sense by a "slave revolution" (emancipation) and the enlistment of black soldiers.[44]

While Marx himself, who construed the war not as one between agrarianism and industrialism but between slave and free labor, never addressed the cotton South's capitalist maturity (or lack thereof), historians since have smoothed the edges of what some Marxists presented as too rough a feudal/capitalist binary. Though much of the Old South's "ruling race" identified as what Eugene Genovese saw as market-averse paternalists, in cotton they produced a proletariat-creating commodity that remade global capitalism. What Walter Johnson terms "slave racial capitalism" exhibited many capitalist features: sanctified private property, least-cost efficiency, complex systems of credit, workplace adaptability, the commodification of labor power, and brutal discipline of workers. Despite working in the service of capitalist development, the South's "factories in the fields" nevertheless threatened to block advanced capitalism due to both its political unreliability (secession) and slowness to self-transform (turn chattel slaves into wage workers). White settler-colonials backed by the U.S. state persisted in removing pre-capitalist impediments to capitalist development (Native Americans, semifeudal proprietors), and scholars would continue to debate how and the extent to which capitalism would have spread and matured across the continent in the event of Union defeat. However, this "bourgeois revolution" was, according to Barrington Moore, "the last revolutionary offensive on the part of what one may legitimately call urban or bourgeois capitalist democracy."[45]

Yet what Marx called the "permanent revolution" of a continuously radicalizing working class never materialized. Though militant workers would later aspire toward a "second civil war" against "wage slavery," the largest social uprising during the war itself, the New York Draft Riots of July 1863 saw white workers riot in opposition to the war, targeting African Americans in the process. Moreover, despite the decisive impact of workers and slaves on the war's outcome, a bourgeois revolution—a conflict designed to safeguard U.S. capitalism—could not have been expected to "finish" the liberation of either wage workers or a formerly enslaved proletariat. In other words, the black advancements of Reconstruction, driven by pressure from below, were largely temporary concessions rooted in expediency. Their overturning was not a Republican Party "betrayal" of African Americans because, although Republican leadership accepted emancipation as necessary to win the war and thwart the Slave Power, reconciliation between capitalists North and South was highly predictable. War and its aftermath were never intended to protect black freedom at the expense of profits, especially if the democratic-redistributionist aims of freedpeople aligned with those Northern industrial workers. "However distant sharecropping may have been from free labor as conceived in the ideology of the prewar Republican Party," Neil Davidson writes, "it was not incompatible with capitalism."[46]

Written in 1935, Du Bois's *Black Reconstruction* remembered the first civil rights movement as a moment when democratic forces nearly overtook the imperatives of big business. Though most white northerners resisted social revolution, mutiny quickly began on plantations as slaves initiated a "general strike" by withdrawing their labor from the cotton fields and allocating it elsewhere.[47] Du Bois understood the triumph of "abolition-democracy" as a moment of transnational and world historical significance and asserted that an emancipatory internationalism of workers, the vast majority being non-white, depended on widening the wartime "general strike" that had transferred the labor of black workers from the Confederate to the Union cause.[48] He outlined Reconstruction's collapse as both a key stage in the reproduction of racial difference indicative of the "modern labor problem" and central to the development of U.S. capitalism and imperialism. In fact, the great scholar-activist branded opponents of Reconstruction—those who sanctioned the violent overthrow of African-American political and social gains—opponents of labor.[49] In other words, the war on freedpeople was a war on workers. Accordingly, when freedpeople used the memory of the war to call for fair labor contracts, public education, voting rights, or land, they were using the experience of slavery and the war's collective memory to further the cause of labor. Indeed, Reconstruction saw former slaves make claims *as workers*; it also saw workers make claims *as black people and former slaves*.

The overturning of Reconstruction shifted the nation's center of gravity northward, as what Du Bois termed an "Empire of Industry" gave way to a "new feudalism" based on capital concentration and fixed wage-earning.[50] Yet Reconstruction, Du Bois lamented during the height of Jim Crow, "could have rebuilt the economic foundations of Southern society, confiscated and redistributed wealth, and built a real democracy."[51] Highlighting the logic that would eventually be used by socialists to call for reparations for the descendants of slaves, Du Bois maintained that slaves'

> demand for a reasonable part of the land on which they had worked for a quarter of a millennium was absolutely justified, and to give them anything less than this was an economic farce. A forty acre freehold would have made a basis of real democracy in the United States that might easily have transformed the modern world.[52]

The theory of wealth redistribution anywhere, Du Bois insisted, "is that the wealth and current income of the wealthy ruling class does not belong to them entirely, but is the product of the work and the striving of the great millions." In the case of the postwar South, "equitable distribution" was the just result of "theft of labor," as well as wartime loyalty and sacrifice.[53] Political leadership jettisoned land redistribution due to the material interests of capitalists (the slippery slope between freedpeople controlling the plantations and industrial workers controlling the factories), as well as capitalist ideology, in which land reform "came directly in opposition to the American assumption that any American could be rich if he wanted to."[54]

Du Bois's thesis was built on claims to landed proprietorship made by freedpeople and the redistributionist appeals of abolitionists. It was Wendell Phillips who announced in 1868 that the overriding problem of Reconstruction was that "the black man has no capital."[55] Non-Marxist scholars would adopt key parts of this argument. Writing half a century after Du Bois, Eric Foner insisted that land redistribution would have had "profound consequences for Southern society, weakening the land-based economic and political power of the old ruling class" and "affecting the former slaves' conception of themselves."[56] Kenneth Stampp concurred, claiming that the economic vulnerability of former slaves put their social and political rights in jeopardy, particularly after the removal of federal troops from the South, and "strengthened the white man's belief in their infinite superiority."[57] "The failure to advance *economic* democracy lent fragility to the impressive political achievements of African Americans," according to Michael Kazin. "As long as most black people worked directly or indirectly (as sharecroppers) for illiberal whites, they would remain poor—and their influence in government would be vulnerable to attacks, both legal and violent, by the unreconstructed sons and daughters of Dixie."[58]

While the Republican Party proved useful in establishing equality before the law, David Montgomery argued, political rights alone did not translate into social equality and such vast material disparities effectively denied wage workers equal political participation. Reform was needed beyond civic equality.[59]

Other revolutionary intellectuals framed the war as a historical stage that saw black workers in particular as a demonstrable vanguard party. In examining the role of black self-emancipation, Trinidadian C. L. R. James underscored the international impact of the independent action of enslaved black people through continuous revolt. James agreed that the war was "a bourgeois revolution against feudalism" in which landed property gave way to a rising industrial bourgeoisie.[60] Though structural forces pushed the sections toward war, "revolutionary Negroes" (with the assistance of a small number of "white revolutionaries") played the critical role through continuous resistance on the plantation and agitation in the public sphere. James's *A History of Negro Revolt* (1938) argued that beginning with the Haitian Revolution, black people in the Western Hemisphere anticipated and fostered radical social change through unflinching defiance of bourgeois political standards, including direct action and a willingness to respond to violence with violence. Swept by currents of Pan-Africanism, the slave rebels of Saint-Domingue were the forebearers of the 54th Massachusetts Infantry. In other words, enslaved blacks spearheaded, rather than proved subordinate to, larger international class struggles.[61]

Perhaps more than any other major Marxist scholar, Herbert Aptheker adhered to the Second American Revolution interpretation of the Civil War. Like Du Bois, James, and James S. Allen (pen name of Sol Auerbach), Aptheker's analysis spotlighted themes of an unfinished revolution and the collective agency of common people, notably black resisters. Moving well beyond the Beardian dichotomy of industrial capitalism versus plantation agrarianism, Aptheker viewed the conflict as a collection of temporary class and racial alliances: a radical bourgeoisie, black proletariat, and parts of the white proletariat (North and South) against the planter class and its cross-class white allies.[62] His description of the growth of abolitionism as a "Negro-white, radical effort to revolutionize America by overthrowing its dominant class" obscures the movement's variety and bourgeois limitations. However, abolitionism's ideological zeal was part of Aptheker's intricate explanation for the war that centered on socio-economic transformation in the North (and thus contests over the West) and class unrest in the South involving the accumulation of internal contradictions within the slaveholding regime. Writing during the Civil War centennial in 1961, Aptheker reminded his readers that the conflict remained of direct relevance to contemporary Americans because its key issues—black rights, who controls the state and for whom it should function, the status of poor whites, the nature of revolution and international solidarity—were entirely unresolved. As such, he lambasted prevailing Civil War scholarship that reduced the war to either a "senseless tragedy," owing to the failings of individual actors, or an overly determined and mechanistic event that precluded human agency. Further, Aptheker alleged (correctly) that academic works tended to either glorify or exonerate the Confederacy while omitting the stories and contributions of African Americans.[63]

In addition to emphasizing international dynamics and proletarian agency, especially with regard to black slaves, some Marxian historians have echoed countless Gilded Age workers by highlighting how the war gave rise to new systems of domination. Marx himself was quick to assert that despite the fundamental exploitation that lay behind each system, workers should unmistakably support wage labor industrialization over slave labor agrarianism, as the former contained some elements of political liberalism and, with the proliferation of working-class identity and institutions, would prove the next stage in the historical development of socialism. Yet many leftists, along with multitudes of wage earners, sensed the war as a "disillusioning victory."[64] This insight that the capitalist bourgeoisie represented both part of a liberating coalition during the war and an oppressive obstacle to be overcome after the war recognized the reality that untold workers felt the war had, in the form of the industrial workplace, unleashed a novel and especially ravenous potential for exploitation. Indeed, the subsequent rise of the industrial order left many laborers feeling that political-financial consolidation that emerged from the war was to blame for new methods of toil and unprecedented scales of wealth, corruption, and power.

In the *Age of Capital*, published in 1975, Eric Hobsbawm contended that the Civil War arose from competing visions of continental unification (slave labor versus free labor) that finally hemorrhaged when the South decisively lost its influence in the Middle West with the election of Lincoln. "Whatever its political origins," Hobsbawm maintained, the war was "the triumph of the industrialized North over the agrarian South, almost, one would say, the transfer of the South from the informal empire of Britain into the new major industrial economy of the United States." This territorial–economic characterization owed to the Beards' Progressive school of history. But it was also an extension of the assumptions of Gilded Age and Progressive Era workers who consistently proclaimed that while the war had, on the one hand, expanded the boundaries of freedom, proletarianization, and unregulated industry had also circumscribed liberty for "wage slaves" in the urban North.[65] Indeed, the war unleashed both revolutionary potential (emancipation and Reconstruction) *and* new capacities for oppression (industrialization and financialization). For working people, white and black, who had witnessed Jay Gould's plutocracy devour Thaddeus Stevens's democratic ideal, the "Yankee Leviathan" had not merely ushered in a wave of newly enshrined positive rights that conceived the federal government as a "custodian of freedom"; the unprecedented wealth aggregation it engendered had also facilitated spectacularly powerful arrangements of political corruption and social authority.[66] It became increasingly clear that a newly empowered U.S. state would play a central role in legally determining and institutionalizing what "free labor" would mean for former slaves.[67] At its core, Marxist memory, like Marxism, has always existed in the service of that paramount question: "What does it mean to be free?"

But if a socialist understanding of the Civil War was so popularly conceived and disseminated between Reconstruction and the New Deal era, with many of its elements adopted by twentieth-century intellectuals, then why have such narratives been largely dismissed by cultural historians especially concerned with the recovery of subaltern narratives? Decades of neoliberal consensus in U.S. politics, the swift disappearance of unions from American life, and the paucity of labor history in college classrooms, all interrelated, have privileged approaches to understanding the past that favor liberal pluralism over radicalism. Perhaps neoliberalism, with all its horrors, necessitates its own memories of slavery in order to justify bourgeois life as freedom. In this sense, the narratives told by slavery scholars who disembody chattel slavery from both "wage slavery" and broader questions of unfreedom and emancipation engender a type of superficial race radicalism that rightly identifies the evils of nineteenth-century property in man without challenging the basic structures, namely capitalist production, that undergird exploitation in the present. Prevailing political ideology, orientations in training, publishing, and research trends, and the basic assumptions of their class positions offer additional testaments to how capital—and hostility to socialism and social democracy—structures academia. Despite subversive working-class discourses on the meaning of the Civil War and the clear influence of those narratives on critical twentieth-century scholars, topics including worker radicalism, organized labor, and socialism are conspicuously marginal in, or even absent from, the academic writing of Civil War cultural history.

This is notably true of "memory studies," the rise of which in the 1980s and 1990s coincided with the decline of Marxism as an academic method of analysis.[68] Civil War memory scholars have often neglected one of the largest and most influential of peoples from below: organized workers. As in Marx and Engels's *Manifesto* for the "emancipation" of labor and "abolition" of property, antebellum labor movements cribbed the cultural politics of the abolitionist movement, and this antislavery vernacular amplified during the post-conflict era.[69] Although historians have surveyed various modes of war commemoration within partisan politics, veterans' societies, heritage groups, and civil rights organizations, their analyses of labor politics are far scanter. While David Blight and Caroline Janney's interpretations of veterans reconciled and irreconcilable are revelatory, their studies and subsequent works in the subfield rarely (if at all) connect Civil War memory to radical politics, grassroots worker organization, or even trade unions. Many memory historians, their scholarship mirroring the national decline of unions and labor studies during the neoliberal turn, have sought to examine commemoration *in toto* through national models, overemphasizing elites, intellectuals, and middle-class institutions. While these groups had undeniable status as the dominant shapers of collective memory, the omission of working-class history is peculiar given both the ubiquity of Civil War themes in U.S. Gilded Age and Progressive Era labor consciousness *and* the fact that veterans and others with direct ties to the war comprised such a large percentage of the postwar working class.

If a convergence of external factors has conditioned particular sets of cultural scholars to omit serious examinations of radicalism, orthodoxy has also led particular sets of radicals to omit serious examinations of culture. Just as scholars of collective memory have evaded Marx, Marxist scholars have only rarely conceptualized collective memory.[70] But if the war's cultural residue mattered so much to late nineteenth- and early twentieth-century workers (and it did), then why have leftist academics tended to ignore topics of collective memory? The answer partly lies in how leftists understand, explicitly or implicitly, the relations between society's base and the superstructure of culture. Many leftists surely view culture as so far downstream from politics as to neglect it as a substantial intellectual undertaking.

Indeed, why *should* Marxists, who are uniquely attentive to the Civil War, care about the popular remembrance it spawned? Simply because there is reciprocity between memory and consciousness. Speaking on the relation between collective remembrance and the left, Leon Trotsky confirmed that even Marxists "live in traditions," connecting the Russian Revolution with the Paris Commune, the June Days, and French Revolution.[71] In the United States, the culture—symbols, language, tradition, and commemoration—surrounding the Civil War was critical to the identities of workers. In establishing the concept of collective memory, sociologist Maurice Halbwachs recognized the variations in how different groups organize, preserve, and represent the past, including distinctions according to class.[72] The eminent social historians E. P. Thompson, Herbert Gutman, and Eric Hobsbawm expounded, alleging that peasants and proletarians typically construct aspirations and express political aims through traditional symbols of order and virtue, repurposed and reframed. In delineating class as not only a material position or derivative of productive relations, but as a cultural formation, Thompson stressed that such an identity of interests was engendered through rituals, value systems, and stories.[73] As such, the process of class consciousness in the United States was filtered through what David Montgomery termed "a mythology of the war and emancipation."[74]

However, the recovery of this radical memory reveals that adhering to causes neither "lost" nor "won," but causes not yet won, socialist memory makers have consistently used the words and wounds of war to envision left alternatives to structures of nationalism, empire, eugenics, segregation, patriarchy, bourgeois consumerism, and industrial and corporate capitalism—even as they lived within and sometimes reinforced those systems. More than a tangential curiosity, the memory of the "Anti-Slavery War"—reading postwar politics into the war or projecting the war into contemporary politics—has been fundamental to the collective identities of U.S. leftists, and to Marxists in particular. Civil War stories, images, metaphors, and vocabulary remained critical points of reference within the labor movement for decades after Appomattox. A century and a half later, abolitionism, resistance by enslaved people, the plantation economy, the social politics of emancipation, and the revolutionary legacies of Reconstruction remain topics of fascination and acute inquiry on the socialist left. The intellectual genealogy of today's "red memory," with its hallmarks of worker agency, materiality, internationalism, and futurism, began with the wartime writings of Marx and Engels and eventually flowed through the theses of Du Bois, Aptheker, and, by degrees, their social history and New History of Capitalism progeny. Yet their conclusions were responses to the instrumentality of freedpeople and radical workers who shaped the war's outcomes. In the decades after 1865, they commemorated the antislavery struggle to reconfigure the parameters of American democracy and, at their most ambitious, expand the very conceptions of human freedom.

Notes

1 Saul K. Padover, ed. *Karl Marx on America and the Civil War* (New York: McGraw-Hill, 1972), 237.
2 Neil Davidson, *How Revolutionary Were the Bourgeois Revolutions?* (Chicago, IL: Haymarket, 2012), 168; Timothy Messer-Kruse, *The Yankee International: Marxism and the American Reform Tradition, 1848–1876* (Chapel Hill: University of North Carolina Press, 1998), 54–55.
3 Eric Foner and Manning Marable, eds., *Herbert Aptheker on Race and Democracy* (Urbana: University of Illinois Press, 2006), 139; Padover, *Karl Marx*, 211.
4 Herbert Marcuse, *Marxism, Revolution and Utopia* (London: Routledge, 2014), 310–11.
5 Eugene Gogol, *Raya Dunayevskaya: Philosopher of Marxist Humanism* (Eugene, OR: Resource Publications, 2004), 134–35.
6 Padover, *Karl Marx*, 263, xxi; Karl Marx and Friedrich Engels, *The Civil War in the United States*, ed. Andrew Zimmerman (New York: International Publishers, 2016), xxi.
7 Padover, *Karl Marx*, xxii–xxiii.

8 Ibid., 237, 242.
9 Marx and Engels, *Civil War*, xxv, 187.
10 Padover, *Karl Marx*, 244.
11 Andrew Zimmerman, "From the Second American Revolution to the First International and Back Again: Marxism, the Popular Front, and the American Civil War," in Gregory P. Downs and Kate Masur, eds. *The World the Civil War Made* (Chapel Hill: University of North Carolina Press, 2015), 315.
12 Marx and Engels, *Civil War*, 281.
13 Robin Blackburn, *An Unfinished Revolution: Karl Marx and Abraham Lincoln* (London: Verso, 2011), 96.
14 Marx and Engels, *Civil War*, 202.
15 Enzo Traverso, *Left-Wing Melancholia: Marxism, History, and Memory* (New York: Columbia University Press, 2016), 57–58.
16 Ibid., xiv.
17 Davidson, *Bourgeois Revolutions*, 351.
18 Paul Buhle, *Marxism in the United States: A History of the American Left* (New York: Verso, 1987), 56–63.
19 David R. Roediger, *The Wages of Whiteness: Race and the Making of the American Working Class* (New York: Verso, 1991), 175.
20 Sterling Stuckey, *Slave Culture: Nationalist Theory and the Foundations of Black America* (New York: Oxford University Press, 1987), 289.
21 Alison Clark Efford, *German Immigrants, Race, and Citizenship in the Civil War Era* (New York: Cambridge University Press, 2013).
22 Matt Karp, "The Mass Politics of Antislavery," *Catalyst* 3 No. 2 (Summer 2019): 154–63; W. E. B. Du Bois, *Black Reconstruction* (New York: Harcourt Brace, 1935), 716; Eric Hobsbawm, *The Age of Empire: 1875–1914* (London: Weidenfeld & Nicolson, 1987), 138; and C. L. R. James, *A History of Pan-African Revolt* (Chicago, IL: C. H. Kerr, 2012), 58.
23 David Montgomery, *Beyond Equality: Labor and the Radical Republicans, 1862–1872* (Urbana: University of Illinois Press, 1967), 90.
24 Du Bois, *Black Reconstruction*, 57; Blackburn, *An Unfinished Revolution*, 39.
25 Marx and Engels, *Civil War*, 177–78.
26 William H. Sylvis, *The Life, Speeches, Labors, and Essays of William H. Sylvis*, ed. James C. Sylvis (Philadelphia, PA: Claxton, Remsen, and Haffelfinger, 1872), 233, 128.
27 Alex Gourevitch, *From Slavery to the Cooperative Commonwealth: Labor and Republican Liberty in the Nineteenth Century* (New York: Cambridge University Press, 2015), 98–101.

28 Mark A. Lause, *The Civil War's Last Campaign: James B. Weaver, the Greenback-Labor Party, and the Politics of Race and Section* (Lanham, MD: University Press of America, 2001), 134.
29 Carl N. Degler, *The Other South: Southern Dissenters in the Nineteenth Century* (New York: Harper & Row, 1974), 288–91.
30 Eric Hobsbawm, *The Age of Capital, 1848–1875* (London: Weidenfeld & Nicolson, 1975), 145.
31 Leon Fink, *The Long Gilded Age: American Capitalism and the Lessons of a New World Order* (Philadelphia: University of Pennsylvania Press, 2018), 124.
32 *The Alarm*, November 5, 1887.
33 *Fulton County News*, March 2, 1904; Eugene V. Debs and Stephen Marion Reynolds, *Debs: His Life, Writings, and Speeches* (Chicago, IL: Charles H. Kerr, 1910), 371–75.
34 Philip S. Foner, *History of the Labor Movement in the United States*, Vol. II (New York: International Publishers, 1955), 43.
35 *Petroleum Centre Daily Record*, September 17, 1872.
36 Cedric J. Robinson, *Black Marxism: The Making of the Black Radical Tradition* (London: Zed Press, 1983), 208–40.
37 Sharon Smith, *Subterranean Fire: A History of Working-Class Radicalism in the United States* (Chicago, IL: Haymarket, 2006), 134.
38 Nina Silber, *This War Ain't Over: Fighting the Civil War in New Deal America* (Chapel Hill: University of North Carolina Press, 2018), 1.
39 Ibid., 77.
40 Robin D. G. Kelley, *Hammer and Hoe: Alabama Communists during the Great Depression* (1990; Chapel Hill: University of North Carolina Press, 2015), 100.
41 Andre Fleche, *The Revolution of 1861: The American Civil War in the Age of Nationalist Conflict* (Chapel Hill: University of North Carolina Press, 2012), 1–10.
42 Davidson, *Bourgeois Revolutions*, 167.
43 James M. McPherson, *Abraham Lincoln and the Second American Revolution* (New York: Oxford University Press, 1991), 8.
44 Davidson, *Bourgeois Revolutions*, 265–66.
45 Seth Rockman, "Slavery and Capitalism," *Journal of the Civil War Era* 2, no. 1 (March 2012): 5; Sven Beckert, *Empire of Cotton: A Global History* (New York: Vintage Books, 2014); Walter Johnson, *River of Dark Dreams: Slavery and Empire in the Cotton Kingdom* (Cambridge, MA: Harvard University Press, 2013), 14; Davidson, *Bourgeois Revolutions*, 265–66, 611–15.
46 Davidson, *Bourgeois Revolutions*, 169, 640, 615.
47 Du Bois, *Black Reconstruction*, 57.

48 Padover, *Karl Marx*, 247; Blackburn, *An Unfinished Revolution*, 54; Du Bois, *Black Reconstruction*, 55, 16.
49 Du Bois, *Black Reconstruction*, 670.
50 Ibid., 580.
51 Ibid., 584.
52 Ibid., 602.
53 Ibid., 604.
54 Ibid., 601.
55 Messer-Kruse, *The Yankee International*, 29.
56 Eric Foner, *Reconstruction: America's Unfinished Revolution, 1863–1877* (New York: Harper & Row, 1988), 314–15, 109.
57 Kenneth Stampp, *The Era of Reconstruction, 1865–1877* (New York: Vintage, 1965), 129.
58 Michael Kazin, *American Dreamers: How the Left Changed a Nation* (New York: Knopf, 2011), 58.
59 David Montgomery, *Beyond Equality: Labor and the Radical Republicans, 1862–1872* (Urbana: University of Illinois Press, 1967), 446.
60 James, *A History of Pan-African Revolt*, 58–60.
61 Selwyn R. Cudjoe and William E. Cain, *C. L. R. James: His Intellectual Legacies* (Amherst: University of Massachusetts Press), 324; Nicole King, *C. L. R. James and Creolization* (Jackson: University Press of Mississippi, 2001), 83.
62 McPherson, *Abraham Lincoln*, 8–9.
63 Foner and Marable, *Herbert Aptheker*, 128–38.
64 Leon Fink, *Workingmen's Democracy: The Knights of Labor and American Politics* (Urbana: University of Illinois Press, 1983), 22.
65 Eric Hobsbawm, *The Age of Capital, 1848–1875* (New York: Vintage, 1975), 142, 78.
66 Richard Franklin Bensel, *Yankee Leviathan: The Origins of Central State Authority in America* (New York: Cambridge University Press, 1990).
67 Mark A. Lause, *Free Labor: The Civil War and the Making of an American Working Class* (Urbana: University of Illinois Press, 2015), 55.
68 Traverso, *Left-Wing Melancholia*, xiv, 55.
69 Marx and Engels, *Civil War*, 1.
70 Traverso, *Left-Wing Melancholia*, xiv.
71 Leon Trotsky, *Literature and Revolution*, ed. William Keach (Chicago, IL: Haymarket, 2005), 115.
72 Maurice Halbwachs, *On Collective Memory* reprint, ed. Lewis A. Coser (Chicago, IL: University of Chicago Press, 1992).

73 E.P. Thompson, *The Making of the English Working Class* (New York: Pantheon, 1964), 9–11.

74 Stephen D. Engle, "Yankee Dutchmen: Germans, the Union, and the Construction of Wartime Identity," in *Civil War Citizens: Race, Ethnicity, and Identity in America's Bloodiest Conflict*, ed. Susannah J. Ural (New York: New York University Press, 2010), 11–56; David Montgomery, *Citizen Worker: The Experience of Workers in the United States with Democracy and the Free Market during the Nineteenth Century* (New York: Cambridge University Press, 1993), 98.

2

"What *is* the correct revolutionary proletarian attitude toward sex?": red love and the Americanization of Marx in the interwar years

Jesse F. Battan

In his review of V. F. Calverton's *Sex Expression in Literature* in a 1927 issue of the *New Masses*, Floyd Dell applauded the book's contribution to a new form of literary criticism that explored the social context of literary production. He was, however, less convinced by Calverton's argument that the new "sex freedom" in modern literature reflected the development of "a revolutionary working class" and its rejection of an economic system based on private property, or that "the anti-bourgeois attitude in morality" was linked to an "anti-bourgeois attitude in economics." Since the same sorts of changes were occurring in capitalist countries as well as in the Soviet Union, Dell was skeptical that changes in sexual morality were an expression of class interests driven by economic conditions rather than the result of the changes wrought by industrialization and the psychology—the idiosyncratic needs—of the individual. In questioning the explanatory power of the theories of Marx rather than Freud to explain these changes, he concluded his review with a challenge to Calverton and "other philosophers of the revolutionary movement," such as Upton Sinclair, Charles Wood, Scott Nearing, and Mike Gold, to answer the question he finally posed: "What *is* the correct revolutionary proletarian attitude toward sex?"[1]

Ever the provocateur, Dell set off a wide-ranging discussion of the role sexuality and private life would play in the social revolutions envisioned by the various cultural and political movements associated with the American left in the late 1920s and the early 1930s. Central to this discussion was an exploration of the relationship between the emotional and erotic life of the individual—the "psychosexual" dimensions of human experience—and the material conditions in which they existed. It ran the gamut from those who argued that material conditions alone shaped the subjective life of the individual to those who insisted that emotional and erotic desires existed autonomously from the material world and, more to the point, believed their liberation was central to the effort to reshape political and economic life. The effort to answer Dell's question created a dialogue on the left that addressed a series of questions about the means and relations of reproduction as well as production. What role would sexual relations play in the revolutionary struggle to create a new world? How should they be structured in the present, or in the future? Could the insights of modern psychology, especially Freudian depth-psychology, be reconciled with Marxist political and economic theories? In short, does private life have political significance?

Free love, bohemianism, and the left

Surveying the history of revolutionary thought and activity, it is clear that Dell was not the first to raise these questions. As Friedrich Engels argued in 1883, "It is a curious fact that with every great revolutionary movement the question of 'free love' comes into the foreground."[2] In his declaration of the connection between sexual and political revolutions, Engels did not overstate his case. In America, for example, there has been a continuous and enduring connection between spiritual liberation, millennial expectations, and sexual radicalism among sectarian religious groups that led to a host of movements and communitarian experiments dedicated to the destruction of private property, the government, the church, and most pointedly, marriage. Another trend, more secular in origin, emerged in the early nineteenth century. Drawing on the anarchist beliefs of William Godwin, the feminism of Mary Wollstonecraft, and the communitarian visions of Robert Owen, Francis Wright, and Charles Fourier, a segment of the American left—made up primarily of a group of anarchists, anarcho-syndicalists, and "romantic" socialists known as "free lovers"—set out to destroy marriage and the nuclear family. In contrast to Victorian moralists who insisted that these institutions provided a harbor of selfless love that protected men and women from the immoral world of commerce, the free lovers argued instead that they were the breeding grounds for the dangerous emotions—such as greed and jealousy—set loose in the market economy. In other words, the competitive social system that worked to estrange men and women from one another had its roots in a marriage and family system that formed the bedrock of the belief in private property and perverted human emotions at their source.[3] While some free lovers insisted that a sexual revolution would precede social revolution, and a few that economic change would transform private life, all agreed that revolutions in both the public and private sphere were needed to transform society.

Throughout the nineteenth century, then, there was a link between political and cultural radicalism that centered on the idea that changes in emotions and economics went hand in hand. This connection, however, was always uneasy and frequently shattered. Beginning in December of 1871, for example, Victoria Woodhull, the notorious nineteenth-century free lover who proclaimed her right to have sex with any man she desired, published the first American edition of the *Communist Manifesto* in her newspaper *Woodhull & Claflin's Weekly*.[4] As a reward for her efforts, the following year Karl Marx and Friedrich Sorge effectively worked to exclude Sections 9 and 12, which were organized by Woodhull and her sister Tennessee Claflin, from the International Workingman's Association. Citizen Marx contemptuously referred to Woodhull as "a banker's woman, free lover, and general humbug." Marx was fearful of alienating German- and Irish-American workers with talk of women's rights and Free Love, referred to as the "woman question," and the "sex question." He was also afraid the IWA would be identified with these movements by their bourgeois opponents. More to the point, while these questions might be considered at some future time, attention spent on such things only distracted workers from the paramount issues of labor and wages, the true engines of revolutionary change.[5]

This concern with political expediency and the belief that economic struggles alone would lead to social revolution set an enduring pattern that would be replicated throughout the history of American radicalism. During the years between 1850 and 1910, for example, many political radicals in the American left struggled to dispel the notion that there was a connection between economic revolution and the transformation of private life. This position was especially strong among Populists, German–American Socialists, members of the Socialist Party of America, anarcho-communists, and advocates of "scientific" or Marxist socialism (such as the Socialist Labor Party), as well as among the leaders and the rank and file of more mainstream labor and trade-union organizations.[6] Many of the leaders and members of these groups argued that the concern with the woman and sex questions were side issues that did little but distract the true revolutionary from the real struggle at hand—the battle between capital and labor. Economic equality would eliminate all forms of social injustice, including those created by bourgeois domestic institutions and sexual ideology.[7]

In the years immediately preceding the First World War and continuing into the 1920s, the rift between political and cultural radicals was once again mended, if only momentarily. Socialists and anarchists of various stripes joined with a new brand of cultural radicals—the bohemian or "libidinal left"—that emerged by 1910 to challenge industrial capitalism and the bourgeois culture that supported it.[8] Unlike Victorian free lovers, who sought liberation through conscious control of sexual desires, this new generation of cultural radicals argued that sexual liberation and social revolution could only be found by escaping into the netherworld of the unconscious, most notably through Freudian psychoanalysis.[9] Like Victorian free lovers, however, the libidinal left argued for a connection between sexual and political revolution. Their rebellion was not only driven by their concern with class inequalities but attentiveness to the tenor of "business civilization" itself—mechanization, materialism, efficiency, security, and boredom—and the "civilized morality" that supported it, which bred only sexual and aesthetic "starvation."[10]

Yet by viewing "civilized" morality as a bourgeois invention, bohemian sexual radicals framed their battle with middle-class sexual mores as a class struggle.[11] The conflict between capital and labor and the war between the sexes and the generations had the same origins: sexual repression. The bourgeois puritan and the philistine capitalists were the common enemy, and would be overcome by the liberation of desire.[12] Moreover, bohemian sexual radicals drew on the working class for ideas on how this was to be done. Celebrating the "proletarian philosophy" of labor radicals he encountered in Chicago in the early twentieth century, for example, Hutchins Hapgood insisted they had, through experience and their isolation from the bourgeois moral code, crafted a political program that rejected private property in personal as well as economic relationships. In his own efforts to reconcile Freud and Marx, Floyd Dell made a similar observation. Dell's vision of the ideal emotional and sexual relationship that would exist in the socialist future was drawn from his image of working-class life. There has been, he argued, "a non-aristocratic kind of marriage, of plebeian origin, having nothing to do with the conservation of property, a love-marriage, which was instinctively human, and which arose whenever and wherever property considerations were removed."[13]

The 1920s and the left's retreat from sexual topics

The libidinal left's marriage of political and cultural radicalism began to unravel after the Russian Revolution of 1917. Once again Marx, and specifically Marx's historical materialism, was central to this divorce. This conflict within the American left was finally brought to a head in 1927, when Floyd Dell asked his question in the *New Masses* and challenged those on the political left to answer it.[14] Answer it they did, in well-attended public debates as well as in periodicals such as the *New Masses*, the *Modern Quarterly*, and the *Daily Worker*.[15] While they attacked bourgeois marriages based on property considerations rather than love, and saw prostitution and "sexual perversions" as an inevitable byproduct of this corrupt institution, political radicals saw the call for sexual freedom by what were described as the "sex boys" as driven by a middle-class concern for personal freedom, and therefore a frivolous, counter-revolutionary diversion from the real struggle between capital and labor.[16]

Upton Sinclair, for example, argued for monogamy and sexual restraint for workers as they struggled to realize the "Cooperative Commonwealth." Even after the revolution, Sinclair argued for the restricted expression of all appetites, especially sexual desires. Espousing a utilitarian attitude toward sex, Sinclair argued erotic desires should only be expressed in ways that were eugenically sound and that would make men and women "better workers for the cause." The advocates of sexual freedom, he concluded, were more of a reflection of "capitalist decadence than of Socialist renascence." H. M. Wicks, the Torquemada of the Communist Party USA in the early 1930s, writing in the *Daily Worker,* readily agreed with Sinclair's puritanical position. The problem with the working class, he insisted, was not too much repression but too much sex. Drawing on his reading of Marx and Engels, he argued that sexual freedom was a bourgeois demand advocated by decadent "vulgarizers of Marxism," sex anarchists who merely represented "the lunatic fringe of the revolutionary movement."[17]

Scott Nearing, Sender Garland, Benjamin Weiss, Charles Wood, and others on the Communist left went even further, arguing that it was a complete waste of time to even discuss sexual and gender issues in the radical press. Surely there were more important things to discuss, such as agriculture, labor struggles, and foreign events. Weiss, for example, excoriated the *New Masses* for dedicating precious column inches to the discussion of proletarian sexual attitudes, while no mention was made of important geopolitical events. "I realize, of course," he wrote,

> that China has nothing to do with the correct revolutionary proletarian attitude toward sex, but am I cookoo or just a trifle stupid if I venture to suggest that the goings-on in China are vastly more important than any such florid nonsense. Is the *New Masses* a revolutionary working-class magazine of the arts or is it merely another demented offspring of Greenwich Village?[18]

For the political left, especially those aligning with Soviet Communism, "Greenwich Village" was short-hand for those who, like Floyd Dell, were described as dilettantish, "petty-bourgeois," effeminate playboys engaged in a puerile and selfish pursuit of sensual and aesthetic pleasures.[19] Echoing George Bernard Shaw's proclamation "Karl Marx made a man of me," political radicals in the 1920s and 1930s embraced the *realpolitik* of political struggle, and denigrated the libidinal left as "boudoir bards" and "bedroom revolutionaries," lounge lizards who ignored economic issues in their preoccupation with the liberation of emotional and erotic desires.[20]

In the pages of *Class Struggle* in 1934, for example, Albert Weisbord described those who "were gamboling free and footloose, down the green of The Village, masturbating their talents on such questions as Sex, Psycho-neurosis, and literature."[21] The cultural radicals' concern with psychology, especially Freudian psychoanalysis, especially troubled political radicals inspired by Marx's historical materialism. They insisted, for example, that there was no such thing as the "psyche." Consciousness is not created within the individual, but rather through external social relationships between individuals.[22] Psychological problems, then, reflect the material conditions that create them and can only be resolved by transforming the industrial system itself. "We must work on the environment, not merely on the hearts of men," argued George Krinn in the *New Masses* in 1928.[23] Floyd Dell had posited another question, "Is Freudian science counter-revolutionary," as the Communists insist, a "pernicious bourgeois fad" that emphasizes individual neurosis rather than class struggle?[24] The resounding answer in the *New Masses* was yes: Freudian psychoanalysis ignored the social sources of subjective experiences, and worse, worked to reconcile individuals to adjust themselves to the world as it is.

As Malcolm Cowley argued in his 1934 post-mortem of the radical spirit that emerged in America before the First World War, by 1919 the tenuous ties were severed between the revolt against "puritanism" and the revolt against capitalism. Bohemian or cultural radicalism was co-opted by mainstream consumer culture, Cowley noted, "and talk about revolution gave way to talk about psychoanalysis."[25] Even Floyd Dell's case came to insist that political radicalism and the pursuit of sexual freedom were the result of unresolved neurotic fixations. While he understood and supported the connection between the destruction of the patriarchal family, the revolution in morals, and the economic changes wrought by industrialization, as a result of his time in Freudian analysis he ultimately became an ardent defender of monogamy, the nuclear family, and, to some degree, the status quo.

Red love: revolution and sexual freedom

Even though the cultural left's interest in Freud often led to individualistic, apolitical solutions to personal problems that reconciled them to life in the modern world, others, such as V. F. Calverton and

Samuel Schmalhausen, carried on the effort to link economic and sexual revolution throughout the 1920s and early 1930s.[26] While sexual and political radicalism were indeed torn asunder after the Russian Revolution of 1917, Calverton and Schmalhausen tried to reunite them by creating a new ideology that linked Marx and Freud. In doing so, they attacked the Communist left for ignoring the relationship between sex and economics, family life, and modes of production, and for advocating the idea "that sex is an individual and not a social affair" and thus irrelevant to their revolutionary struggles. They also tore into the programs of the bohemian left for stressing sexual issues at the expense of "economic circumstances," and for their vague understanding of the connection between sexual desire and social reality.[27]

Like most on the political left, Calverton and Schmalhausen were skeptical of the individualist approach of Freudian analysis, but they were less wary of mobilizing the link between Marx and Freud. Both Calverton and Schmalhausen, in short, were convinced that Marx needed a psychology—an understanding of human motivation not tied to economic conditions—and that Freudian psychoanalysis needed a radical politics.[28] Going beyond a view of psychoanalysis that dealt only with "the pathology of the individual," they instead advocated a "psychosociological revolution."[29] Radical economic change could only occur if it was accompanied by the reconstruction of our sexual and emotional selves through a re-education of the senses, a transformation of our "nervous system," which can be immune from material conditions. "We can more easily change our ideas than our emotional reactions," Calverton insisted. "It is no exaggeration to say that, in one way or another, we are the slaves of our neurons. While we often find phenomenal changes in the intellectual convictions of a man, we rarely discover anything resembling an emotional revolution."[30] Both Calverton and Schmalhausen argued that economic change often left human nature—the emotional structure of the individual—untouched, and they devised new ways of explaining and overcoming this.[31] As Schmalhausen argued, "It takes two revolutions to make a world: one in the sphere of economics and one in the sphere of erotics."[32] In their effort to meld political and cultural radicalism, their ideas linked sexual revolution with a program for the reconstruction of society and cultural renewal.[33]

Calverton and Schmalhausen celebrated some of the changes associated with sexual revolution in the United States, such as the weakening of the patriarchal family, the emergence of the "New Woman" and her demand for sexual autonomy, the demand for birth control information and technology, liberal divorce laws, sex education, and the open exploration of sexual issues. Even though these changes were paralleled in the Soviet Union, they were critical of their lack of focus and direction. Based on their understanding of the "red love" espoused by Alexandra Kollontai and realized by the new social programs inaugurated in the Soviet Union after the Russian Revolution of 1917, they rejected the American revolution in morals because it led only to narcissistic behavior, sexual excesses, and shallow forms of attachment.[34] As Calverton argued, the social and emotional changes associated with this alteration in manners and morals were merely a reflection of the decay of bourgeois society and not a harbinger of the ideal society to come.[35]

The sexual revolution in Russia, Calverton and Schmalhausen were convinced, was spawned by an economic revolution in which "collectivism and cooperative ownership" replaced "individualism and private-property."[36] For a true sexual revolution to occur, a *proletarian* sexual revolution, economic communism must be matched by an emotional and erotic communism that would lead to a more socialized form of love. With the elimination of monogamy and possessiveness, private life would be reconstructed. Love would be freed from the bondage of the isolated pair and transformed into a socialized form of love. This would lead to a more communal or group-oriented experience of affection, what Kollontai referred to as "love-comradeship."[37] As Schmalhausen argued, this would be "a greater human love, a radiant fellowship" that would integrate the individual into the social world and transform political and economic relationships through a generous sense of "fellowship and affection."[38] Men and women will experience more profound emotional connections not only with their sexual partners but also with their comrades engaged in the struggle to transform society.[39]

In the shift from isolated to communal love, the goal of red love was to transform emotional and erotic energy in a way that would reconfigure intimate relationships to include those beyond the happy couple. It will bind men and women to the social world, and will replace the competitive, selfish spirit of the bourgeois moral order. And most important, the re-education of desire promised by red love would provide a blueprint for the ways new forms of love and erotic relationships could themselves be an effective tool in the struggle to realize the ideal society.[40]

Women on the left: articulations of sexuality and class struggle

As Kathleen Brown and Elizabeth Faue correctly note, women were excluded from the conversations of the sex boys on the left.[41] Explorations of Kollontai's views on red love, however, which included the re-education of desire, along with the rejection of the anti-social nature of romantic love and the personal sacrifices it required and the problem of emotional autonomy it created for women, were common themes explored by women in the periodical literature of the political left from the 1920s through the Popular Front period of the 1930s.[42] In addition, radical and proletarian fiction writers, especially women, whose understanding of class exploitation was shaped by poverty, poor working conditions, and the exploitation and harassment they experienced in the workplace and from alcoholic and abusive husbands in the home, celebrated the creation of a new form of love and family life that would liberate them from such treatment. More importantly, it would link them not just to the family, but to larger social communities and political struggles.[43]

The image of red love supported by women on the political left was created in opposition to what it was not. And what it was not was romantic love. Their rejection of romantic love was, in part, an essential element of the political left's critique of popular culture. It was often argued, for example, that romantic love had replaced religion as the opiate of the masses. That is, it produced private solutions to problems that were created by economic inequities and power imbalances, and it was used to distract women from the structural sources of their discontent.[44] Women on the left viewed their efforts to destroy the power of this delusion as an essential step in the creation of women's class consciousness and their commitment to revolutionary change.

The romances consumed by working women in dime novels, popular "true confession" magazines, and most notably in Hollywood movies were central in this critique. In a 1935 article in *Working Woman*, for example, Barbara Alexander describes flipping through a popular magazine during a visit to a Woolworth department store. She dismissively noted it was filled with little else but cosmetic ads, advice to the lovelorn, and stories on how to "catch a man." What was sold was an image of love that was "slooshy and gushy." In stories such as "She Loved a Stranger," which are filled with "sighings and tender murmurings," women readers are fed the belief that all of their problems will be solved by a handsome prince, who will save them from bill collectors and sexually abusive bosses. In such stories and advice articles, personal unhappiness, crushed dreams, and problems in relationships are chalked up to psychological quirks, bad attitudes, and physiological defects. In the end, salvation could be achieved through the purchase of the beauty products advertised in the magazine and sold at the cosmetic counter at Woolworths. "Reading and believing these fake stories," Alexander concluded, "will only serve to put off the day when women will have to face the fact that they and their men must fight to improve their lives by organizing among themselves." Shaking the shoulders of her readers, trying to bring them out of the low-grade erotomania fostered by popular culture, she asks the question—with all of the social problems in the world, and with another world war on the horizon, is this the time to "sit home and weep softly over these cheesy romances? Romances cooked up by the bosses in their effort to keep us dumb? In the desperate hope of keeping us silent?"[45]

Hollywood films were also vilified as the source of the delusions plaguing working women. Sasha Small insisted that motion pictures have become a "wholesale drugging apparatus" created by the bourgeoisie to delude the masses into believing that love conquers all. Such fantasies were also promoted in Hollywood fan magazines that covered the love lives of the stars rather than the problems created by unemployment and high prices.[46] Small also took the true confession pulp magazines to task for the same reasons. But what was worse was that the emotion they provide is a "shabby" substitute for real love. The form of love they sold was portrayed as little more than "kisses and listening to the birds sing" rather than what it should be—an emotional bond that links two people united in common cause, struggling for social justice, treating one another as comrades with kindness, consideration, and respect.[47]

In order to raise women's class consciousness and, more importantly, to link private life to political struggle in an effective way, alternative love stories were written for working women in periodicals such as *Working Woman*.[48] "Stockyard Stella" is a good example, described in the *New Masses* as "the first American proletarian love story written collectively by a group of workers." This serialized love story broke completely with the traditions of the romance narrative.[49] Stella, the heroine, worked in a packing house. In addition to enduring horrifying and exploitive working conditions, she was also subject to the sexual advances of her supervisors. But there's a bright spot in her life. She's in love with Eddie, a co-worker, who gave her a "thrill" whenever she was near him. On their dates, he talked about someday getting rich. Telling him she loved him as he was, however, she discouraged such aspirations. While their courtship eventually led to talk of marriage, because he had to support his parents and his younger brothers, such plans had to be postponed. One day, the inevitable happened. Stella's foreman grabbed her by the waist. Eddie rushed to her rescue, and he was fired on the spot.[50]

Unemployed, Eddie is crestfallen and despondent. While sharing a chair with Stella at a crowded organizing meeting, Stella felt that things were different between them. "Eddie's body felt somewhat lifeless beside hers, these last few afternoons; he didn't put his arms around her the way he used to. Could it be that losing his job made him feel beaten?"[51] Clearly, a man's deflated pride and his diminished libido went hand in hand. Humiliated, Eddie wants to leave town to find a job elsewhere, but Stella tearfully asks him to stay, to fight it out with the rest of his fellow workers. The solution to their problem, she insists, is class solidarity.[52] The workers band together, stop work, go to the superintendent's office, and demand Eddie's job back, a request their boss quickly grants. To celebrate their victory, Eddie lifts Stella. "This time his arms were strong as steel around her." He wants to kiss her, but because he is "a trifle scared of women," he put her down without the kiss. After everyone got back to work, "the eyes of the workers shone with a new light. They had caught their first sight of the road to liberation."[53] Sexual desire, emotional attachment, respect for women, and concerted political action melded together. In this proletarian love story, the successful combination of true love with class consciousness and the political activism that grew out of both conveys a clear message: red love wins the day.

Exploitation and sexual harassment at work, along with abusive husbands and poverty, were not the only problems the working woman faced as a result of the economic and emotional relationships created by capitalism.[54] The attitudes and behavior associated with "male chauvinism"—possessiveness, jealousy, the disregard for their autonomy, and the double standard—were also problems they faced. And, as they quickly discovered, these were not unique to capitalist domestic relations.[55] Of course, some men insisted they did their utmost to fight for gender equality and companionate relationships based on intimacy, respect, and mutual desire.[56] Influenced by the issues raised by the woman question, the companionate marriage was maintained by some on the left.[57] Transactional and even exploitive sexual relationships between men and women on the political left, however, were common.[58] Celebrating an image of the sexually active, virile masculinity associated with the "tramp bohemian" of the early twentieth century, some men, described by Joseph Barrett as "virile, romantic revolutionary roughnecks," pursued uncommitted, impersonal, if not exploitive sexual and emotional relationships, that would not interfere with their political activism. Some women on the political left ignored the feelings of emotional unhappiness or erotic dissatisfaction these relationships created, and subsumed their discontent to a life lived in service to the cause.[59] Others openly complained of the loneliness and lack of emotional support they experienced.[60]

In an article published in the *New Masses*, for example, Agnes Smedley described the experiences that led her to reject marriage and to embrace socialism and the life of a political revolutionary. Disgusted with the plight of married women, their economic dependence and reliance on abusive husbands, perpetual pregnancies, poverty, and looking old before their time, combined with her understanding of the plight of the working-class woman under capitalism, the anonymous character in Smedley's short story announced that she was determined "never to marry, never to love, never to have children." Yet, in spite of her resolution to live free of entanglements, she realized that her heart hungered "for love, for tenderness and affection," which she described as a "tyrannical" urge. While she viewed love, sex, and marriage as the source of women's loss of autonomy, she was incredibly lonely. She yearned for love and affection. In order to maintain her freedom, she didn't live with one man, but with several. After spending some time with a man, she would break away from the relationship and live a period of ascetic withdrawal. Then she would take up with another man when she could stand it no longer. The result was a state of continual unhappiness and frustration. "I needed some human being to share all things with me, to be a part of me and my life," she confessed, "but this need fought with my fear of men as the subjectors of woman," a fact which her sexual relationships consistently proved true. Her pursuit of autonomy, thus, took its toll on her emotional life.[61]

Smedley expanded on the problems faced by women in her 1929 novel, *Daughter of Earth*. The central character, Marie Rogers, is sickened by the plight of women. Reared on fairy tale images of romantic love, she views sexual desire with fear and suspicion, and eventually, love as well. Love, Marie concluded, "meant only pain and suffering and defeat." It meant the end of women's freedom. "When one loves, one can easily be enslaved; and I would not be enslaved."[62] But this awareness shaped her understanding of a new form of love that would reconcile her desire for autonomy and companionship, a form of love that could be "beautiful and free," that would neither enslave nor weaken the individual. In the end she chooses freedom over love, autonomy over the need for tenderness and companionship.[63] But even though it eludes her, however, Marie never gives up hope that she will find a love based on "understanding, tolerance, [and] freedom," a love that will combine affection, comradeship, and commitment to a common "struggle for freedom of the oppressed." "Perhaps," Smedley concludes, "one day the two will be one."[64]

Soviet Russia and the promise of red love

Even though Smedley was unable to reconcile love and freedom, examples of those who did were celebrated in the reports of those who traveled to Russia to observe or work for the new social and economic system created in the wake of the October Revolution. While Calverton was skeptical of the degree to which the Soviet Union had achieved all of the goals associated with red love, an endless stream of supportive stories that described the transformed private lives that awaited women and men in the socialist future nonetheless celebrated the achievement of red love in the Soviet state.[65] Beginning in the mid-1920s and continuing into the 1930s, numerous reports from American visitors to the Soviet Union portrayed positive images of the changes in women's lives, providing a taste of what awaited those in the socialist future in ways that would be familiar to Americans who were pursuing their own sexual revolution but were failing miserably.

Central to the sexual revolution in the United States, for example, were the feminist goals associated with the aspirations of the "New Woman." A woman's desire to have a personal as well as professional or public life, while unrealized in America, was a reality in the Soviet Union. Fending off the appeal of bourgeois feminism, the proletarian sexual revolution was held up as an example of a new social system that would allow women to enjoy a career as well as a satisfying private life.[66] Medical care for mothers, child nurseries, readily accessible forms of birth control, the legalization of abortion, pregnancy leaves, liberal divorce laws, and economic equality all provided the necessary autonomy for women that allowed them to be more than a wife and a mother.[67]

In a realization of the predictions of Marx, Engels, and Bebel, women's economic autonomy and the support of the state allowed women to marry for love. The young, it was widely argued, no longer had to wait for parental permission, or achieve a measure of financial security, before they could enter into a union. Unlike the bourgeois marriage market, Russians did not marry for social prestige or economic advancement, and their choice of a mate was never hindered by social pressures or racial and religious differences.[68] Moreover, once married, no one was forced to stay in a loveless relationship. The union lasted only as long as love.[69] As Ella Winter reported, the Soviets were creating a new family structure that would, in the future, lead to a "new form of human relationships based on real equality between the sexes, real comradeship between social individuals."[70] Economic revolution and social reconstruction were leading not only to the creation of new relationships between men and women, but also to new ways of feeling and expressing desire. "The Western poetic ideal of romantic love, the tortures and delights, 'sighs and tears and pale wanderings,' have little appeal for the Bolshevik," Winter insisted. There were no states of mystic transcendence as promised by American popular culture.[71] As Anna Louise Strong observed, because Soviet wives were absorbed in the "outer world of war and wonder," they were immune to "both the abysses and great ecstasies of personal life." The classical romances were viewed with skepticism; their heroes and heroines branded as emotionally unstable. Those who gave "all for love," were judged as "anti-social [and] immoral."[72]

Unlike romantic love, this suggested, red love in the Soviet Union did not lead to emotional withdrawal and isolation from the community; economic communism has given rise to a new form of love that connects rather than detaches the individual from the social world outside of the couple bond. The love of comrades—the "community of interest"—that exists in society at large is fueled by the affection and respect men and women feel for one another at home. In fact, Soviet men and women do not lose themselves in their personal relationships. Many find that their love redoubles their efforts and enhances their revolutionary fervor. As Strong insisted, this is only one form of companionship. "Personal love itself is, with us, only one aria in an opera whose complex crashing chords ... leave strictly limited time for mere arias." Disappointments in love are overcome by a recommitment to the public, in working for the Second Five Year plan, for example. And love triangles usually involve a job or a machine as the third party. Love has not disappeared from the scene, she insisted. It has merely been transformed into a more personally fulfilling and socially useful form.[73]

While authors such as Ella Winter would have agreed with Calverton that old feelings and ideas die hard, and that the revolution in private life has proved to be more difficult to effect than the transformation of economic life, they insisted that the effort to eliminate private property in the domestic arena has achieved some notable successes. "No Communist philosopher ever predicted that a Soviet society would be a domestic utopia," Winter conceded. Communist society has not, and perhaps will never, solve all the problems of human intimacy. Domestic "tragedies" will occur when jealousy and envy spring from unrequited love or from the embers of a dying love.[74] But for the Soviets, jealousy is looked on as a sickness, an "atavistic" throwback to an earlier, unhealthy era. It is an emotion that people are ashamed of since it is viewed as an

A revolutionary proletarian attitude toward sex? 59

expression of men's ownership of women. Yet, Soviet citizens are still struggling to overcome it. As one husband confessed to Winter, after his wife left him, he wanted to kill her and her lover. "We are still jealous," he confessed. Such emotions cannot be eliminated overnight; they are not true communists yet. But the next generation, his children, the jilted husband claimed, will be free from this despicable emotion.[75]

Expressing the success of the revolution inaugurated by the Soviet social system in a way that the West would understand, Winter concluded that it "is really a nation-wide system of companionate marriage."[76] The goals of the American sexual revolution—the creation of relationships whose focus was the expression of the erotic and emotional needs of the individual, based solely on a form of love that reconciled intimacy and autonomy—was to be achieved by connecting personal satisfaction to social commitment within the context of an economic system that eliminated private property. The erotic and emotional freedoms sought by men and women in the United States were to be achieved through the creation of a socialist state. For the advocates of the communist revolution, the ideal future was clearly in sight and the realization of the goals of red love was at hand.

The sexual revolution

In spite of the longstanding view that the interwar left ignored gender and sexuality, it is clear that the popular literature of the 1930s political left gave voice to a concern with such personal issues, especially those that reflected the unique forms of inequality women faced under any economic system.[77] Moreover, by the end of the decade, in the transition from the Third Period to the Popular Front, there was a move to once again tie "cultural revolution" to the transformation in material conditions.[78] For example, even as the Soviet sexual revolution of the 1920s was essentially reversed in the 1930s, and Kollontai had fallen out of favor in Russia, red love became an important staple of the print culture of the political left.[79] This version of red love, however, viewed historical transformations in love, sexuality, marriage, and the family as the inevitable results of economic shifts. Confident of this, it refused to consider the role of the subjective self in this transformation of both private and public life. More to the point, as Jeffrey Weeks has argued with regard to the writings of Marx and Engels, in their political ideologies there "was no concept ... of the need for conscious struggle to transform interpersonal relations as part of the transformation necessary for the construction of a socialist society."[80] And they came to the same conclusions that Marx, Engels, and Bebel had arrived at decades earlier: once freed from the economic restraints imposed on emotional and erotic desires by a system of private property, a "natural" condition would be achieved. True love, untainted by material considerations, would be freed to create stable monogamous, heterosexual relations, and jealousy and possessiveness would disappear.

The belief that the problems of private life will be eradicated when new generations are raised without the encumbrances imposed upon them by the system of private property, however, is where the red love celebrated by the political left comes up short. The version celebrated by Calverton and Schmalhausen asked for more. They insisted that a true revolution would be concerned with what Kollontai described as a "revolution in the outlook, emotion and the inner world of working people."[81] More important, they explored the role emotions would play in the resistance to the revolution in private life they envisioned, and insisted that the new morality that would be unleashed by the re-education of desire would help usher in the revolution rather than merely await it.[82] The battle, as Kollontai insisted, was with the "psyche of the old human being" that is untouched by changes in material conditions, a struggle that was to be waged on the "psychological-cultural front" as well as on the "military and labor front."[83]

In the interwar period, however, Calverton's and Schmalhausen's efforts to link Freud and Marx, the private and the public, came to naught. By the 1930s the specter of the demise of capitalism fueled the rebirth of political radicalism, but one that pushed aside the concerns of the cultural radicals, such as sexual liberation.[84] As Mike Gold argued in 1937, with the Depression "hunger came through the door, and *Eros* scrammed through the window."[85] Advocating a narrowly doctrinaire, disciplined, and patriarchal political vision, groups such as the Communist Party USA and the Socialist Workers Party, its Trotskyist antagonist, minimized the importance of private life and completely severed the link between sexual and political revolution.[86] The sexual revolution, with its emphasis on subjective states of being that were immune to changes in material conditions, had been deemed a complete failure. You could follow Marx or Freud, but not both.[87]

While both Calverton and Schmalhausen were jointly referred to as the Karl Marx of the sexual revolution, Schmalhausen has subsequently been referred to as its Groucho because his insights into Freud and Marx were thought to be vulgar and cavalier.[88] In terms of their legacy, however, this is a great mistake. While he was able to make his points with verve and good humor, Schmalhausen's ideas on the connection between political and sexual revolution were profound and insightful. More to the point, his collaboration with Calverton, which supporters of Calverton viewed as a low point in his career, created their most enduring legacy for radical thought in the era after the Second World War.[89] It is Schmalhausen's admonition that a revolutionary program needs to look at human nature, not just through the lens of historical materialism, from the perspective of what he referred to as "a constipated communism," but toward the creation of new "cultural values"—a "revolutionary culturism" to be derived from psychology, anthropology, and cultural history—that lives on.[90] As Mari Jo Buhle has argued, in the 1920s "the popular press quickly labeled their work the 'Americanization of Freud.'"[91] In combining psychology with historical materialism, Calverton and Schmalhausen were also engaged in the Americanization of Marx.

While the sectarian clashes and revolutionary tactics of the interwar political left have been largely, and justly, forgotten, what has lived on is the concern with the link between political and sexual revolution—the concern with the subjective self as a site of revolutionary transformation. Following the admonitions of Calverton and Schmalhausen, in the years after the Second World War sexual and political radicalism were reunited by those who sought to explain why the economic collapse of capitalism in the 1930s did not bring the revolution predicted by Marx. The culprit for this was found in the consciousness or emotional state of the masses. Reconnecting sexual repression with political domination, and "cultural revolution" to the transformation in material conditions, social theorists such as Wilhelm Reich and the critical theorists of the Frankfurt School such as Herbert Marcuse inspired a new generation of cultural radicals in the 1960s and 1970s to pick up where Calverton and Schmalhausen left off.[92] Mixing Marx's historical materialism with revamped Freudian theories, they sought once again to reshape the "psychic structure" of the individual, liberate sexual energy from the oppressive forces of civilization, revive emotional intensity, and inaugurate a social revolution.[93]

The battle against linking Marx and Freud—economic and sexual revolutions—continued into the late twentieth century.[94] But efforts to pursue a politics of desire that combines both have also endured. In the postwar era, the historical materialism of the interwar political left, with its rejection of the importance of the politics of personal life, had fallen out of favor. While remnants of that movement, the Old Left, continued to ridicule the activities of segments of the counterculture—such as the New Left, ethnic nationalists, and hippies and Yippies—they and their concerns became irretrievably irrelevant to the political and cultural struggles of the last half of the twentieth century. And these countercultural groups reshaped Marxism to fit their needs.[95] Sexual radicals, feminists, and advocates for LGBTQ rights, for example, ask two essential questions as they continue to explore the relationship between social "dominance, power, pleasure, and resistance."[96] What is the link between social oppression and the suppression of desire? And can the pursuit of pleasure, the expression of thwarted desires, subvert social hierarchies, and lead to the reconstruction of relationships of power?[97] What they have demonstrated is that as long as there is a politics of pleasure that is concerned with economic life outside the bedroom, and that is correspondingly aware of the ways the material environment shapes the sexual politics of private life, sexual desire will continue to challenge the social world in which it operates. At the same time, the organization of private life will continue to be meaningful to struggles to destroy social and economic inequality.

Notes

1 Floyd Dell, "Revolution and Sex," *New Masses* 2, no. 3 (January 1927): 27. This is a review of V. F. Calverton, *Sex Expression in Literature* (New York: Boni & Liveright, 1926).

2 Karl Marx and Friedrich Engels, *On Religion* (Mineola, NY: Dover Publications, 2008), 206.
3 Moses Harman, "Freedom and Love, versus Marriage and Hate," *Lucifer*, April 14, 1897, 117.
4 It was translated into English by Stephen Pearl Andrews, also a central figure in the American free love movement. Timothy Messer-Kruse, *The Yankee International: Marxism and the American Reform Tradition, 1848–1876* (Chapel Hill, NC: University of North Carolina Press, 1998), 170.
5 International Workingmen's Association, *Documents of the First International, 1871–1872* (London: Lawrence & Wishart, 1963), 323–24; William West, "The International," *Woodhull & Claflin's Weekly*, March 22, 1873, 3–4. See also Messer-Kruse, *The Yankee International*, chapter 6.
6 Mari Jo Buhle, *Women and American Socialism, 1870–1920* (Urbana: University of Illinois Press, 1983), 4–5, 257, 262; Allen W. Ricker, *Free Love and Socialism: The Truth as to What Socialists Believe About Marriage* (Saint Louis, Missouri: National Rip-Saw Publishing Co., 1911, 2–3; John Spargo, *Applied Socialism: A Study of the Application of Socialistic Principles to the State* (New York: B. W. Heubsch, 1912), 237, 271.
7 For a more in-depth discussion of this, see Jesse Battan, "'Socialism Will Cure All But an Unhappy Marriage': Free Love and the American Left, 1850–1910," in *Meetings & Alcôves: Gauches et Sexualités en Europe et aux Etats-Unis depuis 1850/The Left and Sexuality in Europe and the United States since 1850*, ed. Jesse Battan, Thomas Bouchet, and Tania Régin (Dijon, France: Editions Universitaires de Dijon, 2004), 29–46.
8 The term is from Leonard Wilcox, *V. F. Calverton: Radical in the American Grain* (Philadelphia, PA: Temple University Press, 1992), 70.
9 Hutchins Hapgood, *The Story of a Lover* (New York: Boni & Liveright, 1919), 102.
10 Malcolm Cowley, *Exile's Return: A Literary Odyssey of the 1920s* (New York: Viking Press, 1971), 217, 18–19, 61, 77, 94; Leslie Fishbein, *Rebels in Bohemia: The Radicals of* The Masses, *1911–1917* (Chapel Hill, NC: University of North Carolina Press, 1982), 87.
11 Nathan G. Hale, Jr., *Freud and the Americans: The Beginnings of Psychoanalysis in the United States, 1876–1917* (New York: Oxford University Press, 1971), 24–26.
12 Cowley, *Exiles Return*, 66–67.
13 Hapgood, *Story of a Lover*, 103, 105, 108; Floyd Dell, *Homecoming: An Autobiography* (1933; Port Washington, NY: Kennikat Press, 1969),

349; Christine Stansell, "Talking about Sex: Early-Twentieth-Century Radicals and Moral Confessions," in *Moral Problems in American Life: New Perspectives on Cultural History*, ed. Karen Halttunen and Lewis Perry (Ithaca, NY: Cornell University Press, 1998), 290.
14 Dell, "Revolution and Sex," 27.
15 The debate between Dell and Calverton over the issue, "Is Monogamy Desirable?" was announced in the *New Masses* 2, no. 5 (March 1927): 31. Dell took the affirmative, and Calverton attacked it.
16 Malcolm Cowley described those who emphasized the importance of sexual revolution as "Sex Boys" operating in a "balloon of rhetoric," unconnected to material realities of life. See his "The Sex Boys in a Balloon," *New Republic*, January 15, 1930, 227.
17 Upton Sinclair, "Revolution—Not Sex," *New Masses* 2, no. 5 (March 1927), 11; Upton Sinclair, "Is Monogamy Desirable?" *Modern Quarterly* 4, no. 1 (January–April 1927): 34–36; H. M. Wicks, "An Apology for Sex Anarchism Disguised as Marxism," *Daily Worker*, June 9, 1927, 4.
18 "Cookoo," a slang spelling of *cuckoo* at the time, is in the original. Scott Nearing to John Darmstadt [John Armistead Collier], February 17, 1927 (folder "Revolution and Sex"—Miscellaneous Correspondence, 1927, box 2, John and Phyllis Collier Papers [JPCP], Walter Reuther Library, Wayne State University); "More About '*The New Masses*,'" from the *Daily Worker* [?], March 10, 1927 [?], Box 2, Clipping – Relating to Revolution and Sex and Sexual Revolution, JPCP; Charles W. Wood, "Don't Fight With Sex," *New Masses* 2, no. 4 (February, 1927): 8–9.
19 Joseph Freeman, "Greenwich Village Types," *New Masses* 8, no. 9 (May 1933), 18; Michael Gold, "Notes on Art, Life, Crap-Shooting, Etc.," *New Masses* 5, no. 4 (September 1929), 10–11, 27; V. F. Calverton, "Love and Revolution," *New Masses* 1, no. 6 (October 1926), 28; Mike Gold, "Floyd Dell Resigns," *New Masses* 5, no. 2 (July 1929), 10–11.
20 George Bernard Shaw, *The Socialism of Shaw*, ed. James Fuchs (New York: Vanguard Press, 1926), 154; Michael Gold, "America Needs a Critic," *New Masses* 1, no. 6 (October 1926): 7–9; John Neugass, "Bedroom Revolutionaries," *New Masses* 10, no.1 (March 31, 1936): 26.
21 Albert Weisbord, "Pseudo-Communist Intellectuals (1)," *Class Struggle* 4, nos. 4–5 (April–May, 1934). www.marxists.org/archive/weisbord/FourFourFive.htm
22 Wood, "Don't Fight With Sex," 9.
23 George Krinn, "The Houdini of Sex," *New Masses* 4, no. 6 (November 1928): 25.
24 Floyd Dell, "Bob Takes A High Dive," *New Masses* 3, no. 2 (June 1927): 27.

25 Cowley, *Exiles Return*, 66–67. Philip Abbott, *Leftward Ho! V. F. Calverton and American Radicalism* (Westport, CT: Greenwood Press, 1993), 19.
26 Abbott, *ibid.*, 19; Leonard Wilcox, "Sex Boys in a Balloon: V. F. Calverton and the Abortive Sexual Revolution," *Journal of American Studies* 23, no. 1 (1989): 10.
27 V. F. Calverton, "Sex and Economics," *New Masses* 2, no. 5 (March 1927), 11; Calverton, "Love and Revolution," 28; John Darmstadt [John Armistead Collier], "The Sexual Revolution," *Modern Quarterly* 4, no. 2 (June–September, 1927): 137.
28 "Marx (in my humble opinion)," Schmalhausen argued, "was not a great psychologist. The science of psychology was too immature in his Communist Manifesto days." Samuel Schmalhausen to V. F. Calverton, February 6, 1924 (box 14, V. F. Calverton Papers, New York Public Library).
29 V. F. Calverton and S. D Schmalhausen, eds., *Sex in Civilization* (New York: Macaulay Co., 1929), 8–9, 279–84; Samuel Schmalhausen to V. F. Calverton, October 24, 1929 (box 14, Calverton Papers).
30 V. F. Calverton, "Red Love in Soviet Russia," *Modern Quarterly* 4, no. 3 (November 1927–February 1928): 182. See also Samuel D. Schmalhausen, "The Sexual Revolution," in *Sex in Civilization*, ed. Calverton and Schmalhausen, 353, 354.
31 See, for example, Calverton's "cultural compulsive thesis." V. F. Calverton, "Modern Anthropology and the Theory of Cultural Compulsives," in *The Making of Man, An Outline of Anthropology* (New York: Modern Library, 1931), 1–37.
32 Samuel D. Schmalhausen, "Will the Family Pass?" *Modern Quarterly* 4, no. 2 (June–September 1927): 106.
33 Wilcox, "Sex Boys," 18–19.
34 Schmalhausen, "The Sexual Revolution," 363.
35 V. F. Calverton to Mike Gold, April 16, 1930 (box 6, Calverton Papers); Samuel D. Schmalhausen, "Is Contemporary Civilization Neurotic?" *Modern Quarterly* 5, no. 2 (Spring 1929):186.
36 Calverton, "Sex and Economics," 11–12.
37 Alexandra Kollontai, "Make Way for Winged Eros: A Letter to Working Youth [1923]," in Alexandra Kollontai, *Selected Writings of Alexandra Kollontai*, ed. and trans. Alix Holt (New York: Norton, 1977), 287–88.
38 Schmalhausen, "The Sexual Revolution," 378.
39 Schmalhausen, *ibid.*, 363, 365, 378. Schmalhausen would emphasize the power of individual psychology—or, in modern terms, subjectivity—to withstand changes in the economic environment more than Calverton, thus emphasizing the psychological component to change.

40 Calverton celebrates Kollontai's ideas on the ways that sexual and emotional relationships between men and women will tie them to the larger "community of interests." "Red Love in Soviet Russia," 185.
41 Kathleen A. Brown and Elizabeth Faue, "Revolutionary Desire: Redefining the Politics of Sexuality of American Radicals, 1919–1945," in *Sexual Borderlands: Constructing an American Sexual Past*, ed. Kathleen Kennedy and Sharon Ullman (Columbus, OH: Ohio State University Press, 2003), 276.
42 Constance Coiner, *Better Red: The Writing and Resistance of Tillie Olsen and Meridel Le Sueur* (New York: Oxford University Press, 1995), 55, 58–59.
43 Paula Rabinowitz, *Labor & Desire: Women's Revolutionary Fiction in Depression America* (Chapel Hill, NC: University of North Carolina Press, 1991); Barbara Foley, *Radical Representations: Politics and Form in U.S. Proletarian Fiction, 1929–1941* (Durham, NC: Duke University Press, 1993).
44 Barbara Alexander, "Happiness for One Dime," *Working Women* 6, no. 10 (November 1935): 13. "Sex has become a sort of bourgeois opium," argued the crusty Mike Gold. "It is a form of escape." See his "The Loves of Isadora," *New Masses* 4, no. 10 (March 1929): 20.
45 Alexander, "Happiness for One Dime," 13–14. For a similar argument, see John Stuart, "Bernarr Macfadden: From Pornography to Politics," *New Masses*, 19, no. 8 (May 19, 1936): 8.
46 Sasha Small, "Love Bows to the Dollar," *Working Woman* 5, no. 8 (September 1934): 7, 12. See Anna Louise Strong, "We Soviet Wives," *American Mercury* 33, no. 128 (August 1934), 422–23, for a discussion of the ways the "sugary" Hollywood romances are rejected in the Soviet Union, and their heroes and heroines are branded as emotionally unstable.
47 Sasha Small, "The Rosy Road to Romance or, Short Cuts to Happiness," *Working Woman* 5, no. 10 (November 1934): 13.
48 *The Working Woman*, which later became *Woman Today*, was published from 1929 to 1937, by the Communist Party USA Central Committee Women's Department. See also Mary Templin, "Revolutionary Girl, Militant Housewife, Antifascist Mother, and More: The Representation of Women in American Communist Women's Journals of the 1930s," *Centennial Review* 41, no. 3 (Fall 1997): 625–33.
49 Ann Barton, "A Collective Love Story," *New Masses* 14, no. 4 (January 1, 1935): 35.
50 A Group of Workers and Jane Benton, "Stockyard Stella," *Working Woman* 6, no. 1 (January, 1935): 4–5.
51 A Group of Workers and Jane Benton, "Stockyard Stella [part III]," *Working Woman* 6, no. 3 (March, 1935): 5.

52 A Group of Workers and Jane Benton, "Stockyard Stella [part II]" *Working Woman* 6, no. 2 (February, 1935): 4–5.
53 A Group of Workers and Jane Benton, "Stockyard Stella [Concluding Chapter]," *Working Woman* 6, no. 4 (April, 1935): 4–5.
54 Ruth McKenney, "Women are Human Beings," *New Masses* 37, no. 12 (December 10, 1940): 6–7.
55 Vera Buch Weisbord, *A Radical Life* (Bloomington, IN: Indiana University Press, 1977), 167–69, 144. See also Peggy Dennis, *The Autobiography of an American Communist* (Berkeley, CA: Creative Arts Book Co., 1977), 190; and Brown and Faue, "Revolutionary Desire," 293.
56 Brown and Faue, "Revolutionary Desire," 283–84.
57 Vivian Gornick, *The Romance of American Communism* (New York: Basic Books, 1977), 56.
58 Kathleen A. Brown and Elizabeth Faue, "Social Bonds, Sexual Politics," *Left History* 7, no. 1 (Spring 2000): 16–17; Brown and Faue, "Revolutionary Desire," 276, 282–83; James R. Barrett, "Was the Personal Political? Reading the Autobiography of American Communism," *International Review of Social History*, 53 (December 2008): 407–10, 415; and Bryan D. Palmer, *James P. Cannon and the Origins of the American Revolutionary Left, 1890–1928* (Urbana: University of Illinois Press, 2007), 81–83.
59 Barrett, "Was the Personal Political?" 407, 410; Hope Hale Davis, *Great Day Coming: A Memoir of the 1930s* (South Royalton, VT: Steerforth Press, 1994), 1, 14, 81, 223–24. See also Foley, *Radical Representations*, 219. For a discussion of the traits of the tramp bohemian, see Kevin White, *The First Sexual Revolution: The Emergence of Male Heterosexuality in Modern America* (New York: New York University Press, 1993), 7–10, 44–49.
60 Buch Weisbord, *Radical Life*, 144. Unlike the lyrical left before the First World War and the New Left after the Second World War, little time has been spent exploring the private lives, the sexual histories, of those active in the interwar left. Recently, scholars such as Vivian Gornick, Elizabeth Faue and Kathleen Brown, Alan Wald, and James Barrett have attempted to rectify this. While they have not completely upended the lingering images of the rabid "masculinism" and "puritanism" that have long been used to characterize the sexual politics of the men and women associated with the interwar left, they have reshaped our understanding of their emotional and sexual experiences. They have convincingly shown, for example, that their private lives did not follow in the narrow grooves established by political ideology or party platforms. In spite of demands for monogamous, heterosexual relationships there

were many examples of those who lived emotional and erotic lives that challenged these expectations. See Gornick, *Romance of American Communism*; Brown and Faue, "Social Bonds," 9–45; Brown and Faue, "Revolutionary Desire," 273–302; Barrett, "Was the Personal Political," 395–423; and Alan Wald, "Bohemian Bolsheviks After World War II: A Minority within a Minority," *Labour/Le Travail* 70 (Fall 2012): 159–86.

61 Anonymous [Agnes Smedley], "One is Not Made of Wood: The True Story of a Life," *New Masses* 3, no. 4 (August 1927): 5–7.

62 Agnes Smedley, *Daughter of Earth* (Old Westbury, NY: Feminist Press, 1973) [1935], 155, 156, 168, 188, 360.

63 *Ibid.*, 184, 218–19.

64 *Ibid.*, 357, 359, 372, 380, 360.

65 Calverton, "Red Love in Soviet Russia," 181, 190.

66 A good example of this can be found in Theodore Dreiser's description of Ruth Kennell's efforts to escape the conventional life of an American housewife and a loveless marriage, and find an intensely satisfying sexual relationship as well as engage in revolutionary activity. See Theodore Dreiser, *A Gallery of Women*, vol. 1 (New York: Horace Liveright, 1929), 341–46; and Julia L. Mickenberg, *American Girls in Red Russia: Chasing the Soviet Dream* (Chicago: University of Chicago Press, 2017), 148.

67 Peter G. Filene, *Americans and the Soviet Experiment, 1917–1933* (Cambridge MA: Harvard University Press, 1967), 141–42; Mickenberg, *American Girls*, 199. See also Ruth McKenney, "Women are Human Beings: II," *New Masses* 37, no. 17 (December 17, 1940): 9–10; and Theodore Dreiser, "How Russia Handles the Sex Question," *Current History* 29 (1929): 535–43.

68 Nan Allen, "Marriage in the Soviet Union," *Working Woman* (January 1935), 14; Ella Winter, *Red Virtue: Human Relationships in the New Russia* (London: Camelot Press, 1933), 131.

69 Meta Berger, "The New Woman," *Woman Today* 1, no. 1 (March 1936): 20–21; Strong, "We Soviet Wives," 416.

70 Ella Winter, "No Gold Diggers," *New Masses* 10, no. 7 (February 13, 1934): 26–27; Winter, *Red Virtue*, 136.

71 Winter, *Red Virtue*, 123.

72 Strong, "We Soviet Wives," 423.

73 *Ibid.*, 416, 419–21.

74 Ella Winter, "Love in Two Worlds," *New Masses* 16, no. 3 (July 16, 1935): 17–19.

75 Winter, *Red Virtue*, 130; Elias Tobenkin, City of Friends (New York: Milton, Balch & Co., 1934), 158–59.

76 Winter, *Red Virtue*, 123.

77 Faue and Brown, "Revolutionary Desire," 276–77.
78 Michael Denning, *The Cultural Front: The Laboring of the American Culture in the Twentieth Century* (London: Verso, 1996).
79 Constance Coiner, *Better Red: The Writing and Resistance of Tillie Olsen and Meridel Le Sueur* (New York: Oxford University Press, 1995), 55, 58–59.
80 Jeffrey Weeks, *Sex, Politics and Society: The Regulation of Sexuality since 1800*, 3rd ed. (London: Routledge, 2012), 217.
81 Kollontai, "Winged Eros," 276–77.
82 Alexandra Kollontai, "Sexual Relations and Class Struggle," *Selected Writings of Alexandra Kollontai*, ed. and trans. Alix Holt (New York: Norton, 1977), 249; Barbara Evans Clements, *Bolshevik Feminist: The Life of Alexsandra Kollontai* (Bloomington, IN: Indiana University Press, 1979), 71; Brown and Faue, "Revolutionary Desire," 276.
83 Alexandra Kollontai, "The New Woman," in *The Autobiography of a Sexually Emancipated Communist Woman*, ed. Iring Fetscher (New York: Herder and Herder, 1971), 83; Kollontai, "Winged Eros," 278.
84 See George Novack, "Radical Intellectuals in the 1930s," *International Socialist Review* 29, no. 2 (March–April 1968): 22; Daniel Aaron, *Writers on the Left: Episodes in American Literary Communism* (New York: Octagon Books, 1974), 91, 168; and Deborah Rosenfelt, "From the Thirties: Tillie Olsen and the Radical Tradition," *Feminist Studies* 7, no. 3 (Autumn 1981): 401.
85 Michael Gold, "Notes on the Cultural Front, *New Masses* 25, no. 11 (December 7, 1937): 2.
86 Brown and Faue, "Social Bonds," 10–12.
87 Wilcox, "Sex Boys," 22–23; Aaron, *Writers on the Left*, 234.
88 The Karl Marx line is found in Henry James Foreman, "Sex in the Civilization of the Twentieth Century," *New York Times Book Review*, June 9, 1929, BR8.
89 Wilcox, "Sex Boys," 11; Abbott, *Leftward Ho*, 48. See also David Ramsey and Alan Calmer, "The Marxism of V. F. Calverton," *New Masses* 8, no. 6 (January 1933), 10.
90 Samuel D. Schmalhausen, "These Tragic Comedians," *Modern Quarterly* 4 (November 1927–February 1928): 220, 215, 226, 227.
91 Buhle, *Feminism and Its Discontents*, 94.
92 Wilcox, *V. F. Calverton*, 86.
93 Paul Robinson, *The Freudian Left: Wilhelm Reich, Geza Roheim, Herbert Marcuse* (New York: Harper & Row, 1969); Richard King, *The Party of Eros: Radical Social Thought and the Realm of Freedom* (New York: Dell Publishing, 1972); Christopher Turner, *Adventures in the Orgasmatron: How the Sexual Revolution Came to America* (New

York: Ferrar, Straus and Giroux, 2011); Peter Drucker, "Conceptions of Sexual Freedom in Marcuse, Foucault and Rubin," *Journal of the International Network of Sexual Ethics and Politics* 2, no. 2 (2014): 31–38.

94 See, for example, the following works by Christopher Lasch: *Haven in a Heartless World: The Family Besieged* (New York: Basic Books, 1979), xiii–xvii; "The Freudian Left and Cultural Revolution," *New Left Review* no. 129 (September–October 1981): 23–34; "Talking About Sex: The History of a Compulsion," *Psychology Today* (November 1978), 147, 149–50, 158. See also E. J. Hobsbawm, *Revolutionaries: Contemporary Essays* (London: Weidenfeld and Nicholson, 1973), 216–18.

95 Dennis, *Autobiography of an American Communist*, 276–77; Gornick, 52, 59, 82.

96 Susan K. Cahn, "Sexual Histories, Sexual Politics," *Feminist Studies* 18, no. 3 (Fall 1992): 629. For discussions on the relationship between radical sexual politics and the political left in the postwar period, see: D'Emilio, *Sexual Communities*, 59–60, 64; Harry Hay, *Radically Gay: Gay Liberation in the Words of Its Founder*, ed. Will Roscoe (Boston: Beacon Press, 1996), 37–46; Stuart Timmons, *The Trouble with Harry Hay: Founder of the Modern Gay Movement* (Boston: Alyson, 1990); Daniel Hurewitz, *Bohemian Los Angeles: And the Making of Modern Politics* (Berkeley, CA: University of California Press, 2007); Aaron Lecklider, "Coming to Terms: Homosexuality and the Left in American Culture," *GLQ: A Journal of Lesbian and Gay Studies* 18, no. 1 (2011): 179–95; Christopher Phelps, "The Closet in the Party: The Young Socialist Alliance, the Socialist Workers Party, and Homosexuality, 1962–1970," *Labor Studies in Working-Class History of the Americas* 10, no. 4 (2013): 11–38; Peter Drucker, *Warped: Gay Normality and Queer Anti-Capitalism* (Leiden: Brill, 2015); and Emily K. Hobson, *Lavender and Red: Liberation and Solidarity in the Gay and Lesbian Left* (Berkeley, CA: University of California Press, 2016).

97 April Haynes, "How Did It Feel? Open Secrets about Sex and Race in Early America," *Early American Literature* 51, no. 1 (2016): 158.

3

Marxism and Americanism: A. J. Muste, Louis Budenz, and an "American approach" before the Popular Front

Leilah Danielson

In his 1997 book *The Cultural Front: The Laboring of American Culture in the Twentieth Century*, Michael Denning offered a sweeping reinterpretation of the culture and politics of the New Deal era that helped to upend decades of scholarship. In it, he challenged the prevailing wisdom about the cultural production of the 1930s, which scholars, following the lead of the New York Intellectuals, had long described as kitschy and middlebrow, sentimental and populist. Cultural producers who depicted the "common man" had allowed themselves to be duped by the Communist Party (CP) whose Popular Front represented a fake, duplicitous effort to gain control of the liberal left, and use it to promote Stalin's agenda. Denning turned this interpretation on its head, boldly drawing upon Marxist cultural theory and particularly Gramsci's ideas about hegemony. Instead of populist-nationalist schlock, he called the cultural production of the Popular Front era a "second American renaissance" in which working-class ethnics and African Americans—organic intellectuals—claimed cultural space for themselves and developed a counter-hegemonic historic bloc that led to the "laboring" of American culture. The Congress of Industrial Organizations (CIO), and not the CP, occupied the center of his narrative; his horizon was what united the labor left rather than divided it.[1]

Denning's critics charged that he had essentially whitewashed history, recapitulating arguments made since the 1940s. Yet, despite their vociferous dissent, scholarship has largely supported his thesis about the central role of the CIO. Recent work has also been published that attempts to rehabilitate the CP and its Popular Front in the celebratory terms of *The Cultural Front*. Still, the question of the meaning of the Americanist theory and culture of the Popular Front era could use more nuance and complexity. For one, efforts to Americanize Marxism and reimagine American national identity as working-class predated both the CP's Popular Front of 1934–1935 and the CIO by around ten years. Second, in some hands, the "American approach"—as they called it—did indeed devolve into nationalism. In others, it offered an interpretation of the world that centered and validated working-class American experiences and agency, while simultaneously promoting socialism and transnational solidarities. The progressive wing of the labor movement in the 1920s and early 1930s, and particularly its two leading lights, A. J. Muste and Louis Budenz, show how the pioneers of the American approach embodied both its great possibilities and limitations. It also shows that the roots of the cultural front were deeper and the challenges greater than Denning's thesis allows.[2]

Muste and Budenz were prominent figures in the labor left of the interwar period and, as we shall see, assumed even greater prominence in U.S. politics after the Second World War. Perhaps one

Figure 3.1 After catching a gas canister, a worker lobs it back into the lines of the Ohio National Guard during the Electric Auto-Lite strike in Toledo, Ohio, May 1934. Ten thousand workers walked out in the strike, influenced by the "Musteites" who simultaneously organized unemployed workers to support the strike rather than scab. The strike won a wage increase and union recognition. *Photographer George Blount, Courtesy Toledo Lucas County Public Library.*

reason they worked well together initially was that they shared a common background and political orientation. Both were from the Midwest and came from deeply religious families; Muste grew up in a working-class Dutch immigrant household and was an ordained minister in the Calvinist Reformed Church of America, while Budenz was a second-generation Catholic from a lower-middle-class family. Both had drifted out of organized religion to become involved in the working class and revolutionary upsurges of the First World War era. The labor movement became their "Messiah," as Muste liked to put it, destined to build the Kingdom of God on earth. The degree to which their religious upbringing shaped their adult politics is hard to determine, since they worked in ethnically and religiously diverse organizations and movements, but it does seem significant that both men came from churches hostile to liberalism. Although they supported the idea of a labor party, they preferred industrial organization and direct action over the parliamentarianism of the Socialists. They both criticized the Communists for what they saw as their erratic and opportunistic approach to trade unionism, and for their "lack of roots in American soil." Both also argued that the labor movement should frame the struggles of the working class against the "new capitalism" (by which they meant Fordism) as the "third revolution" in American history (the first being the American Revolution, the second the Civil War).[3]

Still, there were important differences between Muste and Budenz that foreshadow their split in the mid-1930s over the question of the meaning of the American approach for the revolutionary labor movement. Muste was more of an intellectual than Budenz; his writing was measured and analytical whereas Budenz offered breathless accounts of working-class heroism and capitalist villainy in a moral language of absolutes. Their personalities were also strikingly different. Muste was even-tempered and equanimous; as one contemporary observed, "Just when the air is thick with critical bullets, you will find A. J. grinning a most winning grin and shooting right back, straight and hard." Budenz, by contrast, was high-strung and insecure, which, as we shall see, could undermine his otherwise exceptional leadership abilities.[4]

During the 1920s, Muste and Budenz assumed leadership positions within the progressive wing of the labor movement. Muste had earned his labor bona fides as leader of the Lawrence textile strike of 1919, which led to victory for some 30,000 workers, and as head of the Amalgamated Textile Workers of America (ATWA). In 1921, he became director of Brookwood Labor College and also served as vice-president of the American Federation of Teachers (AFT). For his part, Budenz worked as a journalist for pro-labor Catholic publications, but after observing working-class poverty and state repression of labor strikes, left the church to work as publicity director of the nascent American Civil Liberties Union. In 1921, he became editor of the newspaper *Labor Age* (later *Labor Action*), through which he became directly involved in several important strikes and earned a reputation as a "genius at organizing mass activities." *Labor Age* was the newspaper of choice for militant unionists and pro-labor intellectuals who were frustrated by American Federation of Labor (AFL) conservatism but also convinced that the CP, then ultra-revolutionary in its approach, was out of touch with reality. Over the course of the 1920s, Muste and Budenz explored labor's problems and practiced new ideas for the organization and mobilization of workers in the context of the decade's vibrant workers' education movement. These efforts culminated in the formation of the Conference for Progressive Labor Action (CPLA) in early 1929, an umbrella organization that functioned as the left wing within the AFL, arguing for militant industrial unionism to replace conservative craft business unionism. Muste served as chair of the CPLA and as the movement's first among equals (hence, "the Musteites"), while Budenz was executive secretary of the CPLA.[5]

The labor progressives who subsequently came together in the CPLA offer the strongest evidence to support Denning's argument about the working-class and indigenous origins of the Americanist turn in contrast to those who credit Moscow. Yet Denning only mentions them briefly, noting that "Brookwood alumni were to serve as key organizers and intellectuals for the CIO" and that the CPLA attracted intellectuals such as V. F. Calverton and Sidney Hook, whom he credits with pioneering "the Popular Front" by infusing Marxism with pragmatism and by revitalizing and reconstituting the American revolutionary tradition. In fact, however, as we shall see, the CPLA anticipated the distinctive features of the Popular Front: the centrality of industrial unionism, engagement with mass culture and the production of working-class culture, a creative mix of Marxism and Americanism, and a non-sectarian spirit.[6]

Labor progressives had come together after the postwar Red Scare to regroup and rebuild. The focus of these efforts was to develop educational programming for labor organizers who would return to their unions with new ideas and new energy. Their pedagogy adapted the ideas of educational theorist and pragmatist John Dewey. Just as Dewey emphasized the importance of experience as the path to knowledge and democratic citizenship, labor pedagogues maintained that ideas and practice should work dialectically to build up the collective knowledge and power of the working class. They were, in short, labor "moderns," eager to engender a more open and experimental approach to labor problems and trade union organization. This involved coming to terms with the fact that the political and economic landscape had changed dramatically from the late nineteenth century when the AFL had developed its craft-based, "bread and butter" approach to unionism. The dynamism of the capitalism demanded a dynamic labor movement, able to evolve "new attitudes, new approaches ... [and] to think and to act in terms of social power," as J. B. S. Hardman put it in 1928. Hardman was the editor of the Amalgamated Clothing Workers' (ACW) organ *The Advance*, which had long advocated the importance of workers' education.[7]

This approach contrasted with that of AFL conservatives, who frequently expressed their hostility to "theory" and called for limiting workers' education to "trade union fundamentals." Indeed, by 1928, the AFL leadership had become so threatened by progressives in the nexus of workers' education and *Labor Age* that they redbaited Brookwood and disaffiliated the college from the Workers' Education Bureau. Rather than back down, however, Muste issued a "Challenge to Progressives" in which he called upon those opposed to the "reactionary" policies of the AFL to fearlessly pursue a "progressive trade union program." His manifesto defined labor progressivism as the aggressive organization of industrial workers, resistance to anti-labor laws, active campaigns for social insurance, formation of a labor party, recognition of the Soviet Union, opposition to American imperialism and militarism, and working-class internationalism. It concluded with the assertion that only a labor movement "marked by idealism, leading American workers on to freedom and independence," could inspire workers.[8]

Muste's challenge served as the basis for the formation of the CPLA in the fall of 1929. Building upon their experiences with workers' education, the CPLA emphasized praxis as a means of organizing and mobilizing workers and building a revolutionary consciousness. As Muste frequently put it, organizers should pursue a "pragmatic policy" of organizing around workers' immediate concerns; class consciousness and solidarity would develop out of the experience of taking collective action. Hardman, who served as the CPLA's head of research and education committee, made this fusion of Marxism and pragmatism explicit: "What has 'made' Marx is above all the fact that he carried his ideas into the 'street,' into the actual struggles of his days," he explained to the CPLA rank and file. "He used theory as an enforcement [sic] to his engagement in the practical revolutionary struggle, and the latter as an intellectual feeder for his theoretical work."[9]

Despite its harsh criticism of the AFL, the CPLA did not support dual unionism (the formation of alternative unions within existing jurisdictions), which it viewed as divisive and disruptive. Instead, it sought to push the AFL to the left by taking constructive "action" and providing "healthy criticism." Indeed, the CPLA was eager to overcome the rampant sectarianism of the labor left in the 1920s. On the right was the AFL leadership, which spotted a Bolshevik behind every new idea. On the left was the CP, which had entered its "Third Period" policy in which Communists were to engage in battle against social democrats and trade unionists as well as capitalists. Somewhere in the middle was the Socialist Party (SP), which advocated working through the electoral process and a deferential relationship with the AFL. The CPLA sought to combine the best of all three tendencies through a commitment to direct action and militant unionism over the parliamentarianism of the Socialists, and a flexible, adaptive Marxism over the dogmatism of the Communists. This approach attracted the so-called "militant" wing of the SP, the left-wing of the AFL, and many of those in amalgamated unions such as the ACW. It did not, however, endear them to the Communists who denounced them as "labor fakers" and actively undermined their efforts in the field. Yet rather than respond in kind, the CPLA stressed the importance of finding common ground and building a united front. "We must be over-patient with the Moscow inspired," Budenz counseled in the pages of *Labor Action*.[10]

The CPLA also had a cultural politics. They argued that the massive economic and cultural changes of the 1920s—the rise of the mass industries, welfare capitalism, mass culture, and the white-collar worker—had combined to make workers "beholden to capitalist culture." The task of militant workers was therefore not only to build strong unions, but also to create a "labor culture and labor idealism." This effort proceeded along two interrelated lines. The first was workers' education, which would develop a counter-hegemonic culture that was "not only of the workers and for the workers but by the workers," as Muste asserted in 1925. This involved the production of working-class knowledge through systematic efforts to research and disseminate the history and practices of working-class organization and mobilization. It also involved developing working-class history, literature, drama, art, songs, radio, journalism, and sports. Indeed, unlike their modernist contemporaries and in anticipation of the cultural front, the Musteites advocated engagement with and appropriation of the new mass culture to the needs and values of the labor movement. As M. H. Hedges, director of research and education for the International Brotherhood of Electrical Workers and CPLA member, theorized in *Labor Age*, communication was a cultural system that engaged "men's profoundest emotions," and he called on union activists to copy the tactics of advertisers to engender a sense of self rooted in working-class history and traditions. In a follow-up article, he praised the literary critic V. F. Calverton for exploring how literature expressed the ideology of the "business class" and for showing that culture and moral codes were contingent, contested, and changing. If the labor movement ever hoped to gain the allegiance of the working class, it needed to develop "labor poets, novelists, and historians," as well as build up the movement's economic and political power.[11]

The second aspect of the CPLA's cultural politics was to speak in an "American language." Partly this was accomplished through fusing pragmatism and Marxism, but it also involved reinterpreting American history in terms that affirmed the organized power of workers and the right of revolution. Budenz had pioneered what he called the "American approach" during the First World War, when he likened the Palmer raids of the Red Scare to the persecution of abolitionists in the antebellum era, and further refined it in 1924. His analysis began with the observation that "main street" labor had not been persuaded of the need to overthrow capitalism and viewed socialism as a European import. The key was to reframe the "class war" as the "Third American Revolution," after the 1776 revolution for political freedom and the 1865 revolution freeing the slaves. As Budenz frequently intoned, "That it should be deemed improper and criminal to speak of 'revolution' in the U.S. is evidence of a changing conception of 'Americanism' ... Thomas Jefferson thought that the tree of Liberty needed to be watered with the blood of revolution every nineteen years or so."[12]

The CPLA quickly became a force to be reckoned with on the labor left. Indeed, it served as a kind of "front," as an organizational center for a mix of relations and mutual influences among Socialists, progressive labor leaders, rank-and-file unionists, Marxist intellectuals, and labor educators. Among them were "traditional" intellectuals associated with *Modern Quarterly/Monthly*, such as V. F. Calverton, James Rorty, Lewis Corey/Louis Fraina, and Sidney Hook. As noted above, these collaborations dated to the mid-1920s. Calverton's ideas, one of his biographers has pointed out, came directly "from his contact with Brookwood Labor College ... during the mid and late twenties, and with A. J. Muste." Similarly, Corey and Rorty worked with stalwarts of workers' education and future members of the CPLA—Muste, Hardman, James Maurer (head of the Pennsylvania American Federation of Labor), John Brophy (a major figure in the United Mine Workers of America), Abraham Epstein (a prominent figure in the movement for social insurance), and Phil E. Ziegler of the Railway Clerks—to produce *American Labor Dynamics* (1928), an edited volume exploring the economic and cultural transformations of the previous decade and their implications for the American labor movement. These collaborations led to the formation of American Labor Associates in 1931, an effort that resulted in the publication of *Our America*, a newspaper committed to building "an integrated and militant movement of manual and intellectual workers rallied around a clear-cut and realistic program of action." Contributors included Corey, Rorty, the Marxist lawyer Louis Boudin, and CPLA members Muste, Hardman, David Saposs, and Ludwig Lore.[13]

More importantly from the CPLA's point of view, its members led countless strikes, unionizing drives, and intra-union progressive insurgencies. These included the famous Piedmont revolt of textile workers that spread like wildfire across the south in 1929 and the "Reorganized" movement within the United Mine Workers of America, which challenged the autocratic leadership of John L. Lewis. Although many of their organizing campaigns and strikes ended in defeat, the CPLA felt that their methods were generally successful in inspiring and mobilizing the rank and file and in building up a counter-hegemonic progressive bloc within the AFL. Among the unemployed, the CPLA had more concrete success; by 1932, it could boast of having several hundred thousand members in its Unemployed Citizens' Leagues (UCL).[14]

The rapid growth of the UCLs, the influx of radical intellectuals, along with the deepening crisis of the Great Depression, and the stubborn refusal of the AFL to organize the mass industries, all combined to convince many in the CPLA that revolution was necessary and imminent. Even though Franklin Delano Roosevelt had just been elected president, Muste recalled of these "lean" and "tumultuous years," that "the nation was in a state of civil war … a war in which every city and section of the country was rent with deep cleavages and in which there was a good deal of fighting, though the guns were almost entirely in the hands of the police and the National Guard." As a result, the CPLA assumed a more revolutionary posture, and in 1933 institutionalized its move to the left by reorganizing as a vanguard party called the American Workers' Party (AWP). We might interpret this in Gramscian terms as a shift from a "war of position" toward a "war of maneuver" insofar as they placed less emphasis on building a counter-hegemonic culture and more on direct action. As Muste rallied his comrades, it was time for revolutionaries to throw themselves "*unreservedly into action* … Forward then with renewed vigor all along the line! In Unemployed work! In strikes! In organizing the unorganized! … Forward to the overthrow of capitalism and the establishment of the workers republic!"[15]

This shift to the left cost the Musteites many of their supporters in workers' education and the Socialist Party, who had been drawn to the movement's inclusive and non-sectarian character. They feared that redefining the CPLA as a political party would undermine its broad appeal to unionists and radicals from across the ideological spectrum, and predicted that it would become the target of other left-wing groups who would attempt to capture and destroy it. Muste, Budenz, Hardman, Ludwig Lore, and other leaders in the newly formed AWP were nonplussed; they pointed out that the CPLA had always been committed to advancing "a particular kind of labor movement," one that aimed, in the last analysis, to overthrow capitalism. They rejected the charge that clarifying the CPLA's "position over and against other groups" was a partisan move, and they reiterated their commitment to united action.[16]

In the end, it was the critics who turned out to be right. With the formation of the AWP, several splinter CP splinter groups called for a merger, including the Communist League of America (CLA), the primary American Trotskyist organization headed by Max Shachtman and James P. Cannon. Intellectual newcomers to the AWP such as Sidney Hook and James Burnham tended to support the merger, while long-time Musteites were deeply skeptical, fearing that the Trotskyists' strict internationalism would compromise the AWP's "American approach," and that the Trotskyists' origins as a faction of the CP had made them destructively sectarian and obsessed with the Soviet Union. Muste appeared to agree with much of this criticism, yet he would ultimately favor the merger over and against Budenz. As we shall see, the dispute reflected longstanding differences in how the two men understood the American approach. These differences had seemed a matter of emphasis rather than substance during the early years of the Great Depression as CPLA members threw themselves into the great industrial battles of the day, but merger negotiations forced the Musteites to clarify the meaning of the American approach, a process that would bring the differences between Budenz and Muste to the surface and serve as a point of departure.[17]

The brewing controversy abated somewhat over the summer of 1934. Both men, as noted above, shared a preference for action over talk and found themselves drawn into strikes, demonstrations, and organizing drives, leaving Hook and Burnham in charge of discussions with the CLA. The most dramatic of these was the famous Toledo Auto-Lite strike (Figure 3.1), which paved the way for the unionization of the auto industry and helped to provide the impetus for supporters of industrial unionism to break from the AFL and found the CIO; it also represented the pinnacle achievement of the AWP and its American approach. Initially, the strike appeared to have little chance of success, but then the AWP's local Unemployed

League joined the struggle. The League had been active in Toledo for several years where it had emphasized working-class solidarity by supporting strikes and dissuading the jobless from scabbing. Reflecting this policy, the League supported the Auto-Lite strikers and stayed on the picket line even after the city issued an injunction. Arrests and more demonstrations followed, with Muste and Budenz arriving on the scene to help lead what was turning into a major confrontation between capital and labor. The strike quickly took on the distinctive features of the Musteite movement, with signs that that said "1776–1865–1934" and "Don't Tread on Me," and with the use of militant, confrontational tactics such as mass picketing and defiance of injunctions as means of inspiring and mobilizing workers. The strategy worked; within a few days, some 10,000 people were on the picket line where they engaged in pitched battles with deputies and strikebreakers. Finally, the National Guard arrived on the scene and the government brokered a collective bargaining agreement that helped lead to the formation of the United Auto Workers.[18]

Both Muste and Budenz left Toledo in high spirits. As they reported in *Labor Action*, the settlement represented "an outstanding victory for the workers" and "tribute" to the Americanist strategy and methods of labor organization that they had long advocated. And yet they came to different conclusions about the strike's implications for the question of whether to merge with the CLA. For Muste, the "battle of Toledo" demonstrated that revolution was on the horizon, which made it imperative that the AWP clarify its theoretical framework and maintain tight discipline over its members, a project that would be served by merging with a group known for putting a high premium on theory and party discipline. For Budenz, however, Toledo showed the need for the AWP to remain exactly as it was: action-oriented, theoretically loose, and distinctly "American." Together with J. B. S. Hardman, Budenz argued that merging with the CLA would destroy the AWP's uniquely pragmatic interpretation of Marxism, as expressed in Hook's *Towards the Understanding of Karl Marx* (1933): "We must stand four-square on WORKERS DEMOCRACY—on testing all our views and actions on the working class and not on the Party." Budenz and Hardman further argued that the CLA's sectarianism, particularly its commitment to destroying both the Communist and

Socialist parties, would inhibit the rejuvenation and reunification of the left.[19]

And yet, despite the merits of his argument, Budenz was unable to lead the opposition. When the CLA first approached the AWP, he had fallen sick with a crippling sinus condition. His "sinusitis" miraculously abated during the Toledo strike, but returned in full force in the fall of 1934, confining him to bed rest. With Budenz out of the way, Muste was able to organize his forces and in December the AWP voted to merge with the CLA and become the Workers' Party of the United States with Muste as executive secretary. Hardman resigned immediately, while most others dutifully took out membership cards only to resign over the next year in disgust over the factionalism that consumed the new party. Many of them concluded that reform and not revolution was the order of the day and took up leadership roles in the newly formed CIO. Some also joined the CP, which had just embraced its Popular Front period of pursuing alliances with social democrats and liberals and promoting the idea that Communism was compatible with American traditions.[20]

Muste knew that Budenz was unhappy with the merger but, if we can trust his memoirs, was genuinely surprised by the latter's very public attack on the new party in the spring of 1935 and especially his decision, announced later that year, to join the CP. In this context, it's important to recognize the Leninist context in which revolutionary parties of the era operated; to take actions or make statements outside of the party line was a violation of party discipline, which they took very seriously. From the perspective of leaders like Muste and Cannon, if Budenz had concerns, he should have brought them up with the Politburo, the political arm of the central committee. But Budenz was in his own world; stuck at home most of the time, he spent his days isolated from party members and musing over how to resurrect his American revolutionary party. The use of cocaine to treat his sinus condition may have contributed to his anxiety and depression; Muste, who met with him in late March, apparently described him as "demented."[21]

Whatever the case, Budenz's attack came suddenly and very publicly in the March issue of *Modern Monthly* and centered, unsurprisingly, on the American approach. His argument depended on a series of oppositions between native-born American workers, who were cast as self-possessed, practical, and strong, and Europeanized radicals, who were masochistic, condescending, and effete. Nativism had long been implicit in Budenz's writing, which often contrasted freedom-loving "main-street" workers with out-of-touch foreigners and intellectuals, but it had been obscured by his journalistic emphasis on documenting and encouraging working-class action. Now it emerged in full force. Auto-Lite strikers had moved beyond immediate demands and "reach[ed] out for power" because organizers appealed to their innate, "natural" affinity for revolution by using symbols and slogans that cast the strike in terms of "a new crusade for American freedom." He invoked pragmatism, not in the experiential sense that had been emphasized in the past, but as realism and authenticity in contrast to the "neurasthenic fictions" of radicals steeped in otherworldly "Mumbo Jumbo."[22]

Budenz's not-so-subtle rebuke of his comrades was probably enough to attract the ire of the party leadership, but he went further. Whereas the Musteites had long disparaged parliamentarianism, he now called on revolutionaries to propose a constitutional amendment abolishing capitalism, an approach that he argued would appeal "to the pragmatism of the American masses." He even—one can imagine the scorn and disdain that must have been expressed by Cannon and Shachtman—went so far as to praise the Communists for their recent turn toward a Popular Front.[23]

Cannon called for Budenz's expulsion, while Muste clarified the meaning of the American approach from a Marxist and internationalist perspective in a brilliant series of articles published over the course of the summer of 1935. Notably, and in contrast to his comrades, Muste scrupulously avoided impugning Budenz's character, even going so far as to allow him to read a draft before it was published. More substantially, his response demonstrates that the Old Left's Americanism—in its most sophisticated incarnations—was neither sentimental nor nationalist, as some historians have argued. According to Muste, Budenz's mistake was not in using the "revolutionary potentialities of American tradition and history," but rather in viewing them as a blueprint for socialist revolution. "The American approach does not in and of itself give us a set of basic revolutionary principles," but rather suggests that "we approach the American scene with certain principles which we want to make effective there." Those principles were Marxist and Leninist, which would be adapted "to the specific culture and traditions of the United States." As an example, Muste pointed to Americans' lack of a feudal experience; while this historical variance made American workers slow to develop class consciousness, it also meant that they did "not have any feeling of inferiority. They are not habituated to oppression and servility. It is a fresh, very vigorous working class." American historical memory, moreover, suggested that the United States was supposed to be different from "the old countries," that it was a nation "conceived in liberty and dedicated to the proposition that all men are created equal." Revolutionaries would be "plain fools" if they did not make use of this factor in American psychology, and use it to suggest that the United States was a nation "in which there were not to be rich and poor, oppressors and oppressed, exploiters and exploited."[24]

Still, they shouldn't be "sentimental" or selective in drawing upon the American past. After all, the "rising capitalist class" developed notions of liberty in its own self-interest, and the "dominant tradition" in American history was "one of constant and severe class-struggle" and imperial conquest. Some radicals seemed to believe that simply by appropriating patriotic symbols and slogans, the left would "get the following instead of the Longs and the Coughlins" (a reference to Huey P. Long and Charles Coughlin, populist rabble-rousers of the Depression era). Yet such symbols and slogans, like religion, existed to tie workers to the existing order, in this case to the "mystical" belief that there was such a thing as a "nation or community ... to which we belong and which protects us" but which really functioned to mask class differences. The task of revolutionaries, therefore, was to *critically* engage with American culture and history in order to *break* the working class's attachment to the nation and replace it with "the emotion of class."[25]

Muste further rejected Budenz's argument that American radicalism had been corrupted by the European left's obsession with questions of theory that served only to confuse workers and enervate revolutionaries. While agreeing that the left had a "lunatic fringe," Muste insisted that questions of the united front, trade union policy, socialism in one country, and the foreign policy of the Soviet Union were vitally important to American workers. The growing threats of fascism and another world war were "neither remote nor abstract issues for American workers"; they were, moreover "international, not national" in their origins and scope. As for Budenz's proposal for a constitutional amendment, it was "clearly and utterly out of accord with the position of the Workers' Party."[26]

Muste's deft critique allows us to revisit the cultural politics of the 1930s. Budenz's American approach was indeed a sort of "Don't Tread on Me" version of working-class militancy, and in moments of mass mobilization—when he was leading strikes or protests by the unemployed—he was often dismayed to discover fascistic and nationalist elements rallying to his cause. As Muste would later observe, Budenz "thought of himself ... as a combination of Patrick Henry and Minute Man, carrying forward the American revolution in the twentieth century. He had only the slightest interest in theory and was inclined to regard theories as 'Europeanisms.'" Muste surmised that this was "the thread of consistency in Budenz's political career," which would evolve from Musteite to Communist to patriotic Catholic eager to inform on his former comrades for the House Committee on Un-American Activities (known as HUAC).[27]

Muste's Americanism, on the other hand, involved a *critical* reckoning with American history and culture in order to forge oppositional and ultimately transformative identities, narratives, and solidarities. At the same time, the tone of Muste's articles suggested that he had departed from the spirit that had galvanized progressive unionists to form the CPLA in the first place. Over the course of 1933, as he incorporated the Leninist notion of a vanguard party into his thinking, his language and approach shifted from openness and contingency toward firmness and rigidity. For example, he had always insisted that mass organizations like unions be open to all regardless of political affiliation, but now he called on party members to deliberately shape their politics and ideology; mistakes and "dangerous tendencies" must be faced and "immediately and ruthlessly" corrected, he instructed. The irony was that he himself became the victim of the same discourse as the Trotskyists accused him of "being reactionary ... on the question of internationalism."[28]

Indeed, despite his vociferous defense of unity with the Trotskyists, Muste found the experience of fusing the two parties deeply traumatic. He had hoped the new WP would assume leadership of an increasingly insurgent working class, but instead found himself beset by factional fights over the question of whether or not the party should pursue the "French Turn" in which Trotskyists would enter the Socialist Party in order to make it part of the Fourth International. Muste deeply opposed the move; he thought it was unethical to enter another party on false premises, and he thought that the SP was hopelessly reformist and therefore unlikely to shift to the left. In the intraparty debates over the French Turn, Muste felt that his opponents used duplicitous methods to undermine his position. Meanwhile, in an ironic twist, his former students and followers in the newly formed CIO did not welcome his far-left perspective, and in fact used his own organizing principles against him. For example, during a sit-down strike in Akron, Ohio, in February 1936, Brookwood alumnus Rose Pesotta, now a CIO organizer, rejected his argument that the agreement be thrown out because it did not contain provisions for the closed shop. "You taught us to organize the mass production workers. You laid stress on both the practical and ethical sides. And you never let us forget that when strikes are settled, they must be settled honorably. I won't fail your teaching now," she perfunctorily informed him.[29]

On the sidelines of the labor movement, on the one hand, and a leader of a political party whose strategy he detested, on the other, Muste faced a predicament. He could have joined the CIO, but that would have involved compromising his revolutionary principles. As he recalled, it would have involved becoming "identified with the New Deal ... and, presently, with support of the war—this would have been for me the abandonment of my deepest convictions." As for the CP, he saw it as hopelessly bureaucratic and Stalinist, and feared that its alliance with liberals and social democrats would lead the country into another world war. A mystical experience in a French church in the summer of 1936 helped him to resolve this political and personal crisis. Once more a devout Christian and pacifist, he adopted Gandhian nonviolence, rather than Leninism, as a means of revolutionizing society. In 1940, he became the head of the Fellowship of Reconciliation, the leading peace organization of the United States, through which he organized early experiments in nonviolent direct action against racism. Later, he would lead the peace movement in opposition to nuclear proliferation, U.S. empire, and the war in Vietnam.[30]

As for Budenz, he remained unpersuaded by Muste's argument and had, in fact, already begun secret talks with the Communists. He publicly announced his CP membership in October 1935;

unlike the AWP, which had "childishly" abandoned the American approach, he wrote, the CP had embraced "revolutionary realism ... the defense of 'bourgeois democratic rights' as a weapon against Fascism and as a mantle for the advancement of the revolution; the use of national revolutionary traditions for the driving forward of Socialism and internationalism."

Because of his Midwestern roots, the party had Budenz operate in the open as labor editor of the *Daily Worker*, where he would do the same work he had as editor of *Labor Action*: publicize and celebrate labor militancy and promote the American approach. As he had in the WP, he sometimes got in trouble for failing to follow the party line, such as the time he suggested that religion was a "private matter." Overall, however, he was known as a loyal party member, even going so far as to inform on his former comrades as part of Joseph Stalin's machinations against Leon Trotsky. But when the Communists formally abandoned the Popular Front in April 1945, he secretly reconverted to Catholicism and began informing on the party to HUAC. When he announced his resignation from the CP and return to the church in October 1945, he faced much of the same criticism he had from the WP for "conceal[ing] his thoughts in a most secretive manner," as Elizabeth Gurley Flynn put it. Budenz would go on to become one of the most notorious anti-Communists of the postwar years.[31]

What, then, are we to make of Muste, Budenz, and the movement they led? We could read their disillusionment with Marxism—one stayed on the left, but not as a Marxist, and the other went right—as a metaphor for the failures of the Old Left. Indeed, their efforts and experiences suggest that Denning is too sanguine about the Popular Front. The Americanist emphasis had pitfalls and limitations that could re-inscribe rather than challenge nationalism, and there were clearly sectarian and dogmatic elements in the politics of the 1920s and 1930s that were ultimately destructive of the labor left's most creative elements.

On the other hand, looking backward, what stands out is the dynamism of progressive unionism in the 1920s, a time usually seen as a quiescent one for American labor. In a period not unlike our own, marked by trade union decline, extreme maldistribution of wealth, and empowered capital, trade unionists and radical intellectuals creatively engaged with American mass culture, philosophy, and history to construct a cultural front and a democratic theory and practice of Marxism. Their efforts helped to give birth to the "age of the CIO," which creatively reimagined what it meant to be American in counter-hegemonic terms. Labor progressives also helped to construct the New Deal state and its unprecedented use of government power to regulate industry and protect workers. At the time, it seemed to many, including Muste and Budenz, that these achievements were irreversible, and that the labor movement had been incorporated into the state. In fact, however, as the work of Nelson Lichtenstein reminds us, labor immediately faced a counterattack and increasingly found itself in a rather subordinate position within the Democratic Party. The spirit of the CPLA thus seems quite relevant for today, as Americans seek to resolve pressing problems of social inequality, fragmentation, and environmental catastrophe. Perhaps this appreciative—yet also unromanticized—history of American engagement with the Marxist tradition offers an instructive and rich resource.[32]

Notes

1 Michael Denning, *The Cultural Front: The Laboring of American Culture in the Twentieth Century* (London: Verso, 1997). For the 1930s as fundamentally middle-class and conservative, see Warren Sussman, *Culture as History: The Transformation of American Society in the Twentieth Century* (New York: Pantheon, 1985). Other works that emphasize the role of the Communist Party (understood as Stalinism) include Theodore Draper, *American Communism and Soviet Russia* (New York: Viking Press, 1957) and Harvey Klehr, *The Heyday of American Communism: The Depression Decade* (New York: Basic Books, 1984).

2 For Denning's critics, see, for example, Adam Schatz, "The Cultural Front," *The Nation* 264, no. 9 (March 10, 1997) and responses by Alfred Kazin and Terry Cooney in "Symposium: Culture and Commitment Reconsidered," *Intellectual History Newsletter* 19 (1997). For the CIO, see Patricia Sullivan, *Days of Hope: Race and Democracy in the New Deal Era* (Chapel Hill: University of North Carolina Press, 1996); Lizabeth Cohen, *Making a New Deal: Industrial Workers in Chicago, 1919–1939* (New York: Cambridge University Press, 1990); Robert H. Zieger, *The CIO 1935–1955* (Chapel Hill: University of North Carolina

Press, 1997); and Nelson Lichtenstein, *State of the Union: A Century of American Labor* (Princeton: Princeton University Press; revised edition, 2013). For recent revisionist accounts of the CP see, for example, Glenda Gilmore, *Defying Dixie: The Radical Roots of Civil Rights, 1919–1950* (New York: Norton, 2008); Brian Dolinar, *The Black Cultural Front: Black Writers and Artists of the Depression Decade* (Jackson: University of Mississippi Press, 2012); and Bill V. Mullen, *Popular Fronts: Chicago and African American Cultural Politics* (Urbana-Champlain: University of Illinois Press, 2015). Notably, much of this scholarship focuses on the CP's antiracism for which it was indeed prophetic.

3   Biographies of Muste include Leilah Danielson, *American Gandhi: A. J. Muste and the History of Radicalism in the Twentieth Century* (Philadelphia: University of Pennsylvania Press, 2014) and Joann Oimann Robinson, *Abraham Went Out: A Biography of A. J. Muste* (Philadelphia: Temple University Press, 1981). For Budenz, see Jimmy Grant, "Louis Francis Budenz: The Origins of a Professional Ex-Communist" (Ph.D. diss., University of South Carolina, 2006) and Louis Budenz, *This is My Story* (New York: McGraw, 1947). Muste and Budenz's approach to working-class organization and mobilization is discussed in more detail below. See, for example, Louis Budenz, "What Main Street Labor Thinks About It," *Labor Age* 11 (October 1922): 5–7; Budenz, "Labor History in the Making," *Labor Age* 15, no. 8 (August 1926): 24–26; and A. J. Muste, "Militant Progressivism," *Modern Quarterly* 4, no. 4 (May–August 1928): 332–41. Labor progressives had worked closely with the CP until 1928, when it entered its Third Period, which involved attacking other left-wing groups and pursuing "dual unionism."

4   Devere Allen, "Labor Must Learn: A. J. Muste," *Adventurous Americans* (New York: Farrar and Rinehart, 1932): 100. For Budenz's personality, see Grant, "Louis Francis Budenz," 23–24, 31, 126–27; Muste to Elmer Cope, July 27, 1931, and August 2, 1931, microfilm reel 5, Elmer Cope Papers, 1903–1965, Ohio Historical Society; Muste, "Sketches for an Autobiography," in *The Essays of A. J. Muste*, ed. Nat Hentoff (New York: Simon & Schuster, 1967), 157, 170–74.

5   Muste, "Sketches," 157. See also Grant, "Louis Frances Budenz," 170–74. Michael Denning and Nelson Lichtenstein emphasize the role of Brookwood in serving as a sort of "cadre school" for the CIO. See Denning, *The Cultural Front*, 68–72 and Nelson Lichtenstein, "Falling in Love Again? Intellectuals and the Labor Movement in Post-war America," *New Labor Forum* (Spring/Summer 1999): 21. Unions and left-wing political groups had long recognized the importance of educating their members in trade union fundamentals and/or socialist

theory, but in the 1920s a social movement emerged, complete with a distinctive theoretical framework and counter-cultural institutions and practices. For the history of workers' education in the 1920s, see Tobias Higbie, *Labor's Mind: A History of Working-Class Intellectual Life* (Urbana-Champaign: University of Illinois Press, 2019); Danielson, *American Gandhi*, esp. chapters 3–5; Karyn Hollis, *Liberating Voices: Writing at the Bryn Maw Summer School for Women Workers* (Carbondale: Southern Illinois University Press, 2004); and Richard Altenbaugh, *Education for Struggle: The American Labor Colleges of the 1920s and 1930s* (Philadelphia: Temple University Press, 1990).

6 See Denning, *The Cultural Front*, 7, 431–32. The vast majority of CPLA members were members or officers of AFL or independent unions. See Leonard Bright, "CPLA Organizes," *Labor Age* 18, no. 6 (June 1929): 3–6.

7 For Dewey and education, see Robert Westbrook, *John Dewey and American Democracy* (Ithaca: Cornell University Press, 1993), esp. 167–73. For the workers' education movement's pedagogy, see, for example, Louis Budenz, "Success! Through Workers' Education," *Labor Age* 14, no. 5 (May 1925): 1–3; Alexander Fichandler, "Our Minds and Behavior," *Labor Age* 15, no. 10 (October 1926): 18–19; Clint Golden, "Across America: A Workers' Education Pilgrimage," *Labor Age* 14, no. 7 (September 1925): 4–5; and Fannia Cohn, "Workers' Education Aims at Power," *Labor Age* 16, no. 11 (November 1927): 9–10. J. B. S. Hardman's comments can be found in Hardman, ed., *American Labor Dynamics in the Light of Post-War Developments: An Inquiry by Thirty-Two Labor Men, Teachers, Editors, and Technicians* (Harcourt, Brace & Co., 1928): 106, 109.

8 William Green, "Workers' Education," *American Federationist* 35, no. 10 (October 1928): 1170–71; Muste, "The Challenge to Progressives," *Labor Age* 18, no. 2 (February 1929): 1–4; and Muste, "Progressives Can Win," *Labor Age* 18, no. 2 (February 1929): 8–9. The AFL had collaborated with labor progressives in the workers' education movement until its attack on Brookwood in 1928. See, for example, Carl Haessler, "A. F. of L. Convention High Lights," *Labor Age* 18, no. 1 (January 1929): 3–4 and Muste, "Workers' Education Bureau Surrenders to Reaction," *Labor Age* 18, no. 3 (March 1929): 5–8. For the AFL's anti-intellectualism, see Richard Hofstadter, *Anti-Intellectualism in American Life* (New York: Vintage, 1966): 284–90.

9 Editorial, "The Job Ahead" *Labor Age* 22, no. 1 (December–January 1933): 3; Muste, "Militant Progressivism?" *The Modern Quarterly* 4, no. 4 (May–August 1928): 333–34; and Hardman, "Marx and Marxism after Fifty Years," *Labor Age* 22, no. 1 (February–March 1933): 4–5.

See also Danielson, *American Gandhi*, 66–67, and Higbie, *Labor's Mind*, 63–64.

10 Muste, letter to the editor, *The Nation* 128, no. 3334 (May 29, 1929), 647; Budenz, "Following the Fight," *Labor Age* 19, no. 1 (January 1930): 15; and Muste, "Mother Throws out the Baby," *Labor Age* 17, no. 10 (October 1928): 20–22. On the AFL's antiradicalism, see the recent book by Jennifer Luff, *Commonsense Anticommunism: Labor and Civil Liberties between the Wars* (Chapel Hill: University of North Carolina Press, 2012). On the CP, see, for example, James R. Barrett, *William Z. Foster and the Tragedy of American Radicalism* (Urbana: University of Illinois Press, 2001). John H. M. Laslett provides a history of the Socialist Party and its relationship with American unions in his *Labor and the Left* (New York: Basic Books, 1970). The CPLA's attempt to mix realism and revolutionism "was then hailed as 'practical labor idealism,'" as Brookwood alumnus Len De Caux recalled in *Labor Radical: From the Wobblies to the CIO* (Boston: Beacon Press, 1971), 101. This approach reflected Muste's commitment to observing "working-class ethics" in their relations with other groups, seeking unity whenever possible and avoiding *ad hominin* attacks. See Muste, "Working-class Ethics," *Labor Age* 21, no. 11 (November 1932): 16–18. For an example of CP attacks on the Musteites, see William Z. Foster, *Little Brothers of the Big Labor Fakers* (New York: Trade Union Unity League, 1931).

11 David J. Saposs, *The Future of Radicalism in the Labor Movement*, copy in folder 12, box 7, David J. Saposs Papers, Wisconsin Historical Society (the CPLA reprinted it in pamphlet form); Muste editorial, "Dramatizing the Labor Movement," *Brookwood Review*, vol. 4, no. 2 (December 1925), 2; Muste editorial, "Are Trade Unionists Human Beings?" *Brookwood Review* 4, no. 5 (March 1926), 2; M. H. Hedges, "Organizing the Hidden Men," *Labor Age* 15, no. 12 (December 1926): 2–3; and M. H. Hedges, "Under the Telescope," *Labor Age* 16, no. 2 (February 1927): 18–19.

12 Budenz, "What Main Street Labor Thinks About It," 5–7; Report of the NEC to the CPLA Convention, September 3–5, 1932, folder 29, box 28, Brookwood Labor College Collection, Archives of Labor and Urban Affairs, Walter P. Reuther Library, Wayne State University. See also Budenz, *This is My Story*, 48–49.

13 Leonard Wilcox, *V. F. Calverton: Radical in the American Grain* (Philadelphia: Temple University Press, 1992), 157–59; Hardman, ed., *American Labor Dynamics in the Light of Post-War Developments*; and Editorial, *Our America* 1, no. 1 (January 1933). See also the following items in the J. B. S. Hardman Papers, Tamiment Library and

Robert F. Wagner Labor Archives, New York University: Lewis Corey, Felix Cohen, J. B. S. Hardman, William, L. Nunn, James Rorty, D. J. Saposs, "The XYZ Monthly," January 22, 1932, folder 3, box 6; CPLA NEC Meeting Minutes, May 10, 1932, folder 4, box 38; and "Report of the NEC to CPLA Convention," September 3–5, 1932, folder 4, box 38. Muste, Hardman, and Calverton had been discussing the idea of the American Labor Associates since 1928. See Hardman to Calverton, January 30, 1928, box 7, V. F. Calverton Papers, Manuscripts and Archives Division, New York Public Library. Not surprisingly, CPLA members found an intellectual ally in Sidney Hook whose *Towards the Understanding of Karl Marx* (1933) systematically integrated pragmatism and Marxism. See Christopher Phelps, *Young Sidney Hook: Marxist and Pragmatist* (Ithaca: Cornell University Press, 1997).

14 For the CPLA's involvement in these labor strikes and the unemployed movement, see Danielson, *American Gandhi*, chapter 5; Tom Tippett, *When Southern Labor Stirs* (New York: J. Cape and H. Smith, 1931), 172, 157–62; Roy Rosenzweig, "Radicals and the Jobless: The Musteites and the Unemployed Leagues, 1932–36," *Labor History* 16, no. 1 (Winter 1975): 52–77; Rosenzweig, and "Organizing the Unemployed: The Early Years of the Great Depression, 1929–1933," *Radical America* 10 (July–August 1976): 37–60; and Bernstein, *The Lean Years* (New York: Penguin, 1966), 30–41, 358–90. See also Melvyn Dubofsky and Warren Van Tine, *John L. Lewis: A Biography* (Urbana: University of Illinois Press, 1986): 157–72.

15 Muste, "Sketches," 155–56; Muste, "Message to CPLA Organizers, Branches and Active Workers," March 10, 1933, folder 4, box 38, Hardman Papers. See also Edmund Wilson, quoted in Leon Edel's Introduction to Wilson's *The Thirties: From Notebooks and Diaries of the Period* (NY: Farrar, Straus and Giroux): xv.

16 Folder 14, box 28, Brookwood Collection, is full of letters from educators, Socialists, and labor organizers opposing this move. See also Muste to Leonard Bright, October 20, 1931, Box 28, folder 14 and Muste to Chas. Gardner, February 17, 1932, folder 15, box 28, Brookwood Collection.

17 For criticism of the merger, see, for example, the following items in folder 5, box 38, Hardman Papers: Howe to Hardman, June 21, 1934; Hardman to Howe, June 28, 1934; Budenz and Hardman memos, appendix to the "Summary of Negotiations," AWP Negotiating Committee to the membership, August 30, 1934. See also "Many groups Discuss AWP Program," *Labor Action* 2, no. 5 (March 15, 1934): 4, and Grant, "Louis Francis Budenz," 220–62. During this period, Muste defended the AWP's American approach against the Trotskyists' charge that

they were nationalistic. See Muste, "Labor Internationalism," *Labor Action* 1, no. 13 (December 20, 1933): 3, and Muste, "Building Labor Internationalism," *Labor Action* 2, no. 13 (July 15, 1934): 5.

18 For the CPLA's prior work in Toledo, see editorial, "Bosses Hit by Militant Food Strike," *Labor Action* 1, no. 7 (July 1, 1933): 2 and "Lehigh City Jobless League Help Strikers," *Labor Action* 1, no. 11 (October 11, 1933): 2. For the strike, see Muste, "The Battle of Toledo," *The Nation* 138, no. 3596 (June 6, 1934): 639–40, and Muste, "Terror in Toledo," *Labor Action* 2, no. 10 (June 1, 1934): 1–3; Editorial, "The Auto-Lite Agreement," *Labor Action* 2, no. 11 (June 15, 1934): 2; Bernstein, *The Turbulent Years* (New York: Houghton Mifflin, 1970), 217–25, 224–29; and Grant, "Louis Francis Budenz," 217.

19 Editorial, "The Auto-Lite Agreement," 2; Budenz, "For an American Revolutionary Approach," *Modern Monthly* 9 (March 1935): 14; and Budenz and Hardman memos, appendix to "Summary of Negotiations."

20 See "AWP Convention Votes Unanimously for Merger," *Labor Action* 2, no. 22 (December 15, 1934): 3; "WP Program of Action," *New Militant* 1, no. 10 (February 9, 1935): 3. Despite the "unanimous vote," there was considerable opposition to the merger. By the end of 1935, most members of the former AWP had resigned from the WP. Many of them joined former Musteites who were becoming leaders in the revitalized labor movement, such as John Brophy, Len De Caux, Julius Hochman, Rose Pesotta, Lucille Kohn, Tom Tippett, Sarah Rozner, Victor Reuther, Clint Golden, Mark Starr, Elmer Cope, Cara Cook, and Sam Pollock. Those who joined the CP included Budenz, Arnold Johnson, Bill Reich, Winslow Hallett, and Anthony Ramuglia. See Danielson, *American Gandhi*, 188–95.

21 Muste, "Sketches," 170; Grant, "Louis Francis Budenz," 252–53, 239.

22 Budenz, "For an American Revolutionary Approach," 14–18.

23 Ibid., 16. See also Budenz, "Winning America," *Modern Monthly* 12 (May, 1935): 142–46.

24 Muste, *The American Approach* (pamphlet). Muste's "The American Approach" appeared in series form over the course of the summer of 1935 in the *New Militant*, and later as a WP pamphlet. A copy of the pamphlet can be found in the A. J. Muste Papers (microfilm edition), Swarthmore College Peace Collection, reel 6. See also Minutes of the Political Committee, March 11, 1935 and April 28, 1935, Max Shachtman Papers (microfilm edition), Tamiment Library and Robert F. Wagner Labor Archives, New York University, reel 12.

25 Muste, *The American Approach*.

26 Ibid.

27 Muste, "Sketches," 123. For Budenz's fears about fascism and Americanism see his editorial comment in *Labor Age* 22, no. 1 (February–March 1933): 2–3.
28 Muste, "The Party and the Leagues," *Labor Action* 2, no. 14 (August 1, 1934): 5; Muste editorial, "Political Strikes," *Labor Action* 2, no. 10 (June 1, 1934): 4; and Minutes of Political Committee, October 28, 1935, Shachtman papers, reel 12. For Muste's reflections on this period, see Muste, "Sketches," 152–53.
29 The debates over the French Turn can be found in the Shachtman papers, reel 12. See also Muste, "Sketches," 162–67; Muste, "Return to Pacifism" (1936), reprinted in *The Essays of A. J. Muste*, ed. Hentoff, 199–201; and James Cannon, *History of American Trotskyism: Report of a Participant* (3rd edition, New York: Pathfinder Press, 1995), 207–35. As Muste predicted, the Cannonites never managed to turn the SP into a movement of the Fourth International but rather found themselves expelled in the summer of 1937 for divisive activities. See George Breitman, Paul LeBlanc, and Alan Wald, eds., *Trotskyism in the United States: Essays and Reconsiderations* (Haymarket Books, 2016 reprint edition), 22–25. For the Rose Pesotta quote, see her *Bread Upon the Waters* (Ithaca, N.Y.: ILR Press, 1987), 223–25.
30 See Muste, "Sketches," 152–53. Apparently, the Steel Workers Organizing Committee wanted to hire him as educational director. See B. J. Widick, letter to the editor, *Labor History* (June 5, 1975): 563–64. For Muste's tenure at the Fellowship of Reconciliation and his postwar career, see Danielson, *American Gandhi*.
31 Grant, "Louis Francis Budenz," 263, 270–71, 314–49, and 379. See also Budenz, *This is My Story*, 126–28 and Robert M. Lichtman, Louis Budenz, the FBI, and "The List of 400 Concealed Communists," *American Communist History* 3, no. 1 (June 2004): 25–54.
32 See Lichtenstein, *State of the Union*. Despite his anti-communism, Budenz always remained a supporter of labor rights. Muste, like other postwar radical intellectuals, believed that labor had traded its independence in exchange for legitimacy, and placed his hopes for social change in groups like pacifists, the young, and African Americans. See, for example, Muste, typescript, "Foundations of Democracy: The Role of Economic Groups," (c. 1945), Muste Papers (microfilm edition), reel 4.

4

Women, the family, and sexuality in U.S. Communist Party publications: refashioning Marxism for the Popular Front era

Jodie Collins

In 1936 a large twenty-page pamphlet entitled *20th Century Americanism* was issued by Workers Library Publishers of the Communist Party of the United States of America (CPUSA). The title, emblazoned across the front page, is followed by a subheading asking, "What does every American family want?" Filling the rest of the cover is a photographic image of Earl Browder, leader of the CPUSA, with a little girl on his shoulders, and his wife, Raissa Browder, alongside him (Figure 4.1).[1]

This pamphlet marked not only the launch of the Party's "Communism is Twentieth Century Americanism" slogan, but the refashioning of the Party's image in relation to the family. The pamphlet is a graphic manifesto for the Popular Front, emphasizing the "American tradition" in the fight against fascism and racial inequality. Towards the end of the pamphlet, "The Land of Socialism" is printed across a page with photos of smiling citizens of the USSR and Stalin, boasting of the successes of socialism in the Soviet Union. But it was the wholesome yet politically ambiguous front cover that set the tone for the Party's approach to the family in future pamphlets and publications.

In the Party's shift to promoting more traditional American family values, publications—especially those aimed at women—appealed to emotion and moralism, often at the expense of a Marxist interrogation of American society. While education of both party members and the masses had previously been a priority when it came to party literature, simplified and stereotypical narratives were now often used to promote and justify the Party line. The pamphlets of the period show how, in contrast to the arguments of a number of scholars, the Party's abandonment of a Marxist analysis of the family, gender, and sexuality during the Popular Front disoriented the fight for women's liberation within the Party and the broader left in which it was so influential.

Marxism and gender

From the period of the first Red Scare of 1919–1920 and persisting in varying degrees throughout the twentieth century, an ideology developed in the United States which centered around a supposed "crisis" of the family, and the "related anxieties over changing gender and sexual norms" which was believed to be inextricably linked to the rise of radicalism in America.[2] "Under the banner of Americanism," writes Erica J. Ryan, "social conservatives, nativists, business elites, society women, settlement workers, and 'super' patriots ... reinforced the patriarchal family as a symbol of patriotism and capitalism, a producer of conservative gender norms, a promoter of assimilation, and a tool of social control in the effort [to] contain sex modernism."[3]

There was a basis for this fear. Radicals had for many decades been challenging traditional ideas about family, marriage, sex, and gender. Indeed, in the *Communist Manifesto* Marx and Engels had proclaimed: "Abolition of the family! Even the most radical flare up at this infamous proposal of the Communists."[4] Marxists had typically seen marriage and the traditional family as institutions developed to sustain private property ownership and reinforce reactionary morality and patriarchy, and socialists around the world were, particularly by the turn of the twentieth century, involved in advancing ideas around female and sexual liberation.[5]

In the words of German Marxist Clara Zetkin, "The materialist view of history did not, it is true, give us ready-made answers to the woman question ... but it gave us something better: the correct and precise method of studying and understanding the question."[6] Engels's *The Origin of the Family, Private Property, and the State* (1884) was the touchstone for a Marxist understanding of the family, marriage, and sex, and August Bebel's *Women and Socialism* (1879)—particularly popular among American

Women, the family, and sexuality in U.S. Communism   97

Figure 4.1 Earl Browder, head of the Communist Party USA, projecting family values and adopting a paternal pose during the Popular Front. *Courtesy Social Movements Collection, University of Hawaii.*

Socialists—positioned the woman question into the larger framework of Marxist theory.[7] Central to the Marxist approach was the historical materialist analysis of the family and its origins and development alongside the changing modes of production, as well as its impact on social relations—particularly the subjugation of women—underlined by the hypocrisies borne out of the contradictions of the bourgeois family under capitalism.[8]

It was this Marxist analysis that guided the Bolsheviks' introduction of radical new laws in the Soviet Union shortly after the October Revolution. Making a concerted effort to abolish patriarchal relations and institutions, the 1918 Code on Marriage, the Family, and Guardianship gave women equal status to men, made divorce easy, abolished the category of "illegitimate" children, and vastly expanded communal facilities for childcare and domestic work to liberate women from the home. Abortion was made legal in 1920, and by 1922 homosexuality was decriminalized. Figures such as Alexandra Kollontai greatly contributed to making these landmark pieces of legislature possible and wrote influential works on sexual liberation.

Throughout the 1920s and 1930s, it was asserted particularly among the religious right that the Bolsheviks had turned Russia into an immoral, depraved cesspit.[9] One American Catholic pamphlet, for example, declared in 1930, "Russia has developed a vast multitude of semi-illiterate, corrupt, immoral, uncontrolled, and uncontrollable young men and women whose highest ideal is to satisfy the cravings of licentious appetite." This had been, according to the author, influenced by the work of pioneering Bolshevik "Madam Kollontai, with her doctrines of free love, free marriage, and jungle promiscuity." The Soviets had, through its "constant war on traditions, on the 'old family'—'old morals,' etc. ... plunged Russia into a complete moral chaos."[10]

Scholars such as Van Gosse have asserted that Marxist "dogma" stunted the women's movement in the Party during the 1920s; that "the focus of Marxists on productive and waged labor excludes women" and "denied the existence" of unwaged housewives and children.[11] However, many American women had been drawn to the CPUSA and Marxism on the basis of the radicalism of the new policies introduced by the Bolsheviks. "This revolution went beyond efforts to get women the vote or to make laws more equitable," explains Julia L. Mickenberg. "It meant professional opportunities for women. It meant psychological emancipation from social expectations. It meant romantic relationships based on mutual attraction and shared values and an end to the sexual double standard. It meant the possibility of women being mothers and also having careers."[12]

Progressive ideas around the roles of women both in society and within the Communist movement were visible throughout various Party publications. Sasha Small's *Women in Action*, for example, is a short but comprehensive pamphlet published for International Women's Day in February 1935—only months before the Popular Front policy was adopted—which begins with a sharp attack against the idea that "a woman's place is in the home" and describes the various valiant ways in which women have fought in strikes and protests throughout the decades. Describing how women textile workers "took their places, battling cops and tear gas" in the 1934 San Francisco General Strike and how women "threw themselves in front of the trucks that tried to take scab goods out of the factory" when 1,500 female cigar makers went on strike in Pennsylvania, the pamphlet also details their organizational skill, for example, in preparing relief kitchens for strikers and their major role in campaigning against war and fascism throughout 1934. In fact, women in this pamphlet are spoken of as being stronger and more valiant than the men. Small recalls how during the textile strike in Lawrence in 1912 police terror was "so fierce" that Bill Haywood, leader of the strike, "advised the women to stay off the picket lines," to which one striking woman responded that "Mr. Haywood can't keep us ladies from the picket line ... just because the cops will be there ... The men are alright but they're not so brave in striking as the ladies."[13]

Significantly, Small consistently calls attention to the many sacrifices made especially by black women in strikes and protests. From the black women who, in the ore-mine strikes in Alabama, "threw themselves on the railroad tracks to block trains carrying scabs," and the mothers of the Scottsboro Boys who traveled around the United States and Europe "mobilizing the millions behind the struggle" to free the falsely accused black teenagers, to the courage of figures like Harriet Tubman and Sojourner Truth in fighting against slavery.[14] The narrative of *Women in Action* clearly seeks to combat the dominant perceptions of women and femininity in American society by portraying them in active and assertive roles. Small concludes the pamphlet with the rallying call:

> We women of today have a splendid heritage of struggle behind us. We can draw courage from what has been before, for carrying on the

battles to come. We must gather strength and rally around us those who still hold back—millions of American women who still hide their slavery by their fireside, timid, fooled by hateful lies to chain them to their present drudgery. Our work has only just begun.[15]

Another pamphlet that illustrates the radicalism in the CPUSA's women's movement before the advent of the Popular Front is Grace Hutchins's *Women Who Work* (1932). Hutchins underlines how capitalism "aims to keep women subordinate" through lower wages which force women into positions of inferiority, "to the interest of the employing class, which knows how to use the schools, the churches, the family, the movies, and the radio to keep women in this subordinate position." Rather than simply rallying women behind "their men," the pamphlet highlights the pressing need for men to fight this propaganda and for solidarity with women, robustly arguing that the labor movement will be chronically weakened if it cannot properly include women. Like Small, Hutchins writes that "women of the working class prove themselves among the best and most determined fighters in the workers' struggles."[16]

Significantly, Hutchins also stresses that the majority of black mothers are unable to be housewives, as they are compelled to work to compensate for the low wages of their husbands:

> A greater proportion of Negro mothers must go out to work for a living, even while the children are still babies, because the husband's earnings are so small that they cannot possibly support the family ... More than half the Negro mothers who were living with their husbands and four-fifths of the other Negro mothers were on paid jobs away from the home, while one-fifth of the white mothers went out to work ... Negro women earned from one-third to one-half less than white women.[17]

The most significant CPUSA publication for women in the pre-Popular Front era was the magazine *Working Woman* (1929–1935), published by the Women's Commission. Written almost entirely by women, it reached a circulation of approximately 8,000 in the 1930s. *Working Woman* often featured dramatic illustrations by notable radical artists like William Gropper, and photography of women at work, on strike together, and even battling against police aggression in demonstrations. Women can be seen on the front cover of the

Women, the family, and sexuality in U.S. Communism 101

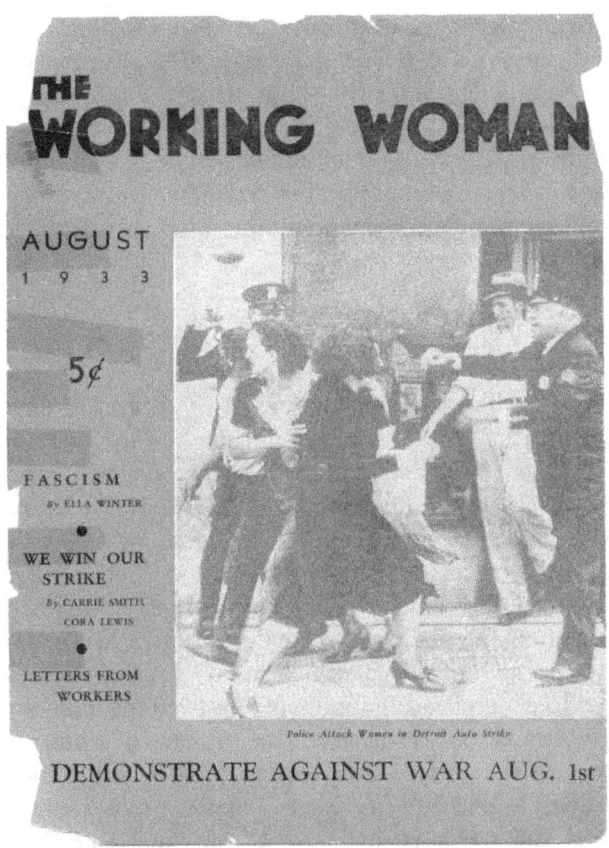

Figure 4.2 Militant action by women was a theme of *Working Woman*, as in this image of police attacking women during the Detroit auto strike of 1933. *Courtesy Marxist Internet Archive.*

August 1933 *Working Woman* being attacked by police during the Detroit auto workers strike (Figure 4.2). The fight against lynching and the call for black and white unity among working women were often promoted. On the front cover of the International Women's Day 1933 issue, a white woman and a black woman stand together making a calling signal similar to the famous image of Lilya Brik by Alexander Rodchenko. *Working Woman*'s June 1930 cover features a dramatic illustration of lynchings in the South, accompanied by the headline "Communist Party in Fight Against Lynching." Articles would frequently boast of women being at the forefront of the struggle of the American working class and vital in the success of strike action and demonstrations. But, fundamentally, the *Working Woman* educated readers and encouraged them to fight for liberation, and to question the values and structures which upheld their oppression. There was no appeal to feminine stereotypes, and discussions of the family, home, and motherhood are addressed firmly within a Marxist framework.

The family and the Popular Front

A key aspect of the Communist Party's new Popular Front approach from 1935 to 1939 was the repositioning of the Party as a paragon of American cultural and moral values, as in the slogan "Communism is Twentieth Century Americanism." While this was on the one hand a response to the pressure of anti-communism, its nationalism and conservatism dovetailed with the Soviet Union's changing laws on sex and the family. Homosexuality was made illegal in the USSR in 1934, then in 1936 the Law "On the Protection of Motherhood and Childhood" was introduced, which imposed strict abortion laws, promoted large families, and tightened restrictions on divorce. The aim of the legislation was to assert the primacy of women's role as mothers and to encourage large, strong families with values similar to those long established in western countries and pre-revolutionary Russia. This was a marked retreat from the Bolsheviks' "earlier laws which had focused on women's liberation and the "dissolution of bourgeois family life."[18] In fact, the classical Marxist idea that the family may "wither away" under communism was denounced under Stalin, who maintained "class enemies" were to blame for the theory. As printed in the official journal of the Commissariat of Justice:

> The state cannot exist without the family. Marriage is a positive value for the Socialist Soviet State only if the partners see in it a life-long union. So-called free love is a bourgeois invention ... Moreover, marriage receives its full value for the State only if there is progeny, and the consorts experience the highest happiness of parenthood.[19]

Parties around the world that were members of the Communist International had embarked upon similar campaigns. Perhaps most striking was an announcement made by a leading member of the French Communist Party (PCF), Paul Vaillant-Courturier, in *L'Humanité* soon after the Popular Front policy was announced in 1935:

> Save the family! Help us in our great inquiry in the interest of the right to love ... The Communists are confronted by a very grave situation. The country which they are to revolutionize, the French world, runs the danger of being crippled and depopulated. The maliciousness of a dying capitalism, its immorality, the egotism it creates, the misery, the clandestine abortion which it provokes, destroy the family. The Communists want to fight in the defense of the French family ... They want to take over a strong country and a fertile race. The USSR points the way. But it is necessary to take active measures to save the race.[20]

In much of the scholarship on the CPUSA's approach to women and the family there is a tendency to romanticize the Popular Front period in the United States; for example, Gosse wrote that the Popular Front approach saw improvements due to the Party's "new awareness of home, family, and neighborhood."[21] In turn, many blame Marxist theory for failures in the Party's approach to women. Denise Lynn indicated that the failures on the woman question during the Popular Front period were in fact borne out of "strict adherence to a Marxian class analysis," and, writing on the Soviet Union specifically, Janet Evans asserted that the increased conservatism in the 1930s was in part due to the limitations of Marxist theory of women's oppression and liberation.[22] Similarly, Rosalyn Baxandall has asserted that the Party "was narrow in its ideas about women, never straying from Marx's early classics or transforming their ideas to suit women's changing position in society."[23]

This blames Marxism for what was, in reality, the Popular Front's dilution and distortion of it. As the CPUSA began to exalt the family as a timeless institution—the "cornerstone of present-day civilization"—the Marxist theory of the family was inverted. Party pamphlets bemoaned that the family was being destroyed by "economic royalists" and "big business" and that, rather, it was the Communists who would "save" the family.[24] The pamphlet *20th Century Americanism* lamented on its first page, "The youth—the hope of America—are themselves without hope. For them America is no longer the land of opportunity. Where will they find jobs?

How will they be able to have a real American home and children? In these questions lies the tragedy of the young people today."[25]

Bearing a remarkable resemblance to right-wing advocacy of a return to traditional family values, the supposed eternal and moral nature of the family became synonymous in CP publications with an imagined ideal of America. Personifying this policy was Party leader Browder, who was portrayed across publications as "an exemplar of marital fidelity"—as seen by the photograph on the cover of *20th Century Americanism*—and repeatedly described as a "plain" man in various pamphlets.[26]

One pamphlet published by the Young Communist League of Massachusetts entitled *The American Way*, illustrated how altered the analysis of the family had become by 1938. Beginning with the question "Are you a good American citizen?" it expounds on the importance of voting before insisting:

YOUTH WANTS TO MARRY

Unemployment and low wages make it impossible for young people to marry. The unhappiness caused by this fact is immeasurable. Young people fall in love now just as deeply as ever. But they cannot be completely happy in their love in the face of poverty and an insecure future ... Population figures reflect the fact that youth is not marrying and having children ... A happy family life is the cornerstone of present-day civilization. Its destruction can only lead to complete demoralization. Let our "100% patriots" ponder that one!

...Youth should demand some sort of federal program that would give them financial assistance and make it possible for them to marry.[27]

This pamphlet illustrates not just the increased use of sentimental platitudes and lack of Marxist analysis in CP publications, but also the great extent to which the Party had tempered its radicalism. This was also visible in references to the family in the discussion of the rights of African Americans in the Young Communist League's pamphlet *Life Begins with Freedom*, authored by Henry Winston:

What do we young Negroes want from life? ... First, we want the right to become useful citizens ... Second, we want a chance to enjoy the good things that life provides. We want to have enough money to have a home that is bright, cheerful, and attractive ... Third, we want a chance to have a family life of our own. We want the chance to find the person we want to marry, to move to a home of our own, to settle down, to raise a family.[28]

In this instance, the fight for liberation for African Americans was softened. Having published powerful pamphlets such as *The Position of Negro Women* by Cyril Briggs and Eugene Gordon only two years earlier, which educated the reader on the multi-faceted historical and economic oppression of black American women and called for concerted organization to fight Jim Crow, this pamphlet conveys a desire not to fight, but to assimilate into existing white patriarchal institutions.[29]

As well as the broad appeal to "average" Americans that the rhetoric of family values potentially had, the CPUSA had particularly hoped that this pro-family campaign could help placate the religious groups which it was attempting to court at this time. As leader Earl Browder explains in the pamphlet *A Message to Catholics*, "To the millions of American Catholics who share such noble and humane ideas, and whose families and homes are threatened by those reactionary forces which have no religion or compassion, we extend our hands in simple friendship."[30] The American Communist Party was obediently mirroring the ideology of the Soviet Union under Stalin, which had begun its own campaign of zealously promoting the institutions of marriage, family, and motherhood, all part of the Soviet state's industrialization objectives.

Browder, however, remained anxious to quell doubts about the Party's dedication to traditional family and marriage. In 1938, the Party published two pamphlets—*The Democratic Front* and the aforementioned *A Message to Catholics*—in which a speech by Browder at the Party's Tenth National Convention was printed. He declared:

> Questions of family and social morality furnish no practical divisions between Catholics and Communists ... Contrary to much slander distributed by reactionary politicians in Catholic circles, the Communists are staunch upholders of the family. We consider sexual immorality, looseness and aberrations as the harmful product of bad social organization, and their increase in America today as largely products of the crisis of the capitalist system, of the demoralization among the upper classes which affects the masses by contagion, and we combat them as we combat all other harmful social manifestations.[31]

These pamphlets—particularly *A Message to Catholics*—were primarily intended for the American public, but this conservative message had already been outlined to Party members in an article by Browder in *The Communist* a year earlier:

> Any manifestation of looseness or penetration into our ranks of bourgeois habits, particularly with respect to personal life, must be rooted out, because it is precisely from such things as this that the enemies recruit in our ranks. It has been an almost invariable result of examination of political degeneration that it almost always is accompanied by personal degeneration. We must begin to examine the private lives of our leading cadres as a necessary and unavoidable part of the guarantee of the political integrity of our Party.[32]

It would have been clear to readers that sexual aberrations and degeneration were references to homosexuality. Although the CPUSA had historically been largely silent on the issue of homosexuality, it attracted a number of lesbian and gay members who, often socially ostracized and faced with state repression, were drawn to the Marxist tradition of challenging norms and oppression.[33] Moreover, there were instances of vocal support within the Party; for example in 1932 when John Pittman, a black Communist journalist, wrote an editorial for the newspaper he founded and edited, the *San Francisco Spokesman*, condemning prejudice against homosexuals and insisting that the Left should be at the forefront of the fight for their liberation.[34] Though homosexual members remained in the Party after Browder's pronouncements, this formalization of the CPUSA's position on sexuality was a tipping point for others. This included Los Angeles gay rights activist Harry Hay, who left in the same year. In a 1939 letter to an ex-lover, writer Harold Norse explained that he had left the Party as it "doesn't take kindly to Writers and queers anyway. And what if they found out about David and me? To the salt mines, dear."[35]

Denunciation of homosexuality and the policing of members' sex lives was a logical extension of the Party's increasing social conservatism which held up the monogamous family as the heart of civilization.[36] Though certainly in line with American anxieties about homosexuality and "sexual deviancy," the Party's decisive stance against homosexuality echoed the changed policy of the Soviet Union, which in 1934 made homosexuality illegal. Soon after, in a

March 1936 speech, People's Commissar of Justice N. V. Krylenko added homosexuals to the list of "class enemies, declassed elements, and criminal elements."[37] Engels's assertion that sexual life should be free from state interference was, much like his theory of the family, now dismissed as "bourgeois" under Stalin.[38]

Originally, the Bolsheviks had decriminalized homosexuality on the basis that it was both harmless and not a legal matter but a personal one. The young Soviet republic sent delegates to the International Congresses of the World League for Sexual Reform and was held up as a "model for world sexual reform" among Austrian and German sex reformers.[39] The spirit of the Bolsheviks' early reforms was summarized in a pamphlet by Dr. Grigorii Batkis, the Director of the Moscow Institute of Social Hygiene, written in 1923:

> The revolution let nothing remain of the old despotic and infinitely unscientific laws; it did not tread the path of reformist bourgeois legislation which, with juristic subtlety, still hangs on to the concept of property in the sexual sphere, and ultimately demands that the double standard hold sway over sexual life ... Concerning homosexuality, sodomy, and various other forms of sexual gratification, which are set down in European legislation as offenses against public morality—Soviet legislation treats these exactly the same as so-called "natural" intercourse. All forms of sexual intercourse are private matters. Only when there's use of force or duress, as in general when there's an injury or encroachment upon the rights of another person, is there a question of criminal prosecution.[40]

In stark contrast to Batkis's summary, the CPUSA's appeal to bourgeois morality and hypocrisies led to the Party publishing denunciations of homosexuality, closing off any alternatives to the heteronormative family unit.[41]

How the Party conveyed the image and role of women in its publications was inevitably affected by the Party's embrace of the traditional family and denunciation of sexual "immorality." Although the number of women working in industry was on the rise, the Party focused on attracting more middle-class housewives. This was not in and of itself a conservative policy; for example, Zetkin had in 1922 underlined the need to engage with and educate even "bourgeois" housewives:

> Under the pressure of inflation, of the glaring discrepancy between income and the cost of living, more and more housewives, including bourgeois housewives, are awakening to a recognition that present conditions—the continued existence of capitalism—are incompatible with their most basic interests in life ... Especially now I consider it particularly necessary to be concerned with the clearest, deepest, and most fundamental education of women.[42]

However, as the Popular Front policy began to permeate pamphlet publications, women began to be spoken of in terms of their relation to the family and home, moving away from discussions about empowering women to fight for liberation or as fellow comrades. Pamphlets accepted the complete economic dependence of women on their husbands and encouraged them to help empower their men so they could tend to the house and feed the children.[43] Party member Jenny Elizabeth Johnstone underlined this in the pamphlet *Women in Steel*: "This little pamphlet has been written in the hope that it will arouse more women to think of the need to go out and fight for the maintenance of their homes, for a better life for their families and children."[44]

Women in Steel was just one example of a trend of pamphlets written for and by women in a "relatable" manner, sometimes as dialogue, where women would chat about the struggles of modern life, and invoke an idea of a once-great America now being torn apart by the ravages of so-called "big business" and "economic royalists." As Johnstone writes, "We can regain our birthright of life, liberty and the pursuit of happiness."[45] The front page of the 1937 pamphlet, *The High Cost of Living*, features an illustration of a woman chasing milk and bread upwards in the style of a chart symbolizing the increase in prices. Written by Margaret Cowl as an imagined dialogue, it begins, "Hello, Kate. Been doing your shopping?" "Oh, hello, Sue; yes, as much as I could. But my heavens, prices are so high I just don't know how we're going to get through this winter." Kate's husband Dick eventually joins in the discussion, and Kate suggests "a baby parade" where women "march to City Hall in with our kids in their buggies" to "counteract the pressure on Congress from big business." "Boy, oh, boy," Dick exclaims, "I'd love to be there when that baby parade rolls up to the Mayor's office!"[46] While these pamphlets include some valuable discussion of wealth inequality, analyses remain shallow and concerned with mild social reform and appeals to government institutions over the advancement of any radical Marxist ideas.

Perhaps the best visual indicator of the CP's changing approach to women could be seen in the rebranding of the monthly magazine *Working Woman* to the glossier *Woman Today* (1936–37). Though a handful of scholars have discussed *Working Woman* and *Woman Today*, the stark differences between these publications remains unaddressed.[47] When *Working Woman* relaunched as *Woman Today* in 1936, the magazine began its first four months with a front-page illustration of a fashionable young woman in a hat (Figure 4.3). The first issue's leading story was titled "The Permanent Wave," a dull tale of a seventeen-year-old girl who wished to have her hair curled in a perm, but her father would not allow it. Each issue had features on beauty, cooking, and fashion. "Show us a woman completely devoid of interest in her appearance and we'll show you the woman who considers herself hopelessly unattractive … There is no such thing as a woman whose appearance cannot be improved to some extent." It perhaps need not be said that you wouldn't find similar columns aimed at men in the *Daily Worker* or *The Communist*.[48]

Woman Today was still more progressive than any other women's magazine in America, dealing with issues such as economic insecurity, sex discrimination, participating in unions, fascism, war, and immigration. Yet within the same pages it promoted stereotypes and, when compared to its predecessor *Working Woman*, had noticeably cooled its rhetoric and erased any trace of Marxist political theory. One letter from a pair of readers published in the August 1936 issue encapsulated the confusion that had been caused by Party publications among women in the Communist movement:

> As for the contents of the magazine—is it really necessary to lure women readers with cooking recipes and style and beauty notes? We are rather overwhelmed with that sort of thing already, it seems to us. But the really important thing about your publication, we feel, is that it does tend to perpetuate that most evil segregation of the sexes, in the matter of working-class organization and solidarity.[49]

While Marxists had sought to liberate women from their oppression within the family, the CPUSA publications of the Popular Front characterized women primarily in terms of their relation to the family unit and the gender stereotypes that reinforced it. Women

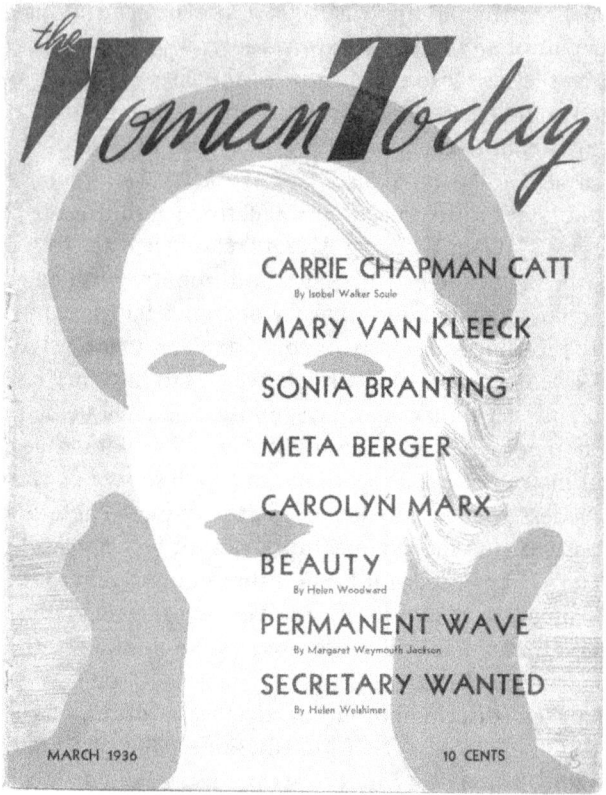

Figure 4.3 Conventional standards of women's beauty and fashion were celebrated in the first issue of *Woman Today*, issued in 1936. *Courtesy Marxist Internet Archive.*

were now differentiated and spoken of less as comrades and more as wives and mothers. This was underpinned by a conscious orientation towards a conciliation with American values and norms by Party leaders, vindicated and encouraged by the changing politics of the Soviet Union under Stalin, and disseminated to membership and the public through the publications for women. This left a legacy in that the same approach to women persisted in the Party's subsequent phases. After the Molotov–Ribbentrop pact in August 1939, when the CPUSA abandoned the Popular Front policy and began to tirelessly campaign against war, pamphlets made emotive appeals to maternal instinct to encourage anti-war sentiment:

"Women are funny. They care more for their dear ones—children and husband, or maybe sweetheart or father and brothers—than for anything else in the world. Women want to keep their dear ones, to take care of them, to do for them, to protect them."[50] When the Soviets joined the Allied war effort in 1941, this emotive appeal to supposed maternal instincts was abandoned. The war was now wholeheartedly endorsed by the Party as its pamphlets' tone shifted to emphasizing the strength and capabilities of women and their importance in the fight against fascism as they were encouraged to enter the workforce for war production. Now, as Elizabeth Gurley Flynn declared, "The glamor girl of today ... is the working woman ... They do not worry about their appearance. 'Feminine vanity' does not balk at dirty faces, greasy hands, hair plastered down under a protective cap ... a lunchbox instead of a fancy purse."[51]

What links all of these uses of gender conservatism is the justification of policies corresponding to the Soviet Union's wider policy shifts.

The CPUSA, the USSR, and abortion rights

It was perhaps the issue of abortion in the Soviet Union that best illustrated the extent to which Stalinization had disoriented the women's movement in the Party. In 1935 the Soviet government began charging for abortions, and in 1936 the procedure was completely prohibited. Abortion in the Soviet Union had, until this point, been free and regarded as a health matter, while in America abortion was linked to communism ideologically and *ipso facto* just another example of radicals' "sexual license and deviance."[52]

As the legislation which would outlaw abortion in the USSR was being finalized, the CPUSA published the pamphlet *Love—Family Life—Career: Behind the Soviet Law Limiting Abortions and Increasing Aid to Mothers* through the Woman Today Publishing Company, which produced *Woman Today* magazine. It contained the text of the Draft Law on Abortions and Aid to Mothers and an anonymously written introduction which explained to readers that in the Soviet Union, "abundance, security, [and] confidence in the future" meant that women no longer needed to have abortions.[53] Towards the end of its introduction, the pamphlet reveals sexual moralism and state control in the ideas supporting the ban: "In such a situation [of economic and social security] there can be no room for light-mindedness and irresponsibility in sexual relationship—all the more since their consequences bear most heavily upon the children of the offenders—hence the provisions of the new law designed to enforce parental responsibility."[54]

Love—Family Life—Career was the only pamphlet ever to be published through *Woman Today*, which suggests an urgency within the party to clarify its position on the question and quell any doubts women may have had about the new policy. Indeed, confusion over the law can be seen across Party publications. The September 1936 issue of *Health and Hygiene* opened with the statement: "It seems that whenever three people congregate these days the conversation invariably drifts to the new Soviet laws on abortion ... Quite a few of our friends, however, are honestly upset."[55] In one article by Sender Garlin, entitled "Every Day is Mother's Day in U.S.S.R.," Garlin writes how a "young American social worker ... failed to see the distinction between the law prohibiting abortions in the USSR and the official ban which exists in her own state."[56] Similarly, a reader wrote to the *Daily Worker*,

> Since the new Soviet law against abortions has gone into effect ... How can we justify the making illegal of abortions? Won't this simply put the abortionist doctors underground as they are in this country? ... Don't you think a woman has the right to choose for herself whether or when she will have a family?[57]

The only article-length protest against the law to be published in any Party publication was written in *Woman Today* by Dr. Hannah M. Stone. Stone was forthright in declaring the new abortion law as a "definite backward step" and clarified that Russia had legalized abortions in 1920 "because it frankly and realistically recognized the fact that women who do not wish to bear children will resort to any measure to have their pregnancy interrupted, and because they accepted the concept that parenthood should be conscious and voluntary."[58] Stone goes on to cite the Russian physician Dr. Vera Lebedeva, who had proclaimed that "the laws of procreation

... must be placed under human control. Conception must be subjected to the free will of the woman. Motherhood must be made conscious!" At the end of this article, an editor's note confirmed that *Woman Today* did "not wholly agree with" the author. Officially, every Party publication wholeheartedly supported the USSR's banning of abortion.

After 1936, discussion started to move towards the criticism of women who would possibly ever *want* an abortion. In a 1937 article in *Woman Today*, Beatrice Blosser asserts:

> I do not believe any normal woman wants to have an abortion. For the average working-class woman, it is purely a matter of economy. The professional woman does not want a child because it will interfere with her career. Yet every childless woman approaching the age of 35 wishes she had or could have a child ... Capitalism has created a selfishness in the middle class and professional woman which leads her to curb her natural instincts. Neither force operates in a socialist society. The only people who, living in a socialist society, could fail to see the progressive character of the new abortion law, would be those containing within themselves remnants of this old selfishness carried over from capitalism.[59]

In 1938, when the journalist Dorothy Dunbar Bromley criticized the Soviet Union's banning of abortion, an article by Louise Mitchell in the *Daily Worker* unequivocally stated, "Dorothy Dunbar Bromley stuck her head in the sand again the other day and started wailing [on] behalf of the Soviet women who had lost the *sweet rugged individualism of countless abortions* and had accepted happy motherhood instead."[60] The idea that a woman might not want children was now explained as a kind of bourgeois decadence. Such an interpretation would likely provoke American Communist women who questioned the new law to self-criticism. Nevertheless, the clear uneasiness among Communists upon the introduction of the law indicates that the abortion issue was tied to what many in the Party had believed the foundations of women's liberation under Communism to be. Free and accessible abortion was one of the revolutionary laws introduced in the earlier years of the Soviet Union designed to form the basis of equality between men and women; it was a measure frequently hailed by the Party in previous years, progressive even from the standpoint of reproductive rights by today's feminist standards.

Women, the family, and American Communism

Few organizations in America in the 1920s and 1930s could claim to be more progressive than the American Communist Party when it came to the roles of women. As Bryan D. Palmer writes, there is "no denying that women in the ranks of the revolutionary Party promoted progressive, feminist causes and struck important blows not only for female emancipation, but for women's public involvement in political struggle."[61]

The loss of a Marxist analysis in the approach to the family, women, and sexuality, however, caused disorientation and undermined the struggle for women's liberation. And indeed, while the Party made significant gains in recruiting women during the Popular Front period—with the numbers of women around 30–40 percent of CP membership—there is an absence of evidence that women were joining the Party because of its portrayal as a bulwark of heteronormative sexuality and traditional family values rather than their campaigns for equal pay and anti-fascism.[62] Moreover, the grassroots work done by women in the Party and progressive ideas which were developed by individual Communist women in the years that followed, as Bettina Aptheker has argued, grew precisely out of their application of Marxism, "with its emphasis on class and race and its dialectical analysis of social moments ... in spite of Party dogma."[63]

Central to Marxist analysis is the concept that the family is not a timeless, unchanging institution, but a social relation subject to historical change. But during the Popular Front, the American Communist Party abandoned this interrogation of capitalist relations and dismissed analysis of the historical and material origins of the family unit and the position of women. Importantly, it was not strictly its striving to "be American" per se which was to blame for the Party's conservatism in the latter half of the 1930s, but rather the Party's unfailing support for and imitation of the Soviet Union's changing policies under Stalin. This was underlined by the desire of the CPUSA's leadership to follow Comintern policy and ally with liberal forces in America by trimming its radicalism and embracing a conservative ideal of "Americanism." The CPUSA was filled with women who had admired the advances made in the Soviet Union. But when the USSR shifted its position on the family in the mid-1930s, Party members now had to adapt to what they

Women, the family, and sexuality in U.S. Communism 115

had previously understood to be conservative ideas and policies. The Party's pamphlets and magazines for women—usually written by women—attempted to reorient women's aspirations to fit the changing Party line. To do so was to compromise the Marxist foundations of the Party on questions of women, sexuality, and the family. In the words of Kate Millet, "Marxism was stood on its head."[64]

Notes

1 The identity of the young girl is something of a mystery, as Browder and his wife had three sons and no daughters.
2 Erica J. Ryan, *Red War on the Family: Sex, Gender and Americanism in the First Red Scare* (Philadelphia: Temple University Press, 2015), 169.
3 Ibid., 167.
4 Karl Marx and Frederick Engels, "Manifesto of the Communist Party," in *Karl Marx and Frederick Engels Collected Works*, Vol. 6 (London: Lawrence & Wishart, 1976), 501.
5 John Lauritsen and David Thorstad, *The Early Homosexual Rights Movement, 1863–1935* (New York: Times Change Press, 1974), 33.
6 Clara Zetkin, cited in Richard Stites, *The Women's Liberation Movement in Russia: Feminism, Nihilism, and Bolshevism, 1860–1930* (Princeton, NJ: Princeton University Press, 1978), 233.
7 Stites, *The Women's Liberation Movement in Russia*, 233.
8 This is summarized well in Richard Weikart, "Marx, Engels and the Abolition of the Family," *History of European Ideas* 18, no. 5 (1994), 658.
9 These sorts of rumors about depravity under Bolshevik rule were also popularly promoted in the UK, see for example Gisela C. Lebzelter, *Political Anti-Semitism in England, 1918–1939* (London: Macmillan Press, 1978), 16–17.
10 Edmund A. Walsh, *Why Pope Pius XI Asked Prayers for Russia on March 19, 1930* (New York: Catholic Near East Welfare Association, 1930), 19–20.
11 Van Gosse, "'To Organize in Every Neighborhood, in Every Home': The Gender Politics of American Communists between the Wars," *Radical History Review* 50 (1991), 109–10, 117, 134.
12 Julia L. Mickenberg, *American Girls in Red Russia: Chasing the Soviet Dream* (Chicago and London: University of Chicago Press, 2017), 6–7.
13 Sasha Small, *Women in Action* (New York: Workers Library Publishers, 1935), 8.

14 Ibid., 5.
15 Ibid., 12.
16 Grace Hutchins, *Women Who Work* (New York: International Publishers, 1932), 5.
17 Ibid., 7.
18 Lauren Kaminsky, "Utopian Visions of Family Life in the Stalin-Era Soviet Union," *Central European History* 44, no. 1 (2011), 71, 65.
19 *Sotsialisticheskaya Zakonnost*, 1939, no. 2, cited in Nicholas S. Timasheff, *The Great Retreat* (New York: E. P. Dutton & Co., 1946), 198.
20 Paul Vaillant-Courturier, *L'Humanité*, 31 October 1935, cited and translated in Kate Millet, *Sexual Politics* (London: Hart-Davis, 1971), 176.
21 Gosse, "'To Organize in Every Neighborhood,'" 109–10, 117, 134.
22 Denise Lynn, "Anti-Nazism and the Fear of Pronatalism in the American Popular Front," *Radical Americas* 1, no. 1 (2016), 27; Janet Evans, "The Communist Party of the Soviet Union and the Women's Question: The Case of the 1936 Decree 'In Defence of Mother and Child,'" *Journal of Contemporary History* 16, no. 4 (1981), 766.
23 Rosalyn Baxandall, "The Question Seldom Asked: Women and the CPUSA," in *New Studies in the Politics and Culture of U.S. Communism*, ed. Michael E. Brown, Randy Martin, Frank Rosengarten and George Snedeker (New York: Monthly Review Press, 1993), 142.
24 *The American Way* (Boston: Young Communist League, n.d., c. 1938), 5–6; Ann Rivington, *Women—Vote for Life!* (New York, Workers Library Publishers: 1940), 7, 8, 15; Maurice Thorez, *Catholics and Communists* (New York: Workers Library Publishers, 1938).
25 *20th Century Americanism* (New York: Workers Library Publishers, 1936), 1.
26 James G. Ryan, *Earl Browder: The Failure of American Communism* (Tuscaloosa: University of Alabama Press, 1997), 143. See for example M. J. Olgin, *That Man Browder* (New York: Workers Library Publishers, 1936) and A. B. Magill, *America Needs Earl Browder* (New York: Workers Library Publishers, 1941).
27 *The American Way* (Boston: Young Communist League, n.d., c. 1938), 5–6.
28 Henry Winston, *Life Begins with Freedom* (New York: New Age Publishers, 1937), 19.
29 Cyril Briggs and Eugene Gordon, *The Position of Negro Women* (New York: Workers Library Publishers, 1935).
30 Earl Browder, *A Message to Catholics* (New York: Workers Library Publishers, 1938).

31 Ibid., 9; Earl Browder, *The Democratic Front Jobs, Security, Democracy and Peace* (New York: Workers Library Publishers, 1938), 54.
32 Earl Browder, "The People's Front Moves Forward," *The Communist*, December 1937, 1101.
33 Aaron Lecklider, "TWO Witch-hunts: On (Not) Seeing Red in LGBT History," *American Communist History* 14, no. 3 (2015), 242.
34 John Pittman, "Prejudice Against Homosexuals," *The Spokesman*, November 3, 1932, cited in ibid.
35 Kathleen A. Brown and Elizabeth Faue, "Revolutionary Desires: Redefining the Politics of Sexuality of American Radicals, 1919–1945," in *Sexual Borderlands: Constructing an American Sexual Past*, ed. Kathleen Kennedy and Sharon Ullman (Columbus: Ohio State University, 2003), 288.
36 *The American Way* (Boston: Young Communist League, n.d., c. 1938), 5–6.
37 Julia M. Allen, *Passionate Commitments: The Lives of Anna Rochester and Grace Hutchins* (New York: State University of New York Press, 2013), 187; Dan Healey, *Homosexual Desire in Revolutionary Russia* (Chicago and London: University of Chicago Press, 2001), 195.
38 Millet, *Sexual Politics*, 175.
39 Lauritsen and Thorstad, *The Early Homosexual Rights Movement*, 66–67; Wilhelm Reich, *The Sexual Revolution* (New York: Farrar, Straus and Giroux, 1945), 157.
40 Grigory Batkis, *Die Sexualrevolution in Russland* (Berlin: Der Syndikalist, 1925). The original Russian was published in 1923. English translation from Lauritsen and Thorstad, *The Early Homosexual Rights Movement*, 64.
41 Elsa Jane Dixler, "The Woman Question: Women and the American Communist Party, 1921–1941" (Ph.D. diss., Yale University, 1974), 43.
42 Clara Zetkin, "Communist Work Among Women," in *Toward the United Front: Proceedings for the Fourth Congress of the Communist International, 1922*, ed. John Riddell (Chicago, IL: Haymarket, 2012), 850.
43 Dixler, "The Woman Question," 51.
44 Jenny Elizabeth Johnstone, *Women in Steel* (New York: Workers Library Publishers, 1937), 2.
45 Ibid., 29.
46 Margaret Cowl, *The High Cost of Living: How to Bring it Down* (New York: Workers Library Publishers, 1937), 12, 13.
47 See, for example, Mary E. Triece, *On the Picket Line: Strategies of Working-Class Women during the Depression* (Chicago: University of

Illinois Press, 2007) and Robert Schaffer, "Women and the Communist Party," *Socialist Review*, 45 (May–June 1979), 95.
48 *Woman Today,* March 1936, 25.
49 *Woman Today,* August 1936, 22.
50 Ann Rivington, *Women—Vote for Life!* (New York, Workers Library Publishers, 1940).
51 Elizabeth Gurley Flynn, *Women in the War* (New York: Workers Library Publishers, 1942).
52 Leslie J. Reagan, *When Abortion Was A Crime* (Berkeley: University of California Press, 1997), 172.
53 *Love—Family Life—Career* (New York: Woman Today Publishing, 1936), 5.
54 Ibid.
55 *Health and Hygiene* was a monthly magazine tied to the CPUSA which ran from 1935 to 1938 and was written by doctors offering left-wing perspectives on health matters.
56 Sender Garlin, "Everyday is Mother's Day in the U.S.S.R.," *Daily Worker*, June 18, 1936, 7.
57 "Questions and Answers," *Daily Worker*, July 3, 1936, 7.
58 Hannah M. Stone, "Soviet Russia's New Family Welfare Laws," *Woman Today,* September 1936, 8.
59 *Woman Today,* January 1937, 26.
60 Louise Mitchell, "Abortion in the U.S.S.R.: A reply to doubting (Thomas) Bromley," *Daily Worker*, July 13, 1938, 7. Emphasis my own.
61 Bryan D. Palmer, "Rethinking the Historiography of United States Communism," *American Communist History* 2, no. 2 (2003), 146.
62 Susan Ware, *Holding their own: American women in the 1930s* (Boston: Twayne Publishers, 1982), 120.
63 Bettina Aptheker, "Red Feminism: A Personal and Historical Reflection," *Science & Society* 66, no. 4 (Winter, 2002/2003), 522.
64 Millet, *Sexual Politics*, 175.

5

Rethinking Karl Marx: American liberalism from the New Deal to the Cold War

Andrew Hartman

Capitalism almost went bust in the 1930s. It was one of the worst crises the mighty economic system had known since its advent in the English countryside some three centuries prior. In the United States, the richest and most industrialized nation on the planet, 25 percent of workers were without jobs by 1933. Whole industries were on the brink of destruction. Automobile manufacturers shed over half their workforces. Small farmers across the vast continent, already beleaguered by falling prices and other chronic difficulties prevalent to an international system of economic competition, were forced off their land and conscripted into the rapidly multiplying armies of the unemployed. Breadlines and soup kitchens popped up to feed the hungry in city after city, where the homeless constructed shantytowns they christened "Hoovervilles" in honor of a president who would not lift a finger to help them. Hobos rode the rails in search of work, sleeping in boxcars and begging for a bite to eat from one stop to the next. Stories of babies dying of hunger in the arms of their mothers were not uncommon. Neither were food riots.[1]

The calamity of the Great Depression left millions of Americans wounded. Countless Americans discovered the name for the system that was to blame for their troubles: *capitalism*. Many also learned the name of the theorist who had prophesized capitalism's demise: *Karl Marx*. For most left-wingers of the early 1930s, Marx became the key to answering some of the most pressing questions of the time. Was capitalism on the verge of ultimate collapse? Were the American people up to the task of socialist revolution? No matter where someone stood on these questions, almost everyone on the left turned to Marx for answers. Several notable intellectuals hid themselves away in libraries in an obsessive effort to redefine Marx for America. If the genius of Marx could be made to fit America, perhaps all the difficult questions about capitalism and socialist revolution could be answered. Intellectuals who emphasized Marx in the 1930s include Sidney Hook, James Burnham, V. F. Calverton, Mike Gold, Lewis Corey, W. E. B. Du Bois, C. L. R. James, Reinhold Niebuhr, and Claudia Jones—the list goes on.

One such thinker who turned to Marx was Kenneth Burke, a brilliant autodidact and influential Marxist literary critic. Burke spent the decade developing a Marxist theory of ideology that was meant to help overcome the barriers to socialist revolution. He not only wanted to understand how people came to believe things, but also how such beliefs might be transformed. In his breakthrough 1935 book, *Permanence and Change*, Burke wrote that "the mere fact that something is to a man's interest is no guaranty that he will be interested in it." Most Americans ignored revolutionary writings or what was called "proletarian literature" and instead had a habit of reading escapist fiction. To this problem Marx was not exactly a guide, since he "tended to confuse the *is* and *ought to be*, so that we sometimes feel that class-consciousness is inevitable, and at other times feel that it must be coached." But the problem was not just Marx. For Burke, such confusion was embedded in the very logic of political consciousness: did our ideas emerge organically from our social situation, or did we need to be taught how to think about our new situation? Burke believed there was a place for pedagogy. "Class morality may rise spontaneously," Burke wrote, "but class-consciousness must be *taught* by accurate appeal to the class morality." This was a revolutionary role for intellectuals.[2]

In 1935, Burke gave an infamous speech before the American Writers' Congress, "Revolutionary Symbolism in America," in which he argued that "the people" ought to be adopted as the essential symbol of revolutionary agency. Burke believed the term would be politically potent in an American context, where there existed a long history of referring to those in need of political redress as "the people." The Communist Party, which had anointed "workers" or "the masses" the subjects of revolution, harshly rejected Burke's suggestion. Rather than a term that clarified the lines of class struggle, "the people" clouded the division. But Burke believed terms had different meanings in different contexts. In his 1937 book, *Attitudes Toward History*, Burke argued that political symbols were often stolen "back and forth" and took on new meanings as "frames of acceptance" shifted.[3]

Burke believed Marx had laid the foundations for a vast new frame of reference. Marx opened up new ideological terrain that allowed more people to imagine a broader framework by rejecting current coordinates and by "organizing the individual mind to confront a present imperfect world by the coordinates of a subsequent better world." Of course, new coordinates did not register with everyone equally. "Capitalism shouted to Marx until the annoyance gave him a diseased liver," Burke wrote, "but it seems to sing a cradle song for some." In other words, not everyone had developed a properly revolutionary class consciousness. This was a problem that Burke believed cultural producers could solve. He wrote:

> If we are to revise the productive and the distributive patterns of our economy to suit our soundest desires, rather than attempting to revise our desires until they suit the productive and distributive patterns, it would surely be in the region of poetry that the "concentration point" of human desires should be found.

For Burke, poetry was not a term limited to the formal literary form. It was something that could be expressed in our political actions. Burke believed that Marx's vision of communism was an expression of poetry in that "we must realize the highly humanistic or poetic nature of its fundamental criteria."[4]

When capitalism crashed down on itself in the 1930s, more American thinkers than ever turned to Marx. But this Marx surge was not enduring. A primary reason, though one not always emphasized, is that a great many Americans found a living savior to rescue them from cataclysmic times. Franklin Delano Roosevelt, the scion of a wealthy upstate New York family, was elected President of the United States in 1932 and three more times because he promised a government that would ease the suffering caused by the Great Depression. He called this government "a new deal for the American people." Considered a traitor to his class by capitalists who thrived on the laissez-faire economic policies of his Republican predecessors, Roosevelt chastised the "economic royalists" who spared nobody in carving out "new dynasties" of wealth and privilege. In a speech before the Democratic Party National Convention in Philadelphia in 1936, Roosevelt lamented that the "whole structure of modern life ... corporations, banks and securities, new machinery of industry and agriculture, labor and capital," had been pressed into serving greedy capitalists. The only solution was a democratic revival that would conquer the new royalists in the same way American revolutionaries had overthrown the old royalists in 1776.[5]

Roosevelt's renowned Philadelphia speech might have made Marx proud with its evocations of "mercenaries" who "sought to regiment the people, their labor, and their property." He gave voice to working-class anger that had persisted through his first term as president. Roosevelt spoke on behalf of a New York City woman who wrote to his wife Eleanor to emphasize that his landslide victory in 1936 was "a mandate from the people ... to redistribute wealth" and to warn that "anyone who trifles with the people at this time had better be careful." Roosevelt also spoke for a Columbus, Georgia man who wrote to thank him for government aid, which was necessary because he was evicted from his home after he was fired from his job for having "the nerve to ask for or 'demand,' better working conditions." Another man wrote to Roosevelt to let him know that "all of the working men are for you." "Saint Roosevelt," as his working-class admirers often called him, gave hope to the forgotten Americans who had been beaten down by capitalism. He became a symbol of hope, even revolution.[6]

But was the Roosevelt presidency revolutionary? Was the New Deal, the Roosevelt administration's massive effort to end the depression and reform the American system, a dramatic move towards socialism? Had Marx been snuck into the corridors of American power? Or, did Roosevelt save capitalism from itself? Did the New Deal sop up revolutionary energies that had seemed so promising, that had given life to such a robust reception of Marx? In comparison to Nazi Germany, fascist Italy, or Stalin's Soviet Union, was the New Deal a more humane approach to countering the vagaries of capitalism? Answers to these questions help illuminate the fate of Marx in midcentury America. As the Great Depression gave way to another World War, which then gave way to a Cold War against the only nation deliberately organizing itself in the image of Marx's ideas, an affirmative American reception of Marx quickly became marked by disillusion.

Any understanding of the New Deal must begin with an understanding that it was a program for industrial recovery. In order to achieve recovery, the New Deal state forcefully regulated corporations to restrain runaway competition. Equally important, the state also guaranteed workers the right to form independent unions and collectively bargain. This meant that for the first time in its history, the U.S. government ended its reflexive alignment with capital against labor. On the whole, the New Deal made the capitalist economy more rational and more predictable. It also made the system fairer to working people. But the New Deal was by no means socialist in the Marxist sense of the term. Roosevelt had no intention of handing over to workers control of the means of production. In the words of a key member of Roosevelt's vaunted Brain Trust, the New Deal was "a democratic and a truly American solution" that distinguished it from the "the socialist doctrines of Karl Marx." Put simply, the purpose of the New Deal was to save capitalism.[7]

It is important to note that there was nothing inherently contradictory in the fact that the New Deal both made life fairer for the working class *and* saved capitalism. At the very moment of revolutionary possibility, at the very moment of what Mike Davis calls "the highwater mark of the class struggle in modern American history," the New Deal state embraced the working class. In doing so, it dispersed the radical energies that made Marx such a powerful symbol. Roosevelt was both the man who challenged capitalists on behalf of workers, and the president who saved capitalism for future capitalists. No wonder he was such a source of cognitive dissonance for Marxists.[8]

Plenty of people on the left admired Roosevelt. Writing from the perspective of a Communist, the famed historian Eric Hobsbawm reflected that "Roosevelt was passionately loathed and denounced by American big business, that is to say by the very people who more than any others represented the evils of capitalism to us." But not all leftists remembered Roosevelt with such affection. An Industrial Workers of the World obituary depicted Roosevelt as "hated by those he had helped and loved by those he had harmed." In 1938, the Trotskyist James Burnham labeled Roosevelt's pro-labor policies "a class collaborationist device" meant to restrain working-class militancy "firmly within the framework of the bourgeois state."[9]

Historians might reserve judgment on whether or not it was a good thing that the New Deal captured the labor movement, but it did—and paradoxically, it did so with the help of the American Communist Party. The history of the American left is rife with such ironies. By 1935, the Party had moved away from its previous "third period" policy of tarring anyone to its right as "social fascists." The Moscow-directed Communist International, or Comintern, ordered the American Communist Party to moderate its position with regard to trade unions and other liberal democratic institutions. All of a sudden "the people" were good (Burke, it seems, was a premature champion of the people). That this shift took place at precisely the moment Roosevelt moved left on labor issues precipitated a left-liberal coalescence known as the Popular Front. It is important to note the crucial international dimension of the Popular Front. It was an uneasy alignment between the Soviet Union and liberal democracies in a common struggle against fascism. But the domestic and international components of the Popular Front went hand-in-glove for American Communists. Historian Maurice Isserman notes that support for the Soviet Union allowed Communists to retain their Marxist credentials even as "they immersed themselves in reform-oriented day-to-day politics." The Popular Front persisted through the Second World War, temporarily interrupted by the Nazi–Soviet pact of August 1939, an agreement the Nazis broke when they invaded the Soviet Union in June 1941. In the Popular Front era, the American Communist Party acted as the left-wing of the labor movement and as a junior partner in the New Deal coalition.[10]

As the Communist Party made tenuous peace with American liberalism, it underwent an ideological shift represented by Party leader Earl Browder's slogan, "Communism is Twentieth Century Americanism." When intellectuals like Sidney Hook sought to Americanize Marx in the early 1930s, Marx's ideas remained at the forefront of such efforts. America served as backdrop or context. But Popular Front impulses downplayed Marx and elevated America. The midcentury erasure of Marx is typically assumed to have been a byproduct of political repression. Burke, for instance, removed traces of Marx from his 1930s books for new editions that were published in the midst of the 1950s Red Scare. But the Popular Front anticipated this development at a time when such self-censorship had little to do with repression. Rather, the deemphasizing of Marx was a consequence of the Popular Front's compulsion to Americanize. For the radical children of Eastern European immigrants, "Communism

Figure 5.1 In claiming that "Communism is Americanism of the 20th Century," the Popular Front sought to portray the Communist Party USA as the embodiment of American national-patriotic destiny. An image of the American Revolution is on the lower left, and Abraham Lincoln in the lower center, but Marx is nowhere in sight. *Communist Party, USA, 1936.*

is Twentieth Century Americanism" (Figure 5.1) was a ticket to assimilation. The motto connected the socialism that their parents first discovered in faraway lands, in books authored by exotic philosophers like Marx, to the millions of progressive Americans who supported the New Deal. Such Americanization, as with all cultural assimilation, was a two-way street. Just as foreign radicals adapted to American political culture, so too was America transformed. As historian Michael Denning argues, the fact that immigrant and plebeian cultural accents had become mainstream by the 1950s, seen in the popularity of films such as *On the Waterfront*, would not have been possible without the Popular Front. Yet given the immense cultural power of America as an idea, we should not overestimate these cultural changes. The American reception of Marx is sobering in this regard. The idea of America leaves little room for Marx.[11]

American Studies, which emerged in the 1940s as a formal inquiry into the idea of America, was part of a larger ideological project that sought to define American culture as distinct from Marxism yet still vital—even revolutionary. In this way, American Studies was perfectly positioned to gain traction during the early

Cold War, when anti-Marxism meshed neatly with an ascendant American nationalism. American Studies is thus often remembered, at least in its early years, as a field dominated by a nationalist strain. Daniel Boorstin's classic trilogy *The Americans* nicely represents this type of analysis. In the hands of Boorstin and other Cold War liberal scholars, the study of America became a study in American exceptionalism. The United States seemed exempt from the laws of history to which Europe seemed bound. As the liberal historian Henry Steele Commager wrote, "That by some alchemy, out of the blending of inheritance, environment, and experience, there came a distinctive American character, cannot be doubted."[12]

Even though American Studies deftly complemented Cold War liberalism, especially in its American exceptionalism, it originated as a Popular Front project. In this, American Studies was intertwined with the Popular Front suppression of Marx. F. O. Mathiessen, author of the influential 1941 book *American Renaissance: Art and Expression in the Age of Emerson and Whitman*, sought a usable past not in European letters—not in Marx—but rather in nineteenth-century American writers like Emerson, Thoreau, Whitman, Hawthorne, and Melville. The men of the American Renaissance, in the words of Mathiessen, "felt that it was incumbent upon their generation to give fulfillment to the potentialities freed by the Revolution, to provide a culture commensurate with America's political opportunity." Their body of work represented nothing less than the "undiminished resources" of American democracy. For a Popular Front thinker like Mathiessen, the cultural resources of American Renaissance writers might prove capable of sustaining the promise of the New Deal. Even more, "their devotion to the possibilities of democracy" could help build a world that would provide dignity to all Americans, including workers. But such a revolutionary world, if it were to come into being, had to first be imagined in an American dialect. Emerson, not Marx.[13]

In short, the New Deal and the Popular Front both worked to water down the American reception of Marx. But so too did the growing awareness of monstrous developments in Stalin's Soviet Union. James Burnham's intellectual course is indicative of how revelations about Stalinist Russia made the American reception of Marx far less favorable. Burnham began his academic career in 1929 when he took a position in the New York University philosophy department, where he hoped to cultivate his budding talents in literary criticism. But the Great Depression wreaked havoc on his worldview, and in 1930 he began reading Marx. Sidney Hook, Burnham's colleague in the NYU philosophy department who was in the midst of writing *Towards the Understanding of Karl Marx* (1933), one of the most important books about Marx ever written by an American, was formative in this regard. But it was ultimately Leon Trotsky who converted Burnham to full-throated Marxism. Burnham came to Trotsky's style of Marxist analysis after reading his 1932 book, *The History of the Russian Revolution*. Burnham was particularly influenced by Trotsky's emphasis on dialectical materialism.[14]

The dialectic is shorthand for the method Marx had appropriated from Hegel to explain how capitalism was generating contradictions that were paving the way for communism. Revolution would spring forth from the conditions of capitalism that had cast people into one of two antagonistic classes, the bourgeoisie and the proletariat. Hegel theorized that, in the unfolding of history, a time was fast approaching in which a rational, absolute ideal—something like divine truth—will have revealed itself in the progressive development of human consciousness as manifested in philosophy, as manifested especially in the mind of a genius philosopher like Hegel. Marx famously flipped this on its head. Marx, too, had a teleology, or a sense of where the future was headed based on the direction of history. But the endpoint for Marx was not found in human consciousness, rather in social relations, in the material world. Hegel, right side up.[15]

In the hands of Soviet theorists and other orthodox Marxists, what came to be called dialectical materialism rationalized the Bolshevik Revolution. This total theory provided the Soviets with powerful ideological vindication. Their revolution was foretold, and thus any action they took to defend it was historically necessary. But in the hands of Trotsky, 1917 was not the culmination of dialectical materialism. Trotsky took issue not with Soviet grandiosity but rather with its parochial view of the dialectic. For Trotsky, socialism could never survive in one country alone, much less in an economic backwater like Russia. The revolution had to be permanent, and it had to be brought to the rest of the world, especially rich countries like the United States. Trotsky's version of dialectical materialism remained in motion, and it included a role for Americans.[16]

From 1933 through 1939 Burnham was a respected member of the Trotskyist movement that sought to build an anti-Stalinist left in the United States. Although never a committed organizer, he was one of the more perceptive intellectuals in the movement. He wrote a string of clear-headed criticisms of American capitalism, Soviet communism, and the American Communist Party. His articles often appeared in the pages of the *Partisan Review*, the unofficial organ of intellectual Trotskyism. But in 1940, in the midst of debates about what became known as the "Russia Question," Burnham quit the Trotskyist movement and declared he was no longer a Marxist.

The debate surrounding the Russia Question was actually an argument about a series of important questions: Was the Soviet Union a worker's state? Or was it ruled by a tiny, brutal elite that represented the proletariat in name only? Was Stalinism a deformation of the Russian Revolution? Was it a betrayal of Marx? Or was Stalinism the logical conclusion of Marxism? Trotsky's position was that Stalin's inner circle was a bureaucratic clique that had wrested control of the revolution and centralized its authority over the proletariat. Stalin had betrayed the revolution, and Stalinist Russia had devolved into what Trotsky labeled a "degenerated workers' state."[17]

At first, Trotskyists like Burnham accepted Trotsky's formulation, since it allowed them to rather effortlessly combine Marxism with anti-Stalinism. But when Trotsky argued the Soviet Union remained a workers' state that demanded support in the face of imperialist aggression, Burnham and several other American Marxists began to peel off from the movement. Backing the Soviet Union grew less and less tenable in light of the Moscow Trials, which provided evidence that Stalin had murdered all surviving Bolshevik Revolutionaries, not to mention the Nazi–Soviet Pact and the ensuing Soviet occupation of Eastern Europe and Finland. Given that Stalin coveted putting Trotsky on trial in Moscow more than anyone else, Trotsky's persistent defense of the degenerated workers' state seemed rather remarkable. Given that an agent of Stalin murdered Trotsky in 1940 by sticking an ice ax in the back of his skull, such a defense was an even more tragic irony.[18]

In the context of the Nazi–Soviet Pact, Burnham broke with Trotsky over the Russia Question and with Marxism itself. He theorized that the Soviet Union, as opposed to needing protection from imperialist powers, was in fact no different from them. He contended that the Marxist dialectic, in predicting a coming socialist revolution, was a lousy way to think about the United States, where the New Deal had stabilized capitalism. Dismissing the Marxist dialectic as a flimsy philosophy led to a snide yet comical exchange with Trotsky. "Burnham does not recognize the dialectic," Trotsky wrote, "but the dialectic recognizes Burnham." Burnham responded in kind: "Comrade Trotsky, I will not match metaphors with you. In such a verbal tournament, I concede you the ribbon in advance. Evidence, argument, proof: these only are my weapons." Trotskyists like Burnham were predisposed to distrust the Soviet Union. Unlike devout members of the Communist Party, or even Popular Front thinkers like Kenneth Burke, Trotskyists were much more inclined to believe the horror stories coming out of Stalinist Russia. But when the full scope of Stalin's murderous regime became apparent, even *they* were traumatized. As a result, many anti-Stalinists, from Max Eastman to John Dos Passos, grew increasingly disillusioned with Marxism and the entire left-wing project more generally. An attenuated, tiny band was all that was left of the "Left Opposition."[19]

By the Second World War and in the Cold War that followed, Marx seemed increasingly implicated in the chaos that had swamped the world. That said, midcentury American intellectuals could not simply ignore Marx, especially since so many of them had long engaged his ideas, often in favorable fashion. Rather, in order to make clear their disenchantment, they had to perform an exorcism of sorts. A new Marx had to be fashioned for the demands of a drastically altered world. Within the course of a decade, a vastly different Marx had appeared on the American scene.

The project of rethinking Marx helped define Cold War liberal thought. Cold War liberals used Marx as an integrative force for calibrating their views to a world in flux. Marx became the bane of liberal democracy. It is difficult to pinpoint when exactly this project began, or who it began with. One crucial beginning was the publication of Edmund Wilson's 1940 book, *To the Finland Station*. This book is a dramatic narrative history of socialism from the storming of the Bastille until that fateful moment when Lenin arrived at Finland Station in St. Petersburg to lead the Bolsheviks to power. Prior to writing this book, Wilson was a well-known left-wing essayist who moved in Trotskyist circles. In this capacity during the 1930s, he had grown disgusted with capitalism, and it showed in his prose. But by 1940, disillusion with Marx also began to seep into Wilson's writing.[20]

Marx is an ironic, if central, figure on the long and winding road to the Finland Station. In his single-minded quest to slay the horrible beast known as capitalism, Marx himself became a beast of a man. Wilson, ever the clever stylist, used Marx's friendship with Engels as a literary device for exploring this paradox. Marx, the calculating rhetorician, endowed the world with metaphors that surgically captured the sweep of history. Engels, the more compassionate figure, added human texture to Marx's abstract structures. Whereas an unsentimental Marx thundered on about the means of production (when he was not thundering on about how "the last capitalist we hang shall be the one who sold us the rope"), Engels showed basic human decency when he wrote about how the Manchester working class was "being shoveled into the mines and the mills like so much raw materials for the prices their finished products would bring, with no attempt even to dispose of the waste." Wilson's distinction is of course exaggerated. Marx wrote movingly of working-class conditions. The novelist F. Scott Fitzgerald insisted to his daughter that she read "the terrible chapter in *Das Kapital* on The Working Day, and see if you are ever quite the same." Moreover, although Engels had indeed written sympathetically about the English working class, he was also the person chiefly responsible for whittling down Marx's theories into abstractions. Nevertheless, distinguishing between Marx and Engels in this way helped Wilson make an important point that would become central to how Cold War liberals framed Marx.[21]

The portrait of Marx as an unsparing exponent of rigid abstractions foregrounded Wilson's criticism of the Marxist dialectic. For Wilson, the dialectic was proof that Marx was a determinist. This is one of the longstanding complaints about Marx made by liberals, conservatives, anarchists—basically anyone who's not a Marxist—that his dialectical theory of capitalism left no room for freedom of human action. Wilson argued that Marx never really worked out the precise nature of causal relations in his dialectical system. Marx never dealt effectively with the relation between human will and the web of material conditions in which humans are situated. How did Marx reconcile the existence of himself as a revolutionary philosopher, for instance, with a materialist conception that human consciousness was constrained by social relations? Wilson contended that Marx's apparent failure to solve this contradiction was grounded in his inability to escape his German roots. Wilson wrote:

> Karl Marx, with his rigorous morality and his international point of view, had tried to harness the primitive German Will to a movement which should lead all humanity to prosperity, happiness and freedom. But insofar as this movement involves, under the disguise of the Dialectic, a semi-divine principle of History, to which it is possible to shift the human responsibility for thinking, for deciding, for acting—and we are living at the present time in a period of decadence for Marxism—it lends itself to the repressions of the tyrant. The parent stream of the old German Will, which stayed at home and remained patriotic, became canalized as the philosophy of German imperialism and ultimately of the Nazi movement.

American socialists, in this view, should have discarded the dialectic and instead embraced a less deterministic, more humanistic form of socialism: Marx leavened with Emerson. In a world in which Stalinism existed as a blood-soaked legacy of the Marxist dialectic, such a proposal was not uncommon nor unreasonable. But it was based on a misunderstanding of the dialectic, whether in its Hegelian or Marxist form.[22]

The most important thing to know about the Hegelian dialectic is that, for Hegel, history was a process of unfolding in which, as Louis Menand writes, "every paradigm contains the seed of its own undoing." Just as we detect some semblance of the present in the past, we seek to detect some semblance of the future in the present. That said, dialectical thinking is a way of recognizing that the future will not be more of the same, it will be something completely different. Hegel focused his lens on ideas. He thought a different future could be found in philosophy. Marx concentrated on social relations. He thought a different future could be found in the economic modes of production. On its surface, there is nothing particularly deterministic about any of this. Just because the future is conditioned by the present does not mean there is a definitive path to it. Nor does it mean that humans have no role in carving out such a path. In both the Hegelian and Marxist dialectics, humans do not sit idly by awaiting the unfolding of history. Humans *are* the unfolding of history.[23]

The idea that the Marxist dialectic erased human will and was thus a forerunner to totalitarianism seemed a perfect paradigm for explaining the world of Hitler and Stalin. Wilson was hardly alone in this. Such anti-Marxism had become a powerful and capacious liberal tendency for understanding totalitarianism. Moreover, the idea that America represented a powerful alternative to Marx—a powerful alternative to totalitarianism—was a bedrock assumption of Cold War liberalism. This point was central to Arthur Schlesinger, Jr.'s 1949 book, *The Vital Center*. For Schlesinger, that the United States was a centrist nation meant that it was a "New Deal country," which also meant that it was best positioned to fight off totalitarianism. Because the New Deal ran "contrary to Marx's prediction of increasing proletarian misery," because it "vastly increased the wealth and freedom of the ordinary worker," the United States was best able to ward off Marxism and other dangerously utopian ideologies.[24]

Most Cold War liberals came to believe that a liberal consensus was one of the defining features of American history, and that this consensus was a key aspect of what distinguished American history from European history. For the political scientist Louis Hartz, author of the 1955 book *The Liberal Tradition in America*, any analysis of American political thought had to begin with what he termed the "storybook truth about American history," that is, the United States had no feudal past. The United States, unlike Europe, lacked "a genuine revolutionary tradition." The philosopher who embodied American political thought was not Marx but rather John Locke. The idea that the United States had never been beholden to the historical restraints that shaped Europe functioned as the bedrock of American exceptionalism. In the hands of some American Cold Warriors, especially conservatives, American exceptionalism was an ideology of national superiority. Not only was America different, it was better. But there was nothing inherently conservative or nationalistic about the notion that American history was defined by consensus. As the liberal historian Richard Hofstadter argued, the idea of an American consensus "owed almost as much to Marx as to Tocqueville." Hofstadter wondered how "any realistic Marxist historian could fail to be struck at many points by the pervasively liberal-bourgeois character of American society in the past." Arguably, neither was there anything inherently conservative or nationalistic about American exceptionalism, at least as a theory of American history. As a point of fact, although Alexis de Tocqueville had posited a version of American exceptionalism, modern usage of the phrase owed to left-wing sectarianism. In 1927, when the American Communist Jay Lovestone argued the United States was not ready for socialist revolution due to the unique power of American capitalism, Stalin accused him of "the heresy of American exceptionalism."[25]

Although Stalin undoubtedly thought he was defending Marxist doctrine when he labeled Lovestone a heretic for suggesting that America was exceptional, Marx himself put forward a concept of American exceptionalism. Marx wrote that American capitalism developed "as in a greenhouse," and he described the United States as the first fully realized bourgeois country because its people were conditioned to the idea that "work is the key to wealth, and wealth the only object of work." More remarkable to Marx was that even though the United States had become an industrial giant, it had not yet developed fixed class distinctions. In Marx's view, this was largely due to the fact that, since the United States did not have a feudal past, it was able to avoid the pathologies that accompanied such a past, including the class hatred that seemed so prevalent in Europe. Marx, in other words, anticipated Hartz.[26]

To most Cold War liberals, American exceptionalism served as proof that Marx's theory of capitalism did not stand up to the weight of evidence. But Marx had anticipated such objections. Whereas Tocqueville argued that America represented Europe's future because Europe was inexorably transforming into a post-feudal, democratic society of the American type, Marx argued instead that Europe was America's future. American exceptionalism was a temporary condition. Marx attributed the exceptional nature of American class consciousness to the fact that there did not yet exist a surplus population in the United States as there did in Europe. He assumed that with massive European migration, a persistent fact for much of Marx's life, the United States would soon boast its own surplus population. Predicting Frederick Jackson Turner's famous "frontier thesis," Marx also contended that as the American frontier closed, European immigrants would no longer be welcomed with land and the autonomy that came with land ownership. The nineteenth-century equivalent of the American dream would soon be dead. Workers would be obligated to work for wages as part of a blossoming American proletariat. If American exceptionalism was the negation of Marx's theory of socialist revolution, Marx negated the negation. He applied his dialectical mode of thought to America. But for Cold War liberals living in a New Deal landscape, such thinking this was more evidence that Marx's dialectical approach was flat-out wrong.

The Cold War liberal vision of Marx was a caricature. Going at least as far back as Edmund Wilson's *To the Finland Station*, liberals had been in the habit of selectively interpreting Marx. The Marx of the Cold War liberal imagination was stripped of all nuance and complexity. The Marx of *Capital* who grappled with the intricate relationship between capitalism and slavery was nowhere to be found. The Marx of *The Eighteenth Brumaire* who struggled with understanding how the forces of reaction captured the popular will had disappeared. Instead, Cold War liberals presented a rigid Marx that gave the world Stalin. "In pulverizing the barriers to political power, in sneering at the instruments of 'mere formal freedom,' in stripping the family of its private character," the Cold War liberal historian Clinton Rossiter wrote, "Marx opened the way to the dynamic, all-pervading collectivism of Soviet totalitarianism." The Cold War liberal interpretation of Marx was a Cold War apologia. As Rossiter wrote: "What we come down to in the end is a fundamental conflict between two bodies of principle, two faiths, two ideologies, a conflict so severe that peace between them has always been and remains today impossible to achieve." Rossiter was talking about the conflict between Marx and the American tradition. But he might also have been talking about the conflict between the Soviet Union and the United States. In his eyes, they amounted to the same thing.[27]

From the late 1930s until the early 1960s, the reception of Marx tracked Cold War liberalism's narrative arc. As assorted left-wing and liberal intellectuals grew disillusioned with Marx, they slowly grew enamored with America, and not just any America. Liberals came to love the America of their own imagination. This America was not merely a military powerhouse that could stand up to Soviet aggression, though that was important to them. It also represented an anti-totalitarian political culture. The America of the liberal imagination was a beacon that endowed the world with a pluralist political philosophy defined by its embrace of human difference. But liberal pluralism, even if more prescriptive than descriptive, more aspirational than actual, was marred by an enormous chasm. Cold War liberalism ignored race.[28]

The liberal celebration of an alleged American pluralism commenced against the backdrop of Jim Crow, which denied basic civil rights to black Americans at a time when the American government was trying to convince non-white people across the globe to align with the United States in the Cold War. This hypocrisy helps explain why most black Americans never felt entirely comfortable with Cold War liberalism. It certainly explains why some black thinkers bucked powerful intellectual trends by sticking with Marxism, even at risk of their freedom. Of course, other black thinkers, most notably Richard Wright and Harold Cruse, did turn away from Marxism out of disillusion with the Communist Party. But such a rightward U-turn was less common among black intellectuals on the left. Mid-twentieth-century Western capitalism looked vastly different to those who experienced it as refracted through white supremacy. W. E. B. Du Bois was far from alone among major American intellectuals when he used Marx to help him interpret American history and society in the 1930s. But during the 1940s and 1950s, as former Marxists like Burnham zigged right, Du Bois zagged left. In 1961, he joined the Communist Party. With this symbolic act, the ninety-three-year-old Du Bois told America to go to hell.[29]

Another major black intellectual who never grew out of love with Marx, even at the cost of his political freedom in the United States, was C. L. R. James, dubbed the "Black Plato" by the *New York Times* in 1980. James was a Trinidadian living in London when he wrote his 1938 masterpiece of Marxist historical scholarship, *The Black Jacobins: Toussaint L'Ouverture and the San Domingo Revolution*, which explained the Haitian Revolution in ways that have influenced anti-colonial and anti-slavery thought ever since, with particular power in the pan-African diaspora. Upon visiting the United States that year, initially intending to stay briefly, he wound up remaining for fifteen years, helping lead various Marxist groups until his 1953 deportation.[30]

As a prominent Trotskyist who developed his own idiosyncratic outlook in 1940, James might have joined the likes of Burnham and Hook in their travels away from Marxism. But living in America as a black man was a radically different experience that led to a radically different trajectory. Being a black man in Europe had already made James a different sort of Marxist, one who brought black and colonized peoples into a mostly European Marxist framework. After moving to the United States in 1938, and especially after traveling across the country on a bus, James undertook to do the same with American culture. This would not be an easy task, although he was well suited to it. As James wrote:

> From the first day of my stay in the United States to the last, I never made the mistake that so many otherwise intelligent Europeans made of trying to fit that country into European standards. Perhaps for one reason—because of my colonial background—I always saw it for what it was, and not for what I thought it ought to be. I took in stride the cruelties and anomalies that shocked me and the immense vitality, generosity and audacity of those strange people.[31]

Despite being a Marxist, and despite being black, James was fascinated by America. He not only staved off disillusionment with Marx, he also managed to remain somewhat optimistic about the strange country he called home for fifteen years. These sensibilities gave James a unique perspective on the United States that permitted him to produce an unknown masterpiece of American Studies. *American Civilization*, which James wrote in 1950 but which went unpublished until 1993, represents a compelling counterfactual. How would the study of America have been different had Cold War liberals not done everything in their power to exorcise Marx? James was convinced that bringing Marx and America together was crucial if the United States was going to have any chance at a socialist future. More than that, he thought bringing Marx to bear on America was necessary to a fuller understanding of the United States. He thus accepted the challenge posed by Charles and Mary Beard in their 1942 book, *The American Spirit: A Study of the Idea of Civilization in the United States*. "The utterly alien nature of Marxism was illustrated by the fact," the Beards wrote, "that neither foreign born nor native Marxists produced any significant contributions to thought in relation to American history or economy." James wanted to prove the Beards wrong.[32]

The overriding concern James expressed in *American Civilization* was with capitalist automation and what this meant for freedom.

James argued that American civilization had reached a threshold unlike any since the Civil War. Modern industrial relations had curtailed individual freedoms to an almost unprecedented degree. Like some of his fellow ex-Trotskyists, James stressed that totalitarianism was not a horror limited to people in far off lands like Russia. The workplace, where Americans spent the majority of their lives, was a totalitarian institution due to advances in mechanization. "The modern worker is a cog in a machine," James argued. "All progress in industry consists of making him more and more of a cog and less and less of a human being." These developments represented a civilizational threshold because of the vast gulf that separated liberal democratic expectations from the experience of work in a capitalist economy. James wrote:

> Upon a people bursting with energy, untroubled by feudal remains or a feudal past, soaked to the marrow in a tradition of individual freedom, individual security, free association, a tradition which is constantly held before them as the basis of their civilization, upon this people more than all others has been imposed a mechanized way of life at work, mechanized forms of living, a mechanized totality which from morning till night, week after week, day after day, crushed the very individualist which tradition nourishes and the abundance of mass-produced goods encourages. The average American citizen is baffled by it, has always been. He cannot grasp the process by which a genuine democracy escapes him.[33]

Workers were alienated not because of low wages or lack of access to consumer goods. Rather, the American working class wanted autonomy. What this spelled for the future, other than working-class anger that might express itself in a range of unpredictable registers, was left an open question. But James did assume the question of automation would become a problem of almost existential proportions. Perhaps he was wrong about that (at least so far). But one thing is certain. James wrote about American society through a lens that had grown less and less common. He wrote about America through the lens of Marx's dialectic, which conceptualized human happiness as deeply wound up with autonomy.

The fact that it took a black Trinidadian to elaborate on American culture through the lens of Marx's theory of autonomy is no surprise given the constraints of Cold War intellectual culture. Cold War liberalism spoke in universal terms but was white in its sensibilities.

The midcentury rethinking of Marx was also largely undertaken by men, which was even less surprising since few women partook in Marxist theorizing about political economy even going back to the 1930s. That is why it also took a Russian immigrant woman, James's close comrade Raya Dunayevskaya, to endow us with a Marxist analysis of capitalism that melded a humanistic focus on the problems of authoritarianism and racism. Sometimes position helps shape perspective.[34]

Dunayevskaya, who translated sections of the young Marx's *Economic and Philosophic Manuscripts* into English in the 1940s, wrote a 1958 book, *Marxism and Freedom*, that sought to reclaim Marx from the Soviet Union, especially in the wake of Soviet Union's brutal repression of an uprising in Hungary in 1956. For Dunayevskaya, it was the perfect time to introduce the world to the young Marx, who had long ago contended that we "should especially avoid establishing society as an abstraction opposed to the individual. The individual *is* the social entity." Dunayevskaya pointed her readers to the stark contrast between Marx and Soviet Communism. "Today, in the face of the constant struggle of man for full freedom on both sides of the Iron Curtain," she wrote, "there is a veritable conspiracy to identify Marxism, a theory of liberation, with its opposite, Communism, the theory and practice of enslavement." She aimed "to re-establish Marxism in its original form, which Marx called 'a thoroughgoing Naturalism, or Humanism.'"[35]

Dunayevskaya had two objectives with *Marxism and Freedom*. First, she wanted to present Marx not only as a critic of capitalism but also as a beacon of human freedom. Second, and related, Dunayevskaya sought to uncover the American roots of Marx's ideas. Indeed, her book's subtitle—*From 1776 until Today*—signaled that American history would foreground her effort to rethink Marx. "Marxism," Dunayevskaya wrote, "is the theoretical expression of the instinctive strivings of the proletariat for liberation." The American proletariat, struggling for freedom against the most formidable bourgeoisie the world had ever seen, inspired Marx, and if Dunayevskaya had her way, would continue to stir Marxists around the world to action.[36]

Dunayevskaya contended that *Capital*, the apex of Marx's mature thought, built upon Marx's lifelong conceptualization of what it would take for people to be free. Moreover, she argued that Marx owed his fully fleshed out vision of human freedom to the fact that he had turned his attention to the American proletariat. This was particularly noticeable in the section of *Capital* that focused on the working day. With some justification, Dunayevskaya maintained Marx conceptualized those particular passages with the Civil War on his mind. "A new life immediately arose from the death of slavery," he wrote. "The first fruit of the American Civil War was the eight hours' agitation, which ran from the Atlantic to the Pacific, from New England to California, with the seven-league boots of the locomotive."[37]

Capital connected the abolition of slavery to the working day. The enslaved men and women who revolted during the Civil War helped overthrow a system that maintained total control over their working day. This act of defiance demonstrated to workers everywhere that in order to live the good life they needed more autonomy over their time and labor. Shortening the working day was a crucial first step. As the influential German émigré and Marxist Herbert Marcuse wrote in the preface to *Marxism and Freedom*, "A socialist society is a society in which free time, not labor time is the social measure of wealth and the dimension of individual existence."[38]

The Marx who advocated for individual freedom in general and more leisure time in particular might have appeared strange to people who automatically linked Marx with the political repression and daily drudgery that characterized life in the Soviet Union. Correcting this popular misconception was precisely why Dunayevskaya wrote *Marxism and Freedom*. It was also why she used the United States as a canvass for her analysis. The young Marx's conception of labor alienation had come alive for an American working class that, due to advanced automation, had been separated further than ever from the products of their labor. As James wrote about the *Economic and Philosophic Manuscripts*: "The great masses of the American workers feel and think in a way that invest these century-old essays with a meaning and significance that they could never have had." The American working class taught Dunayevskaya and James something about Marx that they could not have learned from reading his words alone.[39]

People who lack control over their own labor remain unfree. This was the logic that undergirded *Capital*, the logic that structured *Black Jacobins*, and the logic that ordered *Marxism and Freedom*. Being a black Marxist who had closely studied the history of slavery and slave rebellion helped James make these connections. Being a woman and an immigrant who had rigorously studied Marx in connection with American history had done the same for Dunayevskaya. When Cold War liberalism exorcised Marx from the American imagination, the logic that grounded the work of James and Dunayevskaya was almost entirely absent from the study of America. James and his book *American Civilization* were lost to American Studies for a long time. Dunayevskaya barely registered. And neither did Marx, despite his persistent notoriety. The repression of Marx and Marxists would only get worse. James learned this the hard way in 1953, when the U.S. government deported him back to London, where he would live the remainder of his life in exile, a lot like Marx.

Capitalism's crisis of the 1930s led to a robust reception of Karl Marx. But the New Deal, which stabilized American capitalism such that it seemed indissoluble by the 1950s, combined with the complications of Communism in the Stalin era, derailed what would otherwise have been a Marxist renaissance. The Marxist dialectic persisted in outliers like James and Dunayevskaya. But their marginalization meant that the 1960s radicalization that they anticipated far better than the Cold War liberals took place in a context in which Marx was a forbidden figure.

Notes

1. Anthony Badger, *The New Deal: The Depression Years, 1933–1940* (New York: Hill and Wang, 1989); Robert Goldston, *The Great Depression: The United States in the Thirties* (New York: A Fawcett Crest Book, 1968).
2. Robert Genter, *Late Modernism: Art, Culture and Politics in Cold War America* (Philadelphia: University of Pennsylvania Press, 2010); Michael Denning, *The Cultural Front: The Laboring of American Culture* (London: Verso, 1997); Kenneth Burke, *Permanence and Change: An Anatomy of Purpose* (New York: New Republic, Inc., 1935), 55, 65.
3. Kenneth Burke, "Revolutionary Symbolism in America" (1935), reprinted in Herbert W. Simons and Trevor Melia, eds., *The Legacy of Kenneth Burke* (Madison: University of Wisconsin Press, 1989); Kenneth Burke, *Attitudes Toward History*, third edition (1937; Berkeley: University of California Press, 1987).
4. Burke, *Attitudes Toward History*, 56; *Permanence and Change*, 93.

5 Franklin D. Roosevelt, "Acceptance Speech for the Re-Nomination for the Presidency," Philadelphia, Pennsylvania, June 27, 1936; Roger Daniels, *Franklin D. Roosevelt: Road to the New Deal, 1882–1939* (Champaign, IL: University of Illinois Press, 2015).
6 Robert S. McElvaine, ed., *Down and Out in the Great Depression: Letters from the Forgotten Man* (Chapel Hill, NC: University of North Carolina Press, 1983), 218–27.
7 Ira Katznelson, *Fear Itself: The New Deal and the Origins of Our Time* (New York: Liveright Publishing Corporation, 2013), 230–34. Rhonda F. Levine, *Class Struggle and the New Deal: Industrial Labor, Industrial Capital, and the State* (Lawrence, KS: University Press of Kansas, 1988).
8 Mike Davis, *Prisoners of the American Dream: Politics and Economy in the History of the US Working Class* (London: Verso, 1986), 54.
9 Eric Hobsbawm, *Interesting Times: A Twentieth-Century Life* (London: Allen Lane, 2002), 388; Studs Terkel, *Hard Times: An Oral History of the Great Depression* (New York: Pantheon, 1970), 309; James Burnham, "Attacks on NLRB Reflect Blows Suffered by Labor," *Socialist Appeal* 2, no. 36 (September 1938), 4.
10 Maurice Isserman, *Which Side Were You On? The American Communist Party During the Second World War* (Middletown, CT: Wesleyan University Press, 1982), 4.
11 James Gilbert Ryan, *Earl Browder: The Failure of American Communism* (Tuscaloosa, AL: University of Alabama Press, 2005); Denning, *The Cultural Front*, 437, 156.
12 Michael Denning, "'The Special American Conditions': Marxism and American Studies," *American Quarterly* 38, no. 3 (1986), 356–80; Lucy Maddox, ed., *Locating American Studies: The Evolution of a Discipline* (Baltimore: The Johns Hopkins University Press, 1999); Daniel Boorstin, *The Americans: The Democratic Experience* (New York: Vintage, 1974); Henry Steele Commager, ed., *America in Perspective: The United States through Foreign Eyes* (New York: Random House, 1947), xii.
13 F. O. Mathiessen, *American Renaissance: Art and Expression in the Age of Emerson and Whitman* (London: Oxford University Press, 1941), ix, xv.
14 Daniel Kelly, *James Burnham and the Struggle for the World* (Wilmington, Delaware: ISI Books, 2002); Leon Trotsky, *The History of the Russian Revolution*, 3 volumes, translated by Max Eastman (Ann Arbor, MI: University of Michigan Press, 1932); Sidney Hook, *Towards the Understanding of Karl Marx: A Revolutionary Interpretation* (New York: The John Day Company, 1933). Far and away the best historical scholarship on Hook's Marxist years is Christopher Phelps, *Young Sidney Hook: Marxist and Pragmatist* (1997; Ann Arbor: University of Michigan Press, 2005).

15 Helmut Fleischer, *Marxism and History* (New York: Harper Torchbooks, 1973); Lucio Colletti, *Marxism and Hegel* (London: Verso, 2011); Karl Marx, *Critique of Hegel's Philosophy of Right* (London: Oxford University Press, 1970).
16 Irving Howe, ed., *The Basic Writings of Leon Trotsky* (New York: Schocken Books, 1976).
17 Trotsky, *The Revolution Betrayed*; "The Workers' State, Thermidor, and Bonapartism," *New International* 2, no. 4 (July 1935), 116–22.
18 Deutscher, *Trotsky: The Prophet Outcast* (London: Oxford University Press, 1963). Timothy Snyder, *Bloodlands: Europe Between Hitler and Stalin* (New York: Basic Books, 2010).
19 Daniel Oppenheimer, *Exit Right: The People Who Left the Left and Reshaped the American Century* (New York: Simon & Schuster, 2016), 141; Leon Trotsky, "Petty-Bourgeois Opposition in the Socialist Workers Party," Trotsky "An Open Letter to Comrade Burnham," and James Burnham, "Science and Style: A reply to Comrade Trotsky," all in Trotsky, *In Defense of Marxism* (New York: Pioneer, 1942).
20 Edmund Wilson, *To the Finland Station: A Study in the Writing and Acting of History* (1940; New York: Farrar, Straus and Giroux, 1972); Lewis M. Dabney, *Edmund Wilson: A Life in Literature* (New York: Farrar, Straus and Giroux, 2005).
21 Wilson, *To the Finland Station*, 161; Richard Greenleaf, "The Social Thinking of F. Scott Fitzgerald," *Science & Society* 16, no. 2 (Spring, 1952), 97–114.
22 Wilson, *To the Finland Station*, 231.
23 Louis Menand, "The Historical Romance: Edmund Wilson's Adventure with Communism," *The New Yorker* (March 16, 2003); Walter Kauffman, *Hegel: A Reinterpretation* (New York: Anchor Books, 2003).
24 Richard Aldous, *Schlesinger: The Imperial Historian* (New York: W. W. Norton & Company, 2017); Alonzo Hamby, *Beyond the New Deal: Harry S. Truman and American Liberalism* (New York: Columbia University Press, 1976); Arthur Schlesinger, Jr., *The Vital Center: The Politics of Freedom* (1949; London: Andre Deutsch Limited, 1970), xxii, 46–47.
25 Louis Hartz, *The Liberal Tradition in America: An Interpretation of American Political Thought Since the Revolution* (New York: Harcourt, Brace & World, Inc., 1955), 3; James Livingston, "On Richard Hofstadter and the Politics of 'Consensus History,'" *boundary 2* 34, no. 3 (2007), 33–46; Richard Hofstadter, *The Progressive Historians: Turner, Beard, Parrington* (1968; New York: Vintage, 1970), 452; John Higham, *Beyond Consensus: The Historian as Moral Critic, The American Historical Review* 67, no. 3 (April 1962), 609–25; Ian Tyrrell, "What, Exactly, Is 'American Exceptionalism,'" *Aeon* (October 21, 2016).

26 Heinz D. Kurz, "Transatlantic Conversations: Observations on Marx and Engels' Journalism and Beyond," *Social Research* (Fall 2014), 646–48; Robert Weiner, "Karl Marx's Vision of America: A Biographical and Bibliographical Sketch," *The Review of Politics* 42, no. 4 (October 1980), 486.
27 Clinton Rossiter, *Marxism: The View from America* (New York: Harcourt, Brace & Company, 1960), 248, 8.
28 Richard H. Pells, *The Liberal Mind in a Conservative Age: American Intellectuals in the 1940s and 1950s* (New York: Harper & Row, Publishers, 1985).
29 Mary L. Dudziak, *Cold War Civil Rights: Race and the Image of American Democracy* (Princeton: Princeton University Press, 2000); Thomas Borstelmann, *The Cold War and the Color Line: American Race Relations in the Global Arena* (Cambridge: Harvard University Press, 2001); David Levering Lewis, *W. E. B. Du Bois: The Fight for Equality and the American Century, 1919–1963* (New York: Henry Holt and Company, 2000).
30 C.L.R. James, *Black Jacobins: Toussaint L'Ouverture and the San Domingo Revolution*, second edition (1962; New York: Vintage Books, 1989).
31 Paul Buhle, *C. L. R. James: the Artist as Revolutionary* (London: Verso, 2017), 4; C. L. R. James, *American Civilization*, Anna Grimshaw and Keith Hart, eds. (Cambridge: Blackwell, 1993), 13.
32 Charles A. and Mary R. Beard, *The American Spirit; A Study of the Idea of Civilization in the United States* (New York: The Macmillan Company. 1942); James, *American Civilization*, 305.
33 James, *American Civilization*, 116–17.
34 Stephen M. Ward, *In Love and Struggle: The Revolutionary Lives of James and Grace Lee Boggs* (Chapel Hill, NC: University of North Carolina Press, 2016). Eugene Gogol, *Raya Dunayevskaya: Philosopher of Marxist-Humanism* (Eugene, OR: Resource Publications, 2004).
35 Paul Lendvai, *One Day That Shook the Communist World: The 1956 Hungarian Uprising and Its Legacy* (Princeton, NJ: Princeton University Press, 2008). Raya Dunayevskaya, *Marxism and Freedom: From 1776 until Today* (1958; New York, Humanity Books, 2000), 60, 21.
36 Dunayevskaya, *Marxism and Freedom*, 89.
37 Dunayevskaya, *Marxism and Freedom*, 81–91. Robert Weiner, "Karl Marx's Vision of America: A Biographical and Bibliographical Sketch," *The Review of Politics* Vol. 42, No. 4 (October 1980), 474.
38 Herbert Marcuse, "Preface to the 1957 Edition" of Dunayevskaya, *Marxism and Freedom*, xxiii.
39 James, *American Civilization*, 314.

6

Black Marxism off the color line: W. E. B. Du Bois and Oliver Cromwell Cox as democratic theorists

Paul M. Heideman

The intellectual history of American Marxism's engagement with race has gone through several distinct and contradictory phases. During the years in which Marxist movements had their greatest impact on American society (roughly from the turn of the twentieth century until the postwar years), race was a question that was debated ceaselessly and in detail. As Philip Foner noted, in the prewar Socialist Party, "apart from the question of the farmers' role in the Socialist Party, the Negro question was the most widely debated issue in American socialist circles during the opening years of the twentieth century." The Communist Party was, if anything, even more focused on understanding the structure of racial inequality in the United States, and certainly more dedicated to destroying it. In the postwar era, however, multiple historiographical currents converged in revising this history. From the perspective of consensus liberalism, the Marxist engagement with the race question was little more than a cynical attempt to recruit African Americans into the party and to use American racism as an additional indictment of American capitalism. At the same time, scholars on the left, dissatisfied with the political heritage of American Marxism on the race question, tended to flatten particularly the Socialist Party's uneven and complex history of confronting and conciliating white supremacy.[1]

As the New Left began to develop its own historiographical consciousness in the 1970s and 1980s, another reversal was initiated. Influenced by the new social history, scholars began unearthing the history of American Marxism at the grassroots, in the process uncovering a legacy of Marxist organizing on the race question that utterly upended the simplistic picture of consensus liberalism. The picture that emerged was one in which local activists negotiated the complex interplay between their theory, their party, and politics on the ground. The organizing that emerged from this negotiation was, of course, highly uneven and often fragile. But the depth of American Marxists' commitment to the struggle against white supremacy (at their best) could hardly be gainsaid.[2]

We are now several decades into this historiographical movement, and the literature on American Marxism's engagement with race at the grassroots is vast. Social history, on the one hand, and cultural and literary studies, on the other, have remained the privileged lenses for understanding American Marxism's history with the race question. Though many of these works have included brilliant investigations on the intellectual roots of various aspects of American Marxist discourse on race, intellectual history has only occasionally been the central mode of investigation of this subject. As a result, the conceptual frameworks for understanding American Marxist discourse on race remain underdeveloped.[3]

Surely the most important such framework is provided by Cedric Robinson's *Black Marxism: The Making of the Black Radical Tradition* (1983). Robinson argues that Marxist theory has failed to account for its origins in the culturally specific racialism of modernizing Europe and has thus acted as something of a loyal opposition to European capitalism. The true negation of capitalism came from the Black Radical Tradition, which Robinson traces from precolonial African cultures to the intellectual work of figures like W. E. B. Du Bois, C. L. R. James, and Richard Wright. Despite the title of his book, Robinson is not interested so much in the Marxism of these thinkers as their journey beyond Marxism to make their contributions to the Black Radical Tradition. Central to this journey was, for each thinker, coming to terms with the essential whiteness of Marxism and Marxist movements.[4]

Since its republication in 2000, *Black Marxism* has been enormously influential, with concepts like "black radical tradition" and "racial capitalism" achieving currency well beyond the specific arguments within which they were developed. In terms of intellectual history, however, the impact of concepts drawn from Robinson's work has been flattening in two respects. First, the notion of a black radical tradition tends to project a much higher degree of theoretical and political consensus across black Marxists than has actually existed. It is only at a very abstract level that, for example, W. E. B. Du Bois, Pauli Murray, and C. L. R. James could be considered part of the same political tradition. Rather than using black radical tradition in a pragmatist fashion to denote self-identified black radicals, interpreters have too often followed Robinson in attributing substantive commonality of thought that marks the thinkers included under the label from other streams in intellectual history. Second, Robinson's framing of black radicals losing faith in Marxism's ability to confront the race question has been widely echoed in the historiography, such that the primary contribution of black Marxists is regularly held to be their theorization of racial inequality. Thus, the intellectual contributions of black Marxists that have received the most attention center race against the alleged class reductionism of the rest of the Marxist movement.

The result of this has been an unfortunate lack of attention to other aspects of the thought of black Marxists. The rewards of such attention are demonstrated by examination of two central black Marxists from the mid-twentieth century, W. E. B. Du Bois and Oliver Cromwell Cox, and their understandings of democracy in the texts most central to their reputations as Marxists, *Black Reconstruction* and *Caste, Class, & Race*. In part, these two figures are chosen for their heterogeneity. Du Bois is, of course, one of the most studied intellectuals of the twentieth century, and hardly any aspect of his storied career could be said to lack attention at this point. Born in Massachusetts shortly after the end of slavery, and educated at Fisk University and Harvard, Du Bois emerged as a key intellectual in the early twentieth century. Over the course of the next five decades, through his own authorship and his editing of the National Association for the Advancement of Colored People's (NAACP) journal, the *Crisis*, Du Bois established himself as by far the country's most important interpreter of the race problem. After visiting the Soviet Union in 1926, Du Bois began a serious engagement with Marxist thought, moving to the left and becoming a supporter and eventually a member of the Communist Party before his death in 1963. Cox's path was rather different. Like Du Bois, he completed a doctorate, in his case at the University of Chicago's famous Sociology Department in 1938. Over the next three decades, he published prolifically on race and the trajectory of capitalism. Unlike Du Bois, his early work is deeply marked by his engagement with Marxism and maintains a consistently assimilationist perspective on race in the United States. While Cox developed a theory of capitalism that in many ways anticipated the perspective of world systems theory, his work, unlike Du Bois's has largely failed to inspire broader theoretical or historiographical allegiance.

In discussions of both thinkers' engagement with Marxism, their understandings of the race question loom large. This is fitting in many respects, but emphasis on this aspect of their work to the neglect of others has hindered a fuller understanding of their thought. In the case of Du Bois, debates over slavery, capitalism, and his account of the "general strike of the slaves" in *Black Reconstruction* have curiously passed over his reservations concerning the freedmen's political capabilities, resulting in an exaggeration of his adoption of a Marxist political perspective. In the case of Cromwell, his theorization of democracy and fascism reveal a thinker whose continuities with Marxist thought are at least as important as his heterodoxies.

W. E. B. Du Bois: reconstructing the *demos*

Few accounts of black Marxism in the United States fail to accord pride of place to W. E. B. Du Bois. While figures like Hubert Harrison or Claudia Jones, now recognized as central to the intellectual history of American Marxism, languished in obscurity for decades before achieving a renewed prominence, Du Bois was lionized by the left even during his lifetime. In particular, the Communist Party, which Du Bois had been close to since the mid-1940s and joined in late 1961, promoted his work vigorously, even establishing the W. E. B. Du Bois Clubs of America as a youth organization shortly after his death. The historiography of black Marxism has followed suit. Robinson's field-defining *Black Marxism* analyzes Du Bois as central to the black radical tradition. More recent treatments have not dissented from this evaluation.[5]

Over his long career, Du Bois wrote frequently on Marxist themes, from his early essay on "Socialism and the Negro Problem" to his unpublished manuscript "Russia and America" to *Dark Princess*, his novel about world revolution. Yet Du Bois's reputation as a Marxist theorist rests, overwhelmingly, on his 1935 book, *Black Reconstruction: An Essay Toward a History of the Part*

Which Black Folk Played in the Attempt to Reconstruct Democracy in America, 1860–1880. Recently described by David Roediger as "the most fully realized work of Marxist history of the United States yet produced," Black Reconstruction places the Civil War and Reconstruction alongside the French Revolution and the revolutions of 1848 as an epoch-making process in the emergence of the modern world. At the center of this process are the black folk, whose "general strike" during the Civil War, Du Bois, argues was what ultimately led to the defeat of the slavocracy. In the new Reconstruction governments, elected with black votes, something like "a dictatorship of the proletariat" was built, as black elected officials administered the state in the interests of the freedmen.[6]

With this conceptual vocabulary, it is not hard to see why the book has come to be seen as a milestone in Du Bois's relationship with Marxism. Cedric Robinson sees Black Reconstruction as the moment when Du Bois came to "a realization of the historical forces emergent from the people, specifically the capacities of the Black masses to take steps decisive to their own liberation." Similarly, Bill V. Mullen argues that "Du Bois's interpretation of the black working class (and portions of the white working class) as seeking its own self-emancipation demonstrated a commitment to socialism from below," in contradistinction to Du Bois's earlier embrace of more Fabian models of socialism.[7]

Yet the appreciation of just how profound a conceptual step Du Bois was making with "the general strike of the slaves" has tended to crowd out recognition of other, more ambiguous treatments of the political capacities of the freedmen that exist in Black Reconstruction. Most significantly, Du Bois expresses significant doubts about the readiness of the freedmen for the exercise of the suffrage they had so recently gained. While Du Bois is at pains to stress the world-historical agency of the slaves in leaving the plantations and joining the Union army, and to defend the Reconstruction governments against the charges of corruption, he is also quite clear that immediate mass universal suffrage was *not* the ideal outcome in the postbellum South. Instead, he embraces a kind of trustee model of citizenship, in which full suffrage rights would only have been granted to the freedmen as they acquired land and education. However, the intransigence of the Southern ruling class, and their utter unwillingness to act as responsible trustees of black citizenship, made this course impossible, and made universal enfranchisement necessary.

This line of argument, strangely unnoticed in the copious body of commentary on *Black Reconstruction*, complicates the arguments of interpreters like Robinson who see the book as a decisive break with Du Bois's earlier embrace of elite-led racial politics. Instead, it tends to confirm the arguments of interpreters like Adolph Reed, Robert Gooding-Williams, and Joy James, who stress the centrality and the persistence of elitist conceptions of political participation in Du Bois's thought. While the narrative of "Du Bois's journey towards Marxism" remains a prominent interpretive frame in understanding his political thought, the vitality of alternative conceptions of politics, even in his most insistently Marxist work, suggests that periodization of his political life might be more profitably conceptualized through attempts to understand the different elements of Marxist and non-Marxist social thought that predominated throughout his career.[8]

It is widely recognized that Du Bois's engagement with Marxism prior to writing *Black Reconstruction* was uneven. He had attended meetings of the German Social Democratic Workers' Party as a student in Berlin and had joined the Socialist Party briefly in 1911. While some interpreters have attempted to make the case that Du Bois possessed a developed socialist worldview in this period, the evidence adduced in favor of this argument is not very compelling, and usually involves conflating standard Progressive Era nostrums about the need for democracy and planning in industry with more specifically Marxist arguments. While Du Bois was clearly sympathetic to elements of the socialist movement, this sympathy co-existed with plainly elitist visions of social change. Most infamously, in a 1903 essay, he argued that "the Negro race, like all races, is going to be saved by its exceptional men," and that successful black politics were contingent on the development of the capacities of race leaders. Of course, Du Bois was hardly alone in this period in yoking black progress to the fortunes of black elites. The politics of uplift were both an expression of the class ideology of the tiny black elite as well as a conscious rebuke of the white supremacist denial of black intellectual capacities. For Du Bois, the egalitarian ideals of socialism were not in contradiction with this broader vision of uplift: it was precisely through the cultivation of the leadership abilities (and sense of racial responsibility) of the black elite that a more egalitarian social order could be achieved.[9]

These twin commitments persisted through the period of the writing of *Black Reconstruction*. Du Bois traveled to the Soviet Union in 1926 and came back declaring that "if what I have seen with my eyes and heard with my ears is Bolshevism, then I am a Bolshevik." He also established contact with the Socialist Party in New York, encouraging socialists to be more proactive in addressing racism in the labor movement. In 1933, he announced an agenda for the *Crisis*, the NAACP journal he edited, that included topics like "Depression, Capitalism and Karl Marx," "The 'Class Struggle' of the Black Proletariat and Bourgeoisie," and "The Dictatorship of the Black Proletariat." At the same time, however, his writings continued to display a clear attachment to the politics of elite-led uplift. His 1928 novel *Dark Princess* combined enthusiasm for the Third International with a fascination with the virtues of the monarchy, ultimately embracing what Arnold Rampersad described as "an aristocracy of merit." Three years later, writing on "The Negro and Communism" for the *Crisis*, Du Bois would declare that the "present organization of industry for private profit and control over government by concentrated wealth is doomed to disaster," while also extolling the leadership of the black elite. Referring, significantly, to the Reconstruction period, he praised "educated American Negroes," arguing that "is their foresight and sacrifice and theirs alone that has saved the American freedman from annihilation and degradation." For Du Bois, socialism was the logical telos of black politics, but the key to black political advance was not the organization of the black working class, but rather the sense of duty of the black elite.[10]

As Du Bois began working on *Black Reconstruction* in 1931, he embarked on a more systematic engagement with Marxist thought. With his graduate students at Atlanta University, he read Marx's *Capital*. His friend Benjamin Stolberg, an independent Marxist journalist, provided feedback on the use of Marxist theory in the text, most centrally concerning Du Bois's description of the Reconstruction governments as a "dictatorship of the proletariat." As Matthew Nichter has recently demonstrated, Du Bois also relied crucially on the advice of Will Herberg, a member of the dissident communist grouping around Jay Lovestone. Herberg introduced

Du Bois to his own pamphlet, *The Heritage of the Civil War*, as well as pointing him to Marx's writings on the conflict.[11]

The result was a text that combined a vindication of black governance in Reconstruction governments with a far-reaching reinterpretation of the period in terms of conflicts between and among divided laboring and exploiting classes. While much of the contemporary historiography imagined the Civil War as a mere sectional conflict, Du Bois saw it as a world-historical conflict over forms of property. Ultimately, labor's defeat and the reconciliation of the Northern and Southern propertied classes laid the foundation for the United States' emergence as a capitalist superpower. Imperialism was the bitter fruit of the working classes' defeat.

This macro-historical perspective, however, did not prove to be the text's most influential contribution. Indeed, as Brian Kelly has recently noted, there has been a marked retreat from conceptualizing the Civil War and Reconstruction in terms of class structures and class conflict. Yet at the same time, other aspects of Du Bois's text have been immensely generative of historiographical agendas. The school of work around "whiteness studies," for instance, traces its theoretical heritage to his arguments about the failures of working-class unity during Reconstruction. His concept of "the general strike of the slaves" has been similarly influential. While debates over what has come to be called "the self-emancipation thesis" have percolated among Civil War historians, the idea of a slave general strike has been taken up with enthusiasm in the humanities more broadly, providing a conceptual anchor for scholarship by historians, literary theorists, and philosophers.[12]

The enthusiasm with which the idea of the general strike of the slaves is received today stands in stark contrast to its reception at the time of *Black Reconstruction*'s publication, particularly by other black Marxists. Though the book was generally well-received by reviewers in the mainstream press, other black Marxists were quite critical of it, and focused their criticism on the general strike of the slaves, as well as the cognate theorization of Reconstruction governments as dictatorships of the proletariat. Abram Harris, the radical economist, while praising Du Bois's analysis of the class conflicts shaping the Civil War and Reconstruction, argued that a general strike "implies a real consciousness not only of the class issues that make its use necessary but also of the ends deliberately sought by those who use it." No such consciousness could be discovered amongst the slaves, Harris concluded. The journalist and lawyer Loren Miller, writing in *New Masses*, thought that Du Bois's usage deprived the term "strike" of all meaning. Ralph Bunche, writing in *The Journal of Negro History*, and Henry Lee Moon, writing in *Race*, both agreed. For the young black Marxists of the 1930s, Du Bois's embrace of Marxism had led to an over-hasty application of concepts to contexts that were unsuited.[13]

Whether valorizing or criticizing Du Bois's use of the concepts of general strike and dictatorship of the proletariat, readers of *Black Reconstruction* have tended to see these concepts as encompassing Du Bois's political vision in the book. Brian Kelly, one of Du Bois's most perspicacious interpreters, sees the book's "unconcealed celebration of black agency" as its "most obvious contribution." Yet just as Du Bois's earlier writings had been defined by a simultaneous embrace of egalitarianism and elite-led politics, *Black Reconstruction* contained, alongside its unquestionable celebration of the world-historic achievements of the slaves during the Civil War, profound reservations about their political capacities as freedmen during Reconstruction. Du Bois announces these reservations virtually as soon as he begins discussing black politics during the period. The chapter "The Price of Disaster," which immediately precedes the four chapters examining the performance of Reconstruction governments, makes these reservations clear. In it, Du Bois argues that the Reconstruction governments were "a dictatorship backed by the military arm of the United States by which the governments of the Southern states were to be coerced into accepting a new form of administration, in which the freedmen and the poor whites were to hold the overwhelming balance of political power."

Du Bois is quite explicit as to the purpose of this dictatorship, arguing that it "must endure until the proletariat or at least a leading united group ... had education and experience and had taken firm control of the economic organization of the South." For Du Bois, the purpose of the dictatorship over the South was not simply to protect democratic governments from mob violence; it was also to provide space for the freedmen in particular to develop their political capacities, through education, to be able to practice democracy effectively.[14]

Du Bois returns to these twin themes of dictatorship and education frequently in the second half of *Black Reconstruction*. Education, or its lack, often assumes pride of place in explaining the fortunes of the freedmen. In comparing the Reconstruction governments of Mississippi and Louisiana, for example, Du Bois notes that "there were far fewer Negroes of intelligence and ability in Mississippi than in South Carolina or Louisiana." Earlier, he describes what seems to be his ideal for successful black leadership in this period, noting that "intelligent, free Negroes" in some pockets of the South "had accumulated some wealth and some knowledge of group cooperation and initiative," and had "accepted the new responsibility of leading the emancipated slaves, unselfishly and effectively." This description evinces considerable similarity with the political agenda Du Bois had previously articulated, in which black political success was dependent upon the educated elite performing their duty to the race as a whole and leading it in the fight for egalitarianism. Later, Du Bois points to the importance of educational institutions in black politics, declaring "had it not been for the Negro school and college, the Negro would ... have been driven back to slavery ... [T]hrough establishing public schools and private colleges ... the Negro had acquired enough leadership and knowledge that would thwart the worst designs of the new slave drivers."[15]

The need for education led directly to the need for dictatorship. Du Bois uses that word liberally in *Black Reconstruction*, embracing a Leninist vocabulary. He describes the plantocracy as "political oligarchy and economic dictatorship in the most extreme form in which the world had seen it for five hundred years," and the Reconstruction governments as a "dictatorship of labor." While he excoriates the dictatorship of property in the North, and of the planters in the South, Du Bois argues that dictatorship had a positive role to play, not merely in suppressing the revanchist Confederates, but in preparing the way for democracy. He discusses the theory behind this evaluation at the beginning of the chapters on the Reconstruction governments. The weight of numbers, Du Bois argues, makes democracy inevitable. There is simply no way to prevent the rule of the masses. Under "the current theory of democracy ... dictatorship is a stopgap pending the work of universal education, equitable income, and strong character," which will allow the masses to rule successfully. However, this dictatorship is easily abused, as a result of a lack of faith in the people's ultimate ability for self-government. The result is fascism, slavery, and rule by junta. If, however, the "high ideal" of seeing "every human being, to the extent of his capacity, escape ignorance, poverty, and crime" is maintained, then there are a variety of roads that can be traveled to democracy. "Monarchy, oligarchy, or dictatorships may rule," but as long as that ideal is held true, "the end will be the rule of All, if mayhap All or Most qualify." Underscoring his theory of a responsible dictatorship, Du Bois warns that "the only unforgivable sin is dictatorship for the benefit of Fools, Voluptuaries, gilded Satraps, Prostitutes and Idiots." Du Bois believed in democracy, but he also believed that a people had to be made ready for democracy, and that dictatorship was an appropriate instrument for this work.[16]

In the context of Reconstruction, Du Bois argued that a dictatorship was indeed necessary to develop black capacities for political leadership. Though the Radical Republicans had embraced universal suffrage, such suffrage "could not function without personal freedom, land and education." Until these conditions were secured, "only a benevolent dictatorship in the ultimate interests of labor, black and white, could establish democracy." Du Bois is quite clear that the incapacity of the masses necessitated this dictatorship. In fact, he argues that such a dictatorship was necessary in the North as well, as the electorate there "was provincial and bigoted, thinned by poverty-stricken and ignorant peasant laborers from abroad, and impregnated with the idea that individual wealth spelled national prosperity and particularly with the American assumption of equal economic opportunity for all." It was impossible for such an electorate to counterbalance the power of property. "Only a vast and single-eyed dictatorship of the nation could guide us up from murder in the South and robbery and cheating in the North" towards an egalitarian social order.[17]

Ultimately, Du Bois's concerns about the political capacities of the freedmen lead him, towards the end of the book, to suggest that universal suffrage was, in fact, not the preferred outcome after the Civil War. Instead, Du Bois argues that a model of trustee citizenship would have been preferable, in which the freedmen were gradually extended the franchise in accordance with their attainment of education and economic independence (in the form of land). "The best transition program for capital and labor," he argues, would have been "an effective public school for black labor in the South, and its gradual enfranchisement, or even beyond that, a property qualification for laborers" (as long as land redistribution and high wages made the acquisition of such property possible). A page later, he reiterates this point, lamenting that the South could have "educated and uplifted the blacks and gradually inducted them into political power and real industrial emancipation." If they had done so, even "without yielding immediate political power ... the results undoubtedly would have been better." Of course, such a course of action was never even considered. As he put it elsewhere, "here were people who knew they knew one thing above all others ... that a Negro would not work without compulsion, and that slavery was his natural condition." For the South to adopt this model of trustee citizenship would have required "an industrial unselfishness which the capitalist organization of production does not for a moment admit." Gradual enfranchisement would have been the optimal outcome, but the South's intransigence made it impossible and left only immediate universal suffrage or a return to slavery on the table.[18]

Du Bois is, of course, perfectly clear that the political infirmities he sees in the black *demos* are entirely the product of slavery. Unlike the racist historiography against which he was writing, he doesn't see any special incapacity in the freedmen. Any people enduring centuries of bondage as brutal as that of American slavery who were suddenly freed without access to land, he argues, would be in similar need of leadership. Indeed, as we saw above, Du Bois even at one point suggests that the Northern working class suffered a similar democratic incapacity and needed dictatorship to protect its interests as well. His support for dictatorship and gradual enfranchisement are not violations of his pledge to the reader to "tell this story as though Negroes were ordinary human beings," but rather an insight into what Du Bois thought the capabilities of ordinary human beings in these circumstances were.

This doubt in democratic capacities, voiced repeatedly throughout the second half of *Black Reconstruction*, has gone unnoticed by the book's interpreters. Both champions and detractors of Du Bois's "general strike of the slaves" have seen that phrase as encompassing Du Bois's vision of black politics in the book. Indeed, their discussions of Reconstruction have tended to assimilate to the book a concern with black politics at the grassroots, such as one finds in work by Steven Hahn or Elsa Barkley Brown. Among more recent Marxian interpreters, in particular, there is a tendency to attribute to Du Bois something like C. L. R. James's summation of Marxist politics: "every cook can govern."[19] However, Du Bois's other writings should give us caution regarding such an interpretation. Throughout his long career, despite changing his mind about a great many things, Du Bois remained committed to a vision of black politics as a practice of what Adolph Reed has called "racial custodianship," in which the black elite safeguard the interests of the race as a whole. His ideas about strategies changed, from the militant interracialism of the early NAACP to the nationalism of his black cooperatives schemes in the 1930s. Similarly, his ideas about the ends of black politics changed over time, as Du Bois became less and less confident that existing American institutions could ever be repurposed to serve an egalitarian society. All of this change took place within a framework in which the race's "exceptional men" were held to be the motive force for political change. This framework also structured Du Bois's argument in *Black Reconstruction*.[20]

In one sense, the failure to recognize Du Bois's vision of elite-led politics in *Black Reconstruction* is a product of the singularity of his broader political vision. Du Bois was indeed a distinctively egalitarian political thinker, both in his racial politics and his belief in the inevitability of universal democracy. However, he circumscribed this egalitarianism in ways that are quite foreign to contemporary political thought, most centrally, with a forthright embrace of a hierarchy of abilities that inevitably translated into a political hierarchy. In *Black Reconstruction* in particular, the radicalism of his egalitarianism has led interpreters to overlook his significant circumscriptions of it. Yet for Du Bois, his egalitarianism and his elitism were coterminous.

If in one sense this combination has seemed too strange to be recognized, in another sense its invisibility is a product of its contemporary ubiquity. As Keeanga-Yamahtta Taylor has recently argued, the goal of "black faces in high places" continues to be a dominating theme in black American politics. Here, as in Du Bois's thought, elite racial custodianship is seen as the vehicle for achieving a more egalitarian social order. Understanding the vicissitudes of black politics today requires grasping the particular combination of egalitarianism and elitism that structures this ideology. Du Bois's political theory, even in *Black Reconstruction*, forms one wellspring for this conception of politics, and cannot be understood without attention to that same dialectic of egalitarianism and elitism.[21]

Oliver Cromwell Cox and the ends of democracy

Unlike Du Bois, Oliver Cromwell Cox's influence on contemporary thought has been limited and indirect. Though Cox was nearly as prolific as Du Bois in the years in which he was active, and if anything a more conscientious system-builder in his thought, no schools of thought or distinct streams of scholarship base themselves on his work. This is not to say his work has been entirely without influence. Most notably, Cedric Robinson's analysis of capitalism as a kind of late-stage feudal mercantilism that informs *Black Marxism* is itself heavily influenced by Cox. Similarly, Immanuel Wallerstein has recognized Cox's analyses of capitalism as an important precursor to world systems theory, though one rooted more in his reading of classical political economy than the *Annales* school of economic history that influenced the world systems theorists.[22]

Cox's theoretical omnivorism is, perhaps, one reason why his work failed to persuade many at the time, but it is this feature of his work that has received by far the most scholarly attention over the years. This attention has focused in particular on one aspect of Cox's intellectual formation: the question of his Marxism. On the whole, commentators on Cox's work have argued that his divergences from Marxism were more intellectually significant than his allegiances. Though Cox's discussions of exploitation, imperialism, and class conflict sound obvious Marxian notes, commentators argue that they mask a fundamental reorientation away from a Marxist theoretical frame. They point to the obviously Weberian elements of his class theory, and more significantly, to Cox's relocation of the locus of capitalism from production to trade as evidence that if Cox began with Marx, he ended elsewhere.[23]

While Cox has been praised for his non-Marxian theory of capitalism, he has been castigated for his all too Marxist theory of race. Roediger holds up Cox as a representative of "traditional" Marxist theories of race, which treat race as less fundamental or important than class, a view "which informed and deformed the practice of the socialist movement during its heyday in the US." Similarly, Bruce Nelson accuses Cox of being "too content with traditional Marxist formulas" and ignoring the power of white workers in producing racial subordination. Cox's work, it seems, was uneven in the distance it took from Marxism.[24]

These two questions—the political economy of capitalism, and the understanding of racial inequality within capitalism—have dominated Cox's intellectual reception. In doing so, however, they have tended to crowd out examination of other aspects of Cox's writing. This is a pity, most centrally because Cox had an unusually wide intellectual range for an American social scientist of his generation and training, but also because other aspects of his thought can shed significant light on the interpretive questions that have been central to understanding Cox's career. Cox's account of democracy, particularly in his first major work *Class, Caste, & Race*, explores its complicated relationship with capitalism. He accompanied this with a polemical engagement with the neoliberal progenitor Friedrich Hayek's *The Road to Serfdom*, in which he takes Hayek's arguments as the paradigmatic critique of democracy. Finally, Cox provides an account of fascism that is notable for its distance from the consideration of fascism given by American social science in the postwar years. In all of this, Cox adopted a resolutely Marxist theoretical and political stance. Consideration of Cox as a political theorist thus provides further evidence for the complicated question of the place of Marxism in his thought, as well as restoring his place in the debate about capitalism and democracy taking place after the Second World War.

Democracy was at the center of the problems that dominated Cox's intellectual life. Racial inequality in the United States was, as he put it, a form of "democratic retardation." The problems of class conflict and imperialism as well were fundamentally problems of democracy. Despite this, Cox never wrote an extended treatment of democracy. Instead, he largely folded it into *Class, Caste, & Race*. About seventy-five pages of this massive text are given over to a series of reflections on the origins and ultimate fate of modern democracy, providing a theoretical and normative anchor for his later discussion of race as a problem of democratization.[25]

Cox's treatment is first distinguished by its account of democracy's origins. For Cox, democracy is essentially a modern phenomenon, no more traceable to ancient Athenian democracy than the industrial revolution is. Instead, modern democracy has its origins in the rise of capitalism. Like most Marxists at the time, Cox saw democracy as developing in the nascent Western bourgeoisie's battle against feudalism. Hemmed in by the landlords, the laws, and the church, the small urban bourgeoisie mounted a guerilla war of ideas, encouraging "a number of philosophers, writers, journalists, and propagandists, who undermined the morale of the people who supported the ruling class." The ideas which so sapped the morale of the feudal ruling class were, quite simply, the enlightenment ideals of democracy. Once the target was softened, the bourgeoisie moved in for the kill, overthrowing the feudal ruling class and establishing liberal democratic regimes in place of the feudal order. As Cox concludes, "democracy, then, was made possible by the achievements of the bourgeoisie."[26]

At the same time, however, complete democracy could not be achieved by the bourgeoisie. In fact, the modern bourgeoisie was "unalterably opposed to democracy." According to Cox, this opposition stemmed from what might be termed "democracy creep." While the bourgeois revolutions, such as the English and French revolutions, introduced liberal democracy, that very institution was used by workers to push beyond it, to economic democracy. The masses will "take hold of this popular support of capitalism and use it for the purpose of transferring economic power to themselves." This dynamic leads the bourgeoisie to abandon its support for democracy, and responsibility for its advance falls into the hands of the proletariat. Today, Cox argues, "whatever fraction of democracy we possess ... has been achieved in increments by and for the masses against the more or less violent opposition of bourgeois" classes.[27] Unsurprisingly, Cox then views socialism as the completion of democracy. Indeed, Cox often uses democracy as a synonym for socialism, as when he contrasts democracy and "bourgeois freedom," arguing "democracy will turn power and freedom over to the people." This will then mark the transition from liberal democracy to "accomplished democracy."[28]

In developing this account of democracy, Cox leans heavily on Marxist writings on the subject. The two key authorities in this section of the text, from whom he quotes liberally, are John Strachey and Lewis Corey. Strachey was a British journalist who had been one of the country's leading Marxist intellectuals. Corey, under his original name Louis Fraina, had been an influential founder of American Communism, but he parted ways with the resulting organization and in the 1930s became one of the leading Marxist writers on political economy. Cox draws from both writers heavily in describing the way the contemporary bourgeoisie has forsaken its democratic heritage. Other prominent Marxists pepper the footnotes of these chapters, including the British writer R. Palme Dutt, whose work on fascism was Third International orthodoxy; Rosa Luxemburg, the Polish revolutionary; Paul Sweezy, the American economist; Arthur Rosenberg, the German historian; and Leon Trotsky, the Russian revolutionary. For Cox, the Marxist literature provided his key orientation on the question of democracy.[29]

Cox was not merely a theorist. He was also an engaged intellectual, commenting on and intervening in contemporary politics. In *Caste, Class, & Race*, Cox responds at some length to the arguments of Friedrich Hayek, whose *The Road to Serfdom* had come out five years earlier, providing new intellectual heft to conservatism. For Cox, Hayek's book is not merely an anti-socialist jeremiad, but a comprehensive repudiation of democracy. His response thus focuses on the virtues of democracy.[30] Cox begins with one of Hayek's most influential arguments, concerning the market and the concentration of power. Hayek argues that private ownership of the means of production actually preserves freedom, because it disperses the social power that accompanies such ownership across multiple people. If all of this power were concentrated in one institutional location, "whether it be nominally that of 'society' as a whole or that of a dictator, whoever exercises this control" would have total control. Cox argues that this line of thought rests on a kind of sleight of hand, where somehow people's power over themselves becomes someone else's power over them. This conceals the actual motivation for the argument, what is "very clearly the great fear: fear of democracy." Moreover, Hayek's picture of the dispersion of the power of property via private ownership ignores the actual structure of incredibly concentrated ownership. In the United States, where 60 percent of industrial workers were employed by 2 percent of manufacturing concerns in 1944, the idea of private property leading to a wide dispersion power was farcical. For Cox, Hayek was ignoring really existing capitalism in making his case against socialism.[31]

Cox saw Hayek's arguments as one of the most important lines of attack against democracy. In an article which became the basis for this section of *Caste, Class, & Race*, he explicitly paired this with the second key line of attack, noting that "Adolf Hitler in *Mein Kampf* and Friedrich Hayek in *The Road to Serfdom* have made the most direct attacks on democracy." Cox devotes significant attention to fascism, arguing that it is the encapsulation of all of the anti-democratic tendencies of the bourgeoisie. While Cox's analysis of fascism has been basically ignored in scholarly discussions of his work, it is deeply revealing about his intellectual orientation, and the particular heterodoxies to which he subscribed.[32]

In the postwar years, fascism (and to a lesser degree, communism) became the privileged case for developing a theory of collective behavior that centered on the dysfunctional integration of "the masses" into modern society. The failures of the Weimar Republic, the Nazi takeover, and the Holocaust were all attributed to the pathologies of mass society. William Kornhauser, who taught at the University of Chicago while Cox was a student there, developed the most elaborate version of this thesis in his 1959 book *The Politics of Mass Society*. Kornhauser argued that societies become "massified" in the process of modernization, as people become unstuck from traditional social roles. This results in a lack of social differentiation, and a cultural leveling that emerges politically "in the guise of *populism*." For Kornhauser, movements like fascism were the result of a kind of unrestrained, relentlessly leveling surplus of democracy. Versions of this thesis, that attributed fascism to the masses, emerged throughout mid-century social science, from Kornhauser's Chicago School modernization theory to Hannah Arendt's republicanism to Theodore Adorno's Marxism. For these thinkers, what was notable about fascism was its implantation in the minds of the masses.[33]

Cox attacked this view with reference to both fascism's intellectual history and its place in the social structure. With regards to fascist thought, Cox highlighted its specifically anti-mass thrust. The material he quotes from Adolf Hitler to explain fascist doctrine all revolve around this point. He notes that Hitler summarized the fascist worldview as "rejecting the democratic mass idea, endeavor[ing] to give the world the best people ... the most superior men ... [fascism] has to start from the principle that for humanity blessing has never lain in the masses." Summarizing the fascist relationship to the masses, Cox notes that "they despise the masses, conceding them neither capacity to think nor to develop their own leadership." For Cox, fascism was centrally an anti-mass politics, directed towards removing their influence over public life.[34]

This explicitly elitist ideology reflected fascism's roots as an elite-driven phenomenon. Following his theory of creeping democracy, in which liberal democratic rights would inevitably be used by workers to procure economic democracy, Cox argued that fascism was the natural response of the elite threatened by these incursions on its economic privileges. As he puts it, the natural constituency of the fascist party includes

> the majority of men who have achieved great business success, of politicians of upper chambers, professional men of the highest order, distinguished scholars, eminent bishops and cardinals, the most powerful newspaper owners and editors, learned judges, the valiant upper crust of the military forces, and so on ... the fascists are the capitalists and their sympathizers who have achieved political-class consciousness.

As this passage suggests, at times Cox takes this argument to a mechanistic extreme, arguing that fascism is the natural form of bourgeois class consciousness. Elsewhere, however, he tempers this impulse, noting that "capitalist reactionaries do not ordinarily admire fascism; they accept it only as a last resort in the face of a serious threat from democracy." In either articulation of the argument, however, fascism is an elite-driven movement that arises in response to the advance of democracy. While the theorists of mass society theorized fascism as bubbling up from the dislocated and alienated masses, Cox argues that fascism grows from the top down, in response not to a dislocated mass, but one that is all too coherent and successful in advancing its interests.[35]

In making this argument, Cox was aligning himself with much of the Marxist scholarship on fascism. The references of the section on fascism reflect this, drawing from John Strachey, the French Trotskyist turned anarchist Daniel Guérin, and the radical economist Robert A. Brady. This alignment marked a decisive rejection of the Chicago approach to social movements in general and fascism in particular. Though Cox is well-known for his critique of Robert

Park and the Chicago school's "caste" theory of race relations, his neglected perspective on fascism demonstrates that he also took his distance from them in his understanding of the foundations of collective behavior.[36]

Cox's approach to the questions of democracy and fascism was thus a resolutely Marxist one. He saw democracy in class terms, as a product of working-class struggle against the bourgeoisie, and saw socialism as the completion of the democratic revolution. He criticized Hayek from this standpoint, arguing that Hayek's critique of planning was really a rejection of democracy itself. And, like many left intellectuals in the postwar years, he saw the emergence of fascism as having revealed something profound about the relationship between capitalism and democracy.

Cox pursued a lonely path through mid-century social science. On subjects like racial inequality and democracy, his Marxist commitments led him to understandings of these subjects that were quite different from the mainsprings of American sociology. While his writings on democracy were little noticed, his critique of Robert Park and Gunnar Myrdal in *Caste, Class, & Race* placed a considerable distance between himself and the rest of the discipline. At the same time, though friendly with Paul Sweezy and the group around *Monthly Review*, Cox saw his work as distinct from theirs and from contemporary Marxism more generally. Though a prolific and engaged scholar, he cultivated no followers, and no schools of thought rooted in his theories developed from his work. Despite this, Cox was clearly an important figure in twentieth-century Marxism. His very singularity testifies to the heterogeneity of thought that is characterized as "black Marxism." Like Du Bois, Cox's thought contained different, sometimes contradictory elements. And like Du Bois, the best way to understand that thought is not to ask whether he was or was not a Marxist, but to try and understand, as fully as possible, the way he combined Marxist and non-Marxist concepts throughout his career.

Race and democracy

Both Du Bois and Cox saw a complete democratization of society as inevitable. They imagined quite different paths to that outcome, however, as a result of their different ways of theorizing the forces responsible for democratization. Subsequent scholarship has both sustained and challenged different aspects of their theories. Du Bois's account of the general strike of the slaves has found substantial support in subsequent research, and his social interpretation of Reconstruction was confirmed by Eric Foner's field-defining synthesis in the 1980s.[37] At the same time, his doubts about the political capacities of the freedmen have been undermined by work on grassroots organizing after the Civil War, which shows that the freedmen displayed considerable ability and sophistication in their political participation.[38] They required the North to protect them from white terrorists, not to teach them how to practice democracy. Cox's account, similarly, has experienced a mixture of confirmation and rejection. His account of the working class's role in democratization has received strong empirical support.[39] However, his emphasis on the importance of fascism in halting democratization is significantly overstated. Like virtually all Marxists of his generation, Cox underestimated the mechanisms built into capitalist accumulation that disorganize and frustrate working-class advance.[40]

Both Du Bois and Cox's theories of democracy were, of course, intimately connected to their thinking on the race question. In light of contemporary thinking on racism, what distinguishes both of them is their insistence on embedding their thinking on race within a larger account of democratization in modern societies. For Du Bois and Cox, understanding how the "democratic retardation" of racism could be confronted required a broader theory of the sources of and obstacles to democracy in modern societies. Today, even the most perceptive accounts of the relationship between race and democracy neglect this question, focusing instead on the ways racial oppression impedes democracy or on how democratic procedures can be more race-conscious.[41] Du Bois and Cox's arguments suggest this is a mistake. Racial oppression is but one kind of antidemocratic structure in the modern world, and Du Bois and Cox's insistence that it cannot be understood apart from other kinds is a valuable corrective to seeing such oppression as *sui generis*. From this perspective, dismantling racism is only one part of a broader movement for societal democratization. In this way, attention to the thinking of black Marxists on subjects besides the color line not only broadens our understanding of the contours of their thought, it provides us with the conceptual resources to invigorate our own thinking on the race question.

Notes

1 Philip S. Foner, *American Socialism and Black Americans: From the Age of Jackson to World War II* (Westport, CT: Greenwood Press, 1977), 103; Mark Solomon, *The Cry Was Unity: Communists and African Americans, 1917–1936* (Jackson: University of Mississippi Press, 1998); C. Wilson Record, *The Negro and the Communist Party* (Chapel Hill: University of North Carolina Press, 1951); William P. Jones, "'Nothing Special to Offer the Negro': Revisiting the 'Debsian View' of the Negro Question," *International Labor and Working-Class History* 74, no. 1 (2008): 212–24; Paul M. Heideman, *The Class Struggle and the Color Line: American Socialism and the Race Question, 1900–1930* (Chicago: Haymarket Books, 2018).
2 James R. Green, *Grass-Roots Socialism: Radical Movements in the Southwest, 1895–1943* (Baton Rouge: Louisiana State University Press, 1978); Mark Naison, *Communists in Harlem During the Depression* (Champaign: University of Illinois Press, 1983); Robin D. G. Kelley, *Hammer and Hoe: Alabama Communists During the Great Depression* (Chapel Hill: University of North Carolina Press, 1990).
3 On the literary and cultural history, see Bill V. Mullen, *Popular Fronts: Chicago and African-American Cultural Politics, 1935–46* (Champaign: University of Illinois Press, 1999); Barbara Foley, *Spectres of 1919: Class and Nation in the Making of the New Negro* (Champaign: University of Illinois Press, 2003); William J. Maxwell, *New Negro, Old Left: African American Writing and Communism Between the Wars* (New York: Columbia University Press, 1999); Carole Boyce Davies, *Left of Karl Marx: The Political Life of Black Communist Claudia Jones* (Durham: Duke University Press, 2008). The neglect of intellectual history is criticized in Adolph Reed and Kenneth W. Warren, "Introduction," in *Renewing Black Intellectual History: The Ideological and Material Foundations of African American Thought*, ed. Reed and Warren (New York: Routledge, 2009), vii–xi.
4 Cedric J. Robinson, *Black Marxism: The Making the Black Radical Tradition* (Chapel Hill: University of North Carolina Press, 2000). For the influence of Robinson's book, see Darryl C. Thomas, "The Black radical tradition—theory and practice: Black studies and the scholarship of Cedric Robinson," *Race & Class* 47:2 (2005), 1–22.

5 On the CPUSA's promotion of Du Bois, see Gerald Horne, *Black & Red: W. E. B. Du Bois and the Afro-American Response to the Cold War, 1944–1963* (Albany: State University of New York Press, 1986), Ch. 20; Robinson, 185–240.
6 W. E. B. Du Bois, *Black Reconstruction in America: An Essay Toward a History of the Part Which Black Folk Played in the Attempt to Reconstruct Democracy in America, 1860–1880* (New York: Atheneum, 1977); David Roediger, *Seizing Freedom: Slave Emancipation and Liberty For All* (London: Verso, 2014), 12.
7 Robinson, 198; Bill V. Mullen, *W. E. B. Du Bois: Revolutionary Across the Color Line* (London: Pluto Books, 2016), 81.
8 Adolph Reed, *W. E. B. Du Bois and American Political Thought: Fabianism and the Color Line* (New York: Oxford University Press, 1997); Robert Gooding-Williams, *In the Shadow of Du Bois: Afro-Modern Political Thought in America* (Cambridge: Harvard University Press, 2011); Joy James, *Transcending the Talented Tenth: Black Leaders and American Intellectuals* (New York: Routledge, 1997). Interestingly, *Black Reconstruction* goes almost entirely unmentioned in all three books.
9 David Levering Lewis, *W. E. B. Du Bois: Biography of a Race, 1868–1919* (New York: Henry Holt and Co, 1993), 143–44; W. E. B. Du Bois, "The Talented Tenth," in *The Negro Problem* (New York: James Pott and Co., 1903); Mark Van Wienen and Julie Kraft, "How the Socialism of W. E. B. Du Bois Still Matters: Black Socialism in the 'The Quest of the Silver Fleece'—and Beyond," *African American Review* 41, no. 1 (2007), 67–85; Kevin K. Gaines, *Uplifting the Race: Black Leadership, Politics, and Culture in the Twentieth Century* (University of North Carolina Press: Chapel Hill, 1996).
10 Mullen, *Du Bois*, 67, 74; Mark Van Weinen, *American Socialist Triptych: The Literary-Political Work of Charlotte Perkins Gilman, Upton Sinclair, and W. E. B. Du Bois* (Ann Arbor: University of Michigan Press, 2012), 280–81; Arnold Rampersad, *The Art and Imagination of W. E. B. Du Bois* (Cambridge, MA: 1976, 217); W. E. B. Du Bois, "The Negro and Communism," *The Crisis*, 38 (1931), 313–15. On the continued centrality of elites to Du Bois's political vision in *Dark Princess*, see Kenneth W. Warren, "An Inevitable Drift? Oligarchy, Du Bois, and the Prospect of Democracy Between the Wars," in *Renewing Black Intellectual History*, ed. Reed and Warren, 80–94.
11 Lewis, 361–63. On Stolberg, see Christopher Phelps, "Heywood Broun, Benjamin Stolberg, and the Politics of American Labor Journalism in the 1920s and 1930s," *Labor: Studies in Working Class History* 15, no. 1 (2018): 25–51. Matthew F. Nichter, "DuBois's Marxist Mentor: Will

Herberg and the Making of Black Reconstruction in America" (paper, Historical Materialism conference, New York, NY, April 22, 2017).

12 Brian Kelly, "Slave Self-Activity and the Bourgeois Revolution in the United States: Jubilee and the Boundaries of Black Freedom," *Historical Materialism* 27, no. 3 (2019), 31–76; Roediger, *The Wages of Whiteness: Race and the Making of the American Working Class* (London: Verso Books, 1991); Roediger, *Seizing Freedom*; Gary W. Gallagher, *The Union War* (Cambridge: Harvard University Press, 2012); Noel Ignatiev, "'The American Blindspot': Reconstruction According to Eric Foner and W. E. B. Du Bois," *Labour/Le Travail* 31 (1993), 243–51; Thavolia Glymph, "Du Bois' *Black Reconstruction* and Slave Women's War for Freedom," *South Atlantic Quarterly* 112:3 (2013), 489–505; Gayatri Spivak, "General Strike," *Rethinking Marxism* 26, no. 1 (2014), 9–14; Amber E. Kelsie, "Blackened Debate at the End of the World," *Philosophy & Rhetoric* 52, no. 1 (2019), 63–70.

13 Claire Parfait, "Rewriting History: The Publication of W. E. B. Du Bois' *Black Reconstruction in America*," *Book History* 12 (2009), 266–94; Abram E. Harris, "Reconstruction and the Negro," *The New Republic* (August 7, 1935), 367–68; Loren Miller, "Let My People Go!" *New Masses* (October 29, 1935), 23–24; Ralphe Bunche, "Reconstruction Reinterpreted," *The Journal of Negro Education* 4:4 (1935), 568–70; Henry Lee Moon, "DuBois [*sic*] Looks at Reconstruction," *Race* 1, no. 1 (1935), 60–61.

14 Du Bois, *Black Reconstruction*, 345.

15 Ibid., 442, 350, 667.

16 Ibid., 382–83.

17 Ibid., 585–86.

18 Ibid., 166, 618–21.

19 Steven Hahn, *A Nation Under Our Feet: Black Political Struggles in the Rural South from Slavery to the Great Migration* (Cambridge: Harvard University Press, 2005); Elsa Barkley Brown, "Negotiating and Transforming the Public Sphere: African American Political Life in the Transition from Slavery to Freedom," *Public Culture* 7 (1994), 107–46; C. L. R. James, "Every Cook Can Govern," *Correspondence* 2:12 (1956). Ironically, the only recognition of democratic hesitation in *Black Reconstruction* that I have found is in an article by one of James's collaborators who argues that its celebration of black agency is tempered by Du Bois's "principle of the guardianship of the masses by the professorial chair, the test-tube laboratory, private or government philanthropy, or an entrenched intellectual caste." William Gorman, "W. E. B. Du Bois and His Work," *Fourth International* 11:3 (1950), 80–86.

20 Reed, "The Jug and Its Content: A Perspective on Black American Political Development," in *Stirrings in the Jug: Black Politics in the Post-Segregation Era* (Minneapolis: University of Minnesota Press, 1999).
21 Keeanga-Yamahtta Taylor, *From #BlackLivesMatter to Black Liberation* (Chicago: Haymarket Books, 2016).
22 Robinson, *Black Marxism*; Immanuel Wallerstein, "Oliver C. Cox as World-Systems Analyst," in *The Sociology of Oliver C. Cox: New Perspectives*, ed. Herbert M. Hunter (Stamford: JAI Press Inc, 2000), 173–84. See also Robinson's more extended commentary on Cox's political economy in Robinson, "Oliver Cromwell Cox and the Historiography of the West," *Cultural Critique* 17 (1990–1991), 5–19.
23 Morton G. Wenger, "Are There Weberian Answers to the Puzzle of Oliver C. Cox's Marxism? A Theoretical Realignment and its Analytical Consequences," in *The Sociology of Oliver C. Cox: New Perspectives*, ed. Hunter, 139–54; Christopher A. McAuley, *The Mind of Oliver C. Cox* (Notre Dame: University of Notre Dame Press, 2004).
24 Roediger, *The Wages of Whiteness*, 7; Bruce Nelson, "Class, Race and Democracy in the CIO: The 'New' Labor History Meets the 'Wages of Whiteness,'" *International Review of Social History* 41, no. 3 (1996), 352.
25 Oliver Cromwell Cox, "Leadership Among Negroes in the United States," in *Studies in Leadership: Leadership and Democratic Action*, ed. A. W. Gouldner (New York: Harper & Brothers, 1950), 269.
26 Cox, *Caste, Class, & Race*, 178, 225. In light of modern scholarship, it appears that Cox, like virtually all Marxists of his time, exaggerates the early bourgeoisie's democratic credentials. See Vivek Chibber, *Postcolonial Theory and the Spectre of Capitalism* (London: Verso, 2013), Chapter 4.
27 Cox, *Caste, Class & Race*, 226–27.
28 Ibid., 230.
29 Ibid., 174–244. On Strachey, see Noel Thompson, *John Strachey: An Intellectual Biography* (London: Palgrave MacMillan, 1993). On Corey, see David E. Brown, "The Political and Social Thought of Lewis Corey" (Ph.D. dissertation, Ohio State University, 1969).
30 On the impact of *The Road to Serfdom*, see Theodore Rosenof, "Freedom, Planning, and Totalitarianism: The Reception of F. A. Hayek's *The Road to Serfdom*," *Canadian Review of American Studies* 5:2 (1974), 149–65.
31 Cox, *Caste, Class & Race*, 232–33.
32 Cox, "Modern Democracy and the Class Struggle," *The Journal of Negro Education*, 16:2 (1947), 155–164.
33 William Kornhauser, *The Politics of Mass Society* (New Brunswick: Transaction Publishers, 2008), 103; Hannah Arendt, *The Origins of Totalitarianism* (New York: Meridian, 1951); Theodor Adorno and

Max Horkheimer, *Dialectic of Enlightenment* (New York: Verso, 1999). For the classic critique of "mass society" theories of fascism, see Bernt Hagtvet, "The Theory of Mass Society and the Collapse of the Weimar Republic: A Re-Examination," in *Who Were the Fascists? Social Roots of European Fascism*, ed. Stein Ugelvik Larsen, Bernt Hagtvet, and Jan Petter Myklebust (Oslo: Universitetsforlaget, 1980), 66–117.

34 Cox, *Caste, Class, & Race*, 189. For a contemporary intellectual history of fascism that parallels Cox's arguments, see Ishay Landa, *Fascism and the Masses: The Revolt Against the Last Humans, 1848–1945* (New York: Routledge, 2018).

35 Cox, *Caste, Class, & Race*, 188–89.

36 For Guérin, see Daniel Guérin, *Fascism and Big Business* (New York: Pathfinder Press, 1973). On Brady, see Dan Schiller, "The Legacy of Robert A. Brady: Antifascist Origins of the Political Economy of Communications," *Journal of Media Economics* 12:2 (1999), 89–101.

37 Bruce Levine, *The Fall of the House of Dixie: The Civil War and the Social Revolution That Transformed the South* (New York: Random House, 2013); Roediger, *Seizing Freedom*; Eric Foner, *Reconstruction: America's Unfinished Revolution, 1863–1877* (New York: HarperCollins, 1988).

38 Michael W. Fitzgerald, *The Union League Movement in the Deep South: Politics and Agricultural Change During Reconstruction* (Baton Rouge: Louisiana State University Press, 1989); Lee W. Formwalt, "The Origins of African-American Politics in Southwest Georgia: A Case Study of Black Political Organization During Presidential Reconstruction, 1865–1867," *The Journal of Negro History* 77:4 (1992), 211–22; Hahn, *A Nation Under Our Feet*.

39 Göran Therborn, "The Rule of Capital and the Rise of Democracy," *New Left Review* I/103 (1977), 3–41; Dietrich Rueschmeyer, Evelyne Huber Stephens, and John Stephens, *Capitalist Development & Democracy* (Chicago: University of Chicago Press, 1992); Adaner Usmani, "Democracy and the Class Struggle," *American Journal of Sociology* 124:3 (2018), 664–704.

40 Joshua Cohen and Joel Rogers, *On Democracy: Toward a Transformation of American Society* (New York: Penguin, 1983); Adam Przeworski, *Capitalism and Social Democracy* (Cambridge: Cambridge University Press, 1986).

41 Eddie S. Glaude, *Democracy in Black: How Race Still Enslaves the American Soul* (New York: Crown Publishers, 2016); Lani Guinier and Gerald Torres, *The Miner's Canary: Enlisting Race, Resisting Power, Transforming Democracy* (Cambridge: Harvard University Press, 2002).

7

"Not picketing in front of bra factories": Marxism, feminism, and the Weather Underground

Sinead McEneaney

In June 1969, a small group of ideological outliers took the floor at the national convention of the Students for a Democratic Society (SDS) in Chicago to proclaim a new war on capitalism.[1] Their manifesto argued that black liberation in the United States was one part of a global Third World movement for decolonization and self-determination, and that white privileged students should act as a support structure for this anti-imperialism, with the ultimate aim of forming a revolutionary political party that would dismantle the American capitalist system. Its title, "You Don't Need a Weatherman to Know Which Way the Wind Blows" borrowed a line from the Bob Dylan song "Subterranean Homesick Blues," and gave the faction their name: Weatherman.[2]

Weatherman, later known as the Weather Underground and subsequently the Weather Underground Organization (WUO), drew its ideological influences from three strands.[3] First, it was a product of the late-stage New Left, by then fraught with tensions between Maoists (who often confusingly called themselves Marxist–Leninists), Trotskyists, and a variety of independent radicals and small local collectives, typified by the in-fighting within SDS between the old guard admirers of C. Wright Mills or Herbert Marcuse and the Marxist–Leninist Progressive Labor Party which had come to prominence since the anti-war turn in SDS by 1965.[4] Many prominent Weatherpeople had been activists in community projects run by SDS, had become somewhat disillusioned about the capacity for change through grassroots organizing, and were convinced that change would only happen through revolution, and specifically violent revolution.[5] The second strand of influence came from black liberation movements, especially the Black

Marxism, feminism, and the Weather Underground 171

Figure 7.1 1970 FBI poster for Cathy Wilkerson, a Weatherwoman who later in life developed a thoroughgoing feminist criticism of Weatherman, the Weather Underground, and its successors. *Courtesy Federal Bureau of Investigation.*

Panthers.[6] Locating "real" revolution in the actions of Third World, anti-colonial revolutionaries in Vietnam, Cuba, and parts of Africa and Latin America, Weatherpeople styled themselves as Marxist anti-war, anti-capitalist radicals, intent on overthrowing the American state through violent interventions (Figure 7.1). And thirdly, Weather oriented itself around a countercultural iconography, drawing on ideas of free love and sexual liberation imported from the hippies in order to "smash monogamy" as part of revolutionary systemic change.

These three ideological strands did not always sit well together. In particular, there were tensions between the Marxist leanings of

Weather and the women's liberationist impulses of some of the prominent women in the group. Liberal or socialist feminism, or what we can broadly term hegemonic or separatist feminism of the second wave, was dismissed as a distraction from the revolution. Speaking in January 1970 before a planned attack orchestrated by Weatherwomen on the Armed Forces Induction Center near Grant Park in Chicago, prominent Weather leader Bernardine Dohrn dismissed the entire project of second-wave feminism as anti-radical. "For the first time in history," she proclaimed, "women are getting themselves together. We're not picketing in front of bra-factories now. We're not a woman's organization engaged in self-indulgent bullshit."[7] This chapter seeks to examine the tensions between Marxism and feminism through the lens of the Weathermen. In particular, why did Weather, and particularly the women of Weather, struggle to align themselves with feminist social and economic critiques? What can this tell us more broadly about the interaction between Marxism and feminism at the end of the 1960s?

Weatherman and Marxism

Although much has been written about the Weathermen, both by historians and former activists, there has been relatively little engagement with Weather as a Marxist collective.[8] Activists turned historians, many of them veterans of SDS or the non-violent civil rights movement, sought to curate an optimistic story of the potential of the sixties, destroyed by the violence of Altamont, the Manson family, and the Weather Underground.[9] In this telling, it is easy to dismiss the Weathermen as an infantile group of putative revolutionaries whose actions were destructive and devoid of serious ideological foundation. To some extent, this is a fair criticism; many of the most prominent Weatherpeople were privileged children of wealthy parents, or at least of solidly middle-class backgrounds, who saw their actions through a romantic lens of radical chic.[10] Bill Ayers's autobiography, published in 2001, did little to counter this criticism by relating his experiences with Weatherman through a series of chaotic youthful antics, sobered only by the terrible tragedy of the New York townhouse bombing that took the lives of his friends.[11] In one of the first memoirs by a prominent Weatherman to be published, Ayers steers clear of any serious engagement with the ideological foundations of the group. Some subsequent memoirs took a more serious, analytic tone, although most retain significant blind spots about the weaknesses and failures of Weatherman.[12] For contemporaries seeking to explain how "the Sixties" disintegrated, Weatherman was easily cast as the villain in the story.[13] For others, the activists of Weatherman were misguided and misunderstood young people who were victims of their own idealism. This is most obvious in former *Vanity Fair* journalist Bryan Burrough's recent treatment of the group, which delves into the detail of their activities without explaining any of the ideological forces behind Weatherman's embrace of violence.[14] Historians also struggle with whether to take Weatherman seriously in ideological terms: Jeremy Varon's treatment of the group within a wider narrative of revolutionary violence engages much less critically with the group's ideological weaknesses than does David Barber's analysis several years later.[15] Most recent treatments of Weatherman have sought to provide alternative readings of Weather's ideological underpinning, often in opposition to the narrative created by both SDS activists like Todd Gitlin, and the hostile perspective documented by FBI infiltrators.[16]

There is no need to rehabilitate the reputation of Weatherman, or to cast them as a late-sixties ideological powerhouse of Marxist thought. Their grasp of Marxism was tenuous at times. So too was their perspective on feminism. However, the ideological positioning of the Weather Underground and its quite difficult relationship with a range of ideological positions—including Marxism and feminism—gives us an interesting route into thinking more broadly about the ways that the white left borrowed from, repurposed, and competed with, currents of feminist thought, intersectionalism, Marxist critiques, and anti-imperialism. Recent work by Mona Rocha casts the Weatherwomen as third-wave feminists out of their time; she argues that the brand of feminism espoused by Weatherwomen is much closer to an intersectional approach taken by third-wave movements than it was to their second-wave contemporaries.[17] There is some merit in this argument, but Rocha begins from a perspective of retrofitting Weather's positions on women into an era disconnected from their present. This also ignores that there were examples of quite coherent critiques of class, gender, and race from within the non-white radical left.[18] These were all much more nuanced than Weatherman's rejection of feminism. In his reassessment of the perceived failure of the sixties, David Barber argues that the Marxist–Leninist ideological framework of Weather reframed the "women's question" in a way that reinforced the primacy of white male leadership, and made a women's separatist movement inevitable.[19] He is correct in his assertion that Weatherman delegitimized separatist women's liberation. Just as Weatherman's interpretations of Marxism were often utilitarian, so too were their interpretations of feminism.

In rejecting hegemonic feminism, however, the group sought to use Marxist ideas to justify its actions, and the women of Weatherman—the Weatherwomen—sought to define themselves as (and in reaction to) feminists, while often trying to reconcile their ideas of international revolutionary left-wing violence with both of these ideological positions. Over a short time, from 1969 through to 1974, Weatherman issued several dozen communiqués, statements, and artistic expressions that sought to justify their actions, and revise and sharpen their political positions. In response to internal criticisms, many of these, from December 1970 (*Changing Weather*) to May 1974 (*Prairie Fire*) sought in different ways to clarify and realign their positions on feminism and Marxism. In the light of these efforts to clarify and reshape their ideological positioning, it is too simplistic to see the collectives, so-called "families" and cells that made up Weather simply as intellectual voids full of delusional or maniacal bombers. Their Marxism was a peculiar utilitarian product of late-sixties leftism, mixed with an anti-racism and anti-war sentiment that made these radicals seek to position themselves in solidarity with Black Power advocates and anti-imperialist revolutionaries in Vietnam and elsewhere. As a result, the group made serious and ongoing attempts to situate their actions within a broad landscape of revolutionary socialism.

By 1968, as SDS grappled with similar ideological challenges, splinter groups that predated Weatherman set the foundations for a more militant, and more overtly Marxist approach than had been part of the New Left tradition. From 1966 onwards, key SDS figures like Mike Klonsky and Mark Rudd were already adopting Marxist critiques of American society to advocate dismantling capitalism, which they saw as the root cause of the Vietnam War, race oppression, and poverty.[20] Criticizing the narrow socio-political viewpoint of the SDS, Klonsky wrote in "Towards a Revolutionary Youth Movement":

> The notion that we must remain simply "an anti-imperialist student organization" is no longer viable. The nature of our struggle is such that it necessitates an organization that is made up of youth and not just students, and that these youth become class conscious. This means that our struggles must be integrated into the struggles of working people.[21]

By 1969, however, the splinters had splintered. Those who would form the Weather tendency had concluded that a student–worker alliance would not produce the revolutionary change these radicals sought. John Jacobs (known as JJ), emerged from the Columbia strikes with a revolutionary zeal that he channeled into Weatherman. Regarded as the most well-versed of Weather leaders in Marxist theory, and often viewed as the intellectual heavyweight behind Weatherman, JJ was the primary author of their founding manifesto, in which he and his co-signatories called for a mass revolutionary movement built around the activities of a small clandestine party.[22] The militant language of "You Don't Need a Weatherman" in 1969 reflects a desire to position the aims and tactics of Weather within revolutionary vanguardism. In this founding manifesto, Weather activists defined their so-called "socialist revolution" as one that went beyond the interests of working people in the United States, and instead sought to serve the interests of those oppressed by what they called the United States "Empire." The phrase they used to describe this analysis was "world communism." The rejection of an alliance with the working classes was a departure from classical Marxism, but Weatherpeople continued to explain their activities within an ostensibly Marxist framework. Marxism was ideologically useful for Weather and became a tool to align the organization's domestic violent activities with international revolutionary movements, especially in Cuba, Laos, and Vietnam.

Six years later, several years after the accidental bombing of a New York townhouse left three activists dead and forced many others underground, and with Jacobs expelled from the Weather Underground, the final Weather manifesto *Prairie Fire* sought to reformulate the ideological basis of the group.[23] Addressing itself to "communist minded people," *Prairie Fire* presents a Fanonesque argument that carefully targeted revolutionary violence provides a personal and cultural catharsis for the colonized (black) peoples of the American state. Framing their position against the political and energy crises of the early 1970s, the authors explicitly adopt dialectical materialism as their analytical approach. Summing up their position in 1974, there are echoes of "You Don't Need a Weatherman": "Socialism is the total opposite of capitalism/imperialism. It is the rejection of empire and white supremacy. Socialism is the violent overthrow of the bourgeoisie, the establishment of the dictatorship of the proletariat, and the eradication of the social system based on profit."[24]

This is a more complex and nuanced position than the often confusing Marxist language used to articulate their founding principles in 1969. It demonstrates that at least within the leadership cadres, there was a sustained desire to frame the Weather project within identifiably Marxist thought. This does not necessarily mean that the rest of the membership shared an adherence to Marxist principles. In broad terms, Weather emerged out of opposition to the Vietnam War. Many of its members had no knowledge of Marx and were originally attracted to Weather because they were frustrated with the war or attracted to the violent promise of the group's actions. Nevertheless, to outsiders the group was identified as Marxist. The FBI, whose Chicago office infiltrated and monitored the group over a number of years, characterized the organization as having "adopted an alien ideology" and following a "Marxist–Leninist conception of armed struggle in the US."[25] Whether we accept Weatherman as a truly Marxist group or not, they were perceived by contemporaries as part of a larger wave of Marxist youth organizations worldwide that sought to position themselves as the revolutionary alternative to traditional communism and communist parties, including the Red Army Faction in Germany.[26]

Whereas other SDS factions, including both the Revolutionary Youth Movement II (in which Klonsky took part) and Progressive Labor, held out for a radicalization of the working classes alongside the youth movement, Weather did not. For Weather, the revolution would come through Third World movements, and aligned domestic revolutionaries: they revered revolutionaries in Cuba and Vietnam, and the Black Panthers at home. By recasting what revolution meant in the context of Third World liberation movements, they could critique a white working class in the United States which was seen to benefit from the structural racism at home, and the exploitation of people of color abroad. By summer 1969, the Weather critique, consciously aligned to that of the Panthers, focused on the potential that a small group of activists had to "smash" the system. Alongside the Panthers, they looked for inspiration to Cuba, where Fidel Castro's small guerrilla force had successfully overthrown a U.S.-backed dictatorship, and to Vietnam, where guerrilla forces were unexpectedly holding back the might of the U.S. military. In a United States where a decade of protest had left the political status quo intact, Weatherman abandoned any hope that revolutionary transformation would come from the masses—who were beneficiaries of racism and imperialism—and instead argued that change would have to come from a small, committed band of guerrillas who would take up arms against the state.

In their claim to represent the revolutionary vanguard, Weatherman distinguished itself from another Marxist tendency, Progressive Labor (PL), which had been steadily extending influence in SDS since 1965 and had by 1969 secured the majority of delegates at the national convention.[27] PL drew its political analysis from a more classical nineteenth-century Marxism that prioritized worker–student alliances, crossed with a reverence for the teachings of Mao. Weatherman defined itself in opposition to PL and represented the views of a tiny, if prominent, minority within SDS. By 1969, what had been the largest New Left student organization of the decade was riven with divisions along a range of ideological lines. Where Weatherman departed from other factions—PL, RYM II, and others—was in its explicit embrace of revolutionary violent action as a tool for domestic change. Their expression of this was quite different from the self-defense of the Black Panthers. The French journalist Regis Debray, who had immersed himself in Latin American guerrilla movements, provided the justification for violence by Weather activists. For Debray, episodes of violence were exemplary: they could encourage and inspire others.[28] A very small number of committed activists could undertake revolutionary actions in small cells, or "focos," and inspire others to follow. Thus, Weather's Marxism was a hybrid, with elements of Maoism and the guerrilla tactics made popular by Che Guevara. Their Marxism was elastic, variations on Marxist theories devised to justify tactics rather than the other way around, but their sense of themselves as righteous revolutionaries left very little room for dissent.

Could this ideological position marry feminism? This question is important because women were instrumental in the organization of Weather. Many of these women identified with the principle of women's liberation (even if they did not like to use the term, or indeed did not call themselves feminist) and as Marxist. Many were previously members of SDS, in which they had railed against its misogyny. Bernardine Dohrn, elected as Interorganizational Secretary of SDS in 1968, was a trained lawyer who was politically active in radical education projects and peripherally involved in the student action at Columbia University. A founder of Weatherman, she would become, through her taped readings of its communiqués, its public face. Another founder, Naomi Jaffe, was a founding member of a New York chapter of SDS, and had been an organizer of the Atlantic City protests against the Miss America pageant in 1968.[29] Kathy Boudin and Cathy Wilkerson had worked together at an SDS-sponsored community project in Cleveland, Ohio, and had mobilized local women to challenge an unfair welfare system. They would both become important members of the New York cell of Weather; the townhouse in Greenwich Village which was destroyed by a Weather bombmaker in an accidental explosion in 1970 belonged to Wilkerson's father.

In her autobiography, Wilkerson recalls that while she was slow to identify as a feminist, she had identified the importance of women's liberation as a distinct political demand and she was dismayed at the lack of real engagement against patriarchal oppression within Weatherman.[30] Seattle-based Weatherwoman Susan Stern describes a deeply misogynist structure, where the demands of the collective (often synonymous with white male leaders) overrode the autonomy of individual (often women) members.[31] Jaffe also recalled, years later, that she found it impossible to align her feminist ideals with Weatherman's Marxism.[32] The way that Weatherman was organized exacerbated this problem. Across four or five main collectives/cells (Oakland, Cleveland, Chicago, New York, Seattle), membership reached three hundred or so before the Days of Rage in October 1969, and about half that between the end of 1969 and their disappearance underground, fleeing the FBI, by 1971.[33] Although it was arranged around small, cell-based collectives based on quite close, but fractious, friendship circles, control of Weatherman remained quite top-down, and the top leadership was male. However, women were often the public face of the group, and ought to have exerted more influence over the group's actions and priorities. When the FBI compiled their lists of the most wanted Weathermen, and posted flyers asking for information, almost half of those featured were women. The mugshots of Kathy Boudin, Judith Clark, Bernardine Dohrn, Naomi Jaffe, Celeste McCullough, Wendy Panken, Caroline Tanner, and Cathy Wilkerson all appeared on FBI Wanted posters in mid-1970.

With this public notoriety of leadership cadre women, Weatherman should have provided a space for Marxist anti-imperialism and feminism to become comfortable bedfellows. It did not. Instead, it was heavily criticized by women radicals outside Weather, who argued that Weatherwomen sold out their feminist sisters in a "desperate grab at male approval."[34] In her sideswipe against what she called the WeatherVain, radical feminist Robin Morgan likened the women of Weather to sadistic cult leader Charles Manson's female groupie slaves, complicit in their own marginalization through their embrace of free love. For Morgan, and for later critics, Weather's policy of non-monogamy served only to allow the men of Weatherman to ignore the systemic oppression of women by men. The failure of the left was that women were "leftover." This was as true within Weather as in the counterculture or contemporary mainstream society.

The look is you: anti-consumerism, feminism, and Marxist critiques

Weather missed the opportunity to merge Marxism and feminism in a way that could have contributed to the development of a more revolutionary and militant feminism in the early 1970s. It is difficult to be certain of the causes of this failure to create more fertile soil for the hybridization of Marxism and feminism in Weatherman. There is an extensive literature on the marginalization of women activists in the student, youth left, and civil rights movements of the 1960s.[35] There is also a small, but growing, critique of the ways revolutionary violence and gender intersect in this period.[36] It is possible that Weatherwomen distanced themselves from hegemonic feminism due to their embrace of confrontation and violence, which remained unattractive to women who had become politicized through the non-violent civil rights and anti-war movements. But this does not fully explain why the women of Weather, many of whom were early critics of sexism in the New Left, did not, or could not, articulate women's oppressions more clearly through the dogma and action of Weatherman. One of the key questions about Weather's relationship with feminism is whether interpretations of Marxism articulated by and in Weatherman produced different opportunities for feminist action, or whether the Marxist influences within Weather stifled the kind of feminism one might have expected to see in a group that was steered by these very experienced, prominent women and self-identified feminists. Did the ideological mix, loosely aligned with this "world communism" view of Marxism, create space for feminist discourse? Or did Weather simply replicate the unhappy marriage we commonly associate with the intersection of Marxism and gendered systems of oppression?

In March 1968, *New Left Notes* carried an article by Naomi Jaffe and Bernardine Dohrn, criticizing the recent decision by *Ramparts* magazine to use the image of a woman's breasts and torso as the cover of a special issue on women's liberation.[37] *Ramparts* was one of the most influential cultural publications of the radical left. In "The Look is You," Dohrn and Jaffe railed against what they saw as the commodification of the female body. But their response was aimed beyond *Ramparts*: they targeted the wider movement where women activists were just as marginalized as were women in society at large. Their criticism was not new. Women in the New Left had become increasingly vocal about their subordinate position—politically and socially—since the circulation by Casey Hayden and Mary King of their "Sex and Caste: a Kind of Memo" in 1965.[38] By late 1967, the SDS national convention had very reluctantly passed a resolution to pay attention to the specific oppression faced by women both within the movement and in wider society. These women adjusted familiar critiques of race and class to articulate their perceptions of gendered oppression within the movement. For many New Left women, the New Left and civil rights movement promised alternative social structures that would prioritize gender equality, but in practice simply didn't deliver on this promise.[39] Few men really took "women's issues" seriously: the oppression of women was deemed far less urgent than more "legitimate" issues like black liberation and opposition to the war in Vietnam. New Left feminists fought hard to be recognized.

One of the ways to gain credence was to frame feminist critiques within familiar leftist, and Marxist, language. In "The Look is You," Dohrn and Jaffe framed their critique of *Ramparts* as an attack on consumerism, and a broader attack on the social, economic, and political system that perpetuated these gendered outcomes. They wrote,

> A strategy for the liberation of women, then, does not demand equal jobs (exploitation), but meaningful creative activity for all; not a larger share of power but the abolition of commodity tyranny; not equally reified sexual roles but an end to sexual objectification and exploitation; not equal aggressive leadership in the Movement, but the initiation of a new style of non-dominating leadership.

Invoking a traditional Marxist critique of consumerism, they asserted that "Woman Power is the power to destroy a destructive system by refusing to play the part(s) assigned to us by it—refusing to accept its definition of us as passive consumers, and by actively subverting the institutions which create and enforce that definition."[40] Woman Power, echoing Black Power, served to combine a strand of feminism with an anti-capitalist rhetoric, organically part of a New Left that was splintering over competing Marxist critiques.

One year later, again in *New Left Notes*, Bernardine Dohrn—by that time Interorganizational Secretary of an ideologically splintering SDS—proposed a pathway "Toward a Revolutionary Women's Movement."[41] In this article, Dohrn creates an opposition between two groups of radical women, split between the "politicos" (full-time organizers cognizant of women's oppression within a broader critical landscape) and the "professional women" (women focused entirely on women's liberation, often separatist). Dohrn viewed these professional "bourgeois" women's groups as counterproductive, separatist, and unconscious of class and race struggles. Their view of liberation was what she would call a few months later "self-indulgent bullshit." Instead, she called for revolutionary women to organize themselves around more pressing issues: imperialism and racism—what we might now call intersectionality, but what she calls the "totality of oppression." For Dohrn, sexist hierarchies would be destroyed through an anti-capitalist, anti-imperialist revolution, where oppressed women of all races would co-operate to smash the capitalist system. This position, in keeping with the spirit of the emerging Weatherman faction, revealed a growing antipathy between Weatherman and the women's movement.

Writing ten years later, Heidi Hartmann described what she called "unhappy marriage" of Marxism and feminism, holding that in their competing political agendas feminism had been consistently subordinated to Marxist priorities.[42] Her criticism highlighted differences of political priorities and what work counted as "important":

> Most feminists who also see themselves as radicals (anti-system, anti-capitalist, anti-imperialist, socialist, communist, Marxist whatever) agree that the radical wing of the women's movement has lost momentum while the bourgeois sector seems to have seized the time and forged ahead ... The left has always been ambivalent about the women's movement, often viewing it as dangerous to the cause of socialist revolution ... The pressures on radical women to abandon this "silly stuff" and become "serious" revolutionaries have increased.[43]

This unhappy marriage between Marxism and feminism in the broad New Left and its descendants in the 1970s reflected the ways that activists like Hayden and King felt marginalized in sexist hierarchies of activism in the early to mid-1960s. By the end of the decade, these tensions between what was perceived as serious revolution, and "silly stuff" dismissed as "self-indulgent bullshit" were key to hierarchies of activism within Weatherman, and was responsible for the estrangement of some Weather women who were growing tired of the macho posturing of the leadership cadre. Susan Stern documents this extensively in her recollections of her time in Weatherman and the Weather Underground. Her observations of patriarchal dominance were echoed elsewhere.[44] In her memoir, Diana Block, a committed feminist who joined Weather after the publication of *Prairie Fire* in 1974, recounts how her excitement at the feminist promise of *Prairie Fire* was not fully realized through her experiences aboveground and underground, which were often characterized by in-fighting, ideological disagreements, and personal attacks.[45]

By 1973, when Weatherman had become the Weather Underground, the vision of radical socialist change that Dohrn and others advocated had lost ground to the liberal, largely white, women's movement typified by the National Organization for Women or the women's health clinic movement. The "progressive union" of Marxism and feminism that Hartmann hoped for was articulated with clarity in Angela Davis's *Women, Race, and Class*.[46] But Dohrn was no Davis: the intersectionality that she, and other women within Weather, had hoped for was never realized within that organization. This failure was not inevitable. In July 1969, Cathy Wilkerson—already a prominent member of the Weather group—launched a scathing criticism of both the Revolutionary Youth Movement's and Weatherman's inability to "include an organic analysis of male supremacy" in their manifestos, alleging that this was primarily because of the weakness of their basic understanding of Marxist analysis.[47] Her position paper, "Toward a Revolutionary Women's Militia," published in *New Left Notes*, suggested that a closer understanding of the specific oppressions faced by women would produce a more robust critique of the interplay between class, privilege, and systems of exploitation. Male supremacy, she argued, could not be disentangled from bourgeois individualism. If men claim to fight imperialism, they should do so at home and in their collectives. This position was in line with other contemporary critiques—especially Roxanne Dunbar's "Female Liberation as the Basis of Social Revolution," which echoed Emma Goldman's critique of marriage and drew heavily on Marx and Engels to argue that fundamental social change can only occur through a socialist revolution in which "female liberation" is foregrounded.[48] Elements of this were picked up by the Weatherwomen, who sought to "smash" patriarchy through nonmonogamy, and to organize women-only militias to carry out revolutionary actions. But they also departed significantly from Dunbar, who chided "radicals" for their dismissal of the legal, liberal strategy of groups like NOW as "counterrevolutionary." This dismissal was the undercurrent of the official position taken by Weather on women's liberation.

Despite Dohrn's assertion that Weather was not a woman's organization, many women within Weather did see themselves as a cadre apart from men. In her autobiography, Wilkerson recalls that many women were drawn to a particular praxis-based approach to achieving a socialist revolution. In focusing on the day-to-day "grunt work," women like Wilkerson embraced active participation rather than ideological development. In doing this, she says, two principal strands emerged in Weather, each speaking a different language: one a practical, action-based group, and the other concerned with rallying support around rhetoric, image, and metaphor.[49] These divisions were exacerbated by the macho posturing many of the Weathermen engaged in. Smashing the system went hand-in-hand with smashing monogamy. Jeremy Varon and others have documented the extent to which sexual permissiveness was viewed as central to the revolutionary impulse.[50] Monogamy was anti-socialist. So-called "criticism-self-criticism" (CSC) sessions were loosely developed from Maoist revolutionary tactics in China and were essentially hazing sessions fueled by drugs and sleep deprivations, aimed at controlling behavior within the collectives. Sexual politics within Weather purported to create space for women to express revolutionary sexualities; when viewed through the brainwashing tactics employed within the collectives, there was a clear risk of sexual exploitation.

At a time of heightened awareness around women's roles within the left, the counterculture, and the wider movement, sexual exploitation was frequently reframed within a language of revolution. For the Black Panthers, upon which Weatherman closely styled itself, the revolution would be served through sexual freedom and rejection of monogamy.[51] The underground press, mainly speaking to an urban countercultural audience, advocated free love and practice of intimacies without boundaries.[52] In practice, departures from monogamy did not produce a revolution in gender equality, and often reinforced sexism in hierarchical groups where women felt pressured to engage in sexual relations with men in order to appear properly revolutionary. This phenomenon affected Weatherman. Although largely ignored by Wilkerson and Ayers in their autobiographies, the "smash monogamy" principle encouraged promiscuity without any discussion of consent.[53] While feminists sought to challenge heterosexual monogamy in order to disrupt gendered hierarchies and undermine narratives of morality that were traditionally used to control female sexuality, the women of Weatherman saw the smash monogamy directive as a logical extension of their understanding of Marxism. Monogamy was bourgeois; sexual liberation was revolutionary. But women's liberation, in the separatist sense, remained "self-indulgent bullshit."

Feminism and changing Weather

When three Weatherpeople were killed in March 1970 in an explosion in a Greenwich Village townhouse, the emotional impact was heavily felt by Weather activists. There are indications that Dohrn's position in relation to women's liberation began to shift soon after. In a December communiqué, called "New Morning; Changing Weather," Dohrn's language echoed the second-wave mantra of the "personal is political":

> People are forming new families ... The revolution involves our whole lives ... It is our closeness and the integration of our personal lives with our revolutionary work that will make it hard for undercover pigs to infiltrate our collectives ... One of the most important things that has changed since people began working in collectives is the idea of what leadership is. People—and especially groups of sisters—don't want to follow academic ideologues or authoritarians. From Fidel's speeches and Ho's poems we've understood how leaders grow out of being deeply in touch with movements ... Many of these changes have been pushed forward by women both in collectives with men and in all-women collectives.[54]

In that section of "New Morning," Dohrn sought to assert Weather's feminist credentials by repositioning the women of Weather alongside female revolutionaries in Vietnam (Nguyễn Thị Bình), Cuba, Ireland (Bernadette Devlin), the black struggle (Afeni Shakur), and the anti-war movement (Mary Moylan, a Catholic activist who was associated with Weather's women's brigades). While feminist separatists were accused of trying to undermine family structures, Dohrn emphasized the family-like networks of Weather collectives. This can be read as a Marxist-informed rebuke to liberal and radical feminisms, despite the suggestion that Weather had reflected on the hierarchical, and often sexist, nature of the group's leadership.

It was clear, though, that against the background of the existentialist crisis produced by the townhouse bombing, Weather sought to defuse criticisms of sexism by highlighting the synergies between feminisms and the aims and practices of a newly reflective Weather.

But this position was not sustained, especially as Weather went underground. In their autobiographies, Susan Stern, Diana Block, and Cathy Wilkerson all noted experiences of isolation and marginalization during their time underground. In 1973, responding to criticisms that Weatherwomen were undermining a strengthening mainstream feminist movement, Dohrn made another attempt to recast Weather as feminist. She issued "A Collective Letter to the Women's Movement"—in some ways reflecting a return to the 1971 position—composed by the Women of the Weather Underground, along with a separate letter from Mary Moylan, now declaring herself a radical feminist after a spell living underground with some Weather friends.[55] "Since going underground," Dohrn wrote, "we have never publicly committed ourselves to the right and duty of women to rebel, to the revolutionary content of women's demands, and to the profound feminist critique of Western culture. As communists, we know we can criticize our practice without repudiating or denying our own past." This is a turning point: it appears to be the first place in Weather literature where the term "feminist" is used in a positive manner. This discovery that it was important to pay attention to women as a specific category of analysis in Marxist terms was not news to any socialist feminists outside Weather. But it did represent a change of direction for Weatherwomen. And viewed from the vantage point of the present, the language of discovery in the "Collective Letter" seems to underscore the retroactive nature of assertions by activists forty years later that Weatherwomen were always feminists.[56] Nonetheless, no rapprochement between Weatherman and strands of liberal or radical feminisms were forthcoming; tensions persisted.

Indeed, frustration rose amongst activists who were broadly in favor of Weather's "smash the system" philosophy but sought to force integration of feminism into Marxist rationales. In 1974, radical feminist Jane Alpert penned an attack on the Weatherwomen's lack of feminism. Alpert was never officially a member of Weatherman, but she had been centrally involved in several bombings along with her then-lover Sam Melville, and was sometimes close to both

Bernardine Dohrn and Kathy Boudin. Like Dohrn and Boudin, she spent time underground, evading charges for bombing a New York federal building in 1969.[57] In "Mother Right: A New Feminist Theory" published by *Ms.* magazine, Alpert takes aim at the core ideology of Weather, arguing that it was inconsistent with feminism.

> Your resistance to discussing your personal experience, your trivialization of your own pain and suffering, your insistence that the oppression of others is more important than your own—these are part of the self-contempt that has been bred in all of us women, and I understand it as I understand myself. As for the frequently heard opinion that Third World women support Third World liberation but not Women's Liberation, I believe this is true chiefly of a few women who are highly regarded by Third World *male* radicals and hence are considered newsworthy by the media.[58]

This indicates the kind of unhappy marriage that existed in Weather between Marxism and feminism. In framing the revolution in Marxist terms—where women as a specific category could not exist if the focus was on anti-racism and anti-imperialism—Alpert argued that Weatherwomen simply could not be feminist. In fact, she went further: the women of Weather simply did not understand their own subordination, and even though there were lots of women in leadership positions in Weather, they were in the thrall of movement men (Ayers, Rudd, Jeff Jones) who were definitely not feminists, and were notorious for their dismissal and disrespect of women.[59] In Alpert's view, Weatherwomen were sellouts.

When *Prairie Fire* was published in 1974, it offered an opportunity for the Weather Underground to reflect upon its past and reclaim space for feminism in their anti-imperialist Marxist ideological stance. Written mostly by Dohrn, Ayers, and Rudd, *Prairie Fire* sought to reach out to the wider movement on the left—most of which had by now disintegrated against the background of state repression, the political crisis of Watergate, and the oil crisis. The one-hundred-and-fifty-page book manifests the desire by its underground authors to reconnect with the left it had abandoned in 1969. The change in language, especially about women, reflects this. In her memoir, feminist Diana Block recalls how she felt drawn to Weather (or, more specifically, the aboveground iteration of Weather that called itself Prairie Fire) precisely because of the way *Prairie Fire* outlined the intersection between feminism and imperialism.[60] Devoting a section towards the end of the book to a discussion of the "Rising of Women," *Prairie Fire* finally came close to articulating a marriage between feminism and Marxism that recognized the importance of women as a category of analysis in a broader critique of imperialism and class. Calling for a revolutionary women's politics, the authors of *Prairie Fire* encouraged women in poverty to eschew bourgeois feminism and recognize its inherent privileging of white experiences.[61] The critique of the "self-indulgent bullshit" of middle-class white feminism remained; but the manifesto explicitly sought to find common ground with the broader women's liberation movement.

Prairie Fire appeared too late to have any lasting impact. By 1974, the Weather Underground was rife with divisions, and *Prairie Fire* did little to mend these acrimonious splits. In a sense, the opportunity had been lost years before. The inability of Weather to articulate by 1970 a vision of radical revolutionary Marxist change which included feminism meant they lost traction with other strands of radical feminism that would claim significant ground within the women's liberation movement. Other radical left-leaning women, including Alpert, Morgan, and even Wilkerson, had seen the opportunity to create a happier marriage between a Marxist social and economic critique and a set of feminist principles. By the time this became part of the Weather ideology, the organization itself had slipped into irrelevance, even within radical circles.

Ideology beyond mythology

What does the case of the Weatherman tell us about what Heidi Hartmann called the unhappy marriage between Marxism and feminism? The potential for Weather to shape an alternative feminist revolutionary discourse was certainly there, and it eventually manifested itself in *Prairie Fire*. It is difficult to see how, in the context of the version of Marxism they claimed to espouse, Weatherman could have avoided an early divorce from feminism. Separatist feminism was not compatible with the Weather strategy for revolutionary change. While some prominent Weatherwomen were much closer to emerging feminisms, as an organization Weather's relationship with hegemonic feminism was always difficult.

Nevertheless, Weather activists have spent the past forty years telling and retelling their stories and claiming a feminism that was not reflected in the original ideological positioning of the group. The creation of Weather mythology has made analysis of its ideological significance difficult. This is as much due to the critical dismissal of Weather as ideologically untethered, as it is due to the hagiographical tendencies of its erstwhile adherents. In one of the only published collections of Weather writings, *Sing a Battle Song*, Bill Ayers tells the story of Weather's involvement in the dismantling of SDS as some kind of passive happening, rather than what it was: a concerted disruption of the founding ideals of the organization.[62] In the same collection, the history of Weather is told as if Weather was an inherently feminist organization; Dohrn assures us, "The women of Weather were feminists to a person. We were a vibrant part of the women's movement."[63] These are distinctly revisionist positions, and at odds with most scholarly analyses. In contrast to Ayers and Dohrn, in her book about notorious Weather activist Kathy Boudin, Susan Braudy paints the women of Weather—particularly Dohrn and Boudin—as unhinged, ideologically confused, oversexed, misguided, and generally unlikeable.

The truth lies somewhere between: the Weatherwomen did frame themselves as feminists, viewing themselves as the "real" iteration of feminism, in contradistinction to both liberal and radical feminisms, which they saw as inextricably linked to capitalism and responsible for "self-indulgent bullshit." Their criticism of second-wave feminism identified separatist feminisms' inability to accommodate the interplay between race, class, and war, and especially the ways in which American foreign policy—imperialism in Vietnam—sustained domestic patriarchal systems. But they also failed to see that their version of Marxist critique ignored gender as a key category of analysis, and that their internal hierarchies and practices reproduced those very patriarchal systems they sought to overturn.

Notes

1 I am grateful to have had the opportunity to present some of this material for discussion at the symposium "Marx and Marxism in the United States" at the University of Nottingham and at a workshop at the

Gender Institute at the Australian National University, both in 2019. I also thank the many people who read and commented on earlier drafts of this chapter, especially Fiona de Londras, Carolyn Strange, Mara Keire, Sage Goodwin, Ella St George Carey, Emma Day, Oenone Kubie, Lynne Foote, Grace Mallon, and Christa Watkins.

2 Karin Ashley, Bill Ayers, Bernardine Dohrn, John Jacobs, Jeff Jones, Gerry Long, Howie Machtinger, Jim Mellen, Terry Robbins, Mark Rudd, and Steve Tappis, "You Don't Need A Weatherman To Know Which Way the Wind Blows," *New Left Notes*, June 18, 1969, 3–7.

3 In regard to the group's name, I tend to use the group designation that fits the timeline of the discussion. For descriptions of the group prior to 1971, I tend to use Weatherman or Weather. For activities after 1971, when activists went underground, I use Weather Underground, or Weather Underground Organization (technically correct from 1973 onwards). From 1974, the non-underground section of WUO began to call themselves Prairie Fire, and issued a position paper that year of the same name. However, in the interest of coherence and consistency, for that phase of the movement I adopt Weather Underground Organization (WUO).

4 There is a wide literature on the growth and collapse of the SDS, starting with Kirkpatrick Sale's *SDS: the Rise and Development of the SDS* (New York: Random House, 1973) published while the story of Weatherman was still emerging. See also James Miller, *Democracy Is in the Streets: From Port Huron to the Siege of Chicago* (New York: Simon & Schuster, 1988); Todd Gitlin, *The Sixties: Years of Hope, Days of Rage* (New York: Bantam Books, 1993); David Barber, *A Hard Rain Fell: SDS and Why It Failed* (Jackson: University of Mississippi Press, 2008); Richard Flacks and Nelson Lichtenstein, eds., *Port Huron Statement: Sources and Legacies of the New Left's Founding Manifesto* (Philadelphia: University of Pennsylvania Press, 2015).

5 For example, Bill Ayers was involved in the SDS Radical Education Project in Chicago, and Cathy Wilkerson had been one of the early members of the SDS Economic and Research Action Project in Cleveland, Ohio.

6 David Barber, "Leading the Vanguard: White New Leftists School the Panthers on Black Revolution," in *In Search of the Black Panther Party: New Perspectives on a Revolutionary Movement*, ed. Jama Lazerow and Yohuro Williams (Durham and London: Duke University Press, 2006), 223–51.

7 John Kifner, "That's What the Weathermen Are Supposed to Be … Vandals in the Mother Country," *New York Times* (January 4, 1970), 27.

8 Ron Jacobs, *The Way the Wind Blew: A History of the Weather Underground* (New York: Verso, 1997); Jeremy Varon, *Bringing the War Home: The Weather Underground, the Red Army Faction,*

and Revolutionary Violence in the Sixties and Seventies (Berkeley: University of California Press, 2004); Dan Berger, *Outlaws of America: The Weather Underground and the Politics of Solidarity* (Oakland: AK Press, 2006); Bryan Burrough, *Days of Rage: America's Radical Underground, the FBI and the Forgotten Age of Revolutionary Violence* (New York: Penguin, 2015).
9. Gitlin, *The Sixties*; Barber, *A Hard Rain Fell*.
10. There are many examples of the privileged background of key Weatherpeople. In their discussion of Weatherman, Howard Brick and Christopher Phelps remind us that Bill Ayers was the son of the president of Commonwealth Edison, and Cathy Wilkerson's father was a wealthy radio station investor: *Radicals in America: the U.S. Left since the Second World War* (Cambridge: Cambridge University Press, 2015), 156–60. Kathy Boudin's father Leonard was a prominent lawyer: Susan Braudy, *Family Circles: the Boudins and the Aristocracy of the Left* (New York: Random House, 2003). Dan Berger reminds us that most Weathermen were of solidly middle-class backgrounds, in *Outlaws of America*, 155.
11. Bill Ayers, *Fugitive Days: A Memoir* (Boston: Beacon Press, 2001).
12. Many memoirs have been published since Ayers's, including Cathy Wilkerson, *Flying Close to the Sun: My Life and Times as a Weatherman* (New York: Seven Stories Press, 2007); Susan Stern, *With the Weathermen: The Personal Journal of a Revolutionary Woman* (New Brunswick and London: Rutgers University Press, 2007); Mark Rudd, *Underground: My Life with SDS and the Weathermen* (New York: William Morrow, 2009); Diana Block, *Arm the Spirit: A Woman's Journey Underground and Back* (Oakland: AK Press, 2009); David Gilbert, *Love and Struggle: My Life in SDS, the Weather Underground, and Beyond* (Oakland: PM Press, 2012).
13. This is particularly the case in Todd Gitlin's telling of the story of the sixties, in which Weatherman is a key agent of the destruction of the "years of hope."
14. Burrough, *Days of Rage*.
15. See especially Barber, 183–98.
16. Arthur Eckstein, *Bad Moon Rising: How the Weather Underground Beat the FBI and Lost the Revolution* (New Haven and London: Yale University Press, 2016). See also Federal Bureau of Investigation, Report on the Weather Underground, 1976, vault.fbi.gov
17. Mona Rocha, *The Weatherwomen: Militant Feminists of the Weather Underground* (Jefferson: McFarland & Co., 2020).
18. Becky Thompson, "Multiracial Feminism: Recasting the Chronology of Second Wave Feminism," *Feminist Studies* 28/2 (Summer 2002): 336–60; Benita Roth, *Separate Roads to Feminism: Black, Chicana,*

and White Feminist Movements in America's Second Wave (New York: Cambridge University Press, 2004).
19 Barber, A Hard Rain Fell, 14, 176–78, 196.
20 On RYM II, see Max Elbaum's Revolution in the Air: Sixties Radicals Turn to Lenin, Mao and Che (New York: Verso, 2002).
21 Klonsky, "Towards a Revolutionary Youth Movement," New Left Notes (December 23, 1968), 3.
22 Varon, Bringing the War Home, 48.
23 Weatherman Underground Organization, Prairie Fire: the Politics of Revolutionary Anti-Imperialism (Oakland: Red Dragon Print Collective, 1974).
24 WUO, Prairie Fire, 24.
25 FBI, Report on the Weather Underground, 2.
26 Varon, Bringing the War Home, 20–62.
27 Andrew Kopkind, "The Real SDS Stands Up," Hard Times (June 30–July 7, 1969); Sale, SDS, 563–79.
28 Régis Debray, Revolution in the Revolution? (New York and London: Monthly Review Press, 1967), 41–42.
29 Becky Thompson explores the development of Jaffe's feminism in her book A Promise and a Way of Life: White Antiracist Activism (Minneapolis: University of Minnesota Press, 2001).
30 Wilkerson, Flying Close to the Sun, 258.
31 Stern, With the Weathermen, 154–79.
32 Berger, Outlaws of America, 291–92.
33 Varon, Bringing the War Home, 140.
34 Robin Morgan, "Goodbye To All That," Rat Subterranean News (February 6–23, 1970), 6–7.
35 See for example Sara Evans, Personal Politics: The Roots of Women's Liberation in the Civil Rights Movement and the New Left (New York: Vintage, 1979); Alice Echols, Daring to Be Bad: Radical Feminism in America, 1967–1975 (Minneapolis: University of Minnesota Press, 1989); Benita Roth, Separate Roads to Feminism: Black, Chicana, and White Feminist Movements in America's Second Wave (New York: Cambridge University Press, 2004).
36 Rocha does this well in The Weatherwomen, but the best work on this is Choonib Lee, "Women's Liberation and Sixties Armed Resistance," Journal for the Study of Radicalism 11, no. 1 (Spring 2017), 25–51.
37 Bernardine Dohrn and Naomi Jaffe, "The Look is You," New Left Notes (March 18, 1968).
38 Circulated in November 1965, it was published several months later as Casey Hayden and Mary King, "Sex and Caste: A Kind of Memo," Liberation 10 (April 1966), 35–36.

39 See for example Evans, *Personal Politics*; Rosalyn Baxandall and Linda Gordon, eds., *Dear Sisters: Dispatches from the Women's Liberation Movement* (New York: Basic Books, 2000); Ruth Rosen, *The World Split Open: How the Modern Women's Movement Changed America* (New York and London: Penguin, 2000); Stephanie Gilmore, *Groundswell: Grassroots Feminist Activism in Postwar America* (New York: Routledge, 2013).
40 Dohrn and Jaffe, "The Look is You," 5.
41 Bernardine Dohrn, "Toward a Revolutionary Women's Movement," *New Left Notes* (March 8, 1969), 4.
42 Heidi Hartmann, "The Unhappy Marriage of Marxism and Feminism," *Capital and Class* 3, no. 2 (Summer 1979), 1–33.
43 Ibid., 22–23.
44 A Weatherwoman, "Inside the Weather Machine," *Rat Subterranean News* (February 6–23, 1970), 5, 25.
45 Diana Block, *Arm the Spirit*, 104–108.
46 Angela Davis, *Women, Race and Class* (New York: Random House, 1981).
47 Cathy Wilkerson, "Toward a Revolutionary Women's Militia," *New Left Notes* (July 8, 1969).
48 Roxanne Dunbar, "Female Liberation as the Basis of Social Revolution," *No More Fun and Games: A Journal of Female Liberation* 2, no. 1 (1969), 112.
49 Wilkerson, *Flying Too Close to the Sun*, 263.
50 Varon, *Bringing the War Home*, 54–55; Berger, *Outlaws of America*, 104–105.
51 Robyn C. Spencer, *The Revolution Has Come: Black Power, Gender and the Black Panther Party in Oakland* (Durham and London: Duke University Press, 2016).
52 Sinead McEneaney, "Sex and the Radical Imagination in the *Berkeley Barb* and the San Francisco *Oracle*," *Radical Americas* 3, no. 1 (2018), 16.
53 Berger, *Outlaws of America*, 106; Stern, *With the Weathermen*, 167–70.
54 Weatherman, "New Morning; Changing Weather," December 6, 1970. Reprinted in Bernardine Dohrn, Bill Ayers, and Jeff Jones, eds., *Sing A Battle Song: the Revolutionary Poetry, Statements and Communiqués of the Weather Underground 1970–1974* (New York: Seven Stories Press, 2006), 161–68.
55 Women of the Weather Underground, "A Collective Letter to the Women's Movement," July 24, 1973, in Dohrn et al., *Battle Song*, 199–207.
56 Dohrn et al., *Battle Song*, 10–12.

57 Jane Alpert, *Growing Up Underground* (New York: William Morrow, 1981).
58 Jane Alpert, "Mother Right: A New Feminist Theory," Atlanta Lesbian Feminist Alliance Archives, David M. Rubenstein Rare Book and Manuscript Library, Duke University. Digital copy at https://idn.duke.edu/ark:/87924/r3869r Accessed December 20, 2019.
59 Stern, *With the Weathermen*, 2007.
60 Diana Block, *Arm the Spirit*, 62.
61 WUO, *Prairie Fire*, 126–33.
62 Dohrn et al. *Battle Song*, 21–42.
63 Ibid., 11.

8

A people's history of Howard Zinn: radical popular history and its readers

Nick Witham

Howard Zinn's *A People's History of the United States* (1980) is both a popular and a controversial book. It has sold more than two million copies, has been translated into multiple foreign languages, and has spawned references in movies such as *Good Will Hunting* (1997) and *Ladybird* (2017), as well as the TV shows *The Sopranos* (1999–2007) and *The Simpsons* (1989–present). Such success has caused consternation among professional historians, many of whom view the book as a simplistic and politically distorted version of the American past.[1] While Zinn is the subject of two groundbreaking biographical studies, neither delves deeply into its subject's thought, preferring instead to use his life to chart the history of mid-twentieth-century American social movements.[2] All too often, then, Howard Zinn exists in the scholarly imagination either as a caricature or as a mere avatar for broader historical phenomena.

A People's History is better illuminated if placed within the development and reception of Marxist ideas in the twentieth-century United States. Zinn's eclectic articulation of historical materialism was influenced by both the Old and New Lefts, as well as by respect for a longstanding and politically heterogeneous radical tradition. It thus represented a multi-generational and deeply American approach to Marxism. To take Zinn seriously as a Marxist intellectual affirms the findings of a range of scholars who have highlighted the complexities and nuances of the generational divide between 1960s radicals and their predecessors, as well as the tensions between nationally inflected American radicalisms and those shaped by internationalist sentiment.[3]

Zinn's skepticism about capitalism was inseparable from his radical analysis of racial inequality. His historical writing and political practice engaged significantly with race as a structural aspect of the American past, especially in the emphasis that *A People's History* placed upon the experiences of slavery and emancipation. He was attuned to the dense linkages between American capitalism and racial inequality and wanted to popularize this way of framing the nation's past. In doing so, he drew on the anti-capitalist black radical tradition. As a white radical historian, he forged allegiances with the black freedom struggle by foregrounding the intertwined oppressions rooted in racial capitalism.[4]

The reception of *A People's History* by non-academic readers, finally, demonstrates the striking influence of Marxism on popular understandings of U.S. history in the closing decades of the twentieth century. The example set by Zinn shows the relationships that developed between academics and popular audiences, a dynamic missing from most histories of the American historical profession.[5] It also demonstrates the marked diversity of American intellectual and cultural life during the 1980s and 1990s. While historians of education have been keen to highlight the conservative dynamics at work in the era's "culture wars," the public reception of *A People's History* indicates that there was also a significant place for Marxism in the period's marketplace of ideas.[6]

To contextualize Zinn's political ideas in this way allows us not only to take them seriously but also to view the historian as part of a dense intellectual web shaped by a range of twentieth-century Marxisms. This, in turn, provides new ways of framing the intellectual cultures of American radicalism in the late twentieth-century United States, pointing to the enduring influence of historical materialism not only in the academy but also among the reading public.

"Je ne suis pas un Marxiste": Howard Zinn's American Marxism

Born in 1922 to Jewish immigrants in Brooklyn, New York, Howard Zinn grew up in a working-class family and came to political consciousness during the late 1930s, when he attended Communist Party of the United States (CPUSA) demonstrations. He went on to serve in the U.S. Air Force during the Second World War, before taking a G. I. Bill-sponsored B.A. at New York University. In 1956,

A people's history of Howard Zinn

Figure 8.1 Howard Zinn speaking against the Vietnam War at a protest against the Kent State shootings, Soldier's Field, Harvard University, c. May 8, 1970. *Courtesy Jeff Albertson Photograph Collection, Special Collections and University Archives, University of Massachusetts Amherst Libraries.*

two years before he completed his Columbia University doctorate, Zinn was appointed chair of the history department at Spelman College, a black women's university in Atlanta. Relocation to the South provided the backdrop for the first of Zinn's major political commitments: his engagement with the civil rights movement as a senior advisor to the Student Non-Violent Coordinating Committee (SNCC). In 1964, he moved north to work at Boston University, where he became involved in the movement against the Vietnam War (Figure 8.1). After the American withdrawal, he remained active as a writer and speaker, as well as a resolute opponent of the Boston University administration, until his retirement in 1988.

Upon his death in 2010, Zinn left a substantial corpus of essays and articles on the subject of Marxism. He discussed his first reading of *The Communist Manifesto* aged seventeen, which allowed him to see "my own life, the lives of my parents, and the conditions in the United States in 1939 … in a historical context, placed under a powerful analytical light."[7] During this period, Zinn's political sensibilities were also shaped by his reading in a range of nineteenth- and twentieth-century literature featuring elements of social realism, which fueled his awareness of political injustice. He learned from Jack London, Upton Sinclair, John Steinbeck, and Richard Wright that "race and class oppression were intertwined" in American society.[8] In arriving at this conclusion, he was a very young member of what Michael Denning has famously termed the "cultural front" that emerged out of immigrant and African American working-class neighborhoods in the 1930s and 1940s "modernist metropolis." This was a culture that was centrally concerned with the overlapping politics of communism, anti-racism, and anti-fascism, and committed to the idea that literary and intellectual culture should be shaped by these explicitly political ideas.[9]

Zinn's first truly serious intellectual engagement with Marxist thought came during and after his service in the Second World War. He joined the U.S. Air Force as a committed anti-fascist and fellow traveler of the CPUSA, but, while in Europe, became fascinated by the arguments of Arthur Koestler, especially his book *The Yogi and the Commissar* (1945). What attracted Zinn to Koestler was the way that the Hungarian writer arrived at a nuanced anti-communist standpoint, in which he was able to criticize Soviet ideology for being rooted in the totalitarian logic of the "Commissar" without slipping towards the relativizing position of the "Yogi," who could only view social inequality through a lens of "passive submission."[10] Koestler's book "shook forever" Zinn's political ideas, and led, several years later, to a sympathetic reading of *The God That Failed* (1950), a set of essays edited by the British Member of Parliament Richard Crossman that drew together anti-communist writers from Europe and the United States.[11] The book contained a range of political insights, including Koestler's own denunciation of Soviet backsliding towards the Nazi–Soviet Pact (1939), after which he found himself able to voice wholehearted opposition to the USSR and "no longer cared whether Hitler's allies called me a counter-revolutionary."[12] These were the foundations of Zinn's anti-Stalinist Marxism.

After this, Marxist ideas continued to play a key role in Zinn's political thinking, especially as they were shaped by his encounter with the black freedom struggle and the anti-war movement in the 1960s and 1970s. This influence is particularly clear in a lecture Zinn gave in 1968 entitled "Marxism and the New Left," in which he argued against the idea of historical materialism as a set of concrete doctrines, and in favor of its "constant redefinitions of theory in the light of immediate reality and insistence on *action* as a way of both testing and reworking history."[13] He went on to suggest that the best way to connect the "young" Marx of the "Theses on Feuerbach" (1845) with the campus politics of the 1960s was to develop an "admixture of pragmatism, empiricism, and existentialism":

> We are not really free, but our strength will be maximized if we act *as if* we are free (this is William James's "as if" merging with Sartre's "freedom") ... The existentialist emphasis on the necessity for action—based on conscience but avoiding careful weight of what passive liberals call "the realities"—is one of the most refreshing characteristics of the New Left in America. It combines Emerson's transcendentalism, Marx's revolutionary actionism, Dewey's pragmatism, and Camus' rebelliousness. It may yet revive the waning spirit of this country.[14]

To make this case was, at least implicitly, to skip over the "mature" Marx of *Capital* and the various generations of political thinking associated with Leninism, Stalinism, and Trotskyism, and instead to fuse Marxist thinking with French existentialism.

For Zinn, these ideas conditioned not only his understanding of committed activism, but also of politicized historical writing. Two years later, in *The Politics of History*, he went back to French existentialism, and in particular his reading of Albert Camus's *The Plague* (1947), when he suggested that "neutrality is a fiction in an unnatural world. There are victims, there are executioners, and there are bystanders ... Not to act is to join forces with the spreading plague."[15] This meant that a politicized history of the United States would focus on the experience and agency of what Zinn saw as its "victims" or "prisoners" instead of the perspectives of the privileged, with a view to challenging the status quo of American social relations.[16]

In addition to developing this commitment to change, however, he drew a deep sense of pessimism from another key New Left thinker: the second-generation Frankfurt School social theorist Herbert Marcuse. In his 1964 book *One-Dimensional Man*, which proved influential among student radicals, Marcuse suggested that the forces of "technological rationality" led under capitalism to "better domination, creating a truly totalitarian universe in which society and nature, mind and body are kept in a permanent state of mobilization for the defense of this universe."[17] In Zinn's 1968 parsing of this set of ideas, American history was conditioned by a deeply "irrational" and entrenched system that allowed "corporate profit, not human need" to shape the outcome of all aspects of political and social life.[18] There were opportunities for rebellion, but individuals who took them were limited in their capacity to change the course of history.

In analyzing the political thought of the New Left, Howard Brick has indicated the significance of a version of Marxism that stressed the importance of the young, humanist Marx, and fused his ideas with those of existentialism. This produced, in Brick's generative formulation, "dual notions of alienation, one concerning the plight of the individual in pursuit of meaning and the other addressing the nature of society as a thing apart, beyond control."[19] This summation provides a useful lens through which to view Zinn's encounter with Marxism during the late 1960s and early 1970s. Indeed, the pull and push between capitalism's totalizing structures and the individual political agency of society's rebels was a dialectic that lay at the heart of *A People's History*.

However, this version of Marxism also owed considerable debts to Zinn's biographical roots in the Old Left, in particular his desire to base his approach to radical politics on distinctly *American* philosophical traditions. In making the argument that the New Left's political thought needed to embrace "Emerson's transcendentalism" and "Dewey's pragmatism" as well as the thought of European thinkers such as Marx and Camus, Zinn echoed a set of arguments made by American Marxists in the 1920s and 1930s. As Leilah Danielson has shown in her work on the thought of A. J. Muste and his radical followers during that period, there was a central concern amongst Old Leftists with the process of "Americanizing Marxism" by fusing it with domestic political and philosophical traditions.[20] This was also a project endorsed by the political philosopher Sidney Hook, who, in his youth, had argued for a synthesis between Marxism and pragmatism that would emphasize the importance of practical action as well as revolutionary theory based on the assumption that, in the words of his biographer Christopher Phelps, the two traditions of thought were "each necessary to the other's fulfilment."[21]

Zinn's wide-ranging Marxism was thus indebted to both the Old Left and the New Left, as well as both domestic and cosmopolitan traditions of political philosophy. It was anti-Stalinist, existentialist, avowedly American, and contained elements of both optimism and pessimism. As such, it is not surprising that the historian has sometimes appeared as a less than systematic political thinker. Indeed, Zinn played into this perception himself, never truly accounting for the role of Marxism in his worldview. "Je ne suis pas un Marxiste," he playfully suggested in a 1988 essay, justifying his use of the recycled maxim by arguing that the German philosopher "had some very useful thoughts" but that to call oneself a Marxist was to fall into the trap of arguing that "every word in Volume One, Two and Three of *Das Kapital*, and especially in the *Grundrisse*, is unquestionably true."[22] Whilst this statement could be read as evidence of Zinn's lack of seriousness about political ideas, a deeper understanding of the roots of the historian's approach to Marxism helps to situate it instead as an example of the distinct eclecticism of radical political thought that emerged in the twentieth-century United States.

Marxism and *A People's History of the United States*

At the same time as he was working on *A People's History* during the mid- to late-1970s, Zinn taught a series of seminars in the political science department at Boston University on "Marxism and Political Theory," "Politics and History," and "Ideology and Social Change." These classes fused readings of "classic" texts by Marx and Engels—the *Economic and Philosophical Manuscripts* (1844), the *Communist Manifesto* (1848), the *Eighteenth Brumaire of Louis Bonaparte* (1852), and *Capital*, Volume I (1862)—with more recent work by thinkers such as Marcuse, Sartre, Hannah Arendt, Paul Baran, and Paul Sweezy.[23] The genesis of the book alongside Zinn's energetic teaching of political theory and philosophy of history thus provides an opportunity to consider the ways in which the ideas he discussed with his students made their way into his political worldview, and, ultimately, into the text of the book itself. Upon publication, *A People's History* stood as the first attempt to synthesize the views of a range of Old Left and New Left historians into a coherent popular narrative, a fact widely discussed in reviews of the book, as well as by Zinn's two biographers.[24] What has not been so thoroughly examined is the manner in which the book went beyond simply regurgitating the findings of these historians to fashion a popular theory of history and political change in the United States that owed much to Zinn's ideas about Marx and Marxism.

A People's History opened with a discussion of the historian's philosophy of history, in which he argued that to "tell the story of the discovery of America from the viewpoint of the Arawaks, of the Constitution from the standpoint of the slaves" was part of the "inevitable taking of sides in history," and that,

> The history of any country, presented as the history of a family, conceals fierce conflicts of interest (sometimes exploding, most often repressed) between conquerors and conquered, masters and slaves, capitalists and workers, dominators and dominated in race and sex. And in such a world of conflict, a world of victims and executioners, it is the job of thinking people, as Albert Camus suggested, not to be on the side of the executioners.[25]

This politicized version of "history from below," shaped by Zinn's fusion of Marxism and existentialism, was the unashamed perspective from which he reached out to readers in order to provide a fundamental alternative to the "history books given to children in the United States."[26]

Again, though, this perspective owed just as much to his Old Left political coordinates as it did to his roots in the New Left. Among the most regularly cited scholars in the book were labor historian Philip Foner and historian of slavery Herbert Aptheker, who were both a generation older than Zinn, closely associated with the CPUSA, and chose to interpret the national past through the politicized lenses of class conflict, the heroism of protest, and the centrality of political struggle to the development of American democracy. Zinn's model of engaged historical scholarship, rooted in the desire to uncover the contributions made to political struggle by workers and African Americans, owed much to conceptualizations of left-wing historical writing forged during the 1930s and 1940s by scholars such as Foner and Aptheker.[27] As such, *A People's History* was by no means a purely New Leftist intellectual project.

To get a deeper sense of how Zinn communicated his interpretation of American history to his readers, it is worth focusing on some examples from the text, the first of which is his coverage of the relationship between slavery, capitalism, and emancipation. In the second chapter of *A People's History*, entitled "Drawing the Color Line," the historian described the roots of slavery in "the frenzy for limitless profit that comes from capitalist agriculture," which, fused with "racial hatred," had created a social system "where white was master, black was slave."[28] This interpretation of the origins of slavery as primarily economic was paired with a discussion, drawn from the work of Aptheker, of slave resistance, in which Zinn argued that the picture of the "docile slave"—painted by historians as otherwise diverse as Ulrich B. Phillips and Stanley Elkins—was inaccurate. "The totality of slave behavior," he suggested, especially "the resistance of everyday life," highlighted the agency of enslaved men and women in their historical situation.[29]

This interpretation of black agency rose to the fore again in the book's chapter on the Civil War. Zinn argued that secession was not "a clash of peoples ... but of elites" in which Northern economic expansionism rooted in "free land, free labor, a free market" confronted the inherent economic conservatism of the South.[30] Then, in describing the role played by enslaved people during the war, he endorsed the "general strike" theory of slave resistance in the Confederate states, in which, by flocking to the Union lines as northern armies made their way southward (and thus withdrawing their labor from southern plantations) black people were conceptualized as making an enormous contribution to the defeat of the South. In making this case, Zinn's intellectual lodestar was another Old Leftist, W. E. B. Du Bois, whose work he referred to consistently throughout the book when writing about race and racism. In discussing the Civil War and Reconstruction, the historian drew particularly heavily on *Black Reconstruction in America* (1935), in which Du Bois articulated a consciously Marxist interpretation of the period. Because of its author's radical politics, the book was largely ignored upon publication, but it was resurrected by a range of New Left historians in the 1960s and 1970s, all of whom took its theoretical coordinates seriously, and, in the words of Thomas C. Holt, provided a range of evidence "that the much-maligned general strike *actually did happen.*"[31] While Holt was referring to historians such as Ira Berlin and Eric Foner, whose deep archival research clarified the details of Du Bois's preliminary observations, Zinn also played a key role by lending this interpretation of American history popular credibility.

Such a dynamic was also on display in the chapter of *A People's History* that covered the history of the Gilded Age and Progressive Era, entitled "Robber Barons and Rebels." Zinn described the government of the United States as "behaving almost exactly as Karl Marx described a capitalist state" to the extent that it maintained political order at the expense of working-class rebellion, which meant that, "whether Democrats or Republicans won, national policy would not change in any important way."[32] This thesis allowed Zinn to provide his readers with a series of other theoretical pronouncements about the modern state. "Control in modern times requires more than force, more than law," he suggested, "it requires that a population dangerously concentrated in cities and factories, whose lives are filled with cause for rebellion, be taught that all is right as it is."[33] This led to the conclusion that the nation's education system was "developed as an aid to the industrial system," and that the teaching of history was "required ... to foster patriotism," all of which was designed to stop individual Americans from "contemplating other possible ways of living."[34] Woven into celebratory accounts of the resistance mounted by Eugene Debs, Edward Bellamy, the Haymarket Martyrs, and Emma Goldman, then, were a set of observations about the nature of the modern state that emphasized its ability to isolate pockets of resistance and maintain individual alienation via methods of cultural and social coercion as well as the rule of force and law.

In making this case, Zinn was adapting Marxist theory to shape his interpretation of American history. In one sense, his argument that the late-nineteenth-century proved Marx's theory of the state "almost exactly" is not surprising: in classes on "The State in Marxian Theory" during the 1970s, he had discussed with students texts such as the *German Ideology*, in which Marx and Engels had argued that the state was "the form in which the individuals of the ruling class assert their common interests," and *The Communist Manifesto*, which had famously described it as a "committee for managing the common affairs of the whole bourgeoisie."[35] While these theories were clearly echoed in Zinn's work, he also went beyond them in his discussion of the coercive potential of education, and, in doing so, drew on the 1970s debates taking place between Marxist theorists of the state such as the British academic Ralph Miliband and the Greek-French intellectual Nicos Poulantzas, both of whose work he also set for his students to read and debate.[36] While these radical analysts disagreed on much about the nature of the modern state, they shared the conviction that the collective efforts of radical theorists should be directed towards a detailed elaboration of Marx's outlines, and Zinn's historical scholarship was clearly influenced by these developments.[37]

Throughout the book, Zinn maintained that his interpretation of the American past would only be productive if it pointed to new forms of social action in the present. Indeed, it was in the final chapter of *A People's History*, entitled "The Coming Revolt of the Guards," that he most fully engaged with contemporaneous political questions. There, he argued that the key statistic for understanding contemporary society was that "one per cent of the nation owns a third of the wealth." However, in suggesting that the remaining two-thirds of the nation's wealth was "distributed in such a way as to turn those ninety-nine per cent against one another," Zinn was expanding his critique to make a specific and important intervention in 1970s American Marxist thought.[38] This would become clear later in the chapter, when he wrote about the social position of Americans employed as "teachers and ministers, administrators and social workers, technicians, doctors, lawyers, nurses": "The establishment cannot survive without the obedience and loyalty of millions of people who are given small rewards to keep the system going ... These people—the employed, the somewhat privileged—are the guards of the system, buffers between the upper and lower classes. If they stop obeying, the system falls."[39] For Zinn, the key to successful radical politics was an alliance between those held "prisoner" by the system, i.e., the working class, and those he defined as "guards," concluding that "if we understand this, and act on it, not only will life be different and more satisfying ... but our grandchildren and our great grandchildren, might possibly see a different and marvelous world."[40]

These arguments echoed those made by Barbara and John Ehrenreich in a pair of classic 1977 articles on the status of the "professional-managerial class" in American society.[41] As defined by the

Ehrenreichs, this new class had developed during the twentieth century, and consisted of "salaried mental workers who do not own the means of production and whose major function in the social division of labor may be described broadly as the reproduction of capitalist culture and capitalist class relations."[42] This social category bore striking similarity to the class of "guards" identified by Zinn three years later, and its status was alarming for the Ehrenreichs because it made up "to a very large extent, the left itself," which had been shorn of working-class adherents during the course of the 1960s.[43] They claimed that the professional-managerial class existed in an antagonistic relationship with the traditional working class, to the extent that it could exist "only by virtue of the expropriation of the skills and culture once indigenous to the working class."[44] But their prescription for future social change nonetheless lay in "developing a politics which can address and overcome the class stalemate of the contemporary left" via the "coming together of working-class insight and militancy with the tradition of socialist thinking kept alive by 'middle class' intellectuals."[45] Again, the links between this theory and Zinn's desire for a unity of struggle between "prisoners" and "guards" are clear.

While there is no textual evidence either in *A People's History* or in the syllabi collected in Zinn's papers to show that Zinn had read the Ehrenreichs' essays, the way in which he concluded his popular history with a statement of the potential political power of the professional-managerial class highlights his status as a popularizer of this type of Marxist political thought. Whether it was in its account of slavery, capitalism, and emancipation, of the Gilded Age, or of the 1970s, the book thus owed clear political debts to the intellectual milieus of twentieth-century historical materialism, which framed Zinn's theory of class-based historical development in fundamental ways.

A People's History and its readers

A People's History sold incredibly well: in 1992, twelve years after publication, Zinn was able to report to his agent that it had sold approximately 260,000 copies, with annual totals rising steadily from 16,000 in 1982 to 44,000 in 1991.[46] Zinn thus reached an

A people's history of Howard Zinn 207

unusually large number of readers for a professional academic. But the book was not only purchased; it was also read and deeply considered. It therefore shaped the minds of its readers in important ways. How did Zinn engage with and conceptualize this readership? How were the book's arguments mediated by reviewers? And how did its non-professional readers respond to the book?

The historian's relationship with his publisher, Harper & Row, was initiated in 1975 when he was first approached by the company's Junior Books Division. The editor who originally engaged Zinn, Elaine Edelman, suggested that the material in high school textbooks was simply not accurate, and that this pointed to the emergence of a generation of students "that's turning away from the consciousness of the 1960s ... It's up to people like you to turn your understanding and talents to these kids – kids three and four years away from voting for the next President."[47] It was out of these conversations that Zinn's relationship with Harper's Trade Division ultimately developed, which led five years later to the publication of *A People's History*, a book the historian conceptualized as a single-volume history of the United States that would be "easy to read, radical in viewpoint."[48] Zinn subsequently elaborated on this point, arguing that he had a strong conception at the outset of who his audience would be: "I wanted to have ... spontaneity, a kind of easy-going conversational style in my writing. And I wanted it to be readable not just for people with college educations but any person who reads."[49] In the minds of both author and publisher, the book's marketability and access to readers originated in its all-new approach to U.S. history, its representation of the values of 1960s activism, and the way it rendered them accessible to school-age readers as well as adults.

Upon publication, the book's readability was immediately highlighted by a range of reviewers. In the words of historian Eric Foner, for example, who wrote about the book for the *New York Times*, Zinn's style conveyed "an enthusiasm rarely encountered in the leaden prose of academic history."[50] But other reviewers saved their praise for the political content of the historian's work. The *Minnesota Tribune* emphasized Zinn's argument that "the American economic system is kept in place by a carefully created consensus which protects the interests of the very rich," predicting that the book would be deeply *un*popular amongst those Americans "scrambling to protect their investments in cheap oil from western Asia and coal from Indian reservations."[51] Writing in the Committee for Non-Violent Action's newsletter, *Win*, another reviewer suggested that Zinn's arguments could provide the "foundation" for "social upheaval" by delivering "the tools we need to tear down the walls that were put up to stop us creating a new world."[52] A decade after its publication, the critic George Scialabba provided a succinct overview of these perspectives, suggesting that in the hands of a "morally imaginative reader" the book would prove to be not only enjoyable but a "vocation," and that it represented "one of the permanent achievements of the New Left."[53] In one way or another, all of these reviewers grappled with what they saw as the unique combination of readability and political analysis provided by *A People's History*. It was recognized as a major contribution to popular historical writing about the United States, as well as to radical political thinking more generally.

This is not to say that every left-wing reader was impressed with Zinn's arguments. Writing in *Monthly Review*, for example, the historian Mike Wallace praised the book as a distillation of the "critical scholarship" of the 1960s and 1970s that made this ground-breaking work "accessible to a general public."[54] Nonetheless, he took the book to task for its imprecise articulation of Marxism. Wallace argued that in narrating the relationship between the capitalist system and grassroots protest, Zinn relied too heavily on the fuzzy notion of "control" to describe the relationship between the powerful and the powerless. This did not do enough justice to the complexities of "the means of production" and the "wage relationship" in the matrix of social relations: "What we lack is the sense of transformation over time crucial to the development of a historical sensibility. What we get instead is a curiously static pageant in which now David, and now Goliath, attains momentary supremacy."[55]

This line of analysis was developed in more detail almost a quarter of a century later by another historian, Michael Kazin, who attacked Zinn from both a professional and a political perspective in a 2004 article in *Dissent*. Describing *A People's History* as "bad history, albeit gilded with virtuous intentions," Kazin criticized the book as a "Manichean fable."[56] This was "history as cynicism" that did the thousands of students who engaged with it each year no good.[57] Kazin also rejected the premise that Zinn could legitimately be described as a Marxist:

> The old Rhinelander never took so static or simplistic a view of history. Zinn's ruling elite is a transhistorical entity, a virtual monolith; neither its interests nor its ideology changes markedly from the days when its members owned slaves and wore knee-britches to the era of the Internet and Armani.[58]

This withering critique represented a powerful rejection of Zinn's ideas from the left of the political spectrum. Along with Wallace's response in 1980, Kazin's diatribe helps us to understand the ways in which *A People's History* has become the subject of such controversy in the four decades since its publication. But it also focuses our attention on the manner in which, throughout the book's history, its implications for Marxist political theory have been discussed, debated, and taken seriously.

In his rebuttal to Kazin's article, Zinn focussed his attention on the responses of his non-academic readers. Rejecting the idea that the book was "fatalistic" the historian suggested that "judging from the huge amount of mail I receive … the overwhelming reaction of readers is that they feel inspired by the book, motivated to become active."[59] This interpretation is borne out by the archival record. Soon after *A People's History* was published, for example, a student at Walden School in New York City wrote to Zinn to suggest that the book showed how "it is incorrect to believe that the conglomeration of the leaders inside a history book is a community which represents a country."[60] This type of message endorsing Zinn's "history from below" was repeated by various other students writing from the same school. Another student probed deeper into the meaning of Zinn's approach to the relationship between history and politics, telling the historian that the key message he took away from the books was that, "To grieve for past victims will deplete our 'moral energy for the present.' I can see how this is true, for if we dwell on the terrible things of the past then we will dissolve in pessimism … and damage our willpower to build a better future."[61] As he was encountered in high-school classrooms, then, Zinn was more than just a reminder that historical writing could never be "neutral" or "objective." He was also an influence on young Americans' decisions to engage in concrete ways with left-wing political ideas. This was rooted not only in his accessible prose, but also his ability to communicate an eclectic version of left-wing history that was rooted in, and deeply respectful of, American political traditions.

Other readers also drew connections between Zinn's book and their dissident understandings of American history and politics. Bruce Rockwell, an undergraduate student at California State University, Fullerton, wrote a response in 1981 that explicitly linked Zinn's ideas to those of Marx, especially his interpretation of American history through the lens of economics and class conflict, and suggested that he was inspired by the historian's "hopeful vision for a future when the masses will unite and love in a world of cooperation rather than exploitation."[62] Writing the same year, Roxanne Dunbar-Ortiz, a historian at California State University and an activist in the American Indian Movement, wrote to Zinn to tell him that she had successfully used the book to "introduce radical ideas" to her students. Ultimately, she wanted to thank him for "this valuable contribution to our social revolution." The influence of *A People's History* on her intellectual development was again registered in 2014 with the publication of her landmark book, *An Indigenous Peoples' History of the United States*.[63]

A 1982 letter written to Zinn by a reader then in graduate school, Gina Maranto, went even further, reflecting and reworking some of the central elements of the historian's political theory:

> I have run through the arguments again and again: the arguments about the way our so-called "free" society diffuses protest; about our entrapment by the system of wage-labor and the sacraments of private property; about the mendacity that has characterized the government of the United States since its beginning; about the various ways in which those at the bottom of the heap are turned against one another, or against external "enemies," are so beaten down that it is hard to believe Faulkner's "they endured." It is good, finally, to find someone who has articulated such feelings and thoughts in so compelling and commanding a fashion.[64]

In each of these reactions to *A People's History*, we can see the book's readers responding in a way that reflected and reworked Zinn's combination of analytical pessimism about the structures confronting advocates of revolutionary political change with a nonetheless full-throated encouragement to take rebellion seriously, both as a historical subject and as a collective mission in the present.

Speaking to an interviewer for *Time Out* magazine in the early 2000s, Zinn reflected on the popularity of *A People's History*:

> Over the years, there have been many polls where they ask, do you believe that this country is run for the benefit of the rich? Overwhelmingly, people say yes. That's the only thing that accounts for the fact that the book has been so popular. It speaks to what people are already thinking and feeling.[65]

This explanation points towards a key factor in the book's impressive sales figures: it aided readers, in particular those who were young adults, in articulating a class-conscious understanding of the American past that they already intuited. Recognizing and taking seriously Zinn's popular version of Marxism, these readers actively engaged with *A People's History*, sometimes criticizing it and at other times making it their own. In doing so, they demonstrated the fundamental receptiveness of non-academic audiences to Marxist ideas in the 1980s and 1990s.

A people's Marxism

Shortly after the publication of *A People's History*, Zinn wrote from Paris to his friend and colleague at Boston University, the sociologist Frances Fox Piven. He compared the book to her co-authored 1977 work *Poor People's Movements*, suggesting that what he had tried to do was "more emotional than analytical," with the aim of showing his readers "enough instances of people continuing to fight, despite repression, despite containment of reform, to suggest that the energy is there for even more." The goal of this work, he suggested, was to convince readers to "take the existential leap of faith ... not wildly and recklessly, but based on what history shows people are capable of doing, based on tactics which scrutiny of history shows as effective."[66] Without a doubt, the emotional resonance of Zinn's popular writing was one of the keys to its success. But in recognizing this point, we should not be blind to the seriousness with which he took his role as a theorist of Marxist politics.

Zinn's roots in the intellectual traditions of both the Old and New Lefts shaped his intellectual identity in a range of important ways. While his articulation of Marxist ideas was not always consistent, he drew deeply on the political thought he read throughout his career, particularly that which he discussed with students during the 1970s. This, in turn, fundamentally shaped *A People's History*. The book's analyses of various episodes in the American past were indebted to the insights of Marxist historians, whose work Zinn successfully synthesized. Furthermore, his integration of race and racism as key structural factors in his analysis of U.S. history showed his instinct to interweave historical materialism with analysis of identity politics. When we look in the right places, then, we can see the influence of an eclectic and distinctly American Marxist political theory on his ideas, and also see that he used *A People's History* to explicate this political theory to his readers.

The response of these readers to Zinn's writing highlights the deep-seated importance of a popularly accented Marxist history on the social and political thinking of young people in the 1980s and 1990s. In reading *A People's History*, they encountered a critical version of their nation's past, often for the first time, and had their ideas about contemporary politics transformed. If we pay careful attention to these readers, then, we find Marxism in unexpected places, such as the high-school social studies classroom. We also see Marxism's deep impact on popular understandings of American history. A people's history of Howard Zinn thus shows us a new side of this intellectual and activist, at the same time as it provides insights into the reading habits of those whose education he shaped, and who were, in turn, influenced by the ongoing legacies of Marxism in America.

Notes

1 For one recent example, see the chapter on Zinn in Sam Wineburg, *Why Learn History (When It's Already On Your Phone)* (Chicago: University of Chicago Press, 2018), 51–79.
2 Davis D. Joyce, *Howard Zinn: A Radical American Vision* (Amherst: Prometheus Books, 2003); Martin Duberman, *Howard Zinn: A Life on the Left* (New York: The New Press, 2012).
3 The classic work on the links between the Old and New Lefts is Maurice Isserman, *If I Had a Hammer: The Death of the Old Left and the Birth of the New Left* (Champaign: University of Illinois Press, 1987), but new life is breathed into the question by Christopher Phelps, "Lefts Old and

New: Sixties Radicalism, Now and Then," in *A New Insurgency: The Port Huron Statement and Its Times*, ed. Howard Brick and Gregory Parker (Ann Arbor: University of Michigan Press, 2015), 143–52. An excellent statement of the national and transnational dynamics at play in the American New Left is Doug Rossinow, "The New Left: The American Impress," in *Reframing 1968: American Politics, Protest and Identity*, ed. Martin Halliwell and Nick Witham (Edinburgh: University of Edinburgh Press, 2018), 15–35.
4 For three useful accounts of this tradition, see Cedric Robinson, *Black Marxism: The Making of the Black Radical Tradition* (Chapel Hill: University of North Carolina Press, 2000); Nikhil Pal Singh, *Black is a Country: Race and the Unfinished Struggle for Democracy* (Cambridge, MA: Harvard University Press, 2004); and Carol Boyce Davies, *Left of Karl Marx: The Political Life of Black Communist Claudia Jones* (Durham, NC: Duke University Press, 2008).
5 Peter Novick, *That Noble Dream: The "Objectivity Question" and the American Historical Profession* (Cambridge: Cambridge University Press, 1988); Kerwin Lee Klein, *Frontiers of Historical Imagination: Narrating the European Conquest of Native America, 1890–1990* (Berkeley: University of California Press, 1997); Ellen Fitzpatrick, *History's Memory: Writing America's Past, 1880–1980* (Cambridge, MA: Harvard University Press, 2002). One notable exception is Ian Tyrrell, *Historians in Public: The Practice of American History, 1890–1970* (Chicago: University of Chicago Press, 2005).
6 Andrew Hartman, *A War for the Soul of America: A History of the Culture Wars* (Chicago: Chicago University Press, 2015); Adam Laats, *The Other School Reformers: Conservative Activism in American Education* (Cambridge, MA: Harvard University Press, 2015); Natalia Mehlman Petrzela, *Classroom Wars: Language, Sex and the Making of Modern Political Culture* (New York: Oxford University Press, 2015).
7 Howard Zinn, "Preface to *Marx in Soho*," in *Three Plays: The Political Theater of Howard Zinn* (Boston: Beacon Press, 2010), 103.
8 Howard Zinn, *You Can't Be Neutral on a Moving Train: A Personal History of Our Times* (Boston: Beacon Press, 1994), 17.
9 Michael Denning, *The Cultural Front: The Laboring of American Culture in the Twentieth Century* (London: Verso Books, 1997), xv.
10 Arthur Koestler, *The Yogi and the Commissar and Other Essays* (London: Jonathan Cape, 1945), 12.
11 Zinn, *You Can't Be Neutral on a Moving Train*, 178.
12 Arthur Koestler in *The God That Failed*, ed. Richard Crossman (London: Hamilton, 1950), 74.

13 Howard Zinn, "Marxism and the New Left," in *Dissent: Explorations in the History of American Radicalism*, ed. Alfred A. Young (DeKalb: Northern Illinois University Press, 1968), 360, italics in original.
14 Ibid., 362, 371.
15 Howard Zinn, *The Politics of History* (Urbana: University of Illinois Press, 1970), 40.
16 Ibid., 36.
17 Herbert Marcuse, *One-Dimensional Man: Studies in the Ideology of Advanced Industrial Society* [1964] (New York: Routledge, 2006), 20.
18 Zinn, "Marxism and the New Left," 369.
19 Howard Brick, *Age of Contradiction: American Thought and Culture in the 1960s* (Ithaca: Cornell University Press, 2000), 17.
20 Leilah Danielson, *American Gandhi: A. J. Muste and the History of Radicalism in the Twentieth Century* (Philadelphia: University of Pennsylvania Press, 2014), 157.
21 Christopher Phelps, *Young Sidney Hook: Marxist and Pragmatist* (Ann Arbor: University of Michigan Press, 2005), 8.
22 Howard Zinn, "Je Ne Suis Pas Un Marxiste," in *Failure to Quit: Reflections of an Optimistic Historian* (Boston: South End Press, 2002), 146. This collection reprints the essay, which originally appeared in *Z Magazine* in June 1988.
23 Details of these courses are contained in Howard Zinn Papers, Tamiment and Robert F. Wagner Labor Archive, New York University (hereafter HZP), box 18, folders 20–22.
24 The historiographical coordinates of the book are discussed in Joyce, *Howard Zinn*, 154–71 and Duberman, *Howard Zinn*, 215–38.
25 Howard Zinn, *A People's History of the United States* (New York: Harper Collins, 2002), 10.
26 Ibid., 7.
27 Melvyn Dubofsky, "Give Us That Old Time Labor History: Philip S. Foner and the American Worker," *Labor History*, 26, no. 1 (1985): 118–37; Gary Murrell, *"The Most Dangerous Communist in the United States": A Biography of Herbert Aptheker* (Amherst: University of Massachusetts Press, 2015).
28 Zinn, *A People's History*, 28.
29 Ibid., 34.
30 Ibid., 189.
31 Thomas C. Holt, "'A Story of Ordinary Human Beings': The Sources of Du Bois's Historical Imagination in *Black Reconstruction*," *South Atlantic Quarterly* 112, np. 3 (Summer 2013): 423, italics in original.
32 Zinn, *A People's History*, 258.
33 Ibid., 262.

34 Ibid., 263–64.
35 Karl Marx, *The German Ideology*, in *Karl Marx: Selected Writings*, ed. Lawrence H. Simon (Indianapolis: Hackett, 1994), 154; Karl Marx and Friedrich Engels, *The Communist Manifesto* (London: Penguin, 2002), 221.
36 Ralph Miliband, *The State in Capitalist Society* (New York: Basic Books, 1969); Nicos Poulantzas, "The Problem of the Capitalist State," *New Left Review* 58 (November 1969): 67–68.
37 For a useful contemporaneous overview of these debates, and one that Zinn had also read and discussed with his students, see David A. Gold, Clarence Y. H. Lo and Erik Olin Wright, "Recent Developments in Marxist Theories of the Capitalist State," *Monthly Review* (October 1975), 29–42.
38 Zinn, *A People's History*, 571.
39 Ibid., 574.
40 Ibid., 582.
41 For an important discussion of the development of this idea, see Gabriel Winant, "The Making of *Nickel and Dimed*: Barbara Ehrenreich and the Exposé of Class in America," *Labor* 15:1 (March 2018), 67–79.
42 Barbara Ehrenreich and John Ehrenreich, "The Professional-Managerial Class," *Radical America*, 11, no. 2 (March–April 1977): 13.
43 Ibid., 7.
44 Ibid., 17.
45 Barbara Ehrenreich and John Ehrenreich, "The New Left and the Professional-Managerial Class," *Radical America*, 11, no. 3 (May–June 1977): 21.
46 Howard Zinn to Richard Balkin (March 10, 1992), HZP, box 11, folder 8.
47 Elaine Edelman to Howard Zinn (May 22, 1975), HZP, box 5, Folder 2.
48 Howard Zinn to Angus Cameron (July 30, 1976), Alfred A. Knopf, Inc. Papers, Harry Ransom Center, University of Texas at Austin, box 447, folder 3.
49 Nate Segloff, "A Q&A with Howard Zinn," audiobookstoday.com (July 28, 2003), transcript in HZP, box 10, folder 24.
50 Eric Foner, "Majority Report," *New York Times Book Review* (March 2, 1980), 10.
51 W. E. Huntzicker, "People's History is Disrespectful of Governments," *Minnesota Tribune* (March 16, 1980), G14–G15.
52 Murray Rosenblith, "Reviews," *Win* (April 15, 1982), 32.
53 George Scialabba, "U.S. History: By the People, For the People," *Christianity and Crisis* (May 13, 1991), 155.

54 Mike Wallace, "A History of Class, Race and Sex Struggle," *Monthly Review* (December 1980), 31.
55 Ibid., 34–36.
56 Michael Kazin, "Howard Zinn's History Lessons," *Dissent* (Spring 2004), 81.
57 Ibid., 82.
58 Ibid., 82.
59 Howard Zinn, "Interpreting History," *Dissent* (Summer 2004), 110.
60 Anonymous response to *A People's History of the United States*, Walden School, New York City, no date (c. 1980–1981), HZP, Box 8, Folder 1.
61 Alan Winchester, response to *A People's History of the United States*, Walden School, New York City, no date (c. 1980–1981), HZP, Box 8, Folder 1.
62 Bruce Rockwell, "An Analysis of Howard Zinn's *A People's History of the United States*" (December 9, 1981), HZP, box 11, folder 5.
63 Roxane Dunbar-Ortiz to Howard Zinn (December 9, 1981), HZP, box 5, folder 7; Roxane Dunbar-Ortiz, *An Indigenous People's History of the United States* (Boston: Beacon Press, 2014).
64 Gina Maranto to Howard Zinn (October 5, 1982), HZP, Box 5, Folder 8.
65 Zinn quoted in B. Aria, "History in the Making," *Time Out* (no date, c. 2003), HZP, box 15, folder 18.
66 Howard Zinn to Frances Fox Piven (August 25, 1981), Frances Fox Piven Papers, Five College Archives and Manuscript Collection, Smith College, box 20, folder 8.

9

Class, commodity, consumption: theorizing sexual violence during the feminist sex wars of the 1980s

Mara Keire

The clashing sides in what are now known as the feminist sex wars of the 1980s shared similar radical roots in the leftist activism of the 1960s. Well-versed in the thought of Marx, Engels, and Freud, feminists engaged with Mao, Fanon, and Marcuse. Disheartened by misogyny within the New Left, a number of radical women departed the organizations to which they had devoted so much time, but when they did they brought with them the New Left's theoretical background on the causes of class oppression, the problems of proletarian false consciousness, and the cultural distortions caused by capitalism. They had also engaged, sometimes with great ambivalence, with Freudian ideas about freeing society from the sexual repression that distorted social relations. As these women established consciousness-raising groups and developed radical feminist perspectives on the world around them, they used a Marxian theoretical background to analyze the materialist origins of gender and sexual oppression.[1]

When Shulamith Firestone and Kate Millett published *The Dialectic of Sex: The Case for Sexual Revolution* and *Sexual Politics*, respectively, in 1970, they sparked a flowering of radical feminist thought, inspiring other women activists to speak, write, and organize, but over the course of the decade, radical feminists increasingly diverged in their thought about the causes and consequences of women's oppression. Those differences crystallized during the 1982 Barnard Conference on Sexuality which Carole Vance coordinated and women belonging to anti-pornography organizations picketed. Although feminists had been fighting sexual violence and pornography since the beginning of the 1970s, the Barnard Conference provided women activists and intellectuals a platform to denounce the direction of the anti-pornography movement and to enunciate what came to be called the pro-sex position. Although often portrayed as having little in common, the pro-sex and anti-pornography feminists shared organizational and intellectual starting points which made their subsequent fights all that much more bitter when they used a common vocabulary to excoriate each other about their differing views on sex, sexuality, gender violence, and pornography.

Most of the histories of second-wave feminism focus on this vicious infighting but spend considerably less time exploring the intellectual genealogies of what "pro-sex" and "anti-porn" meant to participants of the sex wars. Part of the reason resides in the fact that second-wave feminists have written the important histories of the period, and most of these feminists sided with the pro-sex cadre. Ruth Rosen, Sara Evans, and Alice Echols all provide essential insight into the organization and enthusiasms of women's activism, but in general they did not focus on the theory informing women's thoughts.[2] In *Desiring Revolution: Second-Wave Feminism and the Rewriting of American Sexual Thought, 1920 to 1982*, Jane Gerhard addressed this history, but her book ends just as the sex wars commenced.[3] Like the editors of the landmark collections *Pleasure and Danger*, which brought together the papers presented at the Barnard conference, and *Powers of Desire*, which served as a cornerstone to the women's studies curriculum well into the 1990s, Gerhard adopted an unabashedly pro-sex view.[4] Together, this canon represents pro-sex feminists as radical liberationists who countered the reactionary tendencies of prudish anti-porn harridans—and not without reason. Catharine MacKinnon and Andrea Dworkin's ill-conceived cooperation with the Reagan-era Moral Majority irreparably tarnished their reputations and set back the fight against violence against women. Carole Vance correctly connected conservatism's co-option of the anti-pornography fight to the culture wars of the 1990s.[5] Yet as the #MeToo movement today exposes the sheer pervasiveness of image-based sexual abuse, workplace harassment, and men's rape of women, the canonical view of the pro-sex and especially the anti-pornography feminists needs a thoroughgoing reappraisal.

Revisiting the 1980s sex wars, but situating them in the context of feminist views about sexual violence, illuminates the influence Marxist thought had on important anti-porn protestors (such as

Catharine MacKinnon, Andrea Dworkin, and Audre Lorde) and pro-sex thinkers (especially Ellen Willis and Gayle Rubin). Marxism, and to a lesser extent Freudianism, guided how they constructed their arguments and presented their programs for change. Feminists dealt with three core Marxist concepts: class, commodity, and consumption. Through the 1970s, most radical feminists agreed that women were a class unto themselves, although their definitions of class and the mechanisms of oppression were often quite diverse. Over the course of the decade, a core group of feminists developed a critique of gender violence, and pornography in particular, that they grounded in ideas about commodification and fetishization of women's sexuality. Starting in the early 1980s, pro-sex feminists challenged the anti-porn feminists by questioning their contentions about the consumption of pornography and emphasizing women's agency as both producers and consumers of pornography. While pro-sex feminists have earned the reputation as the more radical faction, their analysis of sex and suggestions for change ranged from liberal to libertarian and they readily worked with high-profile pornographers.[6] By contrast, anti-violence feminists were more extreme in both their radical analysis of pornography and their reactionary alliances with the New Right. Both groups adapted leftist theory to suit their purposes; however, anti-pornography feminists hewed much more closely to a Marxist framework than scholars have previously recognized.

Class

Second-wave feminists struggled with the question of class. They wanted to assert that women shared a common oppression, and therefore a group interest, but economic differences among women challenged claims to unity. Most white feminists made analogies between the oppression of women and the oppression of black people to show how people across classes could experience shared subjugation, but as bell hooks observed in her scathing analysis of this comparison in *Ain't I a Woman*, it presumed all black people are men and all women are white, effectively erasing the travails of black women, with racist consequences.[7] Although that was a sound objection, the race analogy was in many ways less important than Marxism to white radical feminist analysis. From Shulamith Firestone's *Dialectic of Sex* to Susan Brownmiller's *Against Our Will*, Friedrich Engels's 1884 opus *The Origin of the Family, Private Property and the State* served as the consistent template for explaining the origins of patriarchy and the repression of women.[8] Marxism, especially historical materialism and class analysis, provided the groundwork for a feminist understanding through most of the 1970s and into the 1980s.

Shulamith Firestone took the lead with *The Dialectic of Sex*. A founding member of New York Radical Women, the Redstockings, and New York Radical Feminists, Firestone had started out as an activist in the New Left. But after William F. Pepper, the chair of the 1967 National Conference for New Politics, literally patted her on the head and told her to "move on, little girl. We have more important issues to talk about here than women's problems," Firestone began to adapt leftist theories of oppression for feminism.[9] Like Engels, she argued that separating the work of men from women served as the first division of labor, and like many feminists who followed her, she made the obligatory observation about women's centrality to the forces of reproduction.[10] Although she started the book with notable panache, literally re-writing Engels's introduction to *The Origin of the Family*, when it came time to unpack family dynamics Firestone turned away from historical materialism and toward Freud. For her, it was the structure and sexual taboos of the nuclear family that caused the repression of women and children. In particular, she emphasized the need for the uninhibited expression of sexual desires as a liberatory first step.

Kate Millett's *Sexual Politics* came out the same year as *The Dialectic of Sex*. It was an expanded, interdisciplinary version of her doctoral thesis in literature from Columbia University. She had been pursuing her doctorate and teaching part-time at Barnard in 1968, but because she and some other junior faculty without tenure supported the student protests, they lost their jobs.[11] This dual influence of literary criticism and sixties radicalism shined through in *Sexual Politics*. Millett opened the book with a close analysis of sexual violence in the work of Henry Miller, Norman Mailer, and Jean Genet. Unlike Firestone, Millett spent considerably more time analyzing the role of rape in maintaining sexual divisions, but like other early radical feminists, she focused more on exposing the cultural work that reinforced the so-called naturalism of gendered divisions than on the violent processes that maintained women's subordination. For example, in her theoretical chapter, "Force" figured as only one out of the eight categories that she argued affected women's oppression.[12] In the introduction to her 2000 reissue of the book, Millett mourned the degree to which she downplayed force in her theoretical chapter:

> When I finished *Sexual Politics* in 1970, feminists were still so intent on a reasonable civil rights argument that it seemed almost "shrill" to look very far into domestic violence and rape, which had always been presented as "aberrant" behavior. Only later did we become aware that there was a normative element in patriarchal violence.[13]

Despite her regrets, Millett established the groundwork for radical feminists exploring the role of rape and its cultural representations in maintaining patriarchy. Using a mix of analytical approaches, *Sexual Politics* represented the early theoretical range many feminists adopted to explore women's oppression, their categorization of women as a class, and the possible directions of liberation.

In 1975, with publication of the landmark volume *Against Our Will: Men, Women and Rape*, Susan Brownmiller situated sexual violence as the central dynamic for maintaining the division between men and women and ensuring women's ongoing oppression. An already established journalist, and an early member of the New York Radical Feminists, Brownmiller decided to write *Against Our Will* after hearing so many women relate their experiences of rape in consciousness-raising groups and public speak-outs.[14] While she embraced Engels's epochal approach to historical periodization, Brownmiller lauded August Bebel as alone among the "great socialist theoreticians" for recognizing the role of rape in the development of class, private property, and the division of labor.[15] In contrast to Firestone and Ellen Willis, one of the foremost pro-sex feminists, Brownmiller repudiated the possibility of a feminist reading of Freud. Right in the second paragraph of her introduction, she denounced Freud: "We can search in vain for a quotable quote, an analysis, a perception. The father of psychoanalysis, who invented the concept of the primacy of the penis, was never motivated, as far as we know, to explore the real-life deployment of the penis as weapon."[16] Later in the book, she described how Freud's followers, notably Helene Deutsch and Karen Horney, built on his premise about women's inherent masochism, enshrining what we would now call a rape myth: that women fantasize about rape, even to the point of making false rape accusations, as a result of their repressed sexuality. Through the cumulative impact of these types of examples, Brownmiller achieved one of her most important analytical contributions: she began to enunciate the idea of "rape culture" and how not just rape, but the threat of rape, including its cultural valorization, limits women's mobility and opportunities. *Against Our Will* still stands as one of the most powerful descriptions of the enforcement of patriarchal norms.

Since the early 1970s, lawyer Catharine MacKinnon sought to combine feminism and Marxism to produce an analytical framework for understanding the oppression of women. In her article, "Feminism, Marxism, Method, and the State: An Agenda for Theory," MacKinnon began with the bold statement, "Sexuality is to feminism what work is to marxism: that which is most one's own, yet most taken away."[17] With this opening salvo, she shifted the analytical terrain away from sex as meaning reproduction and the family and toward sex as meaning sexuality, especially the heteronormative emphasis on male aggression and female submission.[18] In MacKinnon's view, men maintained their patriarchal advantage by intertwining sexuality and sexual violence, and normalizing this connection as "natural." With these observations, MacKinnon fundamentally rejected Freudianism as providing a key to fighting male oppression. Indeed, she argued that the "centrality of sexuality emerges not from Freudian conceptions but from feminist practice on diverse issues, including abortion, birth control, sterilization abuse, domestic battery, rape, incest, lesbianism, sexual harassment, prostitution, female sexual slavery, and pornography."[19] Although best remembered for the falsely attributed quote that "all sex is rape," Catharine MacKinnon carefully evaluated the nuances of sexuality and sexual consent. A radical rethinking that centered violence against women as a fundamental mechanism of control not only shaped MacKinnon's writing, but also her legal practice as she applied her ideas about the subordination of women to defending their civil rights.

MacKinnon's legal training meant she combined a scrupulous consideration of past case law with innovative proposals for how to make a more feminist jurisprudence. Notably, MacKinnon considered sexual coercion along a spectrum that included women's experiences at work, at school, and during their leisure time. In her groundbreaking 1979 book, *Sexual Harassment of Working Women*, MacKinnon effectively argued that sexual harassment counted as sex discrimination under Title VII of the 1964 Civil Rights Act, which prohibited discrimination on the basis of race, color, religion, sex, or national origin. MacKinnon denounced "quid pro quo" harassment where men demanded sex in exchange for guaranteeing women's job security, but her radicalism showed most in her enunciation of harassment caused by a "hostile work environment."[20] By arguing that a sexualized work culture put women at a professional disadvantage, MacKinnon contended that sexual harassment was not just about individual men targeting individual women, but about entrenched workplace dynamics that encouraged discrimination against all women. In 1986, the Supreme Court cemented this argument in *Meritor Savings Bank v. Vinson*. Mechelle Vinson's case was notably horrific—her manager had repeatedly raped her in the bank vault—but the extent of her travails meant that the justices did not just consider quid pro quo sex for work but also the damages caused by the hostile, sexualized work environment.[21] By endangering women's job security and economic opportunities, sexual harassment both produced and reinforced social inequality. Through her intellectual analysis and casework, MacKinnon cogently addressed how sexual discrimination had a disastrous impact on women's lives and their sexual vulnerability as a class. By combining labor law and civil rights legislation to fight sexual harassment, MacKinnon followed a path well respected by many activists on the left.[22]

Much of the case precedent on which MacKinnon and other feminist lawyers relied drew on Marxian ideas of division of labor and mechanisms of class oppression. But in their radicalism, they pushed both their intellectual theory and their legal strategies further. When radical feminists fighting sexual violence singled out pornography as an industry and product that reinforced women's oppression, they staked their movement and reputation on persuading people that pornography contributed to the way men sexually abused, economically exploited, and systematically harassed women. Ironically, their analysis of pornography drew directly on

Marxist conceptions of false consciousness, alienation of labor, and commodity reification. In the late 1970s and early 1980s, feminists ranging from Luisah Teish and Alice Walker to, most notoriously, Andrea Dworkin tried to show how pornography—as a fetishized commodity—involved the exploitation of women in its production and created a false consciousness that obscured the possibilities of authentic, unreified sexuality.

Commodity

In her article, "Misguided, Dangerous, and Wrong: An Analysis of Antipornography Politics," published in 1993, approximately a decade after the sex wars began, anthropologist Gayle Rubin questioned why feminists had targeted porn. She argued that pornography was no more violent than many images broadcast in mainstream movies and television shows and its labor practices no more exploitative than many other jobs.[23] She also refuted the notion that viewing violent pornography made men any more sexually aggressive.[24] What Rubin ignored, however, was the neatness with which the fight against pornography developed out of radical feminists' adaptation of Marxism.

For anti-violence feminists, as anti-pornography feminists sometimes called themselves, pornography epitomized how capitalist patriarchy exploited women's sexuality through the alienation of labor, commodity reification, and the erasure of unequal relations of power (Figure 9.1). Pornography as a product reinforced the "thingification" of women in both its making and its meaning.[25] Applying Marxism to feminism, Andrea Dworkin, who had engaged in sex work and escaped a brutally abusive husband, declared that

> the strains of male power are embodied in pornography's form and content, in economic control of and distribution of wealth within the industry, in the picture or story as a thing, in the photographer or writer as aggressor, in the critic or intellectual who through naming assigns value in the actual use of models, in the application of the material in what is called real life.[26]

For anti-violence feminists, pornography was never just about the representation of women; it was also always about how a

Class, commodity, consumption 225

Figure 9.1 Those feminist social critics of the 1980s "sex wars" who opposed pornography had a method of analysis that mapped onto a famous line in the first paragraph of Marx's *Capital* (1867): "Our investigation must begin with the analysis of a commodity." Andreas Feininger, "1595 Broadway," 1983. *Courtesy of the Museum of the City of New York.*

multi-million-dollar business exploited vulnerable women and deformed their sexuality for profit. They believed that the industry itself through its products and practices inculcated the ideology of male supremacy. For these reasons, anti-pornography feminists advocated the radical destruction of the pornography business, not just its internal reform.

In her 1981 opus *Pornography: Men Possessing Women*, Andrea Dworkin condemned the industry and its outputs. Through a rereading of pornographic artifacts, which she situated within the context of their creation, Dworkin showed how porn perpetuated an endemic misogyny, replicated men's oppression of women, and reinforced the alienation of women from their bodies, their sexuality, and their agency. In the chapter "Power," Dworkin analyzed "Beaver Hunters," an image from *Hustler* that portrayed a woman splayed out and tied down to the hood of a Jeep with two white men carrying rifles seated in the car. The caption read, in part, "These two hunters easily bagged their limit in the high country. They told HUSTLER that they stuffed and mounted their trophy as soon as they got her home."[27] With fiery prose, Dworkin deconstructed the photograph. She reminded readers that photographers filmed real people—real women—in painfully abusive positions. She minced no words describing how set designers stripped, tied up, and contorted women into sexually humiliating poses for the camera. Nor did she shy away from annunciating its meaning:

> Owning is expressed in every aspect of the photograph ... The [hunters] have a woman, bound and powerless, to do with as they like ... Their possession of her extends over time, even into (her) death ... The camera and the photographer behind it also own the woman. The camera uses and keeps her. The photographer uses her and keeps the image of her. The publisher of the photograph can also claim her as a trophy. He has already mounted her and put her on display.[28]

Dworkin did not ignore the issue of consent—or women's agency—but she pointed out the lack of economic opportunities for women.

> The fact of the photograph in relation to its context—an industry that generates wealth by producing images of women abjectly used, a society in which women cannot adequately earn money because women are valued precisely as the woman in the photograph is valued—both proves and perpetuates the real connection between masculinity and wealth.[29]

Men staged the images, made the money, and controlled the economic gains in an industry more profitable than even mainstream Hollywood.

Pro-sex feminists did not engage with anti-pornography feminists' structural critique of the industry. Despite their radical roots, they offered instead a liberal vision of progressive improvement and individual agency. Gayle Rubin, who had participated in the New Left, joined one of the earliest consciousness-raising groups, and helped found Samois, a lesbian–feminist BDSM organization, suggested that "we should encourage more women to enter [pornography] as producers, writers, and directors" and that labor organizing and better contracts would eliminate any abuses on set.[30] Amber

Hollibaugh, another defender of pornography, had taken part in the Freedom Summer, organized for the United Farm Workers, and directed the Lesbian AIDS Project in New York. At various times, she had engaged in sex work and argued that it "may make much more sense to spend eight hours stripping than working in a dry cleaning plant, or as an LPN (Licensed Practical Nurse) or office worker taking home $132.00 a week. Sex industry work may offer a woman not only more money but a greater sense of power."[31] As for the product itself, rock critic and Redstocking co-founder Ellen Willis admitted,

> Over the years I've enjoyed various pieces of pornography—some of them of the sleazy Forty-second Street paperback sort—and so have most women I know. Fantasy, after all, is more flexible than reality, and women have learned as a matter of survival, to be adept at shaping male fantasies to their own purpose.[32]

None of these women saw the need for radical structural change in the pornography industry.

Black feminists were less sanguine. Patricia Hill Collins observed, "the political economy of pornography meshes with this overarching value system that objectifies, commodifies, and markets products, ideas, images, and actual people."[33] Most anti-porn black feminists pointed to how the commodification of black women's bodies had a long history inextricably entwined with centuries of slavery. In "A Quiet Subversion," Luisah Teish, a writer, dancer, and Yoruban priestess, argued that "today we see vestiges of that inheritance in the exploitation of women's bodies through prostitution and pornography and the denial of reproductive rights."[34] Like other anti-violence feminists, Teish argued that the disproportionate number of African-American women in the sex trades "bespeaks an economic and cultural crime. Facing the greatest degree of discrimination in education, jobs, and federal aid, some poor black women have been forced into the streets." She observed how media from pornography to album covers and television miniseries "romanticize the image of the battered black woman."[35] Photographs of African-American women naked, chained, and whipped reinforced their dehumanization, normalized their exploitation, and once again reduced them to "stock." Teish excoriated black activists for ignoring racism in pornography, dismissing their arguments that porn was a white product made and marketed by white men; after all, black men also bought porn and participated in the commodification of black women.

Novelist Alice Walker addressed exactly this point in her 1979 short story, "Coming Apart," which embedded excerpts from antipornography essays by Audre Lorde, Tracey Gardener, and Luisah Teish within a narrative about a husband's use of pornography and his wife's growing awareness of its abuses and how they affected her. When the woman first objected to the pornography to which he masturbated, he thought it was because he spent "a luxurious ten minutes" fantasizing about white women's bodies; however, when he brought home pornography featuring black women, she was even more disturbed. As Walker described it, the magazine, *Jivers*, like a lot of pornography, portrayed body parts separated from faces and personalities, transforming them into symbols of power and degradation:

> On the cover are the legs and shoes of a well-dressed black man, carrying a briefcase and a rolled *Wall Street Journal* in one hand. At his feet—she turns the magazine cover around and around to figure out how exactly the pose is accomplished—there is a woman, a brownskin woman like herself, twisted and contorted in such a way that her head is not even visible. Only her glistening body—her back and derriere—so that she looks like a human turd at the man's feet.[36]

After a trip to Times Square, where the husband felt complimented when pimps ask his wife if she was "workin'," the wife started reading black feminists and shared their insights with him. He resisted their message, not wanting to consider how he'd bought into the "fantasies fed to him by movies and magazines." He "refused to see ... that where white women are depicted in pornography as 'objects,' black women are depicted as animals. Where white women are at least depicted as human bodies if not beings, black women are depicted as shit."[37] The story concluded with their separation, then reunification once he saw her again as an authentic woman and made love to her as an individual in her own body.[38]

Although pro-sex feminists scoffed at the idea of a difference between erotica and pornography, anti-violence feminists tied that distinction to how commercial sexual imagery commodified women as interchangeable, usable objects and made sex into an alienated and alienating act. Ironically, when interviewed for the 1981 documentary *Not a Love Story: A Film About Pornography*, porn producer Ron Martin enunciated exactly this perspective. After observing that "what really happens" would not sell, he explained that when "you see sex in the film, it's just a bang, and so you go home and bang. And so the woman says, 'what the hell is going on here?' ... Pornography doesn't have the responsibility to say to the guy, 'Hello, this is banging and this is making love.'" By drawing a distinction between the commodified "bang" and the authentic "making love," Martin made the documentary's director Bonnie Sheer Klein's point for her.[39] Lesbian feminist and poet Audre Lorde sketched out a similar argument, although with greater elegance and far more attention to the liberatory possibilities, in her essay "Uses of the Erotic: The Erotic as Power." In this piece, first presented in 1978, Lorde connected the erotic to women's spiritual strength and pornography to the repression of women's sexual authenticity:

> The erotic has often been misnamed by men and used against women. It has been made into the confused, the trivial, the psychotic, the plasticized sensation. For this reason, we have often turned away from the exploration and consideration of the erotic as a source of power and information, confusing it with its opposite, the pornographic. But pornography is a direct denial of the power of the erotic, for it represents the suppression of true feeling. Pornography emphasizes sensation without feeling.[40]

Calling pornography "the abuse of feeling," Lorde concluded that "to share the power of each other's feelings is different from using another's feelings as we would use a kleenex."[41] In this allusion to the masturbatory detritus of pornography, Lorde emphasized the alienation of pornography in both its production and consumption.

From the perspective of these radical feminists, pornographers used repetition, reduction, and commercialization to alienate women from their sexuality. By turning sex into a "bang" and separating it from "making love," they encouraged men to see women as less than human. In her 1974 book *Woman Hating*, Andrea Dworkin protested the damage caused by capitalist patriarchy. "It is true, and very much to the point, that women are objects, commodities, and some deemed more expensive than others," she wrote, but she also saw a way out "by asserting one's humanness every time, in all situations that one becomes someone as opposed to something. That, after all, is the core of our struggle."[42] In this formulation, fighting pornography was about more than just suppressing dirty pictures. It was about countering the exploitation of women, resisting the commodification of their sexuality, and guiding society toward a path of more authentic erotic experiences. For these radical feminists, pornography created a false consciousness in both men and women about the naturalness of women's oppression, the necessity of male domination in sexual relationships, and an intimate alienation from erotic equality. Unsurprisingly, as the sex wars developed, feminists fought about what they saw as the consequences of consuming pornography.

Consumption

The ideological differences between pro-sex and anti-violence feminists stood out most starkly when they addressed the consumption of pornography. Pro-sex feminists, many of whom called themselves sexual civil libertarians, embraced a rather straightforward view of individual desire and private consumption. Although anti-violence feminists did not invoke Antonio Gramsci by name, they fought what they saw as the naturalizing effect of cultural hegemony that reduced women to commodified sex objects. In their most obvious criticism, they protested the way men required women to re-enact scenes they had witnessed in pornographic films and magazines. Just as importantly, but significantly less discussed either at the time or in the historical canon, feminists also fought the impact of pornography at work. Building on MacKinnon's scholarship on sexual harassment, women workers and feminist lawyers showed how men as a group used pornography to create hostile work environments that closed out women from well-paid jobs and hindered their professional advancement.

One of the most vocal pro-sex feminists, Ellen Willis, articulated an individualistic view of pornographic consumption. She focused almost solely on the consumption of pornographic images, interpreting their use with a Freudian condemnation of sexual repression. As a self-proclaimed sexual libertarian, she emphasized the utopian possibilities of freely expressed sexual desires. In 1979, the

Village Voice—which, not incidentally, included notorious misogynist Norman Mailer as a founder—published one of Willis's most famous essays, "Feminism, Moralism, and Pornography." In it she argued that "by playing games with the English language, antiporn activists are managing to rationalize as feminism a single-issue movement divorced from any larger political context and rooted in conservative moral assumptions that are all the more dangerous for being unacknowledged."[43] But then Willis herself moved on to discuss language at length, especially the definition of porn and the intrinsic place of eroticism in everyone's psychology. She straight-out condemned the view that porn caused sexual violence or that porn depicted violence, not sex. Willis excoriated "the erotica-versus-porn approach" because it evaded "the (embarrassing?) question of how porn is used."[44] And the way it was used, Willis believed, was to evoke authentic arousal. Moreover, Willis argued, "If feminists define pornography, per se, as the enemy the results will be to make a lot of women ashamed of their sexual feelings and afraid to be honest about them."[45] She held that "if *Hustler* were to vanish from the shelves tomorrow, I doubt that rape or wife-beating statistics would decline."[46] Willis, who saw anti-violence efforts as reformist and saw rape crisis centers, battered women's shelters, and women's health clinics as "a network of self-help projects," believed that subversive readings of pornography would suffice in undercutting any explicit misogyny.[47] In so doing, she repudiated anti-porn's implicitly Gramscian perspective that cultural fantasies affect material realities.

Gayle Rubin, one of the most important pro-sex intellectuals, also rested her argument on a repudiation of cultural hegemony. Rubin, who pioneered queer studies in the academy, eschewed the libertarian label but touted her credentials as a sexual outlaw. She believed that it was possible to draw a clear distinction between reality and fantasy. Consolidating her critiques in her 1993 article "Misguided, Dangerous, and Wrong," Rubin followed Willis's format and took on the anti-porn arguments point by point. And like Willis, Rubin saw porn and its consumption as something private done in the home or among consenting adults in spaces devoted to sexual exploration.[48] Throughout the essay, she repeatedly asserted that anti-porn feminists read pornography wrong and misrepresented it. She argued that "very little porn actually depicts violent acts," but Rubin never addressed anti-pornography arguments about women's objectification and commodification, nor did she propose an alternative reading of what she saw as the average, representative pornographic movie or spread.[49] Instead, she defaulted to the argument that pornography was little different in either its sexism or violence than the mainstream media of advertising, television, Hollywood movies, and fashion magazines, but she resisted speculating about what broader counterhegemonic activism should look like. When addressing the anti-violence feminists' critique of BDSM pornography, Rubin's defense rested on its scarcity and the belief that "S/M materials are aimed at an audience that understands a set of conventions for interpreting them."[50] She even acknowledged that "most commercial S/M porn is produced by people who are not practicing sadomasochists ... [and] reflects the prejudices of its producers rather than common S/M practice."[51] Yet Rubin offered no thoughts on how to counter its misrepresentation in either its production or consumption. Like Willis, Rubin grounded her support of pornography and the sexual play of BDSM on the belief that people easily differentiate fantasy from ideology, and that private sex has little impact on public sexism.

Indeed, Rubin readily granted some of the key contentions of anti-pornography feminists, but she did not see them as having structural consequences. She admitted that "most pornography *is* sexist," designed for male audiences, with women models representing "what the average male consumer wants to think about when he is masturbating."[52] She also conceded, "Most pornography does misrepresent women's sexuality and does not encourage men to learn the arts of seduction or to think of their sex partners as independent people with their own needs."[53] In other words, she recognized the "thingification" of women in porn, but she saw it as having a fantastical quality that had little influence on sex/gender systems. Along with other pro-sex feminists, she dismissed any link between pornography and other "more intractable problems of unequal pay, job discrimination, sexual violence and harassment."[54] Yet, in the late 1980s and early 1990s, just as Rubin was writing, a cadre of feminist lawyers and harassed women workers were making exactly this connection, showing how men used pornography to create job sites hostile to women's participation.

Eschewing the libertarian view that emphasized the private consumption of pornography, feminist lawyers sought to show how men used pornography to intimidate women in male-dominated workplaces. This lengthy battle started in the mid-1970s and culminated with *Robinson v. Jacksonville Shipyards, Inc.* (1991). Cases before *Robinson* allowed that posting pornographic spreads, reading pornographic magazines on the job, and drawing pornographic graffiti could feature as part of workplace harassment. In *Robinson*, however, the circuit court judges from the Florida Middle District affirmed that the presence of porn in and of itself constituted harassment.[55] Like Rubin, the defense attorneys for Jacksonville Shipyards, Inc. (JSI) argued that porn posted around the workplace was no more or less violent than mainstream movies and television, but as Lois Robinson's lawyers pointed out, Robinson did not have any choice about whether she would see the pornography posted. Furthermore, pornography differed from sexually violent movies or television because it was solely about sex—as Title VII requires—with no other possible interpretive context.[56]

Supported by two of her women colleagues, Lois Robinson, who worked at JSI from 1977 to 1988, testified as to how men used pornographic pictures of women to intimidate their co-workers, with many male employees participating in the practice or complicit in its continuation. Indeed, "the often surreptitious nature of the posting and graffiti writings left Robinson incapable of identifying many of her harassers," which the court interpreted as lending "credibility to the broader assertion of pervasiveness."[57] In addition to pornographic calendars, a staple of "masculine" workplaces, they chose to display diverse images that emphasized women's sexual objectification. One graffito illustrated a woman's pubic area with seminal fluid leaking out of her vulva, another showed a woman's torso with the words "USDA Choice" written on it, while a third featured "a life-size drawing of a nude woman on a divider in the sheetmetal shop."[58] Images from magazines included a naked woman with a welding shield posted in the welding trailer, while another showed a "picture of two women engaged in a sexual act while a nude man watched."[59] Significantly, neither the plaintiff's experts nor the judges differentiated between "softcore" and "hardcore" porn. They argued that in a work setting all pornography from *Playboy* pinups to crotch shots from *Hustler* encouraged men to see women as sex objects, not equal workers, and that the objectification of women discounted women's professionalism, hindered their advancement, and limited their economic opportunities.[60] The district court judges concluded that "the presence of the [pornographic] pictures, even if not directed at offending a particular female employee, sexualizes the work environment to the detriment of all female employees."[61] Anti-violence feminists had little success eliminating pornography from private settings, but they succeeded in changing federal case law, establishing important precedents for protecting not just individual women from quid pro quo harassment, but women in the workplace more broadly.

Pro-sex and anti-violence feminists offered dramatically different views on how people used pornography. While pro-sex feminists saw its consumption as something individualistic, liberatory, and open to multiple interpretations, anti-pornography feminists focused on how it affected women as a group. These differences arose because of significant ideological differences, including how these activist intellectuals viewed the sexual revolution and whether they embraced the insights of Freud. For women like Willis and Rubin that meant a turn toward libertarianism, but Dworkin, MacKinnon, and others fighting sexual violence remained committed to a materialist understanding of pornography as a commodified and commercialized tool of women's oppression. Whether perpetuating a false consciousness, or demeaning women at work, pornography contributed to women's enduring second-class citizenship.

Women, violence, and social transformation

Radical second-wave feminists coming out of the New Left built their interpretation of women's oppression on the theoretical foundation of Marx and Marxism. Through the 1970s, in consciousness-raising groups, workshops, and speak-outs, as they analyzed women's inequality in the family and on the job, an important cohort of feminists began to see sexual violence, and the threat of sexual violence, as the primary tool of men's oppression of women. Drawing on traditional Marxist ideas about class, false consciousness, commodity reification, and capitalist consumption, radical feminists adapted these concepts and applied them to sexuality.

Class, commodity, consumption 235

Women like Kate Millett, Susan Brownmiller, Andrea Dworkin, Luisah Teish, and Audre Lorde concluded that while the commodification of sex and the objectification of women occurred in many contexts, it was most egregiously obvious in the making, sale, and consumption of pornography. From their perspective, pornography legitimized men's violence against women. They argued that the persistent portrayal of women as sex objects who relished submission and found pleasure in pain created a false consciousness that justified men's abuse. This rationale prompted Robin Morgan to coin the slogan, "pornography is the theory; and rape is the practice."[62] Over time, however, the nuanced radicalism of anti-violence feminists got lost to stereotype and invective particularly after Dworkin, MacKinnon, and other anti-pornography feminists' ill-considered cooperation with the New Right.[63] Yet, it's important to recognize that while the right adopted some of anti-porn feminism's vocabulary, conservatives focused on consumption, eschewing feminist activists' concerns about the abuse of women within the industry. It is this focus on the corporate exploitation of economically vulnerable women, and the harm caused them in the making of pornographic products, that hews most closely to Marxist analysis. For all the excesses of anti-violence feminists, it's worth revisiting the core considerations of their thought, especially as #MeToo brings sexual violence and workplace harassment back as central issues for progressive activists.

Until #MeToo, the pro-sex position held analytical sway among most feminist and leftist intellectuals: the benefits of sexual adventuring and individual desires outweighed the cost of occasional harm. This neoliberal outlook derived logically from the market solutions offered by radical feminists turned sexual libertarians including Ellen Willis, Gayle Rubin, and Amber Hollibaugh. Although rightly concerned about censorship, they never addressed anti-porn proposals to alter the economic structure of a business where almost all the profit went to men and almost all the damage happened to women. The empowerment that pro-sex feminists envisioned was too often within the context of existing systems; they merely required more women hired at all levels of the industry or subversive readings of the materials produced. They also worked hand-in-hand with some of the most important industry moguls of the pornography business.[64] Thus, while not as overtly reactionary as the anti-porn alliance with the Moral Majority, the pro-sex feminists of the 1980s legitimized a status quo that tolerated anything but the most extreme violence against women. They were only an intellectual generation away from "having it all" and two generations away from the "Lean-In" feminism espoused by Facebook CEO Sheryl Sandberg. By abandoning systemic critiques, Marxist materialism, an analysis of conflict between men and women, and the role of real and representational violence in enforcing misogyny, pro-sex feminists eschewed their radical roots and laid the groundwork for conservative media darlings Camille Paglia and Katie Roiphe.

When #MeToo burst into international consciousness in December 2017, it demonstrated in no uncertain terms that sexual violence is still central to women's oppression. It showed the sheer pervasiveness of men's sexual intimidation of women, but the unmasking of the thoroughgoing misogyny of the United States in the news, networks, and movie industry had a particularly devastating impact. Men in the media have restricted women's voices, controlled cultural representations of sex and sexuality, and used sexual violence to intimidate women into compliance. #MeToo exposed networks of power and challenged hegemonic narratives. Women's stories, in all their cumulative effect, revealed that sexual violence is not about singular individuals—either rapists or victims—but about men abusing multiple women in systems designed to protect harassers and silence survivors. As a new generation of women searches for a way to fight these structural dynamics, they would do well to revisit the Marxian emphasis of second-wave radicals. Further theorizing about the mechanisms of men's abuse of women as a class combined with an innovative feminist jurisprudence that emphasizes groups over individuals will go a long way toward addressing the systems of women's oppression.

Notes

1 I am grateful to Robin Vandome and Christopher Phelps who edited this volume and organized the workshop "Marx and Marxism in the United States" at the University of Nottingham, who reached out to me with the irresistible lure: "surely, you have something to say on

this subject." I would also like to thank Jennifer Luff, Jonathan Bell, Leilah Danielson, Nick Witham, John Munro, Sinead McEneaney, Ella St George Carey, Emma Day, Elizabeth Evens, Lynne Foote, Grace Watkins, Sage Goodwin, Grace Mallon, Gillian Thomas, Moira Donegan, Rhonda Wasserman, Scott Stern, Christopher McKenna, Oenone Kubie, and Charlie Jeffries, whose insights made this chapter better.

2 Ruth Rosen, *The World Split Open: How the Modern Women's Movement Changed America* (New York: Viking, 2000); Sara M. Evans, *Tidal Wave: How Women Changed America at Century's End* (New York: Free Press, 2004); Alice Echols, *Daring to Be Bad: Radical Feminism in America, 1967–1975* (Minneapolis: University of Minnesota Press, 1989).

3 Jane Gerhard, *Desiring Revolution: Second-Wave Feminism and the Rewriting of American Sexual Thought, 1920 to 1982* (New York: Columbia University Press, 2001).

4 Carole S. Vance, ed., *Pleasure and Danger: Exploring Female Sexuality* (New York: Pandora, 1992); Ann Snitow, Christine Stansell, and Sharon Thompson, eds., *Powers of Desire: The Politics of Sexuality* (New York: New Feminist Library, 1983). See also Lisa Duggan and Nan D. Hunter, eds., *Sex Wars: Sexual Dissent and Political Culture*, 10th Anniversary Edition (New York, Routledge, 2006).

5 Carole S. Vance, "More Danger, More Pleasure: A Decade after the Barnard Sexuality Conference," in *Pleasure and Danger*, ed. Vance, xxvii–xxxiii.

6 Victoria Baranetsky, "The Economic-Liberty Approach of the First Amendment: A Story of *American Booksellers v. Hudnut*," *Harvard Civil Rights-Civil Liberties Law Review* 47, no. 1 (Winter 2012): 169–218.

7 bell hooks, *Ain't I A Woman: Black Women and Feminism* (Boston: South End Press, 1981), 8.

8 Shulamith Firestone, *The Dialectic of Sex: The Case for Feminist Revolution* (1970; New York: Verso, 2015), Kindle edition; Susan Brownmiller, *Against Our Will: Men, Women and Rape* (New York: Fawcett Books, 1975).

9 Echols, *Daring to Be Bad*, 49.

10 Firestone, *The Dialectic of Sex*, 164, 195.

11 Kate Millett, *Sexual Politics* (1970; Urbana: University of Illinois Press, 2000), Kindle edition, 131–57.

12 The other seven subheadings in the chapter were Ideological, Biological, Sociological, Class, Economic and Educational, Anthropological: Myth and Religion, and Psychological, see Millett, *Sexual Politics*, 740–1438.

13 Millett, *Sexual Politics*, 109–12.
14 Brownmiller, *Against Our Will*, 405.
15 Ibid., 11–12.
16 Ibid., 11.
17 Catharine MacKinnon, "Feminism, Marxism, Method, and the State: An Agenda for Theory," in *The Signs Reader: Women, Gender and Scholarship*, ed. Elizabeth Abel and Emily K. Abel (Chicago: University of Chicago Press, 1983), 227–56, 227.
18 Ibid., 232, 241.
19 Ibid., 241.
20 Catharine MacKinnon, *Sexual Harassment of Working Women: A Case of Sex Discrimination* (New Haven: Yale University Press, 1979), 32–47.
21 Gillian Thomas, *Because of Sex: One Law, Ten Cases, and Fifty Years that Changed American Women's Lives at Work* (New York: St. Martin's Press, 2016), 81–105.
22 MacKinnon was likely aware of the work of legal scholars, especially Stephen C. Yeazell, who argued that in the seventeenth century, as peasants fought the enclosure movement and parishioners sought to prevent parishes from tying tithing to mining or other commodity production, these economic communities started using group litigation to defend their collective rights. They did not seek financial redress, but rather opportunities for collective bargaining. Indeed, Yeazell saw these cases as a constituent part of class formation: by recognizing previously unconnected masses of individuals as sharing status and economic concerns they helped transform an inchoate group into a class. Although Yeazell did not directly evoke Marx, the timeline he proposed and the groups on which he focused align with Marxist chronologies. See Stephen C. Yeazell, "Group Litigation and Social Context: Toward a History of the Class Action, *Columbia Law Review* 77, no. 6 (October 1977): 866–96; Stephen C. Yeazell, "From Group Litigation to Class Action—Part I: The Industrialization of Group Litigation," *UCLA Law Review* 27, no. 3 (February 1980): 514–64.
23 Gayle Rubin, "Misguided, Dangerous, and Wrong: An Analysis of Antipornography Politics," in *Deviations: A Gayle Rubin Reader* (Durham: Duke University Press, 2011), 260.
24 Ibid., 266.
25 MacKinnon, "Feminism, Marxism, Method, and the State," 228–32.
26 Andrea Dworkin, *Pornography: Men Possessing Women* (London: The Women's Press 1981), 25.
27 Ibid., 26.
28 Ibid., 28.

29 Ibid., 29.
30 Rubin, "Misguided, Dangerous, and Wrong," 264.
31 Amber Hollibaugh, "Desire for the Future: Radical Hope in Passion and Pleasure," in *Pleasure and Danger*, ed. Vance, 401–10, 403.
32 Ellen Willis, "Feminism, Moralism, and Pornography," in *Powers of Desire*, ed. Snitow, Stansell, and Thompson, 460–67, 462.
33 Patricia Hill Collins, *Black Feminist Thought: Knowledge, Consciousness, and the Politics of Empowerment* (1990; Oxford: Routledge, 2014), 139.
34 Luisah Teish, "A Quiet Subversion," in *Take Back the Night: Women on Pornography*, ed. Laura Lederer (New York: William Morrow and Company, 1980), 115–18, 116.
35 Ibid., 117.
36 Alice Walker, "Coming Apart," in *Take Back the Night*, ed. Lederer, 95–104, 96.
37 Ibid., 103.
38 Ibid., 104.
39 *Not A Love Story: A Film About Pornography*, directed by Bonnie Sheer Klein (1981).
40 Audre Lorde, "Uses of the Erotic: The Erotic as Power," in *Sister Outsider* (New York: Penguin Classics Edition, 2019), 42–49, 44.
41 Ibid., 48–49.
42 Andrea Dworkin, *Woman Hating* (New York: E. P. Dutton, 1974), 83.
43 Willis, "Feminism, Moralism, and Pornography," 461.
44 Ibid., 463.
45 Ibid., 462.
46 Ibid., 463.
47 Ellen Willis, "Radical Feminism and Feminist Radicalism," *Social Text* 9/10 (1984): 91–118, 92.
48 Rubin, "Misguided, Dangerous, and Wrong," 266.
49 Ibid., 257.
50 Ibid., 258. The expression "s/M" is Rubin's particular term for what is now typically called BDSM, which covers a range of sexual practices, including bondage, dominance and submission, sadomasochism, and other types of fetish play. See Margot D. Weiss, "Working at Play: BDSM Sexuality in the San Francisco Bay Area," *Anthropologica* 48, no. 2 (2006): 229–45, 230.
51 Rubin, "Misguided, Dangerous, and Wrong," 258.
52 Ibid., 271.
53 Ibid., 271.
54 Ibid., 273. Notably, participants in both pornographic films and non-commercial sex play have tried to write contracts that protect them

from harm by outlining the kinds of sex acts in which they are willing to engage; however, these contracts are notoriously difficult to enforce, see Maria de Cesare, "Rxxx: Resolving the Problem of Performer Health and Safety in the Adult Film Industry," *Southern California Law Review* 79, no. 3 (March 2006): 667–710; Andrew Gilden, "Sexual (Re)consideration: Adult Entertainment Contracts and the Problem of Enforceability," *Georgetown Law Journal* 95, no. 2 (January 2007): 541–64; Andrea E. White, "The Nature of Taboo Contracts: A Legal Analysis of BDSM Contracts and Specific Performance," *UMKC Law Review* 84, no. 4 (Summer 2016): 1163–86.
55 Nell J. Medlin, "Expanding the law of sexual harassment to include workplace pornography: *Robinson v. Jacksonville Shipyards, Inc.*" *Stetson Law Review* 21, no. 2 (1992): 655–80, 662–69.
56 *Robinson v. Jacksonville Shipyards, Inc.*, 760 F. Supp. 1486 (M.D. Fla. 1991).
57 Ibid., 1495.
58 Ibid., 1495–97.
59 Ibid., 1501.
60 Ibid., 1526.
61 Ibid., 1523.
62 Robin Morgan, *Going Too Far: The Personal Chronicle of a Feminist* (1977; n.p.: Open Road Media), Kindle edition, 3248.
63 For the legislative work to limit porn, see Andrea Dworkin and Catharine MacKinnon, *Pornography and Civil Rights: A New Day for Women's Equality* (Minneapolis, Organizing Against Pornography, 1988). On Dworkin's efforts, including her testimony before the Attorney General's Commission on Pornography (The Meese Commission), see Johanna Fateman, "Introduction," in *Last Days at Hot Slit: The Radical Feminism of Andrea Dworkin*, ed. Fateman and Amy Scholder (South Pasadena, CA: Semiotext[e], 2019), 317–31. See also Nancy Whittier, "Rethinking Coalitions: Anti-Pornography Feminists, Conservatives, and Relationships between Collaborative Adversarial Movements," *Social Problems* 61, no. 2 (May 2014): 175–93. For the pro-sex perspective on anti-porn feminists' cooperation with the New Right, see Vance, "More Danger, More Pleasure," xxiv–xxxii; Lisa Duggan and Nan D. Hunter, *Sex Wars: Sexual Dissent and Political Culture* (1996; New York: Routledge, 2006).
64 Baranetsky, "The Economic-Liberty Approach of the First Amendment," 196–99.

10

Will the revolution be podcast? Marxism and the culture of "millennial socialism" in the United States

Tim Jelfs

Television is not quite what it was when Gil Scott-Heron declared, on the best-known track of *Small Talk at 125th and Lenox* (1970), "The Revolution Will Not be Televised."[1] In the intervening years, the technologies and cultural forms that mediate American political life have undergone their own processes of revolution, with new media evolving out of the old without established forms leaving the stage of cultural and media production. In a 1999 study, media theorists Jay David Bolter and Richard Grusin described this process as one of "remediation." No medium, they explained, does "its cultural work in isolation from other media, any more than it works in isolation from social and economic forces."[2] The implications of this are significant. Today, alongside resilient literary forms like novels and poetry, alongside all the long-established visual arts, as well as radio and television, film, and popular music, any analysis of the relationship between cultural production and politics in the United States must take account of both the new forms of cultural "content" that digital technology and social media make possible and how those new forms relate to well-established media.

The political formation and culture of "millennial socialism"— a mass-media suggested term implying both the politics of a new century and a new generation of advocates—has emerged coevally with a trans-medial ecosystem: from new left magazines like *n+1*, *Jacobin*, and *Current Affairs* to a developing twenty-first-century canon of culture written, produced, and performed by Americans with outspokenly socialist politics. That includes what has become one of the signature forms of the latest iteration of the American left, the podcast, which since its inception in 2004 as a means of downloading internet-based audio on demand, has grown rapidly as a way of producing and consuming media content.³ The confluence between recent developments in the cultural and media landscape and the re-emergence of an avowedly leftist politics after decades of neoliberal hegemony raises interesting questions for scholars of the histories of both Marxism and media in the United States. These include how best to understand the left politics espoused by these cultural products in relation to the history of Marxist thought in the United States, as well as how to think about the relationship between that ideology and the media used to disseminate it. This latter question is especially urgent given the doubts one might raise about what media and communications technology, and indeed, cultural production as a whole, can and cannot do in relation to left politics and political action. Does the combination of old and new media that provides the platform for the dissemination of the ideology of the contemporary left offer the would-be revolutionaries of today something that has never been there before? Or has less changed than it might sometimes seem when it comes to the culture of the twenty-first century left in the United States and its commitments to political action?

Much of the culture of twenty-first socialism is not Marxist in any doctrinaire sense, but expressive of a political sensibility whose significance in terms of cultural and intellectual history lies in its

Figure 10.1 *Chapo Trap House*, a podcast of the millennial left, live at the Bell House, New York City, November 17, 2017. *Courtesy Wikipedia Commons.*

performative disambiguation of leftism from an American liberalism that has in recent decades, and especially since the financial crisis of 2007–2008, failed to deliver any prospect of a more prosperous, healthy, or materially and ecologically sustainable future for many Americans. Both the figure of Marx and the invocation of Marxist ideas serve an important function in this culture insofar as leftists of various stripes have used them to differentiate themselves from mainstream liberalism, even if the policy prescriptions they advocate often appear more social-democratic than radically socialist. At the same time, much of this emerging culture also operates as a means of political education, teaching its adherents about the wider global history of the left in a media, technological, and cultural environment that makes possible new forms of counter-hegemonic practice. What remains unlikely is that the content they produce heralds anything more radical from a Marxist perspective than a demand for the long-overdue reform of the ideological assumptions of neoliberalism.

What is "millennial socialism"?

That something answering to the name of socialism has begun to haunt the United States has not escaped the notice of *The Economist*. In a February 14, 2019, leader, the magazine deployed the phrases "millennial socialism" and "resurgent left" to describe the phenomenon of increasing numbers of Americans, particularly young Americans, calling themselves "socialist."[4] *The Economist* had solid enough grounds for concern. As Keir Milburn has documented in *Generation Left*, age appears to have become "the key dividing line in politics" across numerous national polities, as evidenced in the United States by the results of a 2016 Harvard Institute of Politics poll, which found positive views of socialism from 33 percent of respondents aged eighteen to twenty-nine.[5] Some of the likely roots of this left turn on the part of what is still, evidently, a minority of Americans are easy enough to hypothesize: the financial crisis of 2007–2008 and the Great Recession that followed; the crushing disappointment of the Obama administration's promises of a "transformative presidency"; the failure since the 1970s of the market-oriented policies of both major political parties to deliver material improvements in Americans' lives or counter the deleterious effects of lightly regulated, hyper-mobile capital; the fading from memory of the Cold War; the Trump presidency. Those in their turn have brought observable political effects like the Occupy protests, the candidacies of Bernie Sanders for the Democratic Party presidential nomination in 2016 and 2020, and the swelling rolls of the Democratic Socialists of America (DSA), an organization that has grown in membership from 6,500 in 2014 to at least 56,000 today, and one that has begun to score significant electoral successes, from elections to the U.S. House of Representatives of DSA-backed candidates like Alexandria Ocasio-Cortez and Rashida Tlaib to less high-profile victories at the city and state level in places like Chicago and Virginia.[6]

The term "millennial socialism" is itself interesting because of the focus it places on generation as a useful category of political analysis. As *The Economist* correctly noted, not all of today's leftists are millennials, but "millennial socialist" seems to imply a certain demographic figure: not just young, but living in a city, and most likely college-educated. In a 2018 *The New York Times* op-ed, M. H. Miller related what it was like to come of age in the United States as a college-educated member of a generation that "graduated into" the Great Recession. His account tells of his family's downward mobility out of the middle class. Refinancing their Detroit home just before the housing bubble burst in an effort to help Miller pay college tuition at NYU left them financially vulnerable. Once his parents lost their jobs after unemployment spiked, there came the threat of foreclosure and, for Miller, six figures of student-loan debt and a struggle to make rent.[7] It is from this cohort that the new socialism seems to be drawing much of its strength in numbers, a demographic that is better emblematized by Ocasio-Cortez, who was all of twenty-nine when she won election to the House of Representatives, than by Senator Sanders, whose experience on the American left goes back to his time in the Young People's Socialist League in the early 1960s.

Numerous new cultural institutions of contemporary "millennial socialism" emerge out of a milieu similar in class and institutional origins to those that feature in Miller's account of his generation's experience, with elite universities playing a significant role in incubating this culture. In 2004, three Harvard graduates and one from Columbia established *n+1*, a relatively early addition to the existing stable of leftist magazines. In 2010, while he was still a student at George Washington University, Bhaskar Sunkara founded *Jacobin*, less literary in its emphases and more closely associated with DSA. Even more recently, *Current Affairs* has emerged out of Harvard under the editorship of Nathan J. Robinson. The origins of this culture are assuredly a function of the generationally specific experiences of many young, educated Americans today. In a longer version of his account of downward mobility, Miller speaks of coming to understand "the extent to which I was among the most overeducated group of young adults in human history."[8] This is an argument pursued at greater length by Malcolm Harris in *Kids These Days: Human Capital and the Making of Millennials* (2017). Harris contends that once it is understood how his generation has been taught, since birth, to conceive of itself in terms of human capital, the political choice facing millennials becomes clear. "We become fascists or revolutionaries, one or the other," he argues, revising Rosa Luxemburg's "socialism or barbarism."[9]

The elite institutional origins of the producers of much "millennial socialist" culture render the relationship of their own cohort and its cultural productions to other expressions of popular discontent and dissent, as well as to the American "working class" as a whole, the topic of vexed debate. In October 2019, one could trace the fallout of an *n+1* essay by labor historian Gabriel Winant arguing that, for all the recent assailing of those supporting the progressive liberal Elizabeth Warren in the Democratic primary race as representative of the PMC (professional managerial class, as coined by the Ehrenreichs in the 1970s), some of the most prominent producers of the culture of "millennial socialism" hailed from just that class, and that some accommodation with it might in any case be necessary in the future.[10] In some of the responses, which ranged from an anonymized round table discussion on the website NonSite.org to one left-wing commentator declaring, rather peculiarly, that "PMC is a state of mind," it was difficult to discern where the rage of Caliban ended and serious strategic disagreements began.[11] Shortly thereafter, one could also read in the long-running Third Camp publication *New Politics* a critique of *Jacobin* contributor Eric Blanc's account of the wave of teachers' strikes witnessed in Chicago, West Virginia, Arizona, Oklahoma, and California as overstating the influence of Sanders's 2016 campaign in shaping those movements at the expense of the involvement of "many educators in intersecting social movements—including the movements for Black lives, ethnic studies, labor and economic justice, and immigrant justice" in the various teachers' revolts.[12]

At issue in these debates were two concerns related to the production of much "millennial socialist" culture. First, there are the difficulties facing socialism in the United States in the twenty-first century when, after decades of deindustrialization and financialization, a long-term decline in the power of organized labor, and the extension of precarity to ever more sectors of the U.S. economy, the working class is quite different in its composition from that of earlier moments in the nation's history. As a result, while what remains of the industrial working class still plays an important part in twenty-first-century workplace mobilizations of class power, teachers and service workers are now no less significant wielders of that power. With the adjunctification of higher education and declining career prospects in that sector only adding more expensively educated human capital to the pool of those well-placed to produce content, many of those who under different historical circumstances might happily have ascended into (or just remained in) the securer ranks of the PMC now also consider themselves, regardless of their class origins, expectations, or elite educations, part of the working class, effectively "proletarianized" under the peculiar conditions of the contemporary economy.[13] Nevertheless, even under these conditions, those producing cultural and media content in the precarious, digitized economy of the twenty-first century retain significantly more power to narrate and meditate on events than those on the front lines of many contemporary workplace struggles. This is not to diminish their efforts in organizing their own workplaces (whether as graduate students in universities or journalists in the newsrooms of new media institutions). It is, however, to recognize that the discursive power they are able to wield needs to be taken into account when approaching the culture of "millennial socialism," for it is the power to narrate the contemporary history of a class to which they may have only relatively recently been recruited.

Up from liberalism

Bearing these considerations in mind allows us to understand and historicize one of the discursive acts that the culture of "millennial socialism" most consistently engages in: namely, a performative disambiguation of leftism and its politics, history, and traditions from those of liberalism. "Performative" here is not meant pejoratively, but in J. L. Austin's sense of a discursive act that itself *does* something, for a "performative utterance" is one that creates that which it purports to describe.[14] See, for example, the winter 2016 issue of *Jacobin* magazine, an issue entitled "Up From Liberalism." Its cover features the faces of Tony Blair, Hillary Clinton, Jeremy Corbyn, and Bernie Sanders rendered as playing cards: Blair and Clinton as the King and Queen of clubs; Corbyn and Sanders the five and six of hearts. Both the transatlantic purview (Sunkara has also recently revived the magazine *Tribune*, a venerable institution of the British left) and ideological imperative to transcend liberalism and its recent and historic limitations recur throughout the issue. Following an excerpt from the 1891 Erfurt Program of the German Social Democratic Party and British Labour leader Tony Crosland's 1956 call for socialists to give up their historic goal of democratizing ownership of the means of production, the editorial goes on to narrate the declension of "traditional social democracy" into the "new centrist program" of Third Way liberalism in the 1990s.[15] This led to parties of the center-left "undermining their own basis of support ... The mass struggles that provided the basis for both reformist and revolutionary left politics seemed like a thing of the past." The emergence on opposite sides of the Atlantic of Corbyn and Sanders as viable electoral propositions, the editorial concludes, are "stirrings of an alternative," and *Jacobin*'s evident ideological mission is to incubate and disseminate the ideological content of that alternative.[16]

This is typical of the new left-wing culture's performative disambiguation from liberalism, which involves articulating what it means to be socialist in the twenty-first century, how that is distinct as an ideological position from liberalism, and how the histories of these two political traditions relate to and diverge from one another once considered in global context. This in turn is a means to grow the left itself, which, as we will see when it comes to podcasting, is a discursive process that can be traced to the level of the individual. For now, it is sufficient to note how consistently the distinction between liberalism and socialism as rival ideologies provides the key fault line across which negotiations of what it means to be a socialist in the

United States in the twenty-first century take place. Whether or not this is a result of the PMC origins of many who produce the culture of "millennial socialism," or simply because of the historic strength of what Louis Hartz long ago identified as the "liberal tradition" in America, remains a matter of speculation. When *The Economist* conversely warns liberals of the siren call of "millennial socialism," it suggests that it too sees much of the new socialism as an alternative to, if not an ideological shearing away from, mainstream liberalism: "Millennial socialism has a refreshing willingness to challenge the status quo. But like the socialism of old, it suffers from a faith in the incorruptibility of collective action and an unwarranted suspicion of individual vim. Liberals should oppose it."[17]

The emergence of a sizeable and self-avowedly socialist alternative to liberalism after decades of neoliberal hegemony, and one armed with its own new cultural and media institutions, has hardly been an overnight process. Indeed, this emergent culture is perhaps best understood as adding to and reshaping residual institutions like DSA that previous waves of leftism, some of them Marxist, had already established in the United States and that the post-Cold War "end of history" never quite expunged, as weak as left politics has undoubtedly been over that period. This is certainly true in journal publishing, with *Jacobin*, *n+1*, *Current Affairs*, and a revitalized *The Baffler* joining longstanding publications such as *Dissent*, *Monthly Review*, *New Politics*, and *In These Times* to provide platforms for the articulation and dissemination of a diverse leftist political culture that is now finally growing again. But such markers of the ideological resurgence of socialism in the twenty-first-century United States also need to be understood along historical trajectories that include relevant struggles in the 1990s, such as that of the global justice movement. From there to Occupy, and from Occupy to the Sanders campaigns and a resurgence in DSA membership, constitutes just one such trajectory along which this political formation has acquired some of its most recent momentum; intersections with racial justice and migrant rights movements, as well as with local labor, housing, criminal justice, and environmentalist struggles from New York to Mississippi and from California to Kentucky point to multiple others.

Deeper trajectories suggest themselves too. For if many of the producers of today's socialist culture appear anxious about their distance from what the working class ought to be and ought to look like, this is itself just a variation on a familiar theme. As Paul Buhle relates, the campus-based New Left of which he was a part "envisioned speaking at once for ourselves and for the entire society," and yet noticeably failed in their efforts to assist in the organization of working-class communities into anything like a revolutionary subject.[18] By the late 1960s, abundant evidence was already gathering both that, as Buhle puts it, "a now largely absent, bemuscled industrial proletariat, long considered destined to seize the factories, [was] obviously not going to Make the Revolution" and that achieving something like "a reformulation of the concept of revolutionary agency" out of a multiplicity of radical causes was never going to be easy.[19] If it is also true, as Asad Haider has argued, that one of the great successes of neoliberalism has been its co-optation of one of the legacies of the New Left period, namely the discourse on "identity politics" that once explained how, as the Combahee River Collective put it in 1977, "the major systems of oppression are interlocking," then the challenges facing contemporary socialists are clear, but not simple.[20] They have to reanimate some of the class politics of the Old Left while articulating a path to social transformation and simultaneously holding the line on gains won in antiracist and related struggles since the New Left era, and to do this in a historical moment that sees the neo-nationalist right globally resurgent and eager to conclude pacts of convenience with financial and fossil-fuel capital as the hegemony of neoliberalism wanes. In this sense, a performative disambiguation that has the cascading ideological effect of actually disarticulating leftism from liberalism (and more leftists from liberals) is just part of what the complicated legacy bequeathed by earlier phases of history urges contemporary leftists to attend to if dreams of a classless society or even a habitable planet are to be realized.

Marx and Marxism in the new socialist culture

The ways that Marx and Marxism have tended to function in the culture of "millennial socialism" speak to some of the complexity of its historical and ideological inheritance. Outside academic debates, references to Marx are often part of a wider engagement with the global history of socialism in all its variety, rather than a rigid reengagement with specifically American Marxist traditions. At times, indeed, references to Marx may seem merely gestural. Witness young online socialists using the microblogging site Twitter to post birthday greetings to Marx on the two-hundredth anniversary of his birth. Here again, we see the same disarticulation from liberalism that is central to this culture: tweeting birthday greetings to "Karl" performs that disarticulation, signaling pride in one's deviation not just from the anti-communist right but from the liberal center too, which might, one supposes, encourage others to follow suit. Other young socialists, meanwhile, take pains to acknowledge debts to Marx while signaling they belong to alternative traditions within the left. Thus, the recent caveat by Nathan J. Robinson of *Current Affairs* that he sees himself in a more "libertarian socialist" tradition than Marx, or the invocation of such figures as Peter Kropotkin in the Twitter handles of young communists.[21] The Black Socialists in America (BSA) collective is clear as to why it identifies itself as "scientific socialist" rather than simply "Marxist":

> While our praxis does reflect the contributions and theory of Karl Marx, we do not consider ourselves a "Marxist" organization. The term began as a term of abuse for those ill-informed pseudo-revolutionaries who had caricatured Marx's philosophy into a quasi-religious orthodoxy without regard for whether it reflected a genuine Socialist ideology. Even today, many so-called "Marxist" parties replicate this same error.

The BSA's post-Marxist stance allows them to acknowledge the influence of Marx while simultaneously focusing on the long tradition of black socialism in the United States, from the abolitionist Peter H. Clark to the contemporary workers' collective Cooperation Jackson in Jackson, Mississippi.[22] It is in this sense both representative of how lightly bound to Marx twenty-first-century socialism appears to be and illustrative of the diversity of influences with which contemporary American socialists are engaging.

Bhaskar Sunkara's *The Socialist Manifesto: The Case for Radical Politics in an Era of Extreme Inequality* (2019) reinforces the point. For Sunkara, Marxism provides what he calls a "framework" for understanding the centrality of class struggle and the question of ownership or control of the means of production to contemporary socialist politics.²³ His book recommends the pursuit of reformist social democracy as a first step towards transitioning to democratic socialism. For Sunkara, Bernie Sanders, Jeremy Corbyn, and even the assassinated Swedish social democratic prime minister Olof Palme are more obviously relevant to the present situation than Marx, or even very much of the history of socialism in the United States. One short chapter condenses the interwoven histories of socialist, communist, populist, and progressive liberal politics in the United States from the earliest workers' movements of the 1820s to the death of Michael Harrington in 1989.²⁴ Sunkara's, then, is a socialism in which Marx is a distant founding figure, of significant symbolic value, but not all that dominant in relation to more proximate political concerns such as lack of healthcare, stable employment, and the already unfolding climate catastrophe.

It is a sign both of the liveliness that exists in this new left culture and the complex historical legacy that today's leftists must confront that *Jacobin*, Sunkara, and their politics of "class-struggle social democracy" now find themselves critiqued from the left.²⁵ When *Commune* magazine launched in 2019, the editors criticized Sunkara and his prescriptions: "Capitalism can't be made more tolerable under present conditions, couldn't be saved even if we wanted to, and won't be voted away." Indeed, their website scorns those who "offer social-democratic fantasy from a past that cannot return," arguing that, for all their apparent radicalism, neither Sunkara's proposed program nor electoral vehicles like the Sanders campaigns are articulating a feasible path to revolutionary transformation because there is no route to a classless society that begins with social-democratic reformism.²⁶ Instead, they affirm,

> We start by taking direction from the struggles of today with their blockades and occupations and makeshift barricades, their broken glass and ad hoc organization, from multigenerational struggles that have at their center a youth who confront a world uglier and less hospitable to flourishing than anything in the past seventy years.²⁷

Although the editors of *Commune* are far from prescriptive about what follows from such a starting point, their attraction to insurrection is of a piece with the theory and aesthetics of one of their editors, the poet Joshua Clover, whose books, including *Red Epic* (2015) and *Riot. Strike. Riot.: The New Era of Uprisings* (2016), represent another important contribution to the new left culture from its avowedly communist wing. "If what you want is calm/to be restored you are still the enemy," reads "Haeccity," Clover's homage to Diane di Prima's "Revolutionary Letter #19" (1969). The poem ends with the following definition of "revolution":

> it's coming out again night after night more of us
> than there are of them it's saying no
> to every deal remember nothing
> belongs to you because nothing
> belongs to anyone[28]

A future in which "nothing belongs to anyone" is not only within reach; it is present already in the very verb tenses with which the poem closes, albeit contingent on the revolutionaries' resolve not to compromise. The poet seems to want to establish, much as Walter Benjamin claimed all historical materialists should, "a conception of the present as the 'time of the now' which is shot through with chips of Messianic time."[29] By means of such a conception, Benjamin proposed in "Theses on the Philosophy of History," all time might be redeemed, and Marx's secularized messianic dream of the classless society brought into being.

But what cultural form might the imagination of such a process take, if it were rooted not in the reformist path proposed by Sunkara but in present-day insurrectionism? Relevant in this regard is Boots Riley's *Sorry to Bother You* (2018), a movie in which the Marxist–Communist frontman of the hip-hop outfit *The Coup* combines the narrative resources of social realism, surrealism, and science fiction to depict class struggle in present-day Oakland. The movie ends with a vision of an uprising of the twenty-first-century proletariat as the half-human, half-horse outcome of a tech billionaire's drive for profit.[30] Such a vision itself represents the trans-medial extension of an aesthetic that Riley—a veteran of the small Generation X cohort of the radical left who has found an audience among millennials—has been exploring musically since the 1990s. "Dig It," for example, from the album *Kill The Landlord* (1993), includes references to Mao Zedong and Kwame Nkrumah and begins, "Presto, read the Communist Manifesto/Guerillas in the Mist, a Guevara named Ernesto." "We are the ones/We'll seal your fate, tear down your state, go get yo' guns," and "I'm here to laugh, love, fuck and drink liquor/And help the damn revolution come quicker," Riley raps in "We Are the Ones" and "Laugh/Love/Fuck" on the album *Pick A Bigger Weapon* (2006).[31]

Riley's rhymes are representative of a hip-hop project that has long mobilized tropes related to the global history of socialism while articulating dreams of revolution. But Riley's work also speaks to the diverse composition of the ideological, aesthetic, and cultural sensibilities that risk being elided under the sign of "millennial socialism," as well as some of the depth and complexity of that political formation's historical origins. Scholars of contemporary socialism in the United States should therefore be wary of assuming that phrases like "millennial socialism" necessarily imply an especially coherent referent. There are varied approaches, varied emphases, and varied timelines contributing to the flourishing of a new socialist culture in which Marx and Marxism are often subordinate to attempts to synthesize out of the complex legacies of both the recent and more distant past a politics appropriate to the needs of the present. If some of them (like the Black Socialists in America's attempt to promote a "dual power" strategy by fostering the spread of worker-owned cooperatives) seem strongly rooted in an understanding of capitalism as at root a mode of production, while others (like Sunkara's social–democratic route to socialism, or the insurrectionists' calls to understand the politics of riots and street rebellions), stress different strategic priorities, that merely reflects the continued absence of any syncretic socialism around which all contemporary American leftists can unite. In the age of the revitalized DSA and Sanders campaigns of 2016 and 2020, electoral strategies that deploy the rhetoric of revolution seem to have the upper hand, while voices more focused on the primacy of extra-parliamentary forms of class power, especially revolutionary forms of such power, remain firmly in the minority.

Podcasting

Such, then, is the complex cultural, historical, and ideological milieu into which twenty-first-century left podcasting has emerged and to which it is contributing. Listening to the first episode of one of the best-known of these podcasts, *Chapo Trap House* (Figure 10.1), broadcast in March 2016, one finds the characteristic performative disambiguation of contemporary left culture from that of liberalism. Recorded in the midst of the Republican and Democratic primary races of that year, the podcast poured equal scorn on both the Trumpian right and the liberal center before taking aim at liberal "political comedians" in particular. Culture like Comedy Central's *The Daily Show*, argued *Chapo Trap House* hosts Matt Christman, Will Menaker, and Felix Biederman, may engage with political questions, but ultimately produces a merely cathartic effect in its viewers, one which "dissipates" both anger and political energy.[32] Thus highlighting the limits of one of their primary influences, they marked themselves out as both working within an established cultural tradition—that of *The Daily Show* and shows like it—while deviating from that tradition, as if to signal that what they were remediating was not just a specific cultural form, but its presumptive ideological content. For while their first podcast may have been characterized by its low production qualities and open-endedness (it ran for just over an hour and a quarter, but subsequent episodes have varied in both length and format), this was still a species of lo-fi satirical "infotainment" in which, as with *The Daily Show*, the failings of contemporary U.S. media and political ideologies were subject to ironic critical analysis. The difference was, and has remained, that the hosts exploited the ability to produce their own content at minimal cost that new media has presented them with while simultaneously validating mockery, outrage, and anger as legitimate and useful from an avowedly left, as opposed to liberal, perspective.

How the hosts of *Chapo Trap House* do that has provoked criticism, with their often profanity-laden language attracting censorious comment.[33] Left-liberal distinctions are again prominent here, as with the criticism of the June 2017 episode in which an impassioned Menaker argued that the left should certainly be willing to cooperate with liberals in the age of Trump, but on its own terms: "You have been proven as failures, and your entire worldview has been discredited. You bend the knee to us and then let's fucking work together to defeat these things, not with fucking means testing or market-based solutions, but with a powerful social-democratic message," he instructed anti-Trump liberals.[34] *Chapo* co-host

Amber A'Lee Frost has defended vulgarity, "the crass, ugly dispensation of judgment with little to no regard for propriety," as an important mode of political expression: "Reclaiming vulgarity from the Trumps of the world is imperative because if we do not embrace the profane now and again, we will find ourselves handicapped by our own civility."[35] Frost's invocation of the "Trumps of the world" is interesting here, for it suggests that there is more going on than just the performative disarticulation of leftism from liberalism. Of course, for Frost, vulgarity might have the advantage of puncturing contemporary liberal pieties, but it is also a political tool for accessing those who might otherwise fall prey to the allure of the right, especially at a moment in which the "alt-right" has its own media institutions attacking the manners and mores of the liberal center.

For some critics of *Chapo* and other "anti-PC" or "anti-woke" elements of the contemporary left, the vulgar mode is symptomatic of a suspect ideology that has even provoked accusations of neo-Strasserism or "red fascism" against young socialists like Frost.[36] This is a stronger version of a critique that notes how contemporary left podcasting all too often reproduces within the culture of the contemporary socialist movement inequalities present in the culture at large. Hence the superficially self-deprecating Twitter joke of the left podcaster Bryan Quinby that "a group of white men is called a podcast."[37] Debates about the reproduction of such inequalities will no doubt continue, as they feed into and are fed by critiques of the evolution of "identity politics" and race–class–gender dynamics as they apply to both critical theory and political strategy.[38] For the success of *Chapo* (at the time of writing, the podcast attracts nearly 33,000 subscribers on the crowdfunding platform Patreon, netting its creators more than $146,000 per month) only renders more acute concerns about the discursive power of those who provide some of the more prominent voices and faces of the culture of "millennial socialism." Are these authentic voices of a new, twenty-first-century composition of the working class? Or are they the relatively privileged, and now wealthy, "failsons" of the PMC?

The plasticity of the form and ease of production and distribution, especially in the age of crowdfunding platforms like Patreon, make podcasting both accessible and malleable, and even the relatively circumscribed subculture of left podcasting reflects the medium's latent heterogeneity. *Jacobin* magazine's *The Dig*, for example, is a far more academic exercise in political education than *Chapo*. It offers in-depth interviews with "left-wing scholars and activists about politics, history, criminal justice, immigration and more."[39] A podcast like *The Michael Brooks Show* (an audio file of a YouTube show) sits somewhere between education and entertainment, blending political comedy with interviews in a show that emphasizes a global left perspective. Before his sudden death in 2020, Brooks's show featured a segment in which he criticizes some political opponent (Hillary Clinton, Nancy Pelosi) over a recording of the national anthem of the Soviet Union, condemning them to an imaginary gulag.[40] *The Katie Halper Show* displayed a similarly ironic sensibility towards the global history of Marxism when she, a self-proclaimed "red diaper baby," used an icon of a sickle crossed with a champagne flute on the thumbnail of her debut episode.[41] Mining a more homegrown seam of left radicalism and thus giving some sense of the variety of left-wing podcasting culture, *Trillbilly Workers Party* is hosted by three young socialists from Whitesburg, Kentucky. Theirs is an interesting addition to the cultural scene at a time when left podcasting is frequently caricatured as a largely Brooklynite practice, while Appalachia has been written off as "Trump country" by many whose primary insights into the region come from work like J. D. Vance's *Hillbilly Elegy* (2016), a text savaged to persuasive effect in the podcast's first episode.[42]

Entertainment or politics?

Assessing the ideological efficacy of such podcasts and the wider socialist culture they form part of is far from straightforward. For decades now, it has been common to exalt the political or oppositional qualities supposedly inherent in different kinds of cultural production. This has much to do with cultural studies' embrace of aspects of Antonio Gramsci's work on hegemony, and perhaps even more to do with the legacy of the New Left's concern with "cultural politics" as such. There have also been important countervailing arguments about the limits of such approaches. As Adolph Reed, Jr., puts it in *Class Notes* (2000), "Cultural production can reflect and perhaps support a political movement; it can never generate or substitute for one."[43] On this view, contemporary culture that deploys

Marxist vocabularies and iconography, or poetry and rap that paint pictures of insurrection, are not themselves political acts so much as the intermittent flaring of manifestations of political consciousness that may reflect a larger left turn on the part of many Americans, including millennials. They do not and cannot, however, stand in for a political movement that has historically had as its object the difficult tasks of nurturing collective consciousness and then finding a route to social transformation in the inhospitable political terrain of the United States. After all, even if one acknowledges the way that new media provide the opportunity to open up effectively limitless time and space to air left political views, how can the hosts of a popular podcast like *Chapo Trap House* be sure that their "infotainment" is not producing the same kinds of catharsis they argue characterize liberal political comedy?

The web-based technologies on which podcasting depends arguably only reinforce some of the limitations inherent to cultural politics as such. In *Democracy and Other Neoliberal Fantasies* (2009), Jodi Dean warned of the unlikelihood of the internet providing a viable platform for social transformation. It was not, she claimed, that "networked communications never facilitate political resistance," but that the kind of communication engendered by "communicative capitalism" in the digital age tends to "capture resistance and intensify global capitalism."[44] For when "communication serves as the key category for left politics, whether communication be configured as discussion, spectacle, or publicity, this politics ensures its political failure in advance: doing is reduced to talking, to contributing to the media environment."[45] This tendency can be further reinforced by the predominantly one-way, parasocial nature of podcasting, in which for all the interactive affordances of new media, listeners still tend to listen and podcasters talk, modeling political sentiments and affective responses on the listener's behalf in much the same way that Mark Fisher described other forms of culture "performing anti-capitalism" for their consumers.[46]

The fear that their listeners might mistake merely consuming cultural products for political action is one that some left podcasters have openly sought to counter, even as their efforts to propagandize socialism appear to be having some effect. While much of a *Chapo Trap House* episode in which the hosts recalled visiting the 2019 Conservative Political Action Conference (CPAC) was devoted to mocking the right, the closing moments of the podcast were filled with a reflection on the relationship between entertainment and politics. "This is entertainment," Will Menaker said. "We're doing entertainment about politics."⁴⁷ But he then addressed his audience directly, making a recruiter's argument for socialism as the only means to defeat the right: "Socialism is the only thing that is standing against these people and what they stand for. So either you're going to be a part of that, or you're just going to fucking be along for the ride."⁴⁸ A November 2019 episode of *The Antifada*, another left podcast, shows how increasing numbers of Americans may be responding to that choice. The host, Jamie Peck, interviewed the hosts of *Trillbilly Workers Party*, and one of them, Tom Sexton, related how he became "radicalized." He first reflected that "the prison abolition work we were doing locally" was what "pushed [him] from, I guess, liberalism into leftism." But he then added,

> and really just because ... at a certain point, there was [*sic*.] so many cultural products: by the time we got going, *Chapo Trap House* was out, all the left publications were rolling, the Bernie campaign was underway, and so, for me, anyway, it made it easier to sort of have a culture to step into that made more sense to me in terms of how I looked at the world ... Liberalism just didn't really make any sense anymore.⁴⁹

These examples give a sense of the kind of work these podcasts, and the wider culture they are part of, might accomplish. For in some ways, left podcasting, and related projects like *Means TV*, a worker-controlled venture aimed at becoming a "Netflix for the left," represent just the latest in a long history of attempts to create an alternative left media culture in the United States. The political economy of the corporate-owned mass media in the United States, even before the deregulation of broadcasting and emergence of conservative talk radio since the 1980s, has long made the construction of some form of what Nancy Fraser has called "subaltern counterpublics" essential to the promulgation of left-wing and other alternative ideologies.⁵⁰ The resources of print and other forms of culture have played their part in this process, and continue to do so; now digital platforms are providing new spaces for the same purpose. One need not be a cyberoptimist, nor underestimate the extent to which the commercial imperatives of major corporations and various factions of the online right and liberal center dominate internet culture, to see that new media technologies can still provide the means to continue to open up productive spaces for political education. Indeed, Sexton's description of "having a culture to step into" illustrates how the performative disarticulation of leftism from liberalism discussed above works in practice and on the individual level within a set of material historical circumstances in which a left turn on the part of some of the population already looks overdetermined. At the same time, the growing network of left podcasts and other forms of "millennial socialist" culture looks capable at least of performing the educative function of explaining what socialism is and has been in the United States and elsewhere.

None of this minimizes the challenges facing both the culture of "millennial socialism" and the political movement it supports. After all, it is one thing to attempt to perform and entrench an ideological disarticulation from liberalism, another altogether to fuse the diffuse potentialities of political life in the United States into an agent for radical social transformation. Some form of cooptation by the liberal mainstream of both the political energies of twenty-first-century socialism and its cultural preferences remains a real possibility. Now that the op-ed pages of *The New York Times* and *Washington Post* have begun to cede space to young socialists like Sunkara, Meagan Day, and Elizabeth Bruenig, and now that Simon & Schuster have published *The Chapo Guide to Revolution* (2018), one wonders how likely it is that some of today's young socialists will (as Sunkara put it during an interview on *The Dig*) one day look back at "that four or five years when everyone all of a sudden was a socialist."[51] This is to say nothing of the violence that the state has repeatedly shown itself prepared to wield when it comes to suppressing political movements of the radical left, both in the twenty-first century and in earlier eras. For now, as Buhle writes in a preface to the third edition of *Marxism in the United States* published in 2013, it is clear that young socialists are still learning "what to do" and "how to do it."[52] They are aware of their weaknesses and vulnerabilities, especially the lack of really extensive or stable roots in the working class. On the other hand, they are also teaching themselves how to organize workplaces, as the appearance of the labor organizer Jane McAlevey on a host of left podcasts and other left media attests, as well as looking for "jobs in several targeted industries, like logistics and transportation," in an effort to build class power.⁵³ One may well continue to doubt that any form of revolution is imminent, but the culture that the latest resurgence in Marxist and Marxist-influenced modes of thought is producing in the United States shows us some of the uses to which socialists of today are already putting the technological and media tools that history has handed them. And on these grounds, there can be little doubt that they have already been successful in recruiting at least some new converts to the latest iteration of an old cause.

Notes

1. Gil Scott-Heron, *Small Talk at 125th and Lenox* (Flying Dutchman/RCA, 1970).
2. Jay David Bolter and Richard Grusin, *Remediation: Understanding New Media* (Boston: MIT Press, 2000), 14–15.
3. Richard Berry, "Will the iPod Kill the Radio Star?" *Convergence* 12, no. 2 (May 2006), 144.
4. "Millennial Socialism," *The Economist* (February 14, 2019) www.economist.com/leaders/2019/02/14/millennial-socialism
5. Keir Milburn, *Generation Left* (Oxford: Polity Press, 2019).
6. Marc Tracy, "Is 'Bernie or Bust' the Future of the Left?" *The New York Times* (August 6, 2019) www.nytimes.com/2019/08/06/us/politics/bernie-sanders-democratic-socialists-america.html; Doug Henwood, "The Socialist Network," *The New Republic* (May 16, 2019) https://newrepublic.com/article/153768/inside-democratic-socialists-america-struggle-political-mainstream
7. M. H. Miller, "I Came of Age During the 2008 Financial Crisis. I'm Still Angry About It," *The New York Times* (September 15, 2018) www.nytimes.com/2018/09/15/opinion/sunday/financial-crisis-student-loans-recession.html
8. M. H. Miller, "Been Down So Long It Looks Like Debt To Me," *The Baffler*, no. 40 (July 2018) thebaffler.com/salvos/looks-like-debt-to-me-miller
9. Malcolm Harris, *Kids These Days: Human Capital and the Making of Millennials* (New York: Little, Brown, 2017), 227–28.
10. Gabriel Winant, "Professional-Managerial Chasm," *n+1* (October 10, 2019) https://nplusonemag.com/online-only/online-only/professional-managerial-chasm/

11 "N+1 and the PMC: A Debate about Moving On," *Nonsite.org* (October 21, 2019) https://nonsite.org/feature/n1-and-the-pmc-a-debate-about-moving-on; "Adolph Reed, The PMC Class, Neoliberalism & Essentialism," *The Michael Brooks Show* (October 31, 2019) www.youtube.com/watch?v=IiCB-H00r48 (06.32–06.33).
12 E. Dyke and B. Muckian-Bates, "Social Movements Gave Rise to the 'Teachers' Revolt,' Not Bernie," *New Politics* (November 6, 2019) https://newpol.org/social-movements-gave-rise-to-the-teachers-revolt-not-bernie/
13 Jodi Dean, *Crowds and Party* (London and New York: Verso, 2018), 20–21.
14 J. L. Austin, *How To Do Things With Words* (Oxford: Oxford University Press, 1962), 5–6.
15 "Up From Liberalism," *Jacobin* 20 (Winter 2016), 1, 6.
16 Ibid., 6, 7.
17 "Millennial Socialism."
18 Paul Buhle, *Marxism in the United States: A History of the American Left* (London and New York: Verso, 2013), 235.
19 Ibid., xii, 230.
20 Asad Haider, *Mistaken Identity: Race and Class in the Age of Trump* (London and New York: Verso, 2018), 9; "Combahee River Collective Statement" (April 1977) https://combaheerivercollective.weebly.com/the-combahee-river-collective-statement.html
21 Nathan J. Robinson, "How to be a Socialist Without Being an Apologist for the Atrocities of Communist Regimes," *Current Affairs* (October 25, 2019) www.currentaffairs.org/2017/10/how-to-be-a-socialist-without-being-an-apologist-for-the-atrocities-of-communist-regimes; Peter Kro-THOT-kin [pseudonym], *Meme*, https://me.me/i/peter-kro-thot-kin-jamie-elizabeth-peter-kro-thot-kin-jamie-elizabeth-we-are-in-898d1c34c27f4ce58c97a61ffbecf826
22 Black Socialists of America, "Who We Are," https://blacksocialists.us/about
23 Bhaskar Sunkara, *The Socialist Manifesto: The Case for Radical Politics in an Era of Extreme Inequality* (London and New York: Verso, 2019), 2.
24 Ibid., 159–86.
25 Ibid., 216.
26 "Introducing Commune," *Commune* 1 (June 11, 2019) https://communemag.com/introducing-commune/
27 "Introducing Commune."
28 Joshua Clover, *Red Epic* (Oakland: Commune Editions, 2015), 18.
29 Walter Benjamin, "Theses on the Philosophy of History," in *Illuminations* (London: Pimlico, 1999), 255.
30 *Sorry to Bother You*, dir. Boots Riley (Universal Pictures, 2018).

31 The Coup, *Kill My Landlord* (Wild Pitch, 1993); The Coup, *Pick a Bigger Weapon* (Epitaph, 2006).
32 "THA SAGA BEGINS," *Chapo Trap House*, episode 1 (December 3, 2016) https://soundcloud.com/chapo-trap-house/episode-1-31216 (45.50-50.15).
33 One such mainstream complaint is Nellie Bowles, "The Pied Pipers of the Dirtbag Left Want to Lead Everyone to Bernie Sanders," *The New York Times* (February 29, 2020) www.nytimes.com/2020/02/29/us/politics/bernie-sanders-chapo-trap-house.html
34 "Blue Pills and Ham," *Chapo Trap House*, episode 120. https://soundcloud.com/chapo-trap-house/episode-120-teaser-blue-pills-and-ham (0.37-0.52).
35 Amber A'Lee Frost, "The Necessity of Political Vulgarity," *Current Affairs* (August 25, 2016) www.currentaffairs.org/2016/05/the-necessity-of-political-vulgarity
36 Alex Cypher, "The DSA and their Crusade Against 'Strasserism,'" *Medium* (April 24, 2019) https://medium.com/@comradecypher/the-dsa-and-their-crusade-against-strasserism-8b2697b07cc
37 Bryan Quinby (@MurderBryan), "A group of white men is called a podcast" (February 18, 2019) https://twitter.com/murderbryan/status/1097603142869569537?lang=en
38 See Henwood, "Socialist Network" for an account of how such debates fueled divisions in the DSA's Philadelphia chapter.
39 "About *The Dig*," *Patreon.com*, www.patreon.com/thedig
40 "Gulag: All Critics of Ilhan Omar Edition ft. Ben Burgis (TMBS 80)," YouTube (March 11, 2019) www.youtube.com/watch?v=Rjpgx1oyr5E&t=231s
41 "Socialist Feminist Alex Press on Sexual Harassment," *The Katie Halper Show* (November 30, 2017) https://podbay.fm/podcast/1020563127/e/1512067776
42 "JD Vance a Snitch," *Trilbilly Workers Party*, episode 1 (February 23, 2017) https://podbay.fm/ podcast/1227003413
43 Adolph Reed, Jr., *Class Notes: Posing as Politics and Other Thoughts on the American Scene* (New York: New Press, 2000), 170.
44 Jodi Dean, *Democracy and other Neoliberal Fantasies* (Durham, NC. and London: Duke UP, 2009), 24, 2.
45 Ibid., 32.
46 Mark Fisher, *Capitalist Realism: Is There No Alternative* (Winchester: Zero Books, 2009), 12.
47 "CPAC Judgment Days," *Chapo Trap House*, episode 294 (March 4, 2019) https://soundcloud.com/chapo-trap-house/294-cpac-judgment-days-3419 (2.05.31-2.05.34).

48 Ibid. (2.08.33–2.08.44).
49 "The Protracted People's War of Appalachia with Trillbilly Workers Party," *The Antifada*, episode 74 (November 13, 2019) www.patreon.com/theantifada/posts?tag=trillbilly%20workers%20party (04.26–05.16).
50 Nancy Fraser. "Rethinking the Public Sphere: A Contribution to the Critique of Actually Existing Democracy," *Social Text*, 25–26 (1990), 56–80, 71.
51 "Socialist Manifesto with Bhaskar Sunkara," *The Dig* (August 16, 2019) www.thedigradio.com/podcast/socialist-manifesto-with-bhaskar-sunkara/ (08.46–08.56).
52 Buhle, *Marxism*, vii–viii.
53 Henwood, "Socialist Network."

11

Does the American experience refute Marxism?

Kim Moody

The United States appears to be in living contradiction to Marxism. American capitalism represents the world's most developed and unfettered version of capitalism. It displays all the features of the system described and analyzed by Marx, with its outrageous inequality, its mass of unemployed and underemployed workers (Marx's "reserve army of labor"), its repeated and often deep crises, and its drive overseas leading to one war after another. But the United States has a political culture overwhelmingly dedicated to capitalism's survival and expansion. And its working class, assuming we admit it has such a social formation, refuses to organize itself into an independent party, much less pursue the revolutionary goals predicted by Marx.

For decades academics have debated whether the United States was an "exception" to the development of the sort of working-class movement seen in most of the "advanced" capitalist economies. The first wave of American exceptionalist analysis saw this failure to conform to European standards of development as rooted in relative working-class prosperity, the "safety-valve" of America's unique frontier, and upward social mobility. No sooner had the ink dried on this explanation, always dubious, than the plight of American workers began to resemble that of their European and settler-colonial counterparts. The Great Depression with its massive misery, on the one hand, and its working-class upsurge, on the other, put an end to the idea that capitalism in the United States had somehow exempted the American working class from the sort of class consciousness and economic organization that had characterized most developed capitalist nations by that time. Yet, when the Second World War ended, despite some discussion within the powerful labor movement that emerged from that war about the formation of a labor party, organized workers resumed their previous attachment to the very capitalist Democratic Party.[1] Had exceptionalism triumphed after all?

Material analysis, not predestined outcomes

As a philosophy, a theory of history, or an analysis of the dynamics of capitalism as developed by Marx and Engels, Marxism is not a secular version of predestination or a teleology that proposes the outcome of history as inherent from the start. Although Marx and Engels used the term "inevitable," particularly in their earlier works, the *method* that evolved, particularly in Marx's monumental three volumes of *Capital* and his political writings, was both empirical in its evidence and based on contingency and contradiction in the tendencies and dynamics he saw in capitalism. For Marx, capitalism, like all previous socio-economic systems, was a product of historical developments in the manner in which human beings carved out their existence and culture from nature, the "modes of production" as he called them. Inherent in these modes of production were class conflict and struggles resulting from unequal appropriation of the products of human labor. All the pre-capitalist systems—Asian state-centered production, ancient slavery, and feudalism—had run up against the limitations of their production systems, on the one hand, and the often complex class conflict this engendered, on the other. As Marx and Engels put it in the *Communist Manifesto*, these systems engender a "now hidden, now open fight, a fight that each time ended, either in a revolutionary reconstruction of society at large, or in the common ruin of the contending classes."[2] While this latter outcome was probably a reference to the fate of the Roman Empire and the collapse of the civilization it had represented, it also hints that history contains developments that depend on the indeterminate outcome of class struggle, not only on the development or limits of the technology or organization of production of the time.

The place of contingency, of actual events and the relative strength of contending classes, is clear in Marx's political writings, particularly those covering the revolutions of 1848 and the Paris Commune.[3] In these works, the conflicts between the major classes and the factions within them are spelled out and analyzed in terms of actual relative strengths and events. In Marx's works on the revolutions of 1848–1850, the failure of the triumph of the working class and communism that had seemed inherent in those mass revolutionary upsurges described in the *Manifesto* is analyzed in empirical detail, revealing the contingent nature of class struggle. In part this contingency is because such struggles take place in settings the actors do not choose. As Marx reminds us in *The Eighteenth Brumaire*, "Men make their history, but they do not make it just as they please; they do not make it under circumstances chosen by themselves, but under circumstances directly encountered, given and transmitted from the past."[4]

Central to these circumstances in the period of capitalism are the economic and social dynamics of capitalism itself. In its most complete form, Marx's work was developed in the notebooks known as the *Grundrisse* and eventually published as *Capital*, Volumes I, II, and III. In these works and others Marx discovered and analyzed certain laws of motion in the very contradictory dynamics of the system that made it historically different from all previous socio-economic systems and that underlay the class conflict between capital and labor. Even here the concept of the "laws" of development was not a matter of predetermined outcome, but of conflicting tendencies. For example, he called the chapter in Volume III that explained the underlying causes of capitalism's periodic crises "The Law of the Tendential Fall in the Rate of Profits." In this chapter he refers to "the progressive *tendency* for the general rate of profit to fall" (emphasis added), while the following chapter discussed the "Counteracting Factors" that limit this tendency.[5]

In other words, determination exists in the interaction of inherent tendencies in the socio-economic system in which humans play a critical, if not always conscious or voluntary role. The capitalist must expand his capital to compete. To do so he must drive and exploit the workers in order to create a profit, while the workers, in turn, will find ways to resist and rebel in a "now hidden, now open fight."[6] The working class and the struggles it wages, as Marxist historian E. P. Thompson put it, "arise at the intersection of determination and self-activity."[7] And that leaves the questions of working-class consciousness and organization open to a high degree of contingency, some advances, periodic defeats, and, so far, no successful permanently established socialist society as Marx understood this—despite the use of the name by a variety of semi- and post-capitalist regimes.

Some Marxists, however, have interpreted Marx and Engels's philosophy of history as pointing to the inevitability of socialism. This was the view of the Second International led by the German Social Democratic Party from the late 1880s until the International collapsed with the outbreak of the First World War in 1914. This interpretation led to a politics of passivity in relation to the overthrow of capitalism that emphasized "determination" and downplayed "self-activity," relying exclusively on parliamentary reforms of the system while waiting for the final crisis of capitalism. This passivity was challenged in the early twentieth century by revolutionary Marxists such as V. I. Lenin, Rosa Luxemburg, and Antonio Gramsci who put the self-activity of the working class back into the center of Marxism as a revolutionary theory of history and material basis for politics.[8]

The crisis of the socialist movement during the First World War put a further dent in the idea of socialism's inevitability among revolutionary Marxists. In its place, as Luxemburg wrote in 1915, "Capitalist society faces a dilemma, either an advance to socialism or a reversion to barbarism."[9] "Socialism or Barbarism," this admission of historical alternatives, became a slogan for revolutionary socialists throughout the twentieth century.[10] Since Luxemburg's time, capitalism has added at least two even more horrific man-made alternatives to socialism: nuclear annihilation and climate extinction—the former an indirect and the latter a direct result of capital's drive to endless accumulation and expansion.[11]

What is determined in Marx's analysis of capitalism once that system has achieved a certain level of development is the constant reappearance of crises; that is, depressions and recessions of various degrees, that originate in the "tendential fall in the rate of profit" referred to above and spelled out in Volume III of *Capital*.[12] For Marx this tendency lay in the accumulation of capital itself. Crises may be sparked by financial or other causes, but it is the underlying fall in the profit rate that brings investment to a halt, plunging the economy into recession or worse. New technology meant to enhance profitability ultimately contributes to the rise in fixed assets and, barring an even faster increase in the total amount of profits, eventually contributes to the falling rate (i.e., ratio) of profit or rate of return on investment (ROI) as it is conventionally described. Over the decades since the mid-nineteenth century, with ups and downs, profit rates have tended to decrease for the major capitalist countries, revealing a tendency for capitalism as a system to grow more slowly.[13]

In terms of the dynamics of capitalism and its crisis-ridden path of growth and accumulation, the United States, far from being an "exception," is the exemplar of Marx's analysis. Figure 11.1 shows the trend of average profit rates for the Group of Seven (G7) nations since the early 1960s through the 2008–2009 recession, in which the United States is the largest contributor to the average. In other words, Marx's analysis of the direction of capitalism, its profit rates, and crises are just as endemic to the United States as to other developed capitalist nations. In economic terms, America is not an exception.

Since in Marx's analysis, all profits and, indeed, value, are created by collective labor in the production process, conflict over the distribution of this wealth between wages and profits as well as the intensity of work become sources of class struggles in the workplace and beyond. While class struggle is, indeed, inevitable under these conditions, its contours and outcomes are not. In other words,

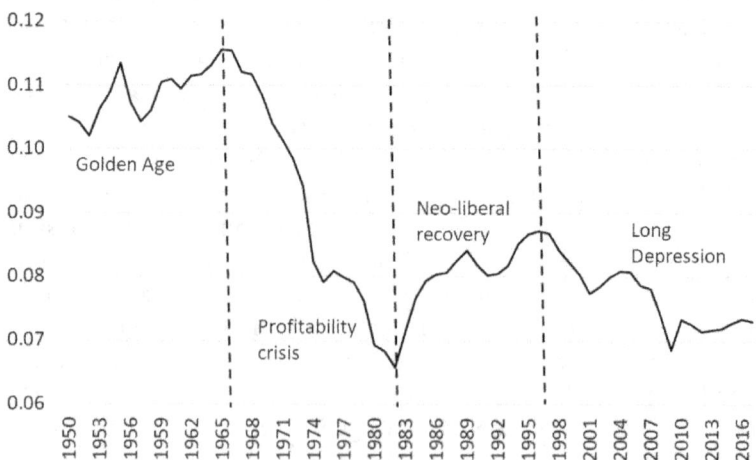

Figure 11.1 Average rate of profit of the G7 nations. *Courtesy Michael Roberts.*

Marxism does not promise the "correct" form of organization, political strategy, or victory at any one point, which is one reason why Marxists of various shades spent much of the twentieth century agonizing over questions of organization and consciousness. These are part of the self-activity that intersects with determination, as Thompson put it. Consciousness, organization, the relative balance in class forces, and the actions of the state all play a role in outcomes that are seldom predictable. It is in this realm that one must discover the failure of socialism to permanently take hold as a mass movement, let alone a revolutionary social outcome.

Stalinism and the derailing of socialism

Nowhere is the reality of contingency more tragically illustrated than in the derailment of revolutionary socialism in the wake of the failure of the Russian Revolution of 1917. In what appeared to be a consummation of Marx's vision, the First World War was followed by revolutionary working-class revolts in Russia, Germany, Italy, and parts of Eastern Europe. Of these, only that in Russia led by the Bolsheviks succeeded in taking power and forming the world's first workers' state. But burdened with a backward agrarian economy, isolated by the failure of revolution in Western Europe, and surrounded and invaded by major capitalist nations, as a young workers' state the Soviet Union soon degenerated into a bureaucratic holding action. Eventually, the party became the state and the growing bureaucracy ruled the party under the increasingly autocratic rule of Stalin.

Stalinism proclaimed itself Marxist and socialist, but by the late 1920s or so the Soviet Union had become in reality a bureaucratic collectivist class society in which the bureaucracy controlled the means of production and the workers became its subordinate employees. Workers' organizations and opposing political currents were suppressed and any shred of socialist democracy eliminated. Stalin and his followers claimed the mantle of Bolshevism and convinced millions around the world that they represented the only hope of "actually existing socialism." The prestige of the Russian revolution and the desire of many for a concrete "home" of socialism gave Stalin and his followers a great deal of authority.[14]

The Communist Parties formed during the revolutionary upsurge that followed the First World War had been the creation of the revolutionary wing of socialism since the split with the older social-democratic and socialist parties during and after the war, but based in part on the prestige of the Soviet Union, in part on lies about the true nature of the regime in Russia, and in part on the ruthless exclusion of critics and oppositionists such as the followers of Leon Trotsky, they eventually came under the leadership of Stalin's supporters. Subsequently, these parties adopted a mechanistic version of Marxism similar to that of the earlier Second International. Communist Party policy and strategy became subordinated to the foreign policy needs of Stalin's Soviet Union. Of course, as workers' parties in the West, their members often acted as militants, building unions, and fighting racism and colonialism, but always within the limits imposed by Stalin and the priorities of Russian foreign policy.

With the Soviet Union and most of the mass Communist Parties now a thing of the past for more than a generation, it requires a feat of retroactive imagination to understand the negative impact the rise of Stalinism had on the international workers' and socialist movement. The redefinition of socialism as a totalitarian one-party state drove many from the ranks of socialism altogether and twisted the meaning of socialism for others. Stalinism drained a large section of the international workers' movement of its revolutionary content and the self-activity that is a key to genuine class consciousness.

Capitalism's "golden years" and the Americanization of politics

The old argument for American exceptionalism was, in the final analysis, a Eurocentric comparison of the United States to Western Europe. As a product of highly uneven development, the world was and is full of countries that failed to follow the European example even as capitalism conquered or absorbed their economies. History, being full of ironies, has seen the tables turned on the notion of an American exception as developments in global capitalism from prosperity to crises to neoliberalism have tended to "Americanize" European politics, while class politics in much of the developing world followed different patterns altogether.

Does the American experience refute Marxism? 271

Beginning in the 1950s, a process unfolded by which European working-class organizations (unions and social-democratic parties) would abandon socialist objectives and anything approaching revolutionary organization to settle for a reform politics not much different from those seen in mid- and late-twentieth-century America, even if America's individualism and market-celebratory expressions often remained more extreme. In other words, the acceptance of capitalism which had previously characterized American working-class politics became the norm of working-class politics throughout the developed capitalist world.

This direction away from revolutionary socialist ideas and politics was fostered by two initial developments in the period following the Second World War that impacted all the major capitalist countries that had previously possessed labor movements with explicitly socialist programs, if not always practices. These were: (1) a nearly quarter-century period of relative prosperity that raised the living standards of large sections of the working class; and (2) the transformation and later collapse of social democracy as a working-class tendency across much of Europe despite their survival as electoral shells in some countries.

The massive destruction of capital during the Second World War in Europe and Japan, on the one hand, and the rise of the United States as the major industrial power, on the other, laid the basis for high profit rates and a period of expanded growth in the developed nations. As recovery unfolded on a world scale, strong labor movements re-emerged in the United States and Western Europe, and real wages rose to levels never seen before. Figure 11.2 shows the growth of real hourly compensation (wages and benefits) and productivity in the United States from 1948 to 2013, revealing the rapid growth of workers' compensation until the early 1970s. The major capitalist countries in Western Europe saw similar rises in real wages as unions revived and took advantage of economic recovery. In the immediate postwar period, Britain's Labour Party would move to establish the modern welfare state, nationalize several key industries, and establish the National Health Service. The German Social Democratic Party (SPD) reorganized on a mass scale, complete with Marxist rhetoric and the older notion of achieving socialism through gradual reforms it had long practiced. By the end of the 1950s, welfare payments composed 10.4 percent of gross national

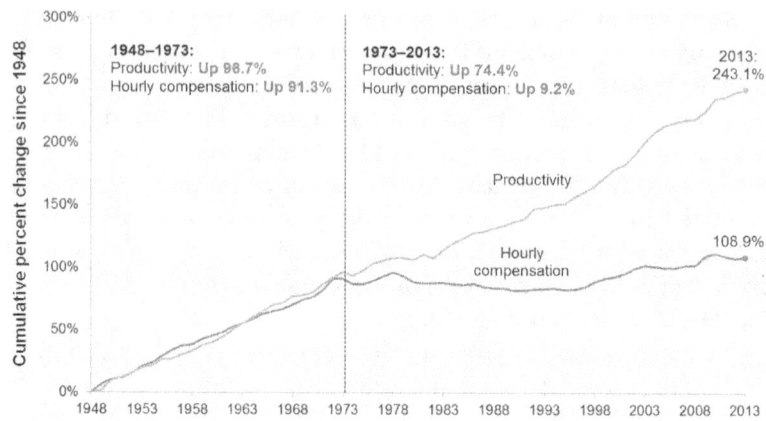

Figure 11.2 U.S. productivity and typical worker's compensation, 1948–2013. *Courtesy Economic Policy Institute.*

product in Germany, those in Austria 9.2 percent, Sweden 9.1 percent, France 8.3 percent, Italy 7.9 percent, and Britain 6.4 percent, compared to just 4.5 percent for the United States.[15]

As prosperity took hold in the 1950s, however, social democracy transformed itself, endorsing capitalism with its new efficiency and welfare state, distancing itself from its traditional working-class base as it sought the votes of the rising professional middle class, and fully embracing the West as the Cold War took shape. The transformation of European social democracy from its traditional notion of gradual movement toward socialism via reforms to a new positive embrace of capitalism was a reflection of the relative prosperity of the period.

In this context, leading social-democratic theorist C. A. R. Crosland argued in the mid-1950s, capitalism had become a corporatist, technocratic, welfare state with its "modern, enlightened methods of personnel management" and "humanized" large-scale industry. In 1958, the Labour Party made this sentiment official when it stated in a glowing reference to the giant corporation that "under increasingly professional managements, large firms are as a whole serving the nation well." Crosland didn't stop there. He saw the unions that emerged in Britain as "masters of the industrial scene," while "In the U.S.A. the Trade Unions have invaded the prerogatives of management in such a way that we might almost speak of industrial democracy there."[16] This was not the view of American union members who fought "the management offensive of 1958–63" described by Mike Davis, nor of British workers whose level of strike action soared after 1953 precisely against this "increasingly professional management."[17]

Probably the most significant and overt sign of the transformation of social democracy in this period, however, was the adoption of the Bad Godesberg Program in 1959 by the German SPD. This program rejected Marxism and no longer saw capitalism as the source of inequality. The party now sought "equality of opportunity" rather than equality of results. Its goal was "the constant growth of prosperity and the just share for all in the national product." Expropriation of capitalist enterprises was no longer necessary since "private ownership of the means of production can claim protection by society as long as it does not hinder the establishment of social justice."[18]

In the eyes of the new generation of SPD leaders who wrote and approved this program, capitalism had been transformed by the "second industrial revolution," i.e., new technology, from an unequal class society to one of liberal pluralism.[19] In policy terms, European social democracy had become almost indistinguishable from American liberalism except in the occasional, ceremonial bow to socialism and the few nationalized industries accomplished in the earlier post-war period. For the social-democratic leaders of the late 1950s onward, hierarchical, technocratic administration in business and the state along with a market economy modified only by limited parliamentary democracy became the foundation of a new social-democratic reformism.

By the second half of the 1960s, the proposition that capitalist prosperity would bring social justice began to wear thin. Under this supposedly reformed capitalism, new technology and "professional management" brought a ruthless speed-up in industry, the first signs of inflation, and growing business resistance to workers' demands. The result was a period of upsurge by workers, students, and others who found that the technocratic rule of capital fell far short of "social justice." This upsurge was a reminder that capitalism not only produces periodic crises and continuous efforts to stunt working-class living and working standards, but also revolts against the regimes that enforce capital's priorities, if not against the system itself. In the United States, where class and race are always tightly intertwined, this revolt began with the civil rights movement in the 1950s by African Americans who had been excluded from the era of prosperity by the system of Jim Crow segregation. The mid-1960s in America brought an upsurge of black, white, and Latino rank-and-file worker actions against employers and often against bureaucratic union leaders who had accepted the logic of the system as well. At the same time millions of public employees in the United States poured into unions for the first time.[20] In Europe, the revolt brought even more radical manifestations such as France's May '68 mass strikes and Italy's "Hot Autumn" of 1969. The reformist Socialist and Communist parties, however, wanted none of this sort of rebellion.[21]

Recurrent crises, neoliberalism, and convergence

The recessions of 1973–74 and 1980–82 and relative "deindustrialization" across the developed economies undermined worker resistance, while business took the opportunity to organize political pressure for deregulation, privatization, and austerity—the core of neoliberal policy. As Margaret Thatcher and Ronald Reagan brought market fundamentalism back into mainstream politics, American liberalism and European social democracy moved further and further to the right in tandem. The leader of this movement in Europe was French Socialist François Mitterrand, who in 1981 reversed his Keynesian policies in favor of neoliberalism. By the 1990s, European social democrats such as the Labour Party's Tony Blair, French Socialist Party leader Lionel Jospin, and the SPD's Gerhard Schroeder joined Democrat Bill Clinton in proclaiming a "Third Way," not between socialism and capitalism, but between the outright conservativism of Thatcher and Reagan and traditional left reformism. A decade or so later, Italy's former Communists followed suit, naming their new center-left party the Democratic Party, and adopting the Obama slogan of "Yes, We Can" for the 2008 Italian elections.

By that time, most of the European social-democratic parties had ceased to see themselves or call themselves parties of the working class. Most, like Clinton's Democratic Party, put the unions at arm's length and sought votes among the educated middle class even where many working-class people still voted for them (as in Britain and Germany). As French Marxist Daniel Singer wrote in the late 1990s, in what he called "A Requiem for Social Democracy," these European social democratic leaders "are all more or less eager to turn their movements into an equivalent of the American Democratic Party."[22]

Furthermore, party membership and participation, once a feature of post-war European, though not American, political parties, virtually collapsed in the last forty years across the political spectrum including the traditional parties of the working class, the exceptions being in Spain, Portugal, and Greece. Despite its large membership, the Labour Party, even under its recent left-wing revival leader Jeremy Corbyn, had the lowest member participation rate in terms of attending a party meeting, handing out a campaign leaflet, or running for party office of any UK political party. This has led to a hollowing out of politics and a passive electorate that has opened to door to the electoral far right across the developed capitalist nations.[23]

The participation of the social-democratic parties in austerity, deregulation, and privatization across Western Europe was universal from the early 1980s through the Great Recession of 2008–2009, emulating in only slightly modified form the direction set by Reagan and Thatcher and soon adopted by the Clinton Administration. While the stronger welfare states in Europe have held up better than the weaker New Deal/Great Society version in the United States, the direction of neoliberal policy in Western Europe, especially in Germany, France, and even Sweden, mirrored that of the United States, with similar results.[24]

European Union policy turned from "Social Europe" to free market Europe. "Gone were the days when 'Europe' was to become a supranational welfare state integrating and improving on, member countries' existing welfare regimes," writes social-democratic intellectual Wolfgang Streeck. In its place in the 1990s and early 2000s, he argues, came the "competition state" with its growing inequality and wage stagnation. Everywhere union membership and strike activity declined significantly and the gap increased between stagnant real worker compensation and rising productivity resulting from lean production, new technology, and government anti-union

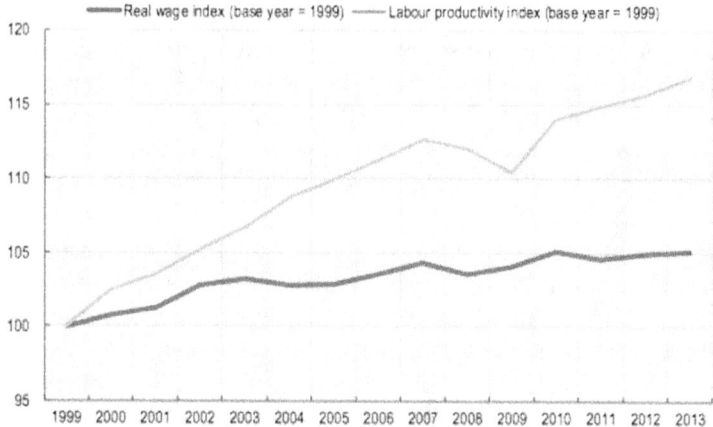

Figure 11.3 Growth in average wages and labor productivity in developed economies (index: 1999 = 100). *Courtesy International Labour Organization.*

policies.[25] Figure 11.2 shows this for the United States, while Figure 11.3 reveals the same pattern for all the developed capitalist nations. Note that over a thirteen-year period real wages rose only 6 percent or less than half a percent per year on average for workers in these major developed economies.

In short, Europe had become more like America not only in economic outcomes but in the politics of its social-democratic as well as its conservative and centrist "bourgeois" parties. This is not to say that the nations of Europe came to look exactly like the United States in every respect, any more than they looked exactly like each other. Their cultures and many institutional arrangements remained distinct even as their economic plight and political behavior converged. Nevertheless, it can be argued that while the Democratic Party never approximated a social-democratic or labor party, with few exceptions European social democracy has come increasingly to imitate the Democratic Party by virtue of its embrace of capitalism, consciously sought multi-class base, lack of member participation, growing financial links with sections of capital in many cases, top-down technocratic approach to elections, and, of course, embrace of much of the neoliberal agenda for nearly four decades.

The abandonment of pro-worker policies and the demotion of working-class voters in the electoral strategies of "Third Way" social-democratic parties as well as the Democratic Party have contributed to the decline of working-class voting and participation across the developed world. As a result, the door has been opened to demagogic "populist" appeals to disaffected workers as well as the sinking petit bourgeoisie and sections of the employed middle classes. If racism has long been a distinguishing feature of American social and political life, it has never been entirely absent from Europe. The rise of fascism in the 1920s and 1930s was enough to demonstrate that. But in the last decade or so in Europe, right-wing populist politicians have had some success in directing working-class anger born of austerity and deindustrialization at immigrants as well as at racial and ethnic minorities across that continent. Like the white working-class supporters of Trump in the United States, the role of white blue-collar workers in the referendum that passed Brexit (the British exit from the European Union), the subsequent election of Conservative Party leader Boris Johnson, and similar right-wing movements in France, Italy, Eastern Europe and elsewhere, though often exaggerated, has underlined the impact of racism on the consciousness particularly of those workers in deindustrialized areas of the developed capitalist nations.

Racism throughout the West is a legacy of slavery, the slave trade, conquest, and colonialism. Marx was fully aware of the negative effects of racism and other forms of bigotry on working-class consciousness and organization, not only in the case of white workers toward blacks in the United States, but also that of English workers toward the Irish, who, Marx wrote, "form a very important section of the working class in England." For this reason and to overcome English antipathy toward the Irish, he urged English workers to support Irish independence, not only in sympathy for the Irish but "in the interests of the English proletariat."[26] The inevitable competition between workers for jobs, wages, housing, education, etc., which becomes more intense in times of crisis or the decline of some industries ("deindustrialization") and the rise of others that disrupts workers lives, is a wedge which today the right exploits to create division and inflame racism and anti-immigrant sentiments. It should be borne in mind, however, that upper- and middle-class voters compose the majority of the actual voting coalitions behind Brexit, Trump, and Boris Johnson. In the case of the victory for Trump in 2016 in midwestern states, the margin of votes provided by white working-class voters was less than the numbers who simply didn't vote in that election.[27]

The convergence of capitalism's dynamics brought a transformation, shrinking, or disappearance of traditional working-class parties in Europe along with their embrace of neoliberalism and austerity to the point where one can no longer speak of "American exceptionalism" in terms of political behavior or policy content, just as one can no longer discern any real difference in the impact of capitalism's dynamics and their social and economic impact on the working class. Convergence, rather than exception, characterizes the state of politics in the United States and Europe.

Post-recession resistance: a changed working class enters the field of class struggle

If, in fact, the working class across the developed capitalist nations had been thoroughly defeated and capital simply triumphant, the convergence of capitalist politics would raise the question of whether Marxism had been proved wrong on an international scale. But if Marx's analysis of the crisis-ridden dynamics of capitalism has been demonstrated all too clearly and with a vengeance in the realm of political economy, so has the "inevitability" of class struggle as a two-sided (or multi-sided) conflict re-emerged, even amidst retreat. As Marx and Engels noted when they wrote of the "now hidden, now open fight," and as historians and sociologists have since pointed out, the level of class conflict is never a constant. Instead, class struggle comes in "leaps" or upsurges as it did in the aftermath of the First World War, the 1930s, and 1960s and 1970s.[28] Since the 2008–2009 recession bottomed-out, we have seen growing signs of resistance in both new and old forms, by both new and old sections of a working class whose composition has been changing throughout the neoliberal period.

Since the 2008 financial crisis, it has become common to see masses of people in the streets and squares of cities across the world protesting government policies or even the governments themselves. Some demonstrations, to be sure, like those in Venezuela or Bolivia were clearly based in middle and upper classes rebelling against left governments. Most, however, were clearly revolts against the

Does the American experience refute Marxism? 279

conditions of years of austerity and soaring inequality brought on by neoliberal policies, the social consequences of wars Western countries had imposed on developing nations notably in the Middle East, or the uprooting of populations and ruthless conditions of work as capitalism deepened its spread to formerly "underdeveloped" nations particularly in China.

The first of these highly visible scenes of rebellion occurred outside the "core" nations of developed (though declining) capitalism. Furthermore, at first glance, as seen on the evening news, many seem to be multi-class or even middle-class in nature. In fact, as David McNally points out, many of these movements involved or are based on mass strikes of workers with other sections of society being drawn into the conflict as the mass strike becomes a method of rebellion for workers, students, feminists, and more. From the Arab Spring of 2011 to its more radical 2019 revival in Iraq, Lebanon, and Algeria, and in France, Chile, and Puerto Rico, among other countries, workers are rediscovering this lost form of collective action.[29] The mass strikes of recent years in China's new industrial areas were clearly working-class in nature. While women have always played an important role in mass strike movements, what makes many of these strike movements *appear* different from most of those of a hundred years ago is the increasingly central role of women in a broad range of industries and the changing composition of the working class itself.

Events across much of Asia, Europe, and North America saw similar upsurges in the mass occupations of urban streets and squares with the Occupy Wall Street movement that spread beyond Zuccotti Park; Spain's Indignados movement and that in Catalonia seeking independence; Greece's mass mobilizations against Troika-imposed austerity; the *gilets jaunes* (yellow vests) in France, the striking West Virginian teachers wearing "RED for ED" T-shirts, the longstanding democracy struggle in Hong Kong in which union organizing became a goal, and the Sardines movement in Italy that packed the squares of major cities "like sardines" in opposition to Matteo Salvini, leader of the right-wing Northern League and, until recently, prime minster. To this we can add the more traditional, militant 2019 strikes and mass demonstrations of French transportation and public sector workers.[30]

Alongside these urban mobilizations have come a variety of new left-wing parties and political movements such as Syriza in Greece,

Podemos in Spain, Die Linke (the Left) in Germany, Left Block in Portugal, La France Insoumise, the Corbyn-led movement to transform the British Labour Party, and Bernie Sanders's presidential primary campaigns in the United States, as well as the election of Alexandria Ocasio-Cortez. Most reflect a similar social base to the mass demonstrations, but unlike those, which sometimes appear leaderless, most of these new party-based movements are characterized by and often dependent on high-profile leaders. Despite the grassroots origins of some of the mass mobilizations, most of these parties have drifted into top-down electoral modes with social-democratic programs that vary in their radicalism. After some initial strong showings, most have lost some or even much of their initial mass base and have fallen into minority party status.[31]

Despite these weaknesses, the upsurge has brought a revival of social democracy in Spain and Portugal where the socialist parties have finally opposed austerity, though not much else. Although the Labour Party under Corbyn, which attempted the most far-reaching transformation of social democracy, was badly defeated in the December 2019 general election, the new Labour left is unlikely to simply disappear. For the most part, however, social democracy has been mortally weakened. In France and Italy, the socialist parties have disappeared, while in Germany the once-proud standard-bearer of reform socialism has seen a much-diminished role as junior partner to the Christian Democrats. In Austria and the Netherlands, the social democrats saw serious defeats. In Sweden, the Social Democrats have become dependent on the Greens, the smaller Left Party, and the sufferance even of the Center Party to form a minority government.[32] The era of social-democratic dominance in Europe has given way to one of political volatility in which the far-right plays a role few imagined possible a decade or so ago. To put it another way, the journey of social democracy to austerity and the limits of American-style liberalism helped open the door to the right.

The American form of this upswing in resistance and opposition to the status quo is found not only in the oft-mentioned Occupy Wall Street, but in the 2011 mass occupation of the Wisconsin state capital by thousands of union members, the strikes and actions of immigrant workers, the mass women's strikes, the Black Lives Matter movement, the mass strikes of teachers across the country, as well as the strikes of nurses and other healthcare workers, telecommunications workers, and hotel and supermarket workers, and the 50,000 General Motors workers who held their strike for forty days in 2019 partly in support of the temporary workers in their midst. In response to this and the rise of right-wing Republicanism, the Democrats have mostly sought refuge in the center, while some presidential candidates in the 2020 primaries have adopted more watered-down versions of left programs like the Green New Deal or Medicare for All.

More surprising is the rebirth of socialism, or at least social democracy, in the United States partly in the form of Bernie Sanders's two runs for the Democratic presidential nomination—both drawing millions of votes, many from working-class voters. Alongside this has come the rise of the Democratic Socialists of America from a moribund group of a few thousand to an active and high-profile organization of 55,000 or more members, with two members in Congress and more in state and local offices, although, like Sanders, mostly as Democrats.

Most surprising of all is the shift in public opinion from the Cold War norms in which socialism was unspeakable to a favorable view of this word by many. In a Gallup poll conducted in April 2019, a remarkable 43 percent thought socialism would be good for the country. Women were more likely to approve of socialism than men, at 48 percent support. As with the demographics of the movements around the world and the United States, it was the young who most thought socialism would be good. Those eighteen to thirty-four years old favored it by 58 percent. If you thought these positive answers came mostly from educated middle-class people, you'd be wrong. Those with a college degree saw socialism as a good thing by 45 percent, but those with only a high-school education or less who make up the bulk of the non-managerial workforce favored it by 46 percent. "Non-whites," who also compose a large percentage of the U.S. working class, favored socialism by 57 percent.[33] Of course, just what those surveyed meant by socialism is unknown. Very likely it was social democracy of the Bernie Sanders type. Nevertheless, this represents a change in political outlook once attributed only to other countries.

To be sure, the more or (increasingly) less peaceful mass assemblies of socially unidentifiable masses do not seem like the classic mass strikes Rosa Luxemburg analyzed, the prelude to the Russian and German revolutions after the First World War, or the labor upheavals of the 1930s in the United States or France. Nor do the new political parties of the left in continental Europe or the social-democratic reform efforts in Britain or the United States resemble in any way the mass revolutionary or near-revolutionary parties that emerged from the First World War. Austerity, inequality, and precarious living standards underlay most of these struggles and eventually became central to their demands. Who, then, are these masses in the streets? What does Marxism tell us about them?

Class formation, re-formation, and proletarianization

Much of the recent rebellion across the world is not only in response to the obvious impact of recurrent crises and neoliberal policies (i.e., class struggle from above) on the majority of people, but the result of changes in class structure—and the structure of classes—that have been a central, if not always visible, part of capitalism's dynamics since the turn toward crises and slower growth in the mid-1970s.

In Marxism, classes are not things—layers of status, education, income, etc.—but evolving relative social formations created, destroyed, and recreated as capital accumulation moves from one industry or sector to another over time in line with the rhythms of profitability. In *Capital*, Volume III, Marx noted the difficulty in locating the demarcation of social classes in England where their "economic articulation is most widely and classically developed." As a result, he continued, "Even here, though, this class articulation does not emerge in pure form. Here, too, middle and transitional levels always conceal the boundaries."[34]

As manufacturing in the West faced rising competition from the East and attempted to offset this by yet more investment in technology, intensification of work through the increased standardization and quantification of work, and the resulting elimination of jobs, its rate of profit fell, leading to more job loss. Even more destructive of manufacturing employment were the four major recessions of the neoliberal period during which over seven million jobs were lost between 1979 and 2019 with only about 1.9 million eventually regained during recoveries.³⁵ Hence "deindustrialization" of the workforce, which was both a result of crises and the classic creation of a "surplus" population analyzed by Marx, meant a decline in the weight of industrial workers in the working class as a whole throughout the West.

Capital, however, did not stand still. As always, it sought and found new areas of investment and worker exploitation in the so-called "service sector"—a term that hides more than it reveals. Millions of jobs have been created in the rising logistics sector of transportation, warehousing, package delivery, and the "big data" that now drives these. Most of these jobs are industrial in nature. In addition, capital has increasingly moved into the realm of social reproduction, again creating millions of new jobs that despite the frequent basis in emotional labor are organized along lean production, algorithm-driven, industrial lines.³⁶

In this context, there are four key aspects of the changing working class in the developed capitalist nations: (1) the decline of the manufacturing workforce; (2) the vast increase in low-wage "service-producing" jobs that are essentially industrial in nature; (3) the proletarianization of formerly middle-class professions; and (4) the disproportionate assignment of millennial youth to the expanding lower-paid sectors of the workforce.

The same trends in lean production, industrialization, and the standardization and quantification of work measurement and management that intensified and eliminated manufacturing jobs and "industrialized" service-producing work have transformed and degraded many professional occupations once thought of as middle-class by virtue of their relative autonomy as well as superior pay. Just as independent artisans were once turned into industrial proletarians by capitalism in the nineteenth century, so in the late twentieth and early twenty-first centuries capitalism has molded many professional employees into proletarians in all but name. The organizations they have crafted or reshaped in the last couple of decades are now unions rather than professional associations. Their demands seek to protect those they serve as well as themselves. A large portion of the workers in these various changing occupations are women and people of color.

The nation's 3.2 million public school teachers have seen their occupations transformed and their autonomy as educators dramatically reduced by lean methods. The "business model" of education reform of recent years has imposed "data-driven" lean methods in the form of "value-added" teacher assessment and ranking based on standardized test results. This business model has brought both work intensification and, for those at the bottom of the bell curve, "involuntary separation." At the same time, classroom sizes in urban schools have grown and merit pay has been introduced to intensify competition among teachers. The result is not improved education, as business-minded reformers claim, but "teaching to the test" and high turnover among teachers. It was the industrialization of education and the proletarianization of its workers that was behind the rebellion of education workers in the United States that erupted from 2018 onward.[37]

Nurses are another example of this process of class reassignment. The nature of hospital-provided healthcare moved from that of independent hospitals acting as charities to an industry composed of hospital corporations and chains which, despite retaining their "non-profit" tax status, act as competing, capital-intensive, profit-making institutions. This industrialization of healthcare has included the full application of lean production and, more recently, advanced methods of worker surveillance and algorithmic task formation. Nurses in nearly 70 percent of all U.S. hospitals, for example, find their work guided by digital "clinical decision support systems" derived from manufacturing-based critical path analysis. This has meant an enormous loss of professional autonomy, on the one hand, and the growing unionization and strike activity of nurses and other hospital workers, on the other.[38]

To these examples of the process of proletarianization must be added the downward social mobility experienced by countless millennials in the past two or so decades as they have moved into a changing, insecure, and lower paid workforce. Millennials, after all, were born into the neoliberal era with its global employment shifts, declining real incomes, and fiscal austerity. Changes in class structure and personnel are often accomplished in part by generational changes, and millennials now compose 35 percent of the U.S. workforce and have become the largest generational group.[39] Millennials, like any generation, are divided by class, with many still entering better-paid professions. But more and more of them face a working-class future even if they have a middle-class background and a college degree. So the millennials have had the misfortune of arriving in the workforce precisely as old middle-income jobs disappeared, high-paid ones became more competitive and difficult to access, and the proportion of lousy jobs increased. As a recent international survey of millennials by Deloitte summarized the results,

> In the United States, millennials who entered the labor market around the recession, or during the years of slow growth that followed, experienced less economic growth in their first decade of work than any other generation. They have lower real incomes and fewer assets than previous generations at comparable ages, as well as higher levels of debt.[40]

More millennial households live in poverty than any other generation, they are mostly renters, more live with parents or friends, and they are more racially diverse just like the working class to which many of them belong.[41] In other words, millennials reflect the economic and social characteristics of the working class more on average than the Gen Xers or Baby Boomers who came before them. The Generation Zers just entering the workforce face even worse prospects. This trend covers much of the developed capitalist world as well as the United States. Indeed, the Deloitte survey cited above covered forty-two nations. America is no exception in this contemporary capitalist world as the rich get richer, the poor poorer, and those once in the middle are pushed down into the working class.

So when we see the streets of cities around the world fill with protesting people who do not all appear to be our stereotype of the working class of yesteryear, what we are seeing is that many of those who have been driven by capital into economic distress and a class position they never expected to experience. To be sure, the real middle class of well-heeled professionals with different interests and cultural complaints have not gone away and may be in the crowd as well. But capitalism's drive to expand creates its crises which, in turn, forces it to grind more of us down under capital's domination to propel its further expansion. The political organizers and enablers of capital's expansion today may be right-wing populists, corrupt dictators, military juntas, or even neoliberal social democrats or American-style liberals. The inevitability of increased exploitation and crisis, however, eventually leads to rebellion. It is here, however, that contingency takes over and organization, consciousness, strategy, etc., matter. In this, America is no exception either. It is here, at the current "intersection of determination and self-activity" that Italian Marxist Antonio Gramsci's famous summary of the state of the world in the 1930s is perhaps appropriate to our own time: "The crisis consists precisely in the fact that the old is dying and the new cannot be born; in the interregnum a great variety of morbid symptoms appear."[42] In this, America is the norm.

Notes

1. C. Wright Mills, *The New Men of Power: America's Labor Leaders* (Urbana: University of Illinois Press, 2001), 155–219.
2. Karl Marx and Frederick Engels, "Manifesto of the Communist Party," in *Selected Works of Marx and Engels* (London: Lawrence & Wishart, 1991), 36.
3. Karl Marx, *Class Struggles in France, 1948–1850* (New York: International Publishers, 1964); Karl Marx, *The Eighteenth Brumaire of Louis Bonaparte* (New York: International Publishers, 1963); Karl Marx, "The Civil War in France," in *Selected Works*.
4. Marx, *Eighteenth Brumaire*, 15.
5. Karl Marx, *Capital*, Volume III (London: Penguin Books, 1991), 315–19, 339–48.
6. Marx and Engels, "Manifesto," 36.
7. E.P. Thompson, *The Poverty of Theory and Other Essays* (New York: Monthly Review Press, 1978), 106.
8. Sidney Hook, *Towards the Understanding of Karl Marx: A Revolutionary Interpretation* (Amherst NY: Prometheus Books, 2002), 18–63.
9. Rosa Luxemburg, "The Junius Pamphlet: The Crisis in German Social Democracy," in *Rosa Luxemburg Speaks*, ed. Mary-Alice Waters (New York: Pathfinder Press, 1970), 269. Luxemburg mistakenly attributed this quote to Engels. In fact, it appeared in the 1891 Erfurt Program of the German Social Democratic Party authored, ironically, by the "father" of inevitability theory, Karl Kautsky. See Ian Angus, "The Origins of Rosa Luxemburg's Slogan 'Socialism or Barbarism,'" *MR Online* (October 22, 2014) https://mronline.org/2014/10/22/angus2210 14-html-2/
10. Hal Draper, "The Inevitability of Socialism: The Meaning of a Much Abused Formula" (December 1947), Marxist Internet Archive. www.marxists.org/archive/draper/1947//12/inevitsoc.htm
11. For a more thorough discussion of Marx's philosophy, see Hook, *Towards the Understanding*.

12 Karl Marx, *Capital*, Volume III, 317–48; for a recent and mercifully brief explanation of the falling rate of profit, see Edward L. Tapia, "The Tendency for the Rate of Profit to Decline—And Why it Matters," *New Politics* 67, Vol. XVII (Summer 2019): 79–88.
13 Anwar Shaikh, *Capitalism: Competition, Conflict, Crises* (New York: Oxford University Press, 2016), 56–74; Michael Roberts, *The Long Depression: How It Happened, Why It Happened, and What Happens Next* (Chicago: Haymarket Books, 2016), 59–61, 223–25; Esteban Ezequiel Maito, "The Tendency of the Rate of Profit to Fall since the Nineteenth Century and a World Rate of Profit," in *World in Crisis: A Global Analysis of Marx's Law of Profitability*, ed. Guglielmo Carchedi and Michael Roberts (Chicago: Haymarket Books, 2018), 129–50.
14 There are numerous Marxist analyses of the rise and consolidation of Stalinism in Russia, including Leon Trotsky, *The New Course*, and Max Shachtman *The Struggle for the New Course* (Ann Arbor: University of Michigan Press, 1965); Ernest Haberkern and Arthur Lipow, eds., *Neither Capitalism nor Socialism: Theories of Bureaucratic Collectivism*. Atlantic Highlands, NJ: Humanities Press, 1996); Leon Trotsky, *The Revolution Betrayed: What Is the Soviet Union and Where Is It Going?* (New York: Pathfinder Press, 1972); Tony Cliff, *Russia: A Marxist Analysis* www.marxists.org/archive/cliff/works/1964/russia/index.htm
15 Michael Kidron, *Western Capitalism Since the War* (Harmondsworth UK: Penguin Books, Ltd, 1970), 20; Council of Economic Advisors, *Economic Report of the President 2011* (Washington DC: U.S. Government Printing Office, 2011), 285, 291; Council of Economic Advisors, *Economic Report of the President 2005* (Washington, DC: U.S. Government Printing Office, 2005), 208.
16 Hal Draper, "The New Social-Democratic Reformism," in Hal Draper, *Socialism From Below*, ed. Ernest Haberkern (New Jersey: Humanities Press, 1992), 92–94.
17 Mike Davis, *Prisoners of the American Dream: Politics and Economy in the History of the US Working Class*. (London: Verso, 1986),121–27; Alan Campbell, Nina Fishman and John McIlroy, *The Post-War Compromise: British Trade Unions and Industrial Politics, 1945–1964* (Monmouth UK: Merlin Press, 2007), 97, 105.
18 Joris von Moltke, *The Great Balancing Act: Explaining the Social Democratic Party's Position Taking on Democracy and Capitalism in Germany, 1871–1959* (B.A. Honors thesis, Department of Political Science, University of Michigan, 2017), 93–94.
19 Von Moltke, *Great Balancing Ac*t, 94.

20 Aaron Brenner, Robert Brenner and Cal Winslow, *Rebel Rank and File: Labor Militancy and Revolt from below during the Long 1970s* (London: Verso, 2010).
21 Daniel Singer, *Prelude to Revolution: France in May 1968* (Boston: South End Press, 2002); Chris Harman, *The First Last Time: 1968 and After* (London: Bookmarks, 1998).
22 Daniel Singer, *Whose Millennium? Theirs or Ours?* (New York: Monthly Review Press, 1999), 58–67; David Broder, "Resurrecting the Italian Left" in *Europe in Revolt*, ed. Catarina Príncipe and Bhaskar Sunkara (Chicago: Haymarket Books, 2016), 81.
23 Vulgar Empiricist, "Into the Void," *Jacobin*, No. 35 (Fall 2019): 66–70; Noel Dempsey, "Membership of UK Political Parties," House of Commons Library, Briefing Paper no. SN05125 (August 9, 2019), 22; Kim Moody, "The UK election: A car crash on the left side of the road," *New Politics* online (December 8, 2019) https://newpol.org/the-uk-election-a-car-crash-on-the-left-side-of-the-road/
24 Wolfgang Streeck, "Progressive Regression: Metamorphoses of European Social Policy," *New Left Review* 118 (July/August 2019): 117–39; Göran Therborn, "Twilight of Swedish Social Democracy," *New Left Review* 113 (September/October 2018): 5–26.
25 Wolfgang Streeck, *Buying Time: The Delayed Crisis of Democratic Capitalism, Second Edition* (London: Verso, 2017), 37; Streeck, "Progressive Regression," 129–30.
26 Karl Marx, Letter to L. Kugelman, November 29, 1869, in *Karl Marx and Frederick Engels: Selected Correspondence* (Moscow: Progress Publishers, 1965), 229–30.
27 Mike Davis, "Election 2016," *New Left Review* 103 (January/February 2017): 5–8; Kim Moody, "Was Brexit a Working-Class Revolt?" *Against the Current* 184 (September/October 2016): 17–22; Kim Moody, *On New Terrain: How Capital is Reshaping the Battleground of Class War* (Chicago: Haymarket Books, 2017), 175–87.
28 Marx and Engels, "Manifesto," 36; E. J. Hobsbawm, *Labouring Men: Studies in the History of Labour* (London: Weidenfeld & Nicolson, 1964), 126–57; Beverly J. Silver, 2003, *Forces of Labor: Workers' Movements and Globalization since 1870* (New York: Cambridge University Press, 2003).
29 David McNally, "The Return of the Mass Strike: Teachers, Students, Feminists, and the New Wave of Popular Upheavals," *Specter*, in press.
30 "Why are so any countries witnessing mass protests?" *Economist* (November 4, 2019) www.economist.com/international/2019/11/04/why-are-so-many-countries-witnessing-mass-protests; "The World is on Fire:

11 of the Biggest Struggles of the Year," *Left Voice* (November 2, 2019) www.leftvoice.org/the-world-is-on-fire-11-of-the-biggest-struggles-this-year; "A shoal of force: Italy's 'sardines' movement takes on takes on the far-right," Reuter videos (November 26, 2019) https://sg.news.yahoo.com/shoal-force-italys-sardines-movement-141239084.html
31 For an early review of most of these, see Príncipe and Sunkara, *Europe*.
32 Anton Jäger, "We Bet the House on Left Populism and Lost," *Jacobin*, 35 (Fall 2019): 124–34; Alan Cafruny, "The European Crisis and the Left" in *Socialist Register 2019*, ed. Leo Panitch and Greg Albo (London: The Merlin Press, 2018), 329–31.
33 Gallup News Service, "April Wave 2" (April 17–30, 2019) https://news.gallup.com/poll/257639/four-americans-embrace-form-socialism.aspx (go to "View complete responses and trends"); Bureau of Labor Statistics, "Table 4-A, Employment status of the civilian population 25 years and over by educational attainment" (February 21, 2020) www.bls.gov/news.release/empsit.t04.htm; Bureau of Labor Statistics, "Profile of the Labor Force by Educational Attainment," *Spotlight on Statistics* (August 2017) www.bls.gov/spotlight/2017/educational-attainment-of-the-labor-force/pdf/educational-attainment-of-the-labor
34 Marx, *Capital*, Volume III, 1025.
35 For an analysis of this see Kim Moody, "Productivity, crises and imports in the loss of manufacturing jobs," *Capital & Class* (2019) https://journals-sagepub-com.ezproxy.nottingham.ac.uk/doi/pdf/10.1177/0309816819852755
36 Moody, *On New Terrain*, 7–69.
37 Bureau of Labor Statistics, "Registered Nurses," *Occupational Outlook Handbook* (September 4, 2019) www.bls.gov/ooh/healthcare/registered-nurses.htm; National Center for Education Statistics, "Fast Facts: Teacher Trends," https://nces.ed.gov/fastfacts/display.asp?id=28; Will Johnson, "Lean Production," in *Class Action: An Activist Teacher's Handbook*, ed. Shawn Gude and Bhaskar Sunkara (Chicago: Jacobin, 2014), 11–18; Shawn Gude, "The Industrial Classroom," in *Class Action*, ed. Gude and Sunkara, 21–31.
38 Kim Moody, "Competition and Conflict: Union Growth in the U.S. Hospital Industry," *In Solidarity: Essays on Working-Class Organization in the United States* (Chicago: Haymarket Books, 2014), 249–74.
39 Pew Research Center, "Millennials are the largest generation in the U.S. labor force" (April 11, 2018) www.pewresearch.org/fact-tank/2018/04/11/millennials-largest-generation-us-labor-force/
40 The Deloitte Global Millennial Survey 2019: Societal discord and technological transformation create a "generation disrupted" (London: Deloitte, Touche, Tohmatsu Limited, 2019), 2.

41 Pew Research Center, "5 facts about Millennial households" (September 6, 2017) www.pewresearch.org/fact-tank/2017/09/06/5-facts-about-millennial-households/
42 Antonio Gramsci, *Selections From The Prison Notebooks of Antonio Gramsci* (New York: International Publishers, 1971), 276.

Index

Note: Literary works by Marx and Engels can be found under their names.

abolitionism 20–22, 24–25, 28, 32–33, 36–38, 77, 250
  see also Civil War; slavery
abortion 57, 98, 102–3, 111–13, 222
  see also reproductive rights
academia see intellectuals; universities
Adorno, Theodor 6, 161
Africa 171
African Americans 10, 18, 20, 26–27, 29–34, 71, 94n.32, 99–101, 104–5, 106, 135, 144, 155, 170, 198, 202, 274, 277
  "general strike" of, in Civil War 17, 22, 31, 147–48, 151–52, 155, 164, 203
  women 99–101, 105, 197, 219, 227–28
  see also Black Lives Matter; Black Panther Party; Black Power; Civil War; Du Bois; slavery
agriculture 48, 122, 203
  see also farmers; land; sharecropping
Alexander, Barbara 53
Algeria 279
alienation 139, 200, 204, 224–25, 228–30
Allen, James S. 33
Alpert, Jane 186–88
Amalgamated Clothing Workers 75

Amalgamated Textile Workers of America 74
"American," meaning of 6
American Civil Liberties Union (ACLU) 74
American exceptionalism xii–xiii, 4, 6–7, 13, 126, 132–34, 264–90
American Federation of Labor (AFL) 26, 74–76, 78–80
American Federation of Teachers (AFT) 74
American Indian Movement (AIM) 210
American Revolution 19, 73, 78, 81, 85, 122, 125
American Studies 8, 125–26, 136, 140
American Workers Party (AWP) 79–82, 87
American Writers Congress 120
Americanism 5–6, 13, 27, 71–96, 102–4, 114, 124–25
  and communism 95–115
Americanization of Marxism 20, 61, 72, 124–25, 200
anarchism 25, 27, 44, 46, 48, 130
anthropology 61
anti-communism 87, 94n.32, 102, 198, 250
  see also McCarthyism; Red Scare
Antifada 258
Appeal to Reason 26
Aptheker, Bettina 114

Aptheker, Herbert 33–34, 38, 202
Arab Spring (2011) 279
Arendt, Hannah 161, 201
art 48, 77, 100, 174
Asia xii, 208, 265, 279
austerity 274–75, 277–80, 282, 284
Austin, J. L. 247
Austria 272, 280
authoritarianism 14, 138, 185
automation 136–37
Ayers, Bill 172–73, 184, 187, 189, 190n.5, 191n.10

Baby Boomers 285
Baffler 248
Baran, Paul 201
Barber, David 173–74
Barrett, Joseph 55
Batkis, Grigorii 106
Baxandall, Rosalyn 103
Beard, Charles and Mary 29, 33–34, 136
Bebel, August 57, 60, 96, 221
Bell, Daniel 14
Bellamy, Edward 204
Benjamin, Walter 252
Berlin, Ira 204
Biederman, Felix 254
Bình, Nguyễn Thị 185
birth control 51, 57, 222
   see also abortion; reproductive rights
Black Lives Matter 2, 280
Black Panther Party 170, 176–77, 184
black people see African Americans
Black Power 174, 181
Black Socialists in America (BSA) 250, 253
Blackburn, Robin 19
Blair, Tony 247, 274
Blanc, Eric 245
Blight, David 36
Block, Diana 182, 186–87
bohemianism 46, 49–50, 55
Bolivia 278
Bolshevism 58, 76, 98, 102, 106–7, 127–29, 150, 269

   see also Lenin; Russian Revolution; Soviet Union
Bolter, Jay David 241
Boorstin, Daniel 126
Boudin, Kathy 178–79, 187, 189
Boudin, Louis 78
bourgeoisie 20, 29, 33–34, 53, 127, 138, 150, 159–61, 163, 176, 204, 277
Brady, Robert A. 162
Braudy, Susan 189
Brexit 277
Brick, Howard 200
Briggs, Cyril 26, 105
Britain 34, 130, 159–60, 198, 205, 247, 271–73, 275, 277, 282
   see also Blair; Corbyn; English Civil War; Labour Party
Bromley, Dorothy Dunbar 113
Brooks, Michael 256
Brookwood Labor College 74–75, 78, 86
Brophy, John 78
Browder, Earl 27–28, 95, 97, 104–6, 115n.1, 124
Browder, Raissa 95
Brown, Elsa Barkley 156
Brown, John 21, 25–26, 28
Brown, Kathleen 52
Brownmiller, Susan 220–22, 235
Bruenig, Elizabeth 259
Budenz, Louis 71–94
Buhle, Paul 20, 249, 259
Bukharin, Nikolai 4
Bunche, Ralph 152
bureaucracy 128, 269
Burke, Kenneth 120–21, 124, 129
Burnham, James 80, 120, 123, 126–29, 135
Burrough, Bryan 173

Calverton, V. F. 9, 43, 49–51, 56, 58, 60–62, 74, 77–78, 120
Camus, Albert 199–200, 202
Cannon, James P. 80, 82–83
capitalism xiii, 1–2, 5–6, 10–14, 18, 19, 24, 27, 29–31, 33, 35, 37–38, 41, 46, 49, 55, 60–61,

Index

73, 77, 79, 80, 83, 96, 103, 105, 108, 113, 119, 121–23, 127–30, 133–38, 140, 147, 150, 157–60, 163, 170, 174, 176, 189, 195–96, 199–200, 203, 206, 217, 224, 251, 253, 257, 264–68, 270–74, 276, 278–79, 282–83, 285
  crises of 267, 273, 278, 282–83, 286
    see also financial crisis; Great Depression; Great Recession
  perceptions of 1
  varieties of xii
capitalists 10, 25, 29–30, 32, 46, 76, 121–23, 162, 202
Castro, Fidel 177, 185
Catholicism 73–75, 85, 87, 98, 105–6, 185
censorship 26, 124, 235
  see also repression
Chapo Trap House 242, 254–59
children 10, 55, 57, 59, 98, 100, 102, 104, 108, 111–13, 124, 172, 202, 205, 220
  see also education
Chile 279
China 48, 184, 279
  see also Mao Zedong; Maoism
Christianity 26, 86, 280
  see also Catholicism; religion
Christman, Matt 254
citizenship 75, 104, 148, 154–55, 234
civil liberties 27, 74, 230
Civil Rights Act (1964) 222
civil rights movement 31, 172, 179–80, 197, 274
Civil War 2–3, 8, 10, 17–42, 73, 78, 137, 139, 148, 151–52, 154, 164, 203
civilization 6, 29, 46, 62, 103–4, 106, 136–37, 140, 265
Claflin, Tennessee 45
Clark, Judith 179
Clark, Peter H. 250
class 2, 8, 10–11, 13, 19, 21, 37, 114, 133, 151, 163, 173–77, 180–83, 188, 198, 205–6, 217, 219–24, 234, 236, 260, 274, 282
  collaboration 123
  conflict 17, 22, 29, 127, 151, 157–58, 202, 210, 265–66, 278
  consciousness xiii, 18, 20, 37, 52, 54, 76, 84, 120–21, 133, 152, 162, 175, 211, 257, 264, 266, 270, 277, 285
  employing 100, 274
  enemies 102, 107
  formation 238n.22, 282
  gender as 11
  hatred 133
  politics 13, 249, 267, 270–71
  reconciliation 27
  reductionism 10, 146
  ruling 32, 148, 159, 204
  solidarity 18, 22, 54, 76, 81
  struggle 2, 4, 7, 10, 25, 33, 49, 84, 123, 250–51, 265–66, 268
  upper 105, 278
  war 26, 78
  see also classlessness; middle class; proletariat; working class
Class Struggle 48
classlessness 7, 249, 251–52
climate extinction 14, 251, 267
  see also environment
Clinton, Bill 274–75
Clinton, Hillary 247, 256
Clover, Joshua 251
Cold War 7–8, 13, 122, 126, 129–30, 132–37, 244, 272, 281
  liberalism 126, 133–37, 140, 244, 272
Collins, Patricia Hill 227
colonialism 136, 171, 176, 277
  see also imperialism
colorblindness 26
Combahee River Collective 249
Comintern *see* Communist International
Commager, Henry Steele 126
Committee for Non-Violent Action 208

commodification 30, 180, 219, 227–30, 232, 235
commodities 11, 29, 181, 224–30, 238n.22
Commune 251
communications *see* media
communism 10, 127, 175–76, 180, 198, 251, 266
  see also socialism
Communist International 8, 27, 102, 114, 124, 150, 270
Communist League of America (CLA) 80
Communist parties, global 176, 270, 274
  see also Communist International
Communist Party of the United States of America (CPUSA) 7, 9, 11, 27, 48–50, 60, 71, 73, 76, 81, 83, 86–87, 95–118, 120, 124–25, 128–29, 135, 144, 146–47, 196, 198, 202
  and African Americans 26–28
  see also Browder; Foster; Lovestone
Confederate States of America *see* Civil War
Conference for Progressive Labor Action (CPLA) 74, 76–80, 85, 88
confiscation 26, 31
  see also expropriation; land, redistribution; redistribution
Congress of Industrial Organizations (CIO) 71–72, 74, 80, 82, 86, 88
consciousness xii, 19, 36–37, 49, 61, 76, 120, 127, 144, 151–52, 196, 207, 236, 257, 269, 277, 285
  false 131, 217, 224, 230, 234–35
  raising 217, 221, 226, 234
  see also class; culture; ideology; philosophy; racism
conscription 30
conservatism 2–3, 7, 26–27, 96, 130, 132, 196, 231, 235–36, 249, 257–58, 274, 276–77
  in Communist Party 102, 106–7, 114–15
  in labor movement 74–75
  see also McCarthyism; Reagan; Thatcher; Trump
Conservative Party (U.K.) 277
Constitution of the United States 5, 83–85, 202
consumerism 5, 37, 49, 137, 179–81
consumption 230–34, 242
Corbyn, Jeremy 247, 251, 275, 280
Corey, Lewis 120, 159–60
  see also Fraina
coronavirus xiii
Coughlin, Charles 84
counterculture 171, 179, 184
Cowl, Margaret 108
Cowley, Malcolm 49
Cox, Oliver Cromwell 10, 144–69
crime 154, 248
  see also prisons
Crosland, C. A. R. 247, 272
Crossman, Richard 198
Cruse, Harold 135
Cuba 171, 175–77, 185
culture xiii, 4, 6–8, 11–13, 20, 36–37, 46, 49, 52–53, 58–59, 71, 74, 77, 79, 84–85, 87, 125–26, 134, 136–37, 145, 196, 198, 206, 218, 220, 222–23, 241–65, 276
  see also counterculture
Current Affairs 241, 245, 248, 250

Daily Worker 47–48, 109, 112–13
Danielson, Leilah 200
Davis, Angela 7, 183
Davis, Mike 272
Day, Meagan 259
De Leon, Daniel 25
Dean, Jodi 257
Debray, Regis 177
Debs, Eugene Victor 4, 5, 26, 204
debt 244, 285
deindustrialization 246, 274, 277, 283
Dell, Floyd 43–44, 47–49
democracy 14, 18, 30–32, 38, 122, 126, 129, 137, 146–49,

152–54, 156–64, 202,
  273, 279
socialist 269
workers 81
see also social democracy
Democratic Party 28, 88, 121, 204,
  254, 265, 274–77, 281
  see also New Deal
Democratic Socialists of America
  (DSA) 1, 244–45, 248, 253,
  281
Denning, Michael 8, 71–72, 74, 87,
  125, 198
deportation 26, 135, 140
depression *see* capitalism; Great
  Depression
determinism 7, 34, 130–31
Deutsch, Helen 222
Devlin, Bernadette 185
Dewey, John 6, 75, 199–200
Di Prima, Diane 252
dialectical materialism 114, 127,
  129–31, 134, 176
  see also historical materialism;
  philosophy
dictatorship 154–55, 160, 177, 285
  see also fascism; Nazism
dictatorship of the proletariat 148,
  150–53, 176
Dissent 248
divorce 96, 102
Dohrn, Bernardine 178–87, 189
Dos Passos, John 129
Douglass, Frederick 28
drama 77
Du Bois, W. E. B. 10, 22, 31–33,
  38, 120, 135, 144–69, 203
Dunayevska, Raya 17, 138–39
Dunbar-Ortiz, Roxanne 183, 210
Dutt, R. Palme 160
Dworkin, Andrea 11, 218–19,
  224–26, 229, 234–35
Dylan, Bob 170

Eastern Europe 124, 128, 269, 277
Eastman, Max 129
Echols, Alice 218
Economist 243–44, 248
Edelman, Elaine 207

education 1, 75, 77, 79, 120, 148,
  153, 196, 204–5, 207, 212,
  245–46, 277, 282
  see also children; teachers;
  universities
Ehrenreich, Barbara and John
  205–6, 245
elections 1, 4, 34, 244, 274,
  276–78, 280
Elkins, Stanley 203
Emancipation Proclamation 26
Emerson, Ralph Waldo 126, 131, 200
emotions 45–46, 58–59, 84, 211
empire 8, 12, 27, 34, 37, 86,
  175–76, 265
  see also imperialism
employment 14, 54, 100, 103–4,
  119, 181, 220, 224, 227, 230,
  244, 251, 259, 264, 277,
  282–83, 285
enclosure 238n.22
"end of history" 248
"end of socialism" (1989) 7
Engels, Friedrich xii, 2–4, 7, 9–10,
  19–20, 23, 28–29, 36, 38, 44,
  48, 57, 60, 96, 107, 130, 183,
  201, 217, 220–21, 265, 267,
  278
  Communist Manifesto xii, 11,
    36, 45, 96, 197, 201, 204,
    252, 265–66
  German Ideology 10, 204
  *Origin of the Family, Private
    Property, and the State* 96,
    220–21
English Civil War 29
environment 1, 88, 248–49
  see also climate extinction; Greens
Epstein, Abraham 78
eroticism 228–31
  see also sexuality
ethnicity 10, 18, 20, 22, 62, 71, 73,
  246, 277
Europe xii–xiii, 2–6, 11–13, 18, 20,
  29, 78, 83–85, 99, 107, 126,
  132–33, 136, 145, 198–200,
  264, 269–80, 282
  "Americanization" of 270
  see also Eastern Europe

European Union 275, 277
Evans, Janet 103
Evans, Sara 218
exceptionalism *see* American exceptionalism
existentialism 13, 199–202, 211
exploitation xiii, 27, 34–35, 52, 54–55, 157, 177, 181, 183, 210, 223–25, 227, 230, 235, 283, 285
   of women 184, 224, 227, 230, 235
expropriation 3, 206, 273
   see also confiscation; redistribution

Facebook 236
   see also social media
family 9–10, 44, 49–52, 57, 59, 95–115, 185, 220, 222, 234
   see also marriage; monogamy; Engels, *Origin of the Family*
Fanon, Frantz 176, 217
farmers 24, 28–29, 119
   see also agriculture; land; sharecropping
fascism 5, 13, 84–85, 87, 95, 99, 109, 111, 114, 122, 124, 147, 154, 158, 160–64, 198, 245, 255, 277
Faue, Elizabeth 52
Faulkner, William 210
Federal Bureau of Investigation (FBI) 171, 173, 176, 178–79
Fellowship of Reconciliation 86
feminism 2, 11–12, 44, 57, 62, 113–14, 171–74, 178–83, 184–89, 217–40, 279
   bourgeois 57, 181–82, 188
   socialist 172, 186
   see also gender; women
feudalism 3, 29–31, 33, 84, 132–33, 137, 157, 159, 265
   see also serfdom
fiction *see* literature
film xii, 53
   see also media
financial crisis (2008) xiii, 1, 243, 278

financialization 13, 35, 246
Finland 128
Firestone, Shulamith 217, 220–21
First International *see* International Workingmen's Association
First World War 26, 46, 49, 73, 77, 267, 269–70, 278, 282
Fisher, Mark 257
Fitzgerald, F. Scott 130
Flynn, Elizabeth Gurley 87, 111
Foner, Eric 32, 204, 207
Foner, Philip 144, 164, 202
force *see* violence
Ford, Henry 5
Fordism 73
Foster, William Z. 27
Fourier, Charles 44
Fourth International 86
Fraina, Louis 78, 160
   see also Corey, Lewis
France 103, 129, 272, 274–75, 277, 279–80, 282
   see also French Revolution; Paris Commune
Frankfurt School 6, 61
   see also Adorno; Horkheimer; Marcuse
Fraser, Nancy 258
"free labor" *see* labor
free love 44–46, 98, 102, 171, 179, 184
freedom 5, 13, 22, 26, 30, 35, 38, 43, 47–49, 56, 59, 75, 78, 83, 104, 130–32, 134–39, 154, 159–60, 184, 196, 198, 199
Freedom Summer 227
French Revolution 29, 37, 148, 159
Freud, Sigmund 9, 43–44, 46–47, 49–50, 60–62, 217, 220–21, 234
Freudianism 219, 222, 230
Frost, Amber A'Lee 255

Gardener, Tracey 228
Garlin, Sender 48, 112
gay *see* homosexuality; sexuality
gender xiii, 8–12, 22, 48, 55, 59, 96, 109, 111, 173, 180–81,

184, 189, 217–19, 221, 232, 255
    see also feminism; masculinity; women
Generation X 252, 285
Generation Z 285
Genet, Jean 220
Genovese, Eugene 29
Gerhard, Jane 218
German Americans 7, 9, 18, 22, 45–46
    see also Lore; Sorge; Weydemeyer
German Social Democratic Party (SPD) 149, 247, 267, 271
Germany 2, 4, 23, 107, 122, 131, 149, 176, 247, 267, 269, 271–73, 275, 280, 282
    1848 revolution 11, 22, 148
    see also Nazism
Ghandianism 86
Gilded Age 4, 23, 34–36, 204, 206
Gitlin, Todd 173, 191n.13
Godwin, William 44
Gold, Michael 43, 60, 120
Goldman, Emma 183, 204
Gooding-Williams, Robert 149
Gordon, Eugene 105
Gorman, William 167n.19
Gosse, Van 98, 103
Gould, Jay 35
Gramsci, Antonio 5–6, 71, 79, 230–31, 256, 267, 286
Great Depression 11, 13, 71–94, 119, 121–22, 127, 150, 264
Great Recession 1, 243–44, 268, 275, 278
    see also financial crisis; recessions
Great Society 275
Greece 275, 279
Green New Deal 281
Greenback-Labor Party 24
Greens 280
Gropper, William 100–1
Group of Seven (G7) 268
Gruson, Richard 241
Guérin, Daniel 162
guerrilla war 177, 252

Guevara, Che 177, 252
Gutman, Herbert 37

Hahn, Steven 156
Haider, Asad 249
Haitian Revolution 33, 135
Halbwachs, Maurice 37
Halper, Katie 256
Hardman, J. B. S. 75–76, 78, 80–82
Harrington, Michael 251
Harris, Abram 151
Harris, Malcolm 245
Harrison, Hubert 26, 147
Hartmann, Heidi 182, 188
Hartz, Louis 15n.8, 132–33, 248
Hawthorne, Nathaniel 126
Hay, Harry 106
Hayden, Casey 180, 182
Hayek, Friedrich 158, 160–61, 163
Haymarket 2, 25, 204
Haywood, Bill 99
healthcare 1, 5, 112, 205, 251, 281, 284
hedge funds 13
Hedges, M. S. 77
Hegel, G. W. F. 127, 131
Henry, Patrick 85
Herberg, Will 150–51
Herndon, Angelo 28
heterodoxy 8–9, 147, 161
heteronormativity 222
higher education see universities
Hill, Christopher 29
hip-hop 252–53
historical materialism 6, 25, 47, 49, 61–62, 97, 132, 195–96, 199, 206, 212, 220, 252
    see also determinism; dialectical materialism; Marxism
historiography 19, 29, 144, 147, 151, 155, 157, 195–216
history xii, 35, 77, 85, 131, 195–216, 265–67, 270
Hitler, Adolf 132, 161, 198
Ho Chi Minh 185
Hobsbawm, Eric 34, 37, 123
Hofstadter, Richard 132
Hollibaugh, Amber 226–27, 235

Holocaust 161
  see also Nazism
Holt, Thomas C. 203
homelessness 14, 119
  see also housing
homosexuality 62, 96, 102, 106–7, 222, 227, 231
  see also sexuality
Hong Kong 279
Hook, Sidney 6, 74, 78, 80–81, 120, 124, 127, 135, 200
hooks, bell 219
Horkheimer, Max 6
Horney, Karen 222
hours *see* workday
House Committee on Un-American Activities (HUAC) 85, 87
House of Representatives 1, 244
housing 14, 244, 248, 277
Hudson, Hosea 28
humanism 13, 121, 131, 138, 200
Hungary 138
hunger 60, 119
Hutchins, Grace 100

identity xiii, 20, 34, 37–38, 72, 85, 211–12, 249, 255
  see also class; gender; nationalism; race
ideology 6, 8, 22, 30, 32, 35, 46, 50, 67, 77, 85, 96, 105, 120–21, 132, 149, 156, 162, 176, 187–88, 198, 201, 209, 225, 232, 242, 250, 255
  see also consciousness; Marx, *German Ideology*
immigration 2, 6–9, 20, 73, 124–25, 133, 138–40, 196, 198, 246, 248, 277, 280
  see also deportation; migration
imperialism 31, 75, 84, 128–29, 131, 151, 157, 170, 173, 176–77, 179, 182–83, 187–89
  see also colonialism; empire
In These Times 248
income 32, 108, 153, 282, 284–85
Indians *see* Native Americans

Industrial Workers of the World (IWW) 26, 123
industry *see* capitalism; manufacturing
inequality 1, 13, 19, 23, 59, 62, 88, 95, 108, 144, 146, 158, 163, 195–95, 198, 205, 223, 234, 264, 273, 275, 279, 282
inflation 108, 273
insurance 14, 75, 78
intellectuals 7, 32, 35–36, 71, 74, 78–80, 83, 87, 119–69, 206, 217, 231, 234–35
  see also New York Intellectuals
International Brotherhood of Electrical Workers 77
International Women's Day 101
International Workingmen's Association 3, 8, 18, 23, 27, 45
internationalism 8, 19–22, 31, 38, 72, 75, 80, 83, 85, 87, 195
Iraq 279
Irish Americans 45
Isserman, Maurice 124
Italy 5, 122, 269, 272, 274, 277, 279–80
  see also Gramsci

Jacobin 2, 241, 244–45, 247–48, 251, 255
Jacobs, John (J.J.) 175
Jaffe, Naomi 178–81
James, C. L. R. 12, 33, 120, 135–40, 146, 156, 167n.19
James, Joy 149
James, William 199
Janney, Caroline 36
Japan 271
Jefferson, Thomas 78
Jews 12, 196
Johnson, Boris 277
Johnson, Walter 29
Johnstone, Jenny Elizabeth 108
Jones, Claudia 120, 147
Jones, Jeff 187
Jospin, Lionel 274
journalism 77, 83, 246
  see also media

Index

Kazin, Michael 32, 208
Kelly, Brian 151–52
Kent State 197
Keynesianism 274
King, Mary 180, 182
Klein, Bonnie Sheer 229
Klonsky, Mike 174–76
Knights of Labor 24, 25
Koestler, Arthur 198
Kollontai, Alexandra 4, 51–52, 59–60, 96
Kornhauser, William 161

labor xiii, 3, 17–22, 25–32, 34–36, 38, 45–48, 60, 71, 74, 77–78, 81, 87, 98, 122–23, 139, 151, 153–55, 203, 224, 226, 246, 248, 265–66, 268, 283, 285
 division of 206, 220–21, 223
 "reserve army of" 264
 see also unions; wage labor; work; working class
Labor Action 74, 76, 81, 87
Labor Age 74–75, 77
labor movement xiii, 7, 13, 21–22, 72–73, 75, 77, 80, 86, 100, 123–24, 150, 265, 271
 see also unions; working class
labor party 4, 19, 73, 75, 265, 276
Labor Reform Association 22
labor unions *see* unions
Labour Party (U.K.) 271–72, 275, 280
land 19–20, 33, 119, 148
 ownership 24, 133
 redistribution 26, 28, 31–32, 154
Laos 175
Latinos 274
law 5, 21, 32, 35, 57, 98, 102, 106–7, 111–13, 159, 178, 204–5, 222–23, 232–34, 236, 238n.22
Lebanon 279
Lebedeva, Vera 112
Lefebvre, Georges 29
Left Opposition 129
 see also Trotskyism
Lenin, V. I. 28, 129, 267

Leninism 82–83, 85–86, 153, 170, 174, 176, 199
Lewis, John L. 79
LGBTQ+ *see* homosexuality; sexuality
liberalism 2, 6, 11, 12, 22, 34, 73, 124, 126, 132–37, 140, 144, 243, 246–48, 250, 254–55, 258–59, 273–74, 285
 see also Cold War; neoliberalism; New Deal; reformism; social democracy
Lincoln, Abraham 17, 18, 21, 25–28, 34, 125
literature 43, 52, 56, 77, 120–21, 130, 145, 147, 150–51, 228, 241, 252
 see also poetry
Locke, John 132
London, Jack 198
Long, Huey P. 84
Lorde, Audre 219, 228–29, 235
Lore, Ludwig 78, 80
Lovestone, Jay 7, 133, 150
Luxemburg, Rosa xiii, 12, 160, 245, 267, 282
lynching 26–27, 101
Lynn, Denise 103

McAlevey, Jane 259
McCarthyism 3, 124
 see also anti-communism; Red Scare
McCullough, Celeste 179
MacKinnon, Catharine 10, 218–19, 222–23, 230, 234–35
McNally, David 279
Mailer, Norman 220, 231
Manson, Charles 172, 179
manufacturing 29, 119, 160, 282–84
Mao Zedong 177, 217, 252
Maoism 170, 177, 184
Maranto, Gina 210
Marcuse, Herbert 7, 17, 61, 138, 170, 199, 201, 217
marriage 44–45, 47, 54–55, 57, 59, 96, 98, 102, 105, 183
 see also family

Martin, Ron 229
Marx, Jenny xii
Marx, Karl xii, 2–4, 7, 17–23, 26, 28, 29–30, 34, 36, 38, 43, 45, 47–50, 57, 60–62, 76, 96, 103, 119–43, 176, 183, 199–200, 204–5, 209, 217, 235, 243, 249–53, 264–68, 269, 277–78, 282–83
   Capital 2, 3, 13, 17, 18, 130, 134, 138–39, 199, 201, 225, 265–67, 282
   Communist Manifesto xii, 11, 36, 45, 96, 197, 201, 204, 252, 265–66
   Economic and Philosophical Manuscripts 138, 201
   Eighteenth Brumaire of Louis Bonaparte 19, 134, 201, 266
   German Ideology 10, 204
   Grundrisse 201, 266
   "Theses on Feuerbach" 199
Marxism, definition of 6–7
Marxism-Leninism 170, 174, 176
   see also Leninism; Maoism
masculinity 55, 67n.60, 226, 233
Mathiessen, F. O. 126
Maurer, James 78
means of production *see* production
Means TV 258
media 227, 232, 236, 241–63
   see also film; journalism
Melville, Herman 126
Melville, Sam 186
memory 19–21, 24, 35–36, 38
Menaker, Will 254, 258
Menand, Louis 13, 131
MeToo movement 2, 218, 235–36
   see also sexual harassment
Mickenberg, Julia L. 98
middle class 3, 27, 29, 36, 46–47, 73, 88n.1, 100, 107, 113, 172, 188, 191n.10, 205–6, 244, 272, 275, 277, 279, 281, 283–85
   see also bourgeoisie; professional-managerial class

Middle East 279
migration 133
   see also immigration
Milburn, Keir 243
Miliband, Ralph 205
militarism 21, 75
millennials 11, 241–63, 281, 284–85
Miller, Henry 220
Miller, Loren 152
Miller, M. H. 244
Millett, Kate 115, 217, 220–21, 235
Mills, C. Wright 170
misogyny 217, 225, 231, 236
Mitchell, Louise 113
Mitterrand, François 274
Modern Monthly 82
Modern Quarterly 47, 78
modernism 77, 96, 198
modes of production *see* production
monarchy 150, 154
monogamy 47, 49, 51, 171, 179, 183–85
   see also family
Montgomery, David 32, 37
Monthly Review 163, 208, 248
Moon, Henry Lee 152
Morais, Herbert 29
Moral Majority 218, 236
morality 43–47, 49, 51, 58, 60, 77, 96, 105, 107
Morgan, Robin 179, 188
Moscow Trials 128
motherhood *see* family
Moylan, Mary 185
Mullen, Bill 148
Murray, Pauli 146
music 6, 77, 241, 252
Muste, A. J. 13, 71–94, 200
Myrdal, Gunnar 163

n+1 241, 244–45, 248
National Association for the Advancement of Colored People (NAACP) 146, 150, 156
National Labor Union 18, 24

National Organization for Women (NOW) 183
nationalism 21–22, 26, 37, 62, 72, 87, 102, 126, 156, 249
nationality 10
Native Americans 30, 210
Nazism 6, 122, 131, 161
 see also fascism; Hitler
Nazi-Soviet Pact 110, 124, 128, 198
Nearing, Scott 43, 48
Nelson, Bruce 158
neoliberalism xiii, 35–36, 158, 235, 242–43, 248–49, 257, 270, 274–75, 278–79, 282, 284–85
Netherlands 280
New Deal 11, 71, 88, 121–27, 129, 132, 134, 140, 275
New Left 7, 12, 62, 144, 170–94, 195, 198–203, 208, 211, 217, 220, 226, 234, 249, 256
New Left Notes 181, 183
New Masses 27, 47, 54–55, 152
New Politics 245, 248
New Right 7, 219, 235
New York Intellectuals 71
New York Radical Feminists 220–21
New York Radical Women 220
New York Times 244, 259
New York Tribune 2, 17
Nichter, Matthew 150
Niebuhr, Reinhold 120
Nkrumah, Kwame 252
nonviolence *see* pacifism
Norse, Harold 106
nuclear weapons 267

Obama, Barack 243, 274
Ocasio-Cortez, Alexandria 1, 244, 280
Occupy Wall Street 1, 244, 248, 279–80
October Revolution *see* Russian Revolution
Old Left 7, 62, 83, 87, 195, 200–3, 211, 249
 see also Communist Party; Trotskyism

opportunism 12, 73
orthodoxy 8–9, 22, 36, 127, 160, 250
Owen, Robert 44

pacifism 86, 94n.32
Paglia, Camille 236
Palme, Olaf 251
Palmer, Bryan D. 114
Pan-Africanism 33
Panken, Wendy 179
Paris Commune 37, 265
Park, Robert 162–63
parliamentarianism 4, 73, 76, 83, 267, 273
Partisan Review 128
partisanship 22
patriarchy 37, 49, 51, 60, 96, 98, 105, 178, 182–83, 189, 220–22, 224, 229
patriotism 22, 26, 84–85, 96, 104, 125, 131, 204
 see also Americanism; nationalism
peasants 37, 154
Peck, Jamie 258
Peck, Raoul xii
Pelosi, Nancy 256
pensions 14
People's Party 24
Pepper, William F. 220
permanent revolution *see* revolution
Pesotta, Rose 86
Phillips, Ulrich B. 203
Phillips, Wendell 32
philosophy 127, 151, 159, 201, 265
 see also consciousness; dialectical materialism; existentialism; morality; pragmatism
Pittman, John 106
Piven, Frances Fox 211
poetry 77, 121, 229, 241, 251–52, 257
Popular Front 9, 11, 52, 59, 71–72, 74, 82–83, 87, 95–115, 124–26, 129

population 104, 133, 204, 279, 283
populism 13, 24–25, 46, 71, 84, 161, 251, 277, 285
pornography 218–19, 222–36
Portugal 275, 280
Poulantzas, Nicos 205
poverty 52, 55, 74, 104, 154, 175, 188, 285
pragmatism 6, 21, 74–77, 81, 83, 146, 199–200
praxis 14, 76, 184, 220, 250
prisons 5, 199, 205, 258
see also crime
production 5, 25, 35, 44, 223–25, 229, 232, 238n.22, 242, 283
  means of 2, 7–8, 10, 130, 208, 250, 269, 273
  modes of 19, 50, 97, 131, 253, 265
productivity 10, 271–72, 275–76
professional-managerial class 205–6, 245, 248, 255
see also class; middle class
profit 10, 19, 30, 150, 176, 200, 203, 225–26, 235, 252, 266–68, 271, 282, 284
Progressive Era 35–36, 149, 204
Progressive Labor (PL) 170, 176–77
proletariat 10, 19, 33, 37, 47, 127–28, 134, 138, 148, 152, 159, 249, 252, 277
see also working class
property 10, 26, 43, 45, 47, 51, 58–60, 96, 151, 154, 160, 210, 226, 264, 273
prostitution 222, 224, 227
psychology 43–44, 49–50, 61–62, 84
see also Freud
Puerto Rico 279
puritanism 46, 48–49, 67n.60

Quinby, Bryan 255

race xiii, 3, 8, 12, 18, 22, 26, 27, 57, 114, 135, 144–47, 149, 157–58, 163, 173–74, 180–83, 189, 195–96, 198, 202–3, 212, 219, 248, 274, 284–85
see also African Americans; segregation; whiteness
racism 24, 26–27, 138, 174, 177, 182, 187, 198, 203, 212, 277
see also segregation; whiteness
radicalism 9, 12, 20, 22, 24–26, 35–36, 44–45, 47, 49–50, 60–61, 84, 96, 98, 100, 104, 119, 156, 195–96, 220, 223, 235, 251, 256, 280
radio *see* media
Ramparts 180–81
rape 218, 220–23, 231, 235
Reagan, Ronald 13, 218, 274–75
recessions 267, 274, 282
see also Great Recession
Reconstruction 18–20, 24, 28, 30–32, 35, 38, 147–57, 164, 203
Red Army Faction 176
Red Scare (1919) 2, 26, 75, 77, 96
see also anti-communism; McCarthyism
redistribution of wealth 1, 30, 32
see also confiscation; expropriation; land, redistribution
Redstockings 220, 227
Reed, Adolph, Jr. 149, 156, 256
reformism 11–12, 14, 28, 86, 107, 231, 247, 251–52, 273–74
see also liberalism; social democracy
Reich, Wilhelm 61
reification 181, 224, 234
religion xiii, 10, 21, 44, 52, 57, 73, 84, 86–87, 96, 98, 105, 205
see also Catholicism; Christianity
religiosity 9
repression
  political 26, 106, 124, 131, 138–40, 187, 211
  see also McCarthyism; Red Scare

Index   303

sexual 48, 61, 217, 220, 229–30
reproduction 44, 220, 222
reproductive rights 227
    see also abortion
Republican Party 22, 26, 30, 204,
    254, 281
republicanism 22, 24, 161
revolution 3–4, 11–14, 19, 22, 24,
    26, 29, 46, 73, 77–79, 82–83,
    87, 120, 127, 134, 245, 249,
    252–53, 260, 265, 269
    of 1848 11, 22, 148, 198, 202–3,
        212, 265–66
    bourgeois 19, 28, 30, 33, 159
    permanent 30, 127
    proletarian 18
    socialist 4, 83, 119–20, 129,
        133–34, 179, 182–84
    see also American Revolution;
        French Revolution; Germany;
        Haitian Revolution; Russian
        Revolution
Revolutionary Youth Movement II
    (RYM II) 176–77, 183
Riley, Boots 252
Robinson, Cedric 145–49, 157
Robinson, Lois 233
Robinson, Nathan J. 245, 250
Rocha, Mona 173
Rockwell, Bruce 210
Roediger, David 148
Roiphe, Katie 236
Roman Empire 265
Roosevelt, Eleanor 122
Roosevelt, Franklin Delano 79,
    121–24
Rorty, James 78
Rosen, Ruth 218
Rosenberg, Arthur 160
Rossiter, Clinton 134
Rubin, Gayle 219, 224, 226,
    231–35
Rudd, Mark 174, 187
Russia 18, 128
    see also Soviet Union
Russian Revolution (1917) 4, 37,
    47, 50, 56, 96, 127, 129, 269
Ryan, Erica J. 96

Sandberg, Sheryl 236
Sanders, Bernie 1, 244–45, 247–48,
    251, 253, 258, 280–81
Saposs, David 78
Sartre, Jean-Paul 201
Schlesinger, Arthur, Jr. 132
Schmalhausen, Samuel D. 9, 50–51,
    60–62
Schroeder, Gerhard 274
Scialabba, George 207
Scott-Heron, Gil 241
Scottsboro Boys 99
Second International 4, 27, 267, 270
    see also social democracy
Second World War 110–11, 122,
    124, 129, 196, 198, 264, 271
sectarianism 11, 44, 61, 74, 76,
    79–81, 87, 133
segregation, racial 31, 37, 135, 274
    see also race
serfdom 18, 158, 160–61
service sector 283
sex work *see* prostitution
Sexton, Tom 258–59
sexual exploitation 184
sexual harassment 52, 55, 218,
    222–23, 230, 232–35
    see also MeToo
sexual objectification 181
sexual revolution 45, 50–51, 57,
    59–62
    see also free love
sexuality xiii, 8–10, 43–70,
    95–115, 171, 181, 184–85,
    217–40
    see also eroticism
Shachtman, Max 80, 83
Shakur, Afeni 185
sharecropping 5, 30, 32
Shaw, George Bernard 48
Silber, Nina 28
Sinclair, Upton 43, 47–48, 198
Singer, Daniel 275
slavery 3, 17–42, 99, 134, 138–40,
    147, 153–55, 196, 202–3,
    206, 209, 222, 265, 277
    see also abolitionism; African
        Americans; Civil War

Small, Sasha 53, 99–100
Smedley, Agnes 55–56
social democracy xiii 1–2, 4, 36, 149, 243, 247, 251, 253–54, 270–77, 280–82, 285
   see also German Social Democratic Party; reformism; socialism
social media 241
   see also Facebook; media; Twitter; YouTube
socialism 2, 7, 12, 24, 36, 78, 95, 125, 127, 138, 148, 150, 174, 176, 241–63, 267, 269, 281
   inevitability of 265, 267–69, 278
   "scientific" 46, 250
   see also "end of socialism"; utopian socialism
Socialist Labor Party (SLP) 25, 27, 46
Socialist Party of America 4, 7, 12, 27, 46, 73, 76, 78–79, 82, 86, 144, 149–50
   see also Debs
Socialist Workers Party (SWP) 60
sociology 146, 157–65, 278
Sombart, Werner 13
Sorge, Friedrich 45
Soviet Union 7, 43, 48, 51, 56–59, 75, 80, 84, 95–96, 103, 105, 107, 110–11, 122, 124, 126–29, 134, 138–39, 146, 150, 198, 256, 269–70
Spain 13, 275, 279–80
Stalin, Joseph 7, 9, 71, 87, 95, 102, 105–6, 110, 126, 128–29, 132–34, 140, 269–70
Stalinism 28, 86, 88n.1, 128–29, 131, 198–99, 201, 269–70
Stalinization 111
Stampp, Kenneth 32
Stanton, Elizabeth Cady 28
state 34, 57, 88, 102, 123, 128, 177, 204–5, 253, 259, 269, 273, 275
   welfare 271–72, 275
   see also Engels, *Origin of the Family*

Steinbeck, John 198
Stern, Susan 182, 186
Stevens, Thaddeus 35
Steward, Ira 22
Stolberg, Benjamin 150
Stone, Hannah M. 112
Strachey, John 159–60, 162
Streeck, Wolfgang 275
strikes 2, 5, 10, 74, 78–79, 85–86, 99, 101, 245–46, 251, 273–75, 279–82, 284
   Electric Auto-Lite (1934) 72, 80–83
   Great Railroad (1877) 24
   Lawrence, Massachusetts (1912) 99
   Lawrence, Massachusetts (1919) 73–74
   San Francisco (1934) 99
   sit-down 86
   slaves' 17, 22, 31, 147–48, 151–52, 155, 164, 203
   students' 175
   teachers' 245, 280
   women's 99–102, 280
Strong, Anna Louise 58
Student Non-Violent Coordinating Committee (SNCC) 197
Students for a Democratic Society (SDS) 170, 172–78, 180–81, 189
suffrage 98, 148, 154–55
Sunkara, Bhaskar 244, 247, 250–53, 259
Supreme Court 222
surplus value 10
Sweden 251, 272, 275
Sweezy, Paul 160, 163, 201
Sylvis, William H. 24

Tanner, Caroline 179
taxation 11, 284
Taylor, Frederick Winslow 5
Taylor, Keeanga-Yamahtta 156
teachers 205, 245–46, 279–80, 283–84
   see also American Federation of Teachers; education

technology 51, 199, 241–43, 252, 257, 259–60, 265, 267, 273, 275, 282
  see also production, means of
Teish, Luisah 227–28, 235
teleology 19, 127, 150, 265
television see media
Thatcher, Margaret 274–75
Third International see Communist International
Third Period 59, 76
Third World 170–71, 176–77, 187
Thompson, E. P. xii, 37, 266
Thoreau, Henry David 126
time see workday
Tlaib, Rashida 244
Tocqueville, Alexis de 132
totalitarianism 6, 132, 134, 137, 198, 200, 270
trade unions see unions
tradition 37
transcendentalism 20, 126
Traverso, Enzo 19
Trillbilly Workers Party 256–58
Trotsky, Leon 4, 6, 37, 87–88, 127–29, 160, 170, 270
Trotskyism 60, 80, 85, 92n.17, 128–29, 199
Trump, Donald J. 13, 244, 254–56, 277
Truth, Sojourner 28, 99
Tubman, Harriet 28, 99
Turner, Frederick Jackson 133
Twitter 250, 255
  see also social media

Unemployed Citizens' Leagues 79–81
unemployment see employment
unions 4, 14, 24, 36, 46, 72–80, 84–85, 87, 109, 123, 246, 271–72, 274–75, 277, 279–80, 283–84
  see also American Federation of Labor; Congress of Industrial Organizations; labor movement; strikes; working class

United Auto Workers (UAW) 81
United Farm Workers (UFW) 227
United Kingdom see Britain
United Mine Workers of America (UMWA) 79
universities 1, 36, 126, 146, 150, 161, 178, 196–97, 201, 210–11, 220, 244, 246
utopian socialism 2, 4

value 10, 268
Vance, Carole 217–18
Vance, J. D. 256
Varon, Jeremy 173, 184
Venezuela 278
veterans 20–21, 24, 27, 36
Vietnam 171, 175–77, 189
Vietnam War 86, 174, 181, 185, 197
Village Voice 231
Vinson, Mechelle 223
violence 20, 26, 31–33, 52–53, 55, 170–77, 180, 204, 218–24, 227–28, 231–32, 234–36, 259
  see also lynching; repression
vote see suffrage

Wade, Benjamin F. 18
wage labor 24, 34, 208, 210, 268
wage slavery 20, 24, 30, 35
wages 10, 45, 100, 104, 134, 137, 155, 266, 268, 271, 276–77
Walker, Alice 228
Wallace, Mike 208
Wallerstein, Immanuel 157
Warren, Elizabeth 245
Washington Post 259
Weather Underground 170–75, 182–83, 186–88
  name variations 190n.3
Weatherman 11–12, 177–88
Weatherwomen 174, 179–80, 183, 186–89
Weeks, Jeffrey 60
Weimar Republic 161
Weisbord, Albert 48
Weiss, Benjamin 48
Weydemeyer, Joseph 22–23

white supremacy *see* race; racism; segregation
whiteness 22, 25–26, 145, 151
   see also race; racism
Wicks, H. M. 48
Wilkerson, Cathy 171, 178–79, 183–84, 186, 188
Willis, Ellen 219, 221, 227, 230–32, 234–35
Wilson, Edmund 129, 134
Winant, Gabriel 245
Winston, Henry 104
Winter, Ella 57–58
Wollestonecraft, Mary 44
women 5, 10, 12, 20, 45, 48, 51–59, 95–118, 138–40, 170–93, 203, 217–40, 279–81, 283
   African American 99–101, 105, 197, 219, 227–28
   see also feminism; gender
Women Today 109–11
Wood, Charles 43, 48
Woodhull, Victoria 45
work 133
workday 14, 138–39, 227
Workers' Party of the United States 82, 85, 87
working class xii–xiii, 2–3, 10, 18, 20, 22, 25–27, 30, 34, 36, 43, 46–48, 71–77, 81, 83–85, 102, 110, 122–23, 130, 137, 139, 150–51, 155, 163–64, 175–77, 196, 198, 204–6, 245–46, 249, 255, 259, 264, 266–67, 269, 271–78, 281, 283–85

black 148, 150, 198
movement xii, 264
organization 3, 109, 266, 269, 271, 285
politics 13, 271
power 12
solidarity 81
white 148, 177, 277–78
women 55, 100, 113, 279
see also class; proletariat
Working Women 53–54, 100–102, 109
workplace 14, 30, 34, 52, 137, 218, 223, 233–35, 246, 259, 268
World League for Sexual Reform 107
World War I *see* First World War
World War II *see* Second World War
Wright, Frances 44
Wright, Richard 135, 145, 198

Yippies 62
Young Communist League 104
Young Marx (film) xii
Young People's Socialist League 244
youth 1, 14, 57, 103–4, 147, 172, 175–76, 179, 200, 251, 283
   see also children; millennials; Revolutionary Youth Movement II
YouTube 256

Zetkin, Clara 96, 107
Ziegler, Phil E. 78
Zinn, Howard 13, 195–216

EU authorised representative for GPSR:
Easy Access System Europe, Mustamäe tee 50,
10621 Tallinn, Estonia
gpsr.requests@easproject.com

www.ingramcontent.com/pod-product-compliance
Lightning Source LLC
Chambersburg PA
CBHW051600230426
43668CB00013B/1924